STUDENT'S BOOK WITH KEY

WITH APP & DIGITAL STUDENT'S BOOK

App

READY FOR

B1 PRELIMINARY

FIONA AISH
ETHAN MANSUR
JO TOMLINSON
with ROY NORRIS

macmillan education

CONTENTS

Reading	Writing	Listening	Speaking
Part 1 Multiple choice Part 5 Multiple-choice cloze	Part 1 Email Part 2 Article	Part 1 Multiple choice	Part 1 Interview Part 2 Extended turn
Part 2 Matching Part 6 Open cloze	Part 1 Email Part 2 Story	Part 2 Multiple choice	Part 1 Interview Part 2 Extended turn Part 4 General conversation
Part 5 Multiple-choice cloze	Part 2 Article Part 2 Story	Part 3 Gap fill	Part 1 Interview Part 2 Extended turn Part 3 Discussion
Part 4 Gapped text Part 6 Open cloze	Part 1 Email Part 2 Article	Part 4 Multiple choice	Part 1 Interview Part 2 Extended turn
Part 3 Multiple choice Part 6 Open cloze	Part 1 Email Part 2 Story	Part 2 Multiple choice Part 3 Gap fill	Part 1 Interview Part 2 Extended turn Part 4 General conversation
Part 2 Matching Part 5 Multiple-choice cloze	Part 1 Email Part 2 Article	Part 1 Multiple choice Part 4 Multiple choice	Part 1 Interview Part 2 Extended turn Part 3 Discussion
Part 3 Multiple choice Part 6 Open cloze	Part 1 Email Part 2 Story	Part 1 Multiple choice Part 3 Gap fill	Part 1 Interview Part 2 Extended turn Part 3 Discussion Part 4 General conversation
Part 1 Multiple choice Part 4 Gapped text Part 5 Multiple-choice cloze	Part 2 Article Part 2 Story	Part 2 Multiple choice Part 4 Multiple choice	Part 1 Interview Part 2 Extended turn
Part 1 Multiple choice Part 6 Open cloze	Part 1 Email Part 2 Story	Part 1 Multiple choice Part 4 Multiple choice	Part 1 Interview Part 2 Extended turn Part 3 Discussion Part 4 General conversation
Part 3 Multiple choice Part 6 Open cloze	Part 1 Email Part 2 Article	Part 3 Gap fill Part 4 Multiple choice	Part 1 Interview Part 2 Extended turn
Part 2 Matching Part 5 Multiple-choice cloze	Part 1 Email Part 2 Article	Part 1 Multiple choice Part 2 Multiple choice	Part 1 Interview Part 2 Extended turn Part 4 General conversation
Part 4 Gapped text Part 5 Multiple-choice cloze	Part 2 Article Part 2 Story	Part 2 Multiple choice Part 3 Gap fill	Part 1 Interview Part 2 Extended turn

INTRODUCTION

Welcome to *Ready for B1 Preliminary*, a course designed to help you prepare for *Cambridge English Qualifications: B1 Preliminary*.

In each unit of *Ready for B1 Preliminary* there are Language focus and Vocabulary sections to help you improve your English, as well as a wide range of activities designed to develop exam skills and strategies and increase your confidence.

The Pronunciation pages at the end of every unit will improve your mark on the Speaking exam by giving you practice with key features of pronunciation, such as individual sounds, word stress and intonation.

Fiona Aish, Joanne Tomlinson,
Ethan Mansur and Roy Norris

Overview of the Examination

Reading 45 minutes

Part	Task Type	Number of Questions	Task Format
1	Multiple choice	5	Five real-world short texts followed by multiple-choice questions with three options.
2	Matching	5	Descriptions of five people which candidates match to eight short texts on a certain topic.
3	Multiple choice	5	A text followed by multiple-choice questions with four options.
4	Gapped text	5	A text from which five sentences have been removed. Candidates match the missing sentences from a choice of eight.
5	Multiple-choice cloze	6	A text with gaps. There is a choice of four options for each gap.
6	Open cloze	6	A text with gaps which candidates must complete with one word.

Writing 45 minutes

Part	Task Type	Number of Tasks	Task Format
1	Email	1 (compulsory)	Candidates are given an email to reply to. There are some notes with information, which they must include in their writing.
2	Article or Story	2 (candidates choose one)	Candidates can choose between two tasks: an article on a particular topic; or a story which must begin with a given opening sentence.

Listening About 30 minutes

Part	Task Type	Number of Questions	Task Format
1	Multiple choice	7	Seven short monologues or conversations. For each question, candidates must choose between three images.
2	Multiple choice	6	Six short dialogues followed by multiple-choice questions with three options.
3	Gap fill	6	Candidates listen to a monologue and complete gaps in a text with words or short phrases.
4	Multiple choice	6	An interview with a single speaker. There are three options for each question.

Speaking 12–17 minutes

Part	Task Type	Time	Task Format
1	Interview	2 minutes	Candidates give personal information in response to questions from the interviewer.
2	Extended turn	3 minutes	Each candidate is given a photo, which they have to describe for about one minute.
3	Discussion	4 minutes	Candidates are given instructions and illustrations, which they first use for discussion, and then for a decision-making task.
4	General conversation	3 minutes	Students answer questions related to the topic in Part 3.

1 IN STYLE

KEY LANGUAGE

Present simple and present continuous
Adverbs of frequency
Clothing
Prepositions of time

PRONUNCIATION

/ʊ/, /uː/ and /ʌ/

EXAM PRACTICE

Reading Parts 1 & 5
Writing Parts 1 & 2
Listening Part 1
Speaking Parts 1 & 2

Speaking Part 1 Interview

Work with a partner. Discuss the questions.

1 What's your favourite colour? Why?
2 What clothes do you wear at the weekend?
3 Are you interested in fashion? Why/Why not?
4 How often do you go shopping?
5 Tell us about a clothing shop near where you live.

What to expect in the exam

- In Part 1, the examiner asks you questions about your likes/dislikes, daily routine and other personal information. The questions are simple to help you feel comfortable at the beginning of the exam.
- You only speak to the examiner in this part of the exam, not to your partner.

1 IN STYLE

a

b

c

d

Speaking Part 2 Extended turn

How to go about it

- In Part 2, you describe a picture for one minute. Keep talking until the examiner stops you.
- Start with general information about the photo, e.g. how many people are in the photograph and what they are doing. Then give more specific details about the people and the place.
- Describe people's clothing. It's an easy way to demonstrate your vocabulary range.

1 Match the descriptions (1–8) to the pictures (a–d).

1 She is wearing jeans.
2 She is wearing a red tracksuit.
3 She is wearing leather sandals.
4 She is wearing a colourful blouse.
5 She is wearing a black jacket.
6 She is wearing red shorts.
7 She is wearing a black skirt.
8 She is wearing a light blue sweater.

2 **SPEAK** Work in pairs. Look at the photographs. They show people spending time together. Describe the people's clothing using words from the boxes.

black blue brown gold green grey orange yellow

boots coat hat shirt shoes sweater T-shirt trousers

In picture 1, the man on the right is wearing a black hat, a sweater, jeans and boots.

3 Student A: Look at photograph 1. Tell your partner what you can see.

Student B: Look at photograph 2. Tell your partner what you can see.

1

2

Vocabulary Clothing

1 Label the pictures of accessories (a–l) with the words in the box.

belt bracelet cap earrings gloves handbag
necklace ring scarf sunglasses tie watch

a

______

b

______

c

______

d

______

e

______

f

______

g

______

h

______

i

______

j

______

k

______

l

______

2 Choose the correct alternative in each sentence.

1 'Where are the changing rooms? I want to *prove* / *try on* these clothes before I buy them.'
2 'These trousers *fit* / *form* me perfectly. They are the right size and length.'
3 'I need to buy a green handbag to *play* / *match* my new green dress.'
4 'My football boots always *break up* / *wear out* fast because I use them a lot.'
5 'I need to *put on* / *dress up* for an important meeting, so I decided to *take up* / *wear* this new suit.'
6 'It's quite hot today. *Quit* / *Take off* those trousers and *turn into* / *put on* some shorts!'

3 Write the correct answers from Exercise 2 next to their definitions (1–8).

1 when clothes are the correct size and shape ______
2 have clothes or accessories on your body ______
3 put clothes on to see if they fit and look good ______
4 wear smart or formal clothes ______
5 when clothes are similar in colour, pattern or style ______
6 use something a lot until it isn't in good condition ______
7 dress yourself with an article of clothing ______
8 remove clothes ______

4 SPEAK Work in pairs. Discuss how true the sentences are for you.

1 I never wear any accessories.
2 I ask people to take off their shoes when they visit my house.
3 It's almost impossible to find jeans that fit me.
4 I never buy clothes online. I like going to shops and trying clothes on.
5 I hate dressing up. I feel uncomfortable in smart clothes.

Reading Part 1 Multiple choice

What to expect in the exam

- In Part 1, there are five short texts. These could be notices, signs, notes, emails, text messages or instructions. For each text, there is a multiple-choice question which tests your understanding of the main message.
- The incorrect options often include wrong information or information that does not appear in the text.
- The correct option repeats the main message of the text, but usually uses different words.

1 Look at the text for the first question in Exercise 3 below, ignoring the options for now. Which of the options (a or b) best describes the purpose of the text?

a to advertise something

b to explain rules people must follow

2 **SPEAK** Work in pairs. Look at the texts in questions 2–5 in Exercise 3 below, ignoring the options for now. Discuss the purpose of each text.

3 Now for questions 1–5, choose the correct answer (A, B or C).

How to go about it

- For each question, look at the design and images to help you understand what type of message it is. Then, carefully read the text to find out what the main message and purpose of it are.
- Compare each option with the meaning of the text. An option may have the same word or phrase as the text but not be the correct answer.
- Check your answer. Read the option you have chosen again to make sure that its meaning matches the text.

1

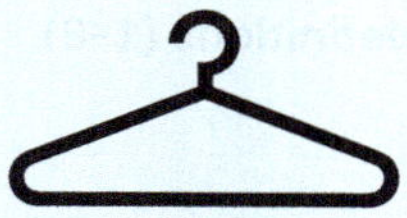

FITTING ROOM POLICY

No more than 5 items in the fitting room

Help our staff by putting all unwanted items on the counter before you leave

A Remember to take your items with you when you leave.

B If you want a different size from the counter, ask the staff.

C You are only permitted to try on five items at a time.

2

TO: Guillermo
FROM: Mark
SUBJECT: Gallery tour

Just to remind you about the urban art gallery tour on Saturday.

I'll wait for you at the entrance from 3.45 pm, but the guide says to be on time – she'll start no later than 4 pm. The tour finishes at 5 pm.

What is Mark doing?

A warning Guillermo not to be late for the tour
B asking whether Guillermo can come to the tour
C helping Guillermo remember an invitation to the tour

3

SNOWBOARD FOR SALE

Not even three years old and in good condition

Quick sale preferred

Offers welcome, but no less than 200 pounds, please

Zack 7975 747 356

A Zack's snowboard needs repairs.
B Zack would accept 200 pounds for his snowboard.
C Zack bought his snowboard three years ago.

4

50 % wool   50% cotton

Think about the Earth while washing this product.

Save energy and wash in cold water.

Hanging your clothes out to dry means more fresh air for your clothes and for the planet.

A Wool clothing must be washed in cold water.
B Drying this product in a machine will cause damage to it.
C Wash at this temperature to help the environment.

5

Hi Ashley
We're walking to the park right now, but it's starting to rain. I think we have to postpone our basketball game. What about tomorrow? I have to work in the morning, but I'm free all afternoon.
Charlotte

Charlotte is writing to

A ask if Ashley is available to play basketball.
B cancel plans she had made with Ashley.
C complain about the bad weather.

4 Go to the **Additional materials** on **page 196**.

Vocabulary Prepositions of time

1 **Look at these sentences from the reading texts and choose the correct alternative.**

1 Just to remind you about the urban art gallery tour *at* / *in* / *on* Saturday.
2 The tour finishes *at* / *in* / *on* 5 pm.
3 I have to work *at* / *in* / *on* the morning, but I'm free all afternoon.

2 **Check your answers in the Reading Part 1 task on page 5.**

3 **Complete each gap with a preposition which can be used before both noun phrases.**

at in on

1 ______ the afternoon the evening
2 ______ midday lunchtime
3 ______ January the month of June
4 ______ weekdays my birthday
5 ______ 1982 the year I was born
6 ______ summer the holiday season
7 ______ 21st May the 7th of November
8 ______ night the weekend
9 ______ (the) future the past
10 ______ half an hour five minutes' time

4 **Complete the table with *at, in* or *on.***

months (e.g. *January*)	
dates (e.g. *1st June*)	
seasons (e.g. *summer*)	
years (e.g. *1995*)	
clock times (e.g. *ten o'clock*)	
days of the week (e.g. *Thursday*)	

5 **We often use *at* in time expressions. Match the sentence beginnings (1–6) to the sentence endings (a–f).**

1 I thought it was a joke **at**
2 Go and get ready **at**
3 When I get paid **at**
4 I'm sorry, but I'm too upset **at**
5 We carried the boxes **one at**
6 Don't you feel nervous **at**

a **the end** of the week, I'll buy a new phone.
b **the thought of** speaking in public?
c **once**! We're going to be late.
d **a time** up the stairs because they were so heavy.
e **first**, but then I realised he was serious.
f **the moment** to discuss this. Can we talk later?

6 **Complete the sentences so that they are true for you.**

On Mondays, ...
In the afternoon, I usually ...
In summer, one of my favourite things to do is ...
At the weekend, I never ...
At the moment, I don't have enough time to ...

7 **SPEAK Discuss your sentences with a classmate. Ask follow-up questions.**

A: At the weekend, I never sleep late. I always get up early and go for a walk.
B: Really? Don't you want to sleep more?
A: I want to, but I can't! I wake up at the same time every day.

Language focus Present simple and present continuous

1 SPEAK In pairs, read sentences 1–5 and decide if the underlined verbs are in the present simple or the present continuous.

1 I go to the hairdresser's at least once a month.
2 Sorry, I can't talk now – I'm packing my suitcase.
3 The sun sets in the west.
4 She still lives in the house she was born in 63 years ago.
5 He's reading *The Lord of the Rings* trilogy. He hopes to finish the second book this week.

2 Match sentences 1–5 in Exercise 1 to uses a–e below.

Use the present simple to talk about:
a things that are always true.
b permanent or long-term situations.
c routines and habits.

Use the present continuous to talk about:
d temporary activities or situations.
e actions in progress at the present moment.

3 Go to **Ready for Grammar on page 202** **for rules, explanations and further practice.**

4 Read the following social media post and choose the correct options.

GREY MATTER

As I sit here and write this post, I (1) *wear / 'm wearing* grey trainers made from wool and a grey cotton T-shirt. My desk and chair? Grey. My car? Yes, you guessed it – grey. As you can probably tell, grey is my favourite colour. My wife (thankfully) loves it, too. Some people (2) *find / are finding* this strange. They think that grey (3) *doesn't count / is not counting* as a colour. For them, grey is unexciting, boring – depressing, even. Okay, I (4) *don't say / 'm not saying* that I don't understand people's dislike of grey. It's not exactly a colourful colour. But, for me, there is so much to love. Grey (5) *looks / is looking* modern and professional, stylish and sophisticated. Stop and think: what colour (6) *do you associate / are you associating* with experience and responsibility? Grey, of course! As you can see, I could talk about grey all day, but, before I finish, I have a question for all my followers: right now my wife and I (7) *search / are searching* for the perfect pair of matching grey slippers to wear around the house. (8) *Does anyone have / Is anyone having* any suggestions?

5 SPEAK Do you agree with the writer's opinions about the colour grey? Why/Why not?

6 Complete each gap with the present simple or present continuous form of the verb in brackets. The subject is always *you*.

1 *Do you listen* (*listen*) to the radio in the morning?
2 When it's cold, ______ (*wear*) a hat and gloves?
3 In general, ______ (*prefer*) your clothing to be fashionable or comfortable?
4 ______ (*watch*) any good TV series right now?
5 Apart from English, ______ (*learn*) any other languages at the moment?
6 ______ (*know*) anybody famous?

7 SPEAK In pairs, take turns to discuss the questions in Exercise 6. Ask follow-up questions.

Listening Part 1 Multiple choice

1 1.1 Read question 1 and look at the three pictures. Then listen to and read the extract from the Audioscript. The underlined sections contain words or phrases which refer to pictures A, B and C. Choose the correct answer (A, B or C).

1 What does the woman decide to order?

A

B

C

Woman:	I'm glad we decided to have Italian food. I really like this restaurant.
Man:	Me too. What do you want to eat? If I know you, it'll be the pizza. That's what you usually have.
Woman:	Yes, this one with mushrooms and peppers looks delicious. But then, well – this pasta with prawns looks really interesting, too. I don't often eat pasta.
Man:	What about the risotto? You like rice.
Woman:	It's true, but you know what? I think I'll have what I normally order.
Man:	Okay, and I think I'll have that pasta you mentioned.

2 SPEAK Work in pairs. Compare and explain your answers. Say why the other two answers are incorrect.

3 1.2 You will hear people talking in six different situations. For questions 2–7, choose the best answer (A, B or C).

What to expect in the exam

- In Listening Part 1, you answer seven questions by choosing the correct picture (A, B or C).
- For each question, you hear a short conversation between two people or just one person talking, e.g. a news report, a voice message or advertisement.
- As with all parts of the listening paper, you will hear distractors. The speakers mention things from all three pictures, but only one picture is correct.

2 How is the man getting to work today?

A

B

C

3 What has the woman lost?

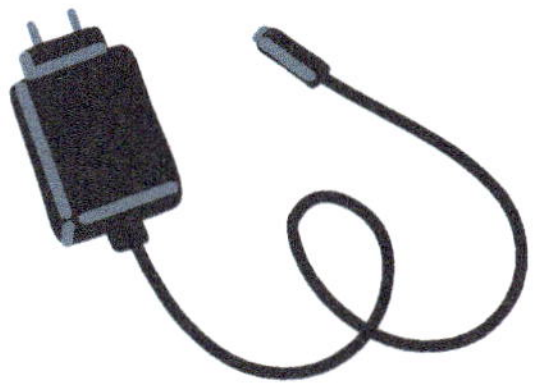
A

B

C

4 What T-shirt is the woman wearing in the photo?

A

B

C

5 What is the price of the newest smartwatch this week?

A

B

C

6 Which magazine does the man decide to buy?

A

B

C

7 Why are the streets around the main square closed today?

A

B

C

4 SPEAK Work in pairs. What kind of clothes would you wear:

- to a dinner at a nice restaurant?
- for a professional office job?
- on an airplane?
- at a farmer's market?
- for a professional photograph?
- to a concert?

Language focus Adverbs of frequency

1 Look at sentences from the listening and underline the correct alternative in the rules 1–4 below.

*I **usually** wear plain white T-shirts.*

1 Put adverbs of frequency *before* / *after* most verbs.

*There are **always** interesting film reviews to read.*

2 Put adverbs of frequency *before* / *after* the verb *be*.

*I don't **often** eat pasta.*

3 Put adverbs of frequency *before* / *after* auxiliary verbs.

*I drive to work **every day**.*

4 Put longer adverbial phrases *at the end* / *in the middle* of the sentence.

2 Adverbs of frequency say how often something happens. Put the adverbs in the box into the correct place in the continuum.

always hardly ever ~~never~~ often sometimes usually

1 *never* 2 ______ 3 ______ 4 ______ 5 ______ 6 ______

0% 50% 100%

3 Go to Ready for Grammar on page 202 for rules, explanations and further practice.

4 **SPEAK** Work in pairs. Talk about how frequently you do the following things:

- buy new clothes
- clean your car
- ride a bike
- play chess

Writing Part 1 Email

1 **Read the Writing Part 1 task below and answer the questions.**

1. Who are you writing to?
2. Why are you writing?
3. What information do you have to include in the email you write?
4. How long should your email be?

Read this email from your English-speaking friend Marc and the notes you have made.

From: Marc
Subject: New clothes
Hi,
It's been a week since I last saw you, so I thought it would be nice to meet up tomorrow. ← Agree.
As you know, I need to buy some new clothes for work. We could go to the shopping centre or the High Street in the city centre. Which do you prefer? ← Say which
Maybe some other friends could come with us. Who should we invite? ← Suggest …
In the evening, we could go to the cinema if you're free. Let me know! ← Thanks, but …
Marc

Reply to Marc using all the notes. Write your email in about 100 words.

2 **Read the following answer. Does Sergio respond to all the notes?**

Hi Marc,
Thanks for writing. Yes, let's meet up tomorrow evening after I finish work.
It's true – I remember you wanted to buy a new suit to wear to the office. I need some new clothes, too. Maybe I'll look at shirts. Mine are all a bit old. You asked about where to go. Personally, I like the shopping centre better. It has more variety.
It's been a long time since I saw Lucas. Why don't we invite him?
About the cinema, I'm sorry, but I can't go. I have plans with my girlfriend.
Bye for now.
Sergio

3 **Add the underlined expressions from the model answer to the table below.**

Responding to an email	Making suggestions	Ending an email
	let's …	

4 **Add the following expressions to the table in Exercise 3.**

Shall we …? | *Nice/Good/Great to hear from you.*
See / Talk to you soon. | *Thanks for your email.*
Take care. | *You/We could …*

5 **Read the information in the *How to go about it* box. Then go to the Additional materials on page 196 and do the Writing Part 1 task.**

For more information on writing emails, see pages 192–193.

How to go about it

- Read the email and think about these questions:
  - **a** Who you are writing to?
  - **b** Why you are writing to this person?
  - **c** What four points do you have to include in your response?
- Plan your email. Think about what you want to say, and in what order. It's easier to write your email if you decide what you want to say first.
- Don't copy words and phrases from the input email.

1 REVIEW

Reading Part 5 Multiple-choice cloze

1 Read the following text, ignoring the gaps for the moment. What kind of business did Iman Abdulmajid start?

2 Now read the text again. For questions 1–6, choose which answer (A, B, C or D) best fits the gap.

How to go about it

- First, read the text quickly to get a general idea of what it's about.
- Read each sentence with a gap, paying close attention to the words that come before and after the gap. Choose the word that best fits.
- Before you finish, read the whole text again to check that all your answers make sense.

A Model Businesswoman

Iman Abdulmajid is a world-famous model and businesswoman, but she didn't always **(1)** .... of working in the fashion industry.

Iman is originally from Somalia, but she **(2)** .... university in Kenya, where she studied political science. One day, a well-known fashion photographer stopped her on the street. Soon after, she moved to New York, where she quickly became a supermodel. In 1992, she married British singer David Bowie. However, Iman was not satisfied with being famous and **(3)** .... beautiful clothes. She decided to create her own cosmetics company, which makes a **(4)** .... range of beauty products for women with all skin colours. It is now a successful global brand.

For many years, Iman has been **(5)** .... in charity work, helping to raise millions of dollars. At the **(6)** ...., she is supporting the CARE association in its fight against world hunger.

1	A imagine	B dream	C hope	D wish
2	A attended	B went	C joined	D made
3	A putting	B dressing	C wearing	D fitting
4	A deep	B long	C high	D wide
5	A involved	B concerned	C decided	D accepted
6	A point	B instant	C minute	D moment

Vocabulary Prepositions of time

1 Complete the sentences with *at*, *in* or *on*.

1. In Europe, the longest day of the year is always ____________ the month of June.
2. After a 35-year career in fashion, Pavel plans to retire ____________ the end of the month.
3. ____________ the rainy season, the river rises by 1.5 metres and covers the surrounding fields.
4. According to the website, the library is busiest from 11 am to 2 pm ____________ weekdays.
5. Attention all customers: the shop will close ____________ half an hour.
6. When you all speak ____________ once, I can't understand anything!
7. I bought this dress to wear ____________ my birthday.
8. Traditionally, they break for tea and biscuits ____________ midday.

Language focus Present simple and present continuous

Underline the correct alternatives.

1 **A:** Has your son found a flat?
B: Not yet. For now, he *stays* / *'s staying* with a friend.

2 **A:** Does the university have a good French department?
B: Yes, it does. We *teach* / *'re teaching* a range of levels every year – from beginner to advanced.

3 **A:** Which one is Simon?
B: That's him over there – the one who *waits* / *is waiting* in line to buy tickets.

4 **A:** Do you always wear trainers to work?
B: No, not usually, but right now I *wear* / *'m wearing* them to help with the pain in my back.

5 **A:** Are your children musical?
B: Yes, they *play* / *'re playing* the piano very well, and this year they're also learning to sing.

6 **A:** Where are you?
B: I *sit* / *'m sitting* on a bench outside that shoe shop we like.

7 **A:** How do you get around the city?
B: On foot or by public transport. We *don't own* / *'re not owning* a car.

8 **A:** Do you have time to help me organise these files?
B: Sorry, but I *leave* / *'m leaving* the office now. Maybe tomorrow?

Writing Part 2 Article

You see this announcement in an online English-language magazine.

> **Articles wanted!**
>
> **New clothes**
>
> - Do you like shopping for new clothes?
> - Do you think people feel different when they wear new clothes?
>
> Write an article answering these questions. The best articles answering these questions will win a prize.

Write your article in about 100 words.

For more information on writing articles, see **page 195**.

Pronunciation /ʊ/, /uː/ and /ʌ/

1 Match the words from the Listening Part 1 task on pages 8–9 to their correct pronunciations. There is an example at the beginning (0).

come cook food good just move put sun true

/ʊ/	/uː/	/ʌ/
0 /kʊk/ *cook*	**3** /fuːd/ ______	**6** /kʌm/ ______
1 /gʊd/ ______	**4** /muːv/ ______	**7** /sʌn/ ______
2 /pʊt/ ______	**5** /truː/ ______	**8** /dʒʌst/ ______

2 1.3 Listen and repeat the words with the /ʊ/, /uː/ and /ʌ/ sounds.

3 Which vowel sound – /ʊ/, /uː/ or /ʌ/ – is longer than the other two?

4 **SPEAK** Work in pairs. Play the game and find three paths across the river.

Cross the river

There is one path for words with /ʊ/ sounds, one for words with /uː/ sounds and one for words with /ʌ/ sounds. Say the words out loud as you play.

wool /ʊ/	**balloon**	**study**	**juice** /uː/	**front**	**through**	**country** /ʌ/
June	**look**	**up**	**number**	**blue**	**colour**	**too**
sugar	**bus**	**pull**	**soup**	**full**	**glove**	**look**
summer	**nut**	**lose**	**could**	**soon**	**foot**	**cut**
would	**suit**	**summer**	**bull**	**does**	**touch**	**boot**
shoe	**must**	**young**	**bush**	**who**	**wolf**	**nothing**

2

TAKING IT EASY

KEY LANGUAGE

Past simple and *used to*
Past simple and past continuous
-ed and *-ing* adjectives
Leisure activities

PRONUNCIATION

-ed endings: /t/, /d/ and /ɪd/

EXAM PRACTICE

Reading Parts 2 & 6
Writing Parts 1 & 2
Listening Part 2
Speaking Parts 1, 2 & 4

Speaking Part 1 Interview

Work with a partner. Discuss the questions.

1 Where do you live?
2 Describe the people you live with.
3 How often do you meet up with friends?
4 Do you play any musical instruments?
5 What kinds of things do you enjoy reading?

Speaking Part 2 Extended turn

Describe the picture and say:

- how many people there are
- what activity they are doing
- what clothes they are wearing

2 TAKING IT EASY

Listening Part 2 Multiple choice

1 Look at the photograph. Where are the people? Why do you think they decided to go to this place?

What to expect in the exam

- Listening Part 2 consists of six short dialogues. As with all B1 Preliminary listening tasks, you will hear each dialogue twice.
- For each dialogue, there is a multiple-choice question with three options. The questions test your general understanding of the dialogue, for example someone's feelings or opinion. You may also have to listen for what two people agree on.

2 Read question 1 in Exercise 3. Look at the shaded Audioscript on pages 236–237 and answer these questions.

1 What synonym of the word 'book' does the woman mention?

2 What activities at the library does the woman mention? How do we know they're free?

3 How do we know the woman does NOT use the library as a quiet place to study?

3 **2.1** **You will hear people talking in six different situations. For questions 1–6, choose the best answer (A, B or C).**

1 You will hear two students talking about their local library.
What does the woman like best about it?
A You can borrow books.
B There are free activities.
C It's a good place to study.

2 You will hear two friends talking about the characters in a TV show they've watched.
What does the woman say about the characters?
A They don't behave like real people.
B It's easy to predict what they will do.
C They have funny conversations.

3 You will hear a man talking about a tourist apartment.
How did he feel?
A tired of cooking all his own food
B satisfied with the help he got from the owner
C pleased with the location of the apartment

4 You will hear two workmates talking on the phone about a report.
The woman calls the man to
A explain to him how to use a computer program.
B remind him to check the information in his reports.
C give him advice on how to improve his writing.

5 You will hear two friends talking about a history museum.
They agree that
A the dinosaur section has improved.
B the food in the café is very expensive.
C teenagers think museums are boring.

6 You will hear two friends talking about an online course.
The woman thinks it was
A challenging to hand in everything on time.
B enjoyable to study with someone else.
C easier to study online than face-to-face.

Language focus Past simple and *used to*

1 **Read the dialogues. Choose the correct alternatives to complete rules 1 and 2 below.**

A: **Did you go** to the concert last night? I **didn't see** you there.
B: No, I **stayed** at home and **studied**.

A: As a teenager, what **did you use to do** in your free time?
B: I **used to meet up** with my friends after school. We often **went** to a park and just **chatted**.

A: Roberto is in much better shape these days.
B: It's true. He **didn't use to be** very fit, but now he exercises three times a week.

1 We use *used to* with the base form to talk about past habits or states that are *still* / *no longer* true in the present. We *can also* / *cannot* use the past simple in these situations.
2 To talk about single completed actions in the past, we can *only use the past simple* / *use either 'used to' or the past simple.*

2 **Look at the dialogues in Exercise 1 again and answer the following questions.**

1 What are the negative and question forms of *used to*?
2 What are the past simple forms of these verbs?

chat go stay study

3 How do we form negatives and questions in the past simple?

3 **Go to Ready for Grammar on page 204 for rules, explanations and further practice.**

4 **For sentence endings 1–5, write two sentence beginnings with *used to* – one positive and one negative. There is an example at the beginning (0).**

0 ... but now I prepare most of my own meals.
When I was younger, I didn't use to like cooking ...
As a university student, I used to buy lots of takeaway food ...
1 ... but now I wake up early.
2 ... but now I can speak and understand the language quite well.
3 ... but now I work in a law firm and I have to wear a suit and tie.
4 ... but now I go to the cinema almost every week.
5 ... but now I take the train every day.

5 **SPEAK** **Work in pairs. Discuss topics 1–6 below. Think about the correct use of the past simple and *used to*. Ask follow-up questions for more information.**

1 the types of films you used to watch
2 a video game or sport you used to play
3 a competition you won or lost
4 a type of music you used to listen to
5 an interesting event you once attended
6 a place you used to go on holiday

A: When I was a teenager, I used to watch a lot of superhero films, but I'm not really interested in those anymore.
B: I used to love those films, too. Did you have a favourite superhero?

Reading Part 2 Matching

1 **SPEAK** What are the advantages and disadvantages of shopping online?

2 You are going to read about eight clothing websites (A–H). For the people below (1–5), decide which clothing website would be most suitable.

What to expect in the exam

- In Part 2, you have to match five descriptions of people to eight short texts (the options), all of which are related to the same topic.
- Three of the options don't match any of the descriptions, but they contain distractors. For example, option A on page 19 does not match any of the descriptions (1–5). It contains the phrase 'offers free returns within 30 days, no questions asked', which relates to description 2, but doesn't mention the other information in the description.
- For this reason, it's important to check that the option you choose correctly matches ALL the information in the description, not just one specific detail.

1 **Josip and Tara** want to buy clothing that will last a long time, and they would like to know about the people who make the clothes. They'd like to buy from a website with good reviews.

2 **Sam** needs to buy new clothes to wear while jogging, and she wants these articles of clothing to be fashionable. She'd like to buy from a website that makes it easy to return things.

3 **Isak** is very tall and needs to find clothing that will fit him. He wants clothing he can wear while doing outdoor activities and he doesn't care about the latest trends.

4 **Florence and Albert** are going to a wedding and need something nice to wear. They want to buy clothes from designer brands, but they don't want to pay full price.

5 **Francesca** is going on a trip to the mountains this winter and needs some warm, comfortable clothes to wear. She'd like to find a website with a lot of options.

3 **SPEAK** Work in pairs. Which of the websites would you prefer to use? Why?

CLOTHING WEBSITES

A FASHIONSHOP.COM

Fashionshop.com aims to connect everyday shoppers with the work of promising new designers. Be the first to wear next year's big trend. If you take a risk and regret it, fashionshop.com offers free returns within 30 days, no questions asked. Plus, it sells more than just clothes: you'll find plenty of beauty products there too.

B FORMACTION.COM

Need something to wear for a special occasion? Head to formaction.com, where you'll find elegant dresses, jackets, suits and so much more. The best part about this website is the sales, you won't find high-fashion clothes at lower prices anywhere else! Attention environmentally minded customers: formaction.com only uses packaging made from 100% recycled paper.

C ATHLETEZ.COM

Gym clothes don't have to be boring! Athletez.com sells stylish clothes to exercise in. The website gives you the option of searching the site by type of workout: boxing, yoga, tennis – you name it. Check out their colourful trainers and matching tracksuit bottoms. If a piece of clothing doesn't fit right, not to worry. Send it back for an immediate refund.

D FAIRCLOTHING.COM

Shop at fairclothing.com and make the world a better place. The site represents 200 small brands. The result? More than 40,000 feel-good products in one place. Each brand has its own profile with detailed information about everything from working conditions to the use of renewable resources. Our recommendation: the super comfortable sweaters, made from 100% New Zealand wool. They're just what you need for outdoor activities in the autumn or spring.

E SIMPLYGOOD.COM

Are you interested in good quality clothing that won't wear out? Check out simplygood.com. It offers an impressive selection of casual clothes like sweaters, shirts and trousers. One thing that sets this site apart is the pictures they provide of the factories where the clothing is made and the employees who work there. Based on the positive comments online, this website has a bright future.

F ENJOYTHEOUTDOORS.COM

The homepage of enjoytheoutdoors.com says, 'Being outdoors brings out the best in us.' As you might expect, it's a great place to find clothes for hiking or camping – or just taking a long walk on a cold day. With so many different choices, you could spend hours on enjoytheoutdoors.com. We recommend their jackets – they will keep you warm all day in low temperatures.

G FASHIONFORLESS.COM

Dress like a model without paying a small fortune. Fashionforless.com has joined forces with popular designers to bring you a low-cost collection of fun and fashionable casual designs. They also have accessories for all occasions, from scarves and gloves to sandals and sun hats. In a rush? Fashionforless.com can deliver select items in 24 hours. Now that's what I call service!

H CLOTHES4EVERYBODY.COM

Do you find the whole idea of fashion annoying? Rather go hiking than shopping? Then clothes4everybody.com is for you. From shirts to trousers, T-shirts to jeans, sports and outdoor clothing, check out the full range of everyday items in plain colours. There is a wide variety of sizes that work for any body type, which has led to many positive reviews. Second-hand items are also available.

Vocabulary *-ed* and *-ing* adjectives

1 Look at the sentences from the reading text on page 19. Choose the correct alternatives to complete rules 1 and 2.

*Gym clothes don't have to be **boring**!*

*Are you **interested** in good quality clothing ...?*

*Do you find the whole idea of fashion **annoying**?*

Some adjectives have two forms (*-ed* or *-ing*):

1 Use adjectives ending in ***-ed / -ing*** to describe the person who experiences an emotion.

2 Use adjectives ending in ***-ed / -ing*** to describe a person or thing that causes an emotion.

2 Underline the correct alternative to complete the sentences.

1 I was *surprised / surprising* to see Jules in the tournament. I didn't even know he played tennis.

2 United suffered an *embarrassing / embarrassed* 4–1 defeat at home on Saturday. The players walked red-faced to their dressing room at the end of the game.

3 Up there on stage, Margot looked completely *relaxed / relaxing*, as if she were talking to five people instead of five hundred.

4 Mum was *disappointed / disappointing* with my decision not to attend university. She wanted me to become a lawyer like her.

5 There's something very *satisfied / satisfying* about preparing a meal using vegetables that come from your own garden.

6 About halfway through the book, I got really *confused / confusing* and didn't understand what was happening in the story.

7 Around the world, animal populations have decreased by almost 70% in just 50 years. That is a *frightened / frightening* statistic.

8 Avoid creating *frustrated / frustrating* experiences for your children, such as making them learn to ride a bike before they are ready.

3 Make notes and prepare to tell your partner about two of the following.

- a travel experience you found frustrating
- a decision you made that you are satisfied or disappointed with
- a leisure activity you find relaxing
- a part of English grammar you find confusing
- an animal you are or used to be frightened of

4 **SPEAK** Work in pairs. Using your notes, tell your partner about the topics you chose from Exercise 3. Ask follow-up questions.

For me, reading is a relaxing leisure activity.

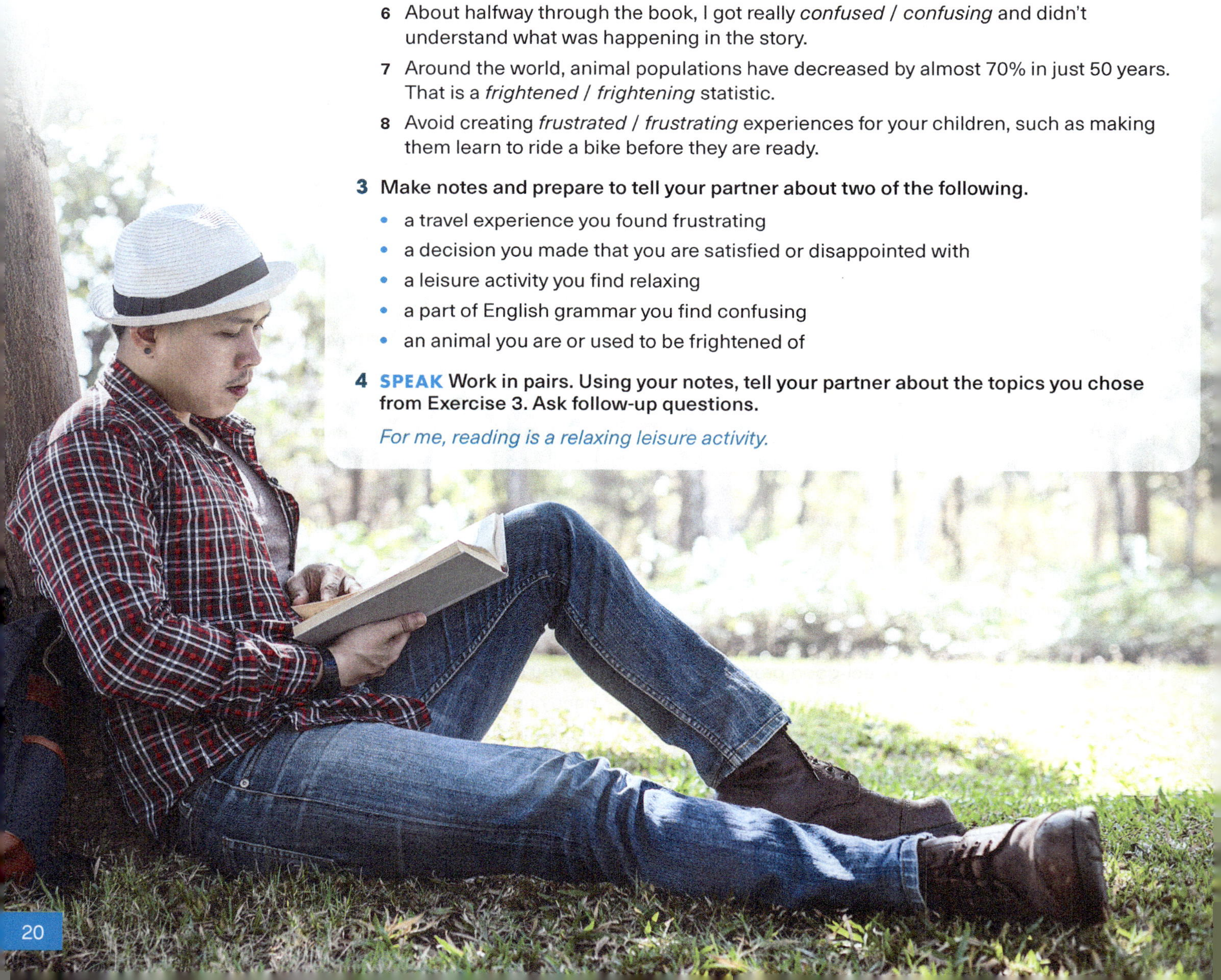

Language focus Past simple and past continuous

1 **Read the embarrassing stories and complete rules 1 and 2 below with the correct tense: past simple or past continuous.**

At my wedding, I **was dancing** with my mother-in-law when I accidently **stepped** on her foot. It really hurt and she **got** quite angry with me. I was really embarrassed!

Last year, I **was studying** Italian and I **decided** to take a trip to Italy. On the first day, I **ordered** a 'latte' at a coffee shop and **received** a glass of milk instead of a cup of coffee. I felt really silly!

1 Use the ______________________ for completed actions in the past.

2 Use the ______________________ for actions in progress at a particular time in the past.

2 **Go to Ready for Grammar on page 204 for rules, explanations and further practice.**

3 **Complete stories A and B by choosing the correct alternative.**

A

You won't believe what happened to me at the vehicle registration agency the other day. I **(1)** *sat* / *was sitting* in the office and the woman who worked there **(2)** *registered* / *was registering* my car when she **(3)** *asked* / *was asking* me a simple question, 'What body type?' I **(4)** *didn't know* / *wasn't knowing* what to say. 'Uh, average, I guess. Maybe a bit overweight?', I **(5)** *answered* / *was answering* finally. 'Of the car!', she said and immediately began to laugh. I felt ridiculous.

B

The most embarrassing thing happened to my boyfriend the other day. He **(6)** *walked* / *was walking* down the high street when he **(7)** *started* / *was starting* to feel hungry. Just then, he **(8)** *saw* / *was seeing* a fried chicken restaurant. There was a woman outside holding a box of free samples. The fried chicken **(9)** *looked* / *was looking* delicious. The woman **(10)** *grabbed* / *was grabbing* his hand while he **(11)** *put* / *was putting* it into the box to take a piece and wanted to know what he **(12)** *did* / *was doing*. They weren't free samples. She was just a customer holding a box of chicken!

4 **Write a story similar to the ones in Exercise 3. Use ONE of the prompts (1–2) below to help you create the story. Pay attention to how you use the past simple and past continuous.**

1 You met somebody for the first time and made a bad impression.
- Who did you meet?
- What were you doing when you met them?
- How did you feel?

2 You sent an email or message to the wrong person.
- Who did you send the email or message to?
- What were you doing when you sent it?
- How did you feel?

5 **SPEAK** **Work in small groups. Take turns to read out each other's stories. Then discuss whose story is the most original or entertaining.**

Writing Part 2 Story

1 Read the following Writing Part 2 instructions and answer the questions.

1 Who is the main character of the story?

2 Where does the story start?

Your English teacher has asked you to write a story. Your story must begin with this sentence.

When Paula walked in, everybody at the party looked surprised.

Write your **story** in about **100 words**.

2 Read a model answer to the Part 1 task in Exercise 1, ignoring the gaps. Does the rest of the story clearly connect with the first sentence?

(1) ____________ Paula walked in, everybody at the party looked surprised. Nobody thought she was coming – even though the party was for her.

It was Paula's birthday, so some friends decided to throw a surprise party. All her friends came. There were presents and decorations, but no Paula. They had forgotten to invite her! As **(2)** ____________ as they realised their mistake, they texted her. 'Sorry, very busy,' Paula responded. Everybody was disappointed. 'What do we do now?', they wondered. Then, all of a **(3)** ____________, Paula walked through the door.

In the **(4)** ____________, instead of being surprised, Paula had surprised her friends!

3 Complete the time expressions (1–4) in the story with the words in the box.

end	when	soon	sudden

4 Match each part of a story (1–3) to its purpose (a–c).

1 beginning
2 middle
3 end

a The action finishes, or the problem or conflict is resolved.
b The characters and setting are introduced.
c An important action takes place, or there is a problem or conflict the characters must deal with.

5 **SPEAK** Work in pairs. Read the Part 2 task below and think about what kind of story you could write. Put your ideas in the table below.

Your English teacher has asked you to write a story. Your story must begin with this sentence.

> **It was my first day on the course and I felt a bit nervous.**

Write your **story** in about **100 words**.

Part of the story	Action/Reason	Good vocabulary to include
1 **Beginning** *painting course*	**Reason for feeling nervous** *It's your first time taking an art course.*	*paintbrush, picture, landscape, detail, studio, beautiful, original, etc.*
2 **Middle**	**What is the problem?**	
3 **End**	**What happened?**	

6 Now do the Part 2 writing task from Exercise 5. Use your ideas from the table.

How to go about it

- Read the task instructions. Identify the main character and the setting in the first sentence of the story.
- Ask yourself: Who is this person? Why are they in this place?
- Plan the beginning, middle and end of your story.
- Start your story with the sentence in the task instructions. Connect the rest of the story to this first sentence. So, if the story starts with *Monica climbed out of the car and ran as fast as she could to the forest*, your story should involve a forest and a woman named Monica.
- Tell your story using the names or pronouns in the first sentence, e.g. using *I*, *they*, or *he/she*.

For more information on writing stories, see page 194.

Vocabulary Leisure activities

1 **SPEAK** Work in pairs. Talk about what you like doing in your free time.

2 Write each verb on the left (A) next to the correct leisure activity on the right (B). The first one has been done for you.

A	B			A	B		
~~go~~	1	______	at a restaurant	use	7	______	events
take	2	*go*	hiking	attend	8	______	shopping
eat out	3	______	photographs	go	9	______	social media
do	4	______	films at the cinema	go	10	______	video games
see	5	______	exercise	read	11	______	the news
spend	6	______	time with friends	play	12	______	for a walk

3 **SPEAK** Work in pairs. Look at pictures 1–4 below. Which of the leisure activities from Exercise 2 are the people doing?

4 **SPEAK** Take turns to describe pictures 1–4 below.

5 Put the expressions in the correct column.

~~I really enjoy ...~~ I'm not really into ... I'm a big fan of ... I can't stand ...

I don't like ... at all. I like ... a lot. I can't live without ...

Likes	Dislikes
I really enjoy ...	

6 **SPEAK** Work in small groups. Discuss the leisure activities in Exercise 2. Use expressions from Exercise 5. Give reasons why you like or dislike the activities.

Personally, I'm a big fan of going for a walk in the evening. I find it very relaxing

Speaking Part 4 General conversation

SPEAK Read the information in the boxes below. Then discuss the questions that follow with a partner.

What to expect in the exam

- In Speaking Part 4, you discuss your habits, opinions, likes/dislikes and personal experiences.
- The examiner may ask you a question to answer individually. They may also ask you a question to discuss together with your partner.
- Listen carefully to your partner while they are answering a question. The examiner may ask you a follow-up question about what your partner said, e.g. 'Do you agree?'
- Ask your partner questions to find out their opinions.

1 What do you usually do after work or school? Why?
2 What did you do last weekend?
3 Do you have enough free time? Why/Why not?
4 Do you prefer spending your free time with your family or with your friends? Why?
5 Is it important to relax in your free time? Why/Why not?

Useful language

Talking about personal experiences

The other day, I started listening to a new podcast.

In my experience, it's hard to make time for exercise.

When I was younger, I used to spend most of my time indoors watching TV.

3

4

2 REVIEW

Reading Part 6 Open cloze

For questions 1–6, read the text below and think of the word which best fits each gap. Use only one word in each gap.

What to expect in the exam

- In Reading Part 6, you read a short text with six missing words. You have to fill each gap with one word – never two. The answer is never a contraction (*it's*, *you're*).
- This task mainly tests grammatical structures, so the missing words are often 'grammar words', such as pronouns (*your*, *it*), prepositions (*in*, *of*) and verb auxiliaries (*have*/*has*/*had*, *was*/*were*).
- The open cloze also tests vocabulary by gapping words in phrasal verbs (*look forward to*, *base on*) and fixed expressions (*in spite of*, *after all*).

STARGAZING

My friend Rory belongs to a stargazing club – a group of people that get together to look at the night sky – and last Saturday he invited me to go with him. The club meets **(1)** .... month in the Galloway Forest Park. This part of Scotland is famous **(2)** .... being a 'dark sky park'. There's no light pollution there, so it's perfect for stargazing.

Rory told me to arrive between 7.30 **(3)** .... 8.00 pm, because it was important to set **(4)** .... the telescopes before it got dark. That night, we looked at Venus, Mars, Saturn and Jupiter. But my favourite was the Moon. I could see its mountains and valleys!

I **(5)** .... to love looking at the night sky when I was child, but **(6)** .... wasn't until my trip to Galloway Forest Park with Rory that I got to see the Moon and the planets up close with a professional telescope.

Language focus Past simple and past continuous

Complete the sentences using the past simple or past continuous form of the verb in brackets.

1 When my train arrived at the station, my parents ____________________ (*wait*) for me on the platform.

2 No, Levi ____________________ (*not meet*) Sara while he was visiting Madrid. They first met in Utrecht.

3 So, what ____________________ you ____________________ (*do*) at 10.05 am on the day of the crime?

4 Sorry, I ____________________ (*not hear*) the phone because I was outside watering the garden.

5 The sun ____________________ (*rise*) over the sea just as we arrived at the coast.

6 Can you believe it? They refused to let us into the restaurant because my husband ____________________ (*not wear*) a suit jacket.

Vocabulary Leisure | *-ed* and *-ing* adjectives

Choose the correct alternatives to complete the sentences.

1 I *saw* / *looked* this horror film at the cinema when it first came out and, let me tell you, it was really *frightened* / *frightening*. It gave me bad dreams.

2 To keep active and *do* / *make* more exercise, we started taking step aerobics classes, but the instructor kept shouting at us to work harder. We quickly got *frustrated* / *frustrating* and quit.

3 After a particularly stressful week at work, Linh finds it *relaxed* / *relaxing* to drive out to the countryside and *go* / *give* for a long walk.

4 I began *making* / *taking* photographs a long time ago, but I had my first exhibition only recently. It felt really *satisfied* / *satisfying* to see my photos up there on the gallery walls.

5 They had plans to *attend* / *assist* a talk by their favourite author, but it was cancelled at the last minute. Lucy was very *disappointed* / *disappointing*; she had very much wanted to go.

Writing Part 1 Email

Read this email from your English-speaking friend Kim and the notes you have made.

From: Kim

Subject: Fancy dress party!

Hi

I'm thinking of having <u>a fancy dress party</u> at my house with some of my good friends – including you, of course! ← Good idea!

We could have the party on Friday or Saturday night. <u>Which one would be better?</u> ← Explain which day and why.

I don't want to cook, so I'm planning to order some takeaway food. <u>What kind of food do you think people would like?</u> ← Suggest …

Let me know if you have <u>any questions</u>. ← Ask about transport to Kim's house.

Talk to you soon,

Kim

Write your **email** to Kim using **all the notes**. Write your answer in about **100 words**.

For more information on writing emails, see pages 192–193.

Pronunciation *-ed* endings

1 2.2 For 1–3 below, listen and repeat the past forms of the regular verbs. Underline the word that ends in a different sound from the others in the group.

1	started	decided	performed	repeated
2	answered	received	ordered	searched
3	checked	divided	fixed	walked

2 There are three possible pronunciations for *-ed*: /t/, /d/ and /ɪd/. Put the words from Exercise 1 in the correct column.

/t/	/d/	/ɪd/
searched	*performed*	*divided*

3 What does the *-ed* ending sound like when it's added to verbs whose base form ends in the letters 't' or 'd', for example, *visit* or *need*?

4 **SPEAK** Work in pairs. Read the rules and play the game.

NOUGHTS AND CROSSES

1 **Player A, you are X. Player B you are O.**
2 **Take turns to say the correct pronunciation of the past tense form of a verb. If you say it correctly, put an X or O in the square.**
3 **The first player to win three squares in a row (up, across or diagonally) is the winner.**

handle	knock	test
end	stop	interrupt
announce	inform	encourage

5 **SPEAK** In your notebook, create your own noughts and crosses board using the words below. With a partner, play the game again.

answer argue follow introduce knock push regret skate wait

3 YOU ARE WHAT YOU EAT

KEY LANGUAGE

Countable and uncountable nouns
Articles
Containers and amounts
Food

PRONUNCIATION

/w/, /h/, /v/ and /z/

EXAM SKILLS

Reading Part 5
Writing Part 2
Listening Part 3
Speaking Parts 1, 2 & 3

Speaking Part 1 Interview

Work with a partner. Discuss the questions.

1 Are you a good cook?
2 Did you like eating fruit when you were a child?
3 How often do you eat takeaway food?
4 Which meal of the day is the most important: breakfast, lunch or dinner? Why?
5 Do you think people in your country eat a healthy diet? Why/Why not?

Speaking Part 2 Extended turn

Describe the picture. What objects can you see? Use these phrases to help you.

In the picture I can see ... *There is/are ...*
The picture shows ...

3 YOU ARE WHAT YOU EAT

Speaking Part 3 Discussion

1 **SPEAK** Work in pairs. Look at the photographs. What are the people in the photos learning to do? Is it an important thing to learn? Why/Why not?

2 3.1 Look at the Part 3 task on page 31. Now listen to two B1 Preliminary candidates doing the task. Which option do they think is best?

3 3.1 Listen again and write the missing word in each gap.

1 **A:** *So,* ____________ *one do you want to talk about first?* There are a few good options, I think.

B: *What* ____________ *this one?* It looks like they are giving people food in front of the school.

2 **A:** I think it's a great idea to put ... a cooking video on social media. *Do you* ____________?

B: Yes, a lot of people will see the video there. *You're* ____________.

3 **A:** *In my* ____________, it makes sense to give a free cooking class – it's fun!

B: *If you* ____________ *me*, it's not the best choice. People just go for the free class.

4 **A:** All right, so ... ____________ *we talk about* the newspaper now?

B: OK. To be honest, *I'm not* ____________ *about that one*. People, uh, people usually read the news online.

5 **A:** Yes, I completely agree. I, uh, *I still think a cooking video on social media is the best* ____________. What about you?

B: OK sure, *let's* ____________ *with that one then.*

4 **SPEAK** Work in pairs. A new cooking school wants to attract students. Here are some ways of attracting students. Talk together about the different ways of attracting students to the new cooking school, and say which would attract the most students. Use some of the expressions in italics from Exercise 3.

What to expect in the exam

- In Speaking Part 3, you discuss an imaginary situation with your partner. The examiner gives you a set of images to help you.
- You do not need to discuss all the options in the task. It's fine to discuss three or four.
- Part 3 lasts 2–3 minutes. You should continue speaking until the examiner stops you.
- The examiner does not take part in your discussion. It's up to you to keep the conversation going by asking your partner questions and responding to their ideas.

Ways to attract students to a new cooking school

5 Think about how well you did the Speaking Part 3 task in Exercise 2. For the questions below, give yourself a mark between 1 and 3.

1 needs improvement 2 satisfactory 3 excellent

	1	2	3
Was my pronunciation clear and easy to understand?			
Did I listen to my partner and respond to what they said?			
Did I give reasons or examples to justify my answers?			
Did I use a good range of grammar and vocabulary?			

6 **SPEAK** With your partner, take turns to explain your marks. Give examples. What would you most like to improve on?

Reading Part 5 Multiple-choice cloze

What to expect in the exam

- In Part 5, you have to read a text with six gaps. For each gap, there are four options (A, B, C and D) to choose from. Only one of the options correctly fills the gap.
- Part 5 tests different types of vocabulary: collocations, phrasal verbs, the meaning of individual words and words with dependent prepositions. It may also test grammar, e.g. which verbs are followed by the *-ing* form or the infinitive.

1 **SPEAK** **Work in pairs. Look at the pictures and the title. What's the topic of the text? What sort of information do you think it will give about this topic?**

2 **Read the text quickly, ignoring the gaps for now, and check your predictions.**

3 **Read the text again. For questions 1–6, choose which answer (A, B, C or D) best fits each gap.**

A is for ...

The apple is one of the most popular fruits in the world. Did you know that half of all trees that produce fruit are apple trees? Apples originally came from Central Asia, east of the Caspian Sea. Later, the fruit (1) ______ popular in the Roman Empire. From there, it didn't (2) ______ long for apples to spread around the world.

Apples come in an amazing variety of different colours, shapes and sizes. It might seem hard to believe, but there are (3) ______ some 7,500 different types of apples! It would be hard to try them all.

There are dozens of (4) ______ to eat apples, which is probably one (5) ______ for their popularity. You can prepare an apple dessert. You can make apple sauce or jam. Or you can simply eat apples raw, perhaps with a bit of honey or cheese. What about you? How do you (6) ______ to eat apples?

1	A went	B began	C won	D became
2	A take	B make	C find	D get
3	A correctly	B actually	C accurately	D entirely
4	A manners	B styles	C approaches	D ways
5	A result	B answer	C reason	D factor
6	A prefer	B consider	C advise	D enjoy

4 **To choose the correct option in Part 5, it can be important to look at the preposition that follows the gap. This is the case in question 5 in Exercise 3 above. For 1–6 below, look at the preposition in bold and choose the correct alternative.**

1 Traditional food in my country is completely *different* / *opposite* **from** the food in other countries I've visited.

2 I never wait more than a day to *answer* / *reply* **to** an email. It's rude to keep people waiting.

3 Personally, I'm not *interested* / *fascinated* **in** political issues. I pay very little attention to politics.

4 I *believe* / *think* **in** the importance of lifelong learning. I want to be a student forever.

5 In general, I don't like *asking* / *requesting* **for** help. I prefer to solve problems on my own.

6 In my view, the government should *deliver* / *provide* every secondary school pupil **with** a free internet connection at their house. Nowadays, they can't study without it.

5 **SPEAK** **Work in pairs. How true are the sentences in Exercise 4 for you?**

Language focus Countable and uncountable nouns

1 Look at these two sentences from *A is for ...* . Then complete the rules with *countable* or *uncountable*.

*You can prepare an **apple dessert**.*

*You can eat apples [...] with **honey** or **cheese**.*

1 ______________ nouns have a plural form. We can use them after *a/an* when they are singular. Examples: *apple*, *chair* and *garden*.

2 ______________ nouns do not have a plural form, and they cannot be used after *a/an*. Examples: *honey*, *traffic* and *health*.

2 Read the dialogues 1–6. Which nouns in bold are countable and which are uncountable? Write *C* or *U* next to each one. The first one has been done for you.

1 A Could you give me a little **help** with this box? It's super heavy. *U*
B Sure, no **problem**.

2 A Dad, I'm hungry. Did you bring any **snacks**?
B Yes, I've got a few **biscuits** here in my bag. Do you want one?

3 A There's a lot of practical **advice** here about how to cook **seafood**.
B That's true. I tried a **recipe** from that site recently and it was really tasty.

4 A There isn't any **pasta** in the cupboard, is there?
B No, I think we finished it all. There's some **rice**, though.

5 A This place has a lot of really interesting **dishes** on the menu.
B I know! I'm surprised it isn't more popular. Not many **people** seem to know it exists.

6 A I don't have much **money** at the moment, but I'd really like to buy some new **shelves** for the bathroom.
B Have you looked on one of those second-hand apps? Some of the **furniture** there is almost brand new.

3 Now look at the underlined words and phrases in Exercise 2, and the nouns that follow them. Put the underlined words and phrases in the correct category below. Some words go in more than one category.

1 Before countable nouns	
2 Before uncountable nouns	*a little*
3 Before countable and uncountable nouns	

4 Go to Ready for Grammar on page 206 for rules, explanations and further practice.

5 **SPEAK** Imagine you have a friend who wants to eat more healthily. How much (if any) of these foods would you recommend eating during a normal week? Practise using the words and phrases from Exercise 3.

bread egg fish fruit hamburger ice cream juice meat milk pasta pizza rice salt seafood soup sweets vegetable yoghurt

Vocabulary Containers and amounts

1 SPEAK Work in pairs and write a list of different types of food that usually come in a packet. For example, biscuits or chewing gum.

2 Match phrases 1–6 to the pictures a–f. Then complete the gaps with the missing food words.

1 a bottle of ______
2 a jar of ______
3 a tin of ______
4 a bag of ______
5 a box of ______
6 a carton of ______

a

b

c

d

e

f

3 Think of at least two more foods that are usually sold in each of the containers from Exercise 2.

4 SPEAK Work in pairs. Which foods from Exercises 2 and 3 do you have in the kitchen at home? Tell your partner if, when and how you eat or drink them. Give as much information as possible.

*There is always **a jar of strawberry jam** in my fridge. I put it on my toast in the morning. Strawberry is my favourite flavour, but I also like ...*

5 Match the sentence beginnings 1–6 to the endings a–f to make complete sentences.

1 After work, could you buy a **loaf of**
2 After a fizzy drink and three **slices of**
3 I gave Paul a **bar of**
4 For the salad, we need to buy a **head of**
5 Why don't we buy a **bunch of**
6 The recipe says to add a **spoonful of**

a **bananas**? Fruit is a healthy snack.
b **bread** from the bakery on the corner?
c **chocolate** and a bouquet of flowers.
d **sugar** and then mix all the ingredients.
e **lettuce**, some tomatoes and carrots.
f **pizza**, my stomach feels a bit upset.

6 SPEAK Work in pairs. Describe the pictures using the phrases in the box below, as well as the phrases from Exercises 2 and 5 above.

a bowl of | a cup of | a glass of | a plate of | a jug of

Listening Part 3 Gap fill

1 3.2 You will hear a man called Chris Molina talking about his job as a professional mushroom hunter. Read question 1 in Exercise 2, and then listen to the first section of the recording. Where does he live *now*?

What to expect in the exam

- In Listening Part 3, you have to listen for specific details. While you listen, you have to complete missing information from the recording (words or numbers) in six notes or sentences.
- The information in the recording is in the same order as the questions.
- When the speaker spells a word out, letter by letter, your spelling must be correct.
- For many questions, there will be distractors, i.e. information that sounds like it might fit the gap but is not quite right.

2 3.3 Now listen to the full recording. For questions 1–6, write the correct answer in each gap. Write one or two words, or a number, a date or a time.

THE MUSHROOM HUNTER

1 Chris now lives in ....
2 Chris did a degree in .... at university.
3 In autumn, Chris starts work at .... in the morning.
4 To be good at mushroom hunting, you have to be ....
5 When Chris finds a mushroom in the forest, he puts it into a ....
6 Chris's website is www...es

3 **SPEAK** Would you like to have a job where you work outdoors? Why/Why not?

Language focus Articles

1 Match rules 1–6 to examples a–f from the listening.

1 We use *a*/*an* to talk about someone's job.
2 We use *a*/*an* before a noun that is one of many.
3 We use *the* to refer to a person, place or thing that we have talked about before.
4 We use *the* when there is only one of something.
5 We use no article to talk in general about plural nouns.
6 We use no article to talk in general about uncountable nouns.

a *I use a basket, though. That way spores ...* ***fall out of the basket*** *...*
b *I've become a bit of an expert in* ***biology ...***
c *Then I drive up to* ***a pine forest*** *near my town.*
d ***Little kids*** *love searching for mushrooms!*
e *I'm* ***a professional mushroom hunter.***
f *At eight,* ***the sun*** *is just starting ...*

2 Go to Ready for Grammar on page 208 for rules, explanations and further practice.

3 Read the article from a food website about poke, ignoring the gaps for now. Why has this dish become so popular?

THE POKE CRAZE

For centuries, poke has been one of **(0)** ___*the*___ main dishes in Hawaii (USA). In recent years, it has become very popular throughout the rest of **(1)** ________ United States as well as **(2)** ________ Southern Europe. With new poke restaurants opening in cities from London to Sydney, it's fair to say that people all over **(3)** ________ world are mad about poke. But why?

The Hawaiian word poke means 'cut into pieces' and **(4)** ________ dish consists of raw fish (usually tuna) with rice, vegetables and a bit of soy sauce. It's easy to prepare – just mix the ingredients together and serve it in **(5)** ________ bowl. Simple as that. So what makes it so special? Well, to begin with, poke looks beautiful in photos on Instagram – **(6)** ________ important advantage in today's world, where everyone is also mad about **(7)** ________ social media. It's also a healthy dish that **(8)** ________ people can feel good about eating. Finally, **(9)** ________ poke bowls are not particularly difficult to make at **(10)** ________ home, so it's easy to enjoy **(11)** ________ poke bowl even if you don't feel like eating out.

So, what about you? Ready to join **(12)** ________ poke craze?

4 Read the text again and complete each of the gaps with *a*, *an* or *the*, or leave it blank. There is an example at the beginning (0).

5 You are going to talk for a minute about a type of food that has become popular where you live. Make notes on:

- where it comes from
- its ingredients
- reasons for its popularity

6 **SPEAK** Work in small groups. Take turns to talk about your food. Then say which foods you like the most or would be most interested in trying.

Vocabulary Food

1 SPEAK What's your favourite dish? What do you like about it?

2 Match the verbs in the box to the definitions (1–5).

bake barbecue boil fry roast

1 ____________ to cook food in water that is 100 degrees Celsius
2 ____________ to cook food in hot oil on top of the cooker
3 ____________ to cook food on a metal frame over an open fire
4 ____________ to cook food, such as bread or cakes, in an oven without liquid
5 ____________ to cook food, e.g. meat or vegetables, in an oven at a high temperature

3 SPEAK Tell your partner about three meals or types of food that you regularly eat in your home. Describe how the food is prepared, using the verbs in Exercise 2.

*When it's cold, my dad often **boils** carrots to eat as a side dish. They're delicious!*

4 Complete each sentence with a word from the box.

bitter sweet

1 There's absolutely no need to add sugar to orange juice. It's naturally ____________.
2 I love dark chocolate, but this kind with 95% cocoa is a little too ____________ even for me.

juicy sour

3 Can we add some sugar to this lemonade? It's really ____________.
4 These peaches are very soft and ____________. You'll have to wash your hands after you eat one!

salty spicy

5 This popcorn is too ____________! I need to drink a glass of water.
6 We serve the chicken with a deliciously ____________ sauce, made from chillies and other hot peppers.

5 SPEAK Work in pairs. Use the adjectives from Exercise 4 to describe the following foods. Say whether you like the food and how often you eat it.

- broccoli
- cake
- cherries
- lemons
- crisps
- curry
- peanuts
- sausages
- yoghurt

Writing Part 2 Article

1 SPEAK Work in pairs. Read the following Writing Part 2 task. Talk about what ideas you would include in your answer.

You see this announcement on an English-language website.

Articles wanted!

A great dish

- What's your favourite traditional dish from your country or region?
- What do you like about it?
- How important is it to learn how to cook the food you like?

The most interesting articles answering these questions will be published on our website.

Write your **article** in about **100 words.**

2 Read the model answer below, ignoring the options in italics. Does the writer answer all three questions from the task instructions?

PASTA AND PEAS, PLEASE

In Italy, there is a traditional dish you should try: *pasta e piselli* (pasta and peas). *I like this dish because it's made with only a few basic ingredients. / There are three good reasons to try this amazing dish*. All you need are peas, an onion, olive oil, pepper, salt, Pecorino Romano cheese and a type of small pasta like ditalini. Everything is cooked together in one pot. Am I making you hungry? *To be honest, I find cooking a bit boring. / My advice is: if you love eating something, learn to cook it.* My father taught me to cook *pasta e piselli* and now I share my love of this dish with everyone. Come to my house and I will make it for you!

3 A topic sentence tells the reader the main theme of a paragraph. Choose the best topic sentence in italics for the second and third paragraphs of the model answer.

4 You are going to write your own answer to the task in Exercise 1. Before you write, use the notes below to organise your ideas.

Paragraph 1

Introduce the dish and catch the reader's attention

Paragraph 2

Answer the question: What do you like about it?

Paragraph 3

Answer the question: How important is it to learn how to cook the food you like?

5 Write topic sentences for paragraphs 2 and 3.

6 Now write your article in three paragraphs using your ideas from Exercise 4 and the topic sentences from Exercise 5.

How to go about it

- Read the instructions and underline the points you have to include in your answer.
- Make a plan. Organise your ideas into paragraphs. Each paragraph should have a theme. At the beginning of each paragraph, use a topic sentence to make the theme clear to the reader.
- Give your article a title that will catch the reader's attention.
- While you write, use a variety of descriptive language, e.g. adjectives and adverbs.

Useful language

Describing feelings

One way to make an article more interesting is to describe people's feelings. Complete sentences 1–6 with a word from the box.

confused grateful keen proud relaxed satisfied

1 Susi never feels __________ with her desserts. She always thinks they could be better.
2 In the kitchen, my grandfather is always calm and __________. He never looks anxious or worried.
3 Wait a minute – I'm getting __________. Can you explain the beginning of the recipe to me again?
4 My sister loved my baked pasta! She even asked me to make it again next week. I felt very __________ of myself.
5 We're __________ to learn how to make bread. Do you think your father could teach us?
6 We are extremely __________ to everyone who has donated food to our charity this week.

For more information on writing articles, see page 195.

3 REVIEW

Vocabulary Containers and amounts

Complete the crossword. You can find all the phrases on page 34.

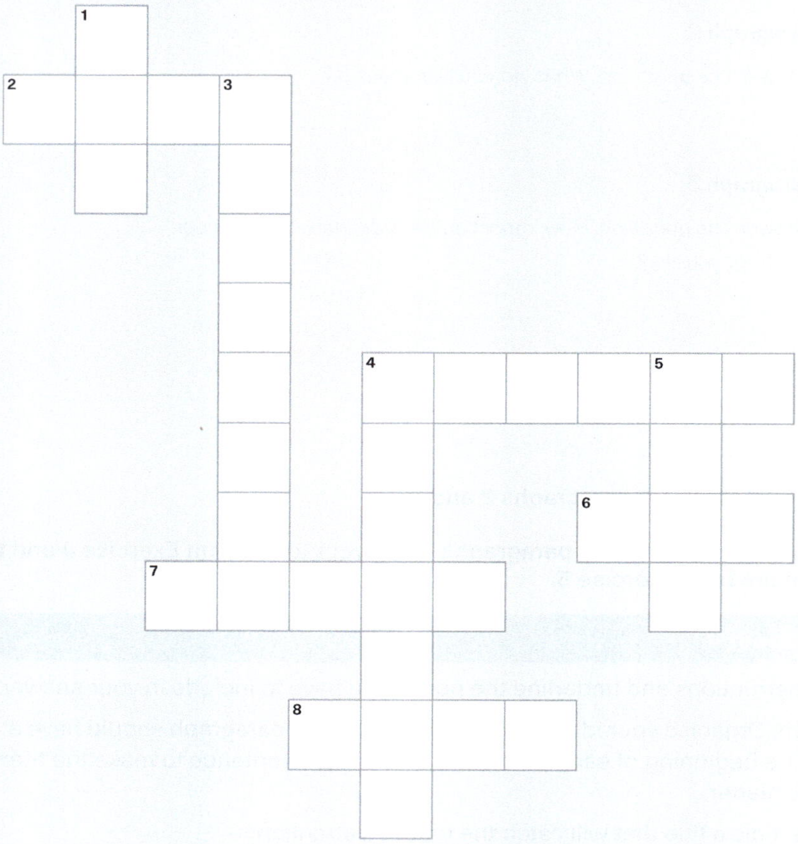

ACROSS

2 Let's buy a few ______ **of popcorn** for the party.
4 Get the biggest ______ **of olive oil** they have. We always run out of it.
6 Can we buy a different ______ **of chocolate**? I'm allergic to nuts.
7 Can I have a ______ **of** cheese **pizza** to take away?
8 Put that ______ **of lettuce** in the compost bin – it's gone off.

DOWN

1 For my birthday, she gave me a ______ **of** her homemade blueberry **jam**.
3 In the film *Mary Poppins*, the children take a ______ **of sugar** with their medicine.
4 There were ______ **of** yellow **bananas** hanging from the trees.
5 One ______ **of** white **bread**, please.

Language focus Countable and uncountable nouns

Underline the correct alternative to complete the sentences.

1 Taleggio and mascarpone are my favourite Italian *cheese* / *cheeses.* Have you tried them?
2 How *many* / *much* chocolate syrup do you want on your ice cream?
3 The truth is that most *chewing gum* / *chewing gums* contains sugar and can be very bad for your teeth.
4 We don't have *any* / *some* milk. Can you pick some up at the supermarket?
5 Our bakery sells a number of homemade *cakes* / *cake* and other desserts.
6 It was nice to have the opportunity to apply the technical *knowledge* / *knowledges* I learnt at university.
7 There were *a little* / *a few* spots of tomato sauce on the kitchen floor.
8 This company does high-level research, and that requires a lot of space and sophisticated *equipment* / *equipments*.

Language focus Articles

Complete the gaps with *a* / *an* / *the*, or leave it blank.

1 It's true that I'm obsessed with ________ speciality coffee.
2 Is there ________ souvenir shop near here?
3 I've always loved ________ cars.
4 My aunt is ________ travel agent.
5 They live in ________ small, cosy cottage in the mountains.
6 I'm rather busy at ________ moment.
7 He has Turkish lessons three times ________ week.
8 She is a famous artist from ________ Netherlands.

Writing Part 2 Story

Your English teacher has asked you to write a story. Your story must start with this sentence:

Ali walked out of the restaurant into the cold rain.

Write your story in about 100 words.

For more information on writing stories, see **page 194**.

Pronunciation /w/, /h/, /v/ and /z/

1 3.4 Listen and repeat the words.

		At the beginning	In the middle	At the end
1	/h/	heat, whole	ahead, unhappy	
2	/v/	valley, value	oven, clever	serve, drive
3	/w/	whether, waiter	always, takeaway	
4	/z/	zero, zone	dozen, busy	amaze, cheese

2 Practise reading the sentences aloud.

/h/
1 There is nothing I **hate** more than **hot**, **humid** air.
2 **Who** is that standing **behind** your **house**?

/v/
3 **Everybody** on the guest list **arrived** before **seven**.
4 Little **Vera** turned **five** in **November**.

/w/
5 The **waiters** in this restaurant are **always wearing** clean, **white** shirts.
6 **When** did you **win** this **award**?

/z/
7 The **zoo** is **closed** on **Tuesday**.
8 The **quiz** was not as **easy** as I hoped!

3 SPEAK Work in pairs. Read the rules and play the game.

FOUR IN A ROW

1 Take a pencil and use the table below as your board.
2 To win a space, you have to correctly pronounce the word. The object of the game is to win four spaces in a row. Try to stop your partner from winning four spaces in a row before you.
3 After playing one game, rub out your marks and play again.

behave	believe	raise	weather	happen	leave
Brazil	amaze	unhelpful	awake	waste	perhaps
vote	heart	work	visit	as	cheese
pleasant	jazz	voice	welcome	eleven	host
unhealthy	weigh	please	Switzerland	backward	improve
which	heavy	microwave	whose	available	takeaway

4

WHAT'S ON

KEY LANGUAGE

Present perfect simple
Present perfect simple and past simple
Live entertainment
Social media

PRONUNCIATION

Suffixes *-sion* and *-tion*

EXAM SKILLS

Reading Parts 4 & 6
Writing Parts 1 & 2
Listening Part 4
Speaking Parts 1 & 2

Speaking Part 1 Interview

Work with a partner. Discuss the questions.

1 What did you do last weekend?
2 Describe a video game or a board game that you like.
3 What's your favourite kind of music?
4 Do you enjoy visiting museums?
5 How often do you use social media?

Speaking Part 2 Extended turn

Describe the picture. Use the adjectives in the box to help you.

boring	enjoyable	exciting	interesting
popular	relaxing	stressful	unusual

4 WHAT'S ON

Vocabulary Live entertainment

1 SPEAK Do you like going to live shows or events? Why/Why not?

2 Match questions 1–7 to answers a–g.

1 Surely you're not going to **miss** this ***opportunity*** to see your favourite band live?
2 Why did you **cancel** the ***show*** on opening night?
3 The show didn't **attract** a very big ***audience,*** did it?
4 How did he get a job **designing** ***costumes*** for Hollywood movies?
5 Did Paul's comedy show **get** good ***reviews***?
6 Did they **charge** ***admission***?
7 Is this musical **enjoying** the same ***success*** in other parts of the world?

a A famous director saw him wearing a shirt he made himself.
b Yes, people everywhere seem to love the songs, whatever the language.
c We had to make that decision because half the cast fell ill.
d Yes, we had to pay to get in, but it was only five euros.
e You're right. There were lots of empty seats.
f I'd love to go to the concert, but the tickets are just too expensive.
g No, unfortunately they were quite negative. One critic said he didn't get half the jokes.

3 Match each pair of verbs in 1–7 below to one of the nouns in *italics* in Exercise 2. The first one has been done for you.

1 give (someone) / see an *opportunity*
2 rent / wear a ________
3 entertain / surprise the ________
4 attend / host a ________
5 post / read a ________
6 pay / refuse ________
7 achieve / celebrate ________

4 Complete the gaps using the correct form of one of the verbs from Exercise 3. The first one has been done for you.

A director friend recently **(1)** *gave* me the **opportunity** to **(2)** ________ her new musical **show** for free on opening night. The tickets were expensive, so I was pleased I didn't have to **(3)** ________ **admission**!

I absolutely loved it. One thing that seemed to **(4)** ________ the **audience**, but also entertain them, was the fact that the actors **(5)** ________ modern **costumes**, even though the story took place in the 16th century. For me, it was the perfect way to show that we have the same problems today as people did five hundred years ago.

The next day, theatre critics **(6)** ________ extremely positive **reviews** of the musical online. I called my friend to congratulate her and invite her out to lunch to **(7)** ________ her **success**, but she said she was going to be too busy giving interviews to the press.

5 Rank the following live shows or events in order from the most interesting (1) to the least interesting (10) for you.

ballet circus comedy show fashion show magic show
musical opera parade play pop concert

6 **SPEAK** Work in pairs. Compare and discuss your lists from Exercise 5.

Speaking Part 2 Extended turn

1 Using the words in the box, complete phrases 1–7, which are used for describing where things are in a picture.

bottom bottom left corner left middle right ~~top~~ top right corner

1 at the *top*
2 in the ______
3 on the ______
4 in the ______
5 on the ______
6 in the ______
7 at the ______

Don't forget!

As you describe the objects you see in the picture, say *where* they are.

2 **SPEAK** Work in pairs. Look at photographs 1 and 2. Use the phrases from Exercise 1 to say where things are in the photos.

In the first photo, I can see a stage in the middle of the photo.

3 Student A: Look at photograph 1. It shows people at an outdoor performance. Tell your partner what you can see in the photograph.

Student B: Look at photograph 2. It shows people at a music festival. Tell your partner what you can see in the photograph.

1

2

Listening Part 4 Multiple choice

1 SPEAK Look at the picture. What kind of museum can you see?

What to expect in the exam

- In Listening Part 4, you listen to an interview and answer six multiple-choice questions. This exam task tests your ability to understand attitudes and opinions, as well as detailed information.
- As in all B1 Preliminary listening tasks, you hear the recording twice. Remember to check your answers the second time you listen.
- The options (A, B and C) usually paraphrase the information in the text – that is, they say the same thing in different words. For example, in question 1 below, 'well-known musicians' appears in option B, but the speaker talks about 'rock stars.'

2 4.1 You will hear an interview with a man called Danny O'Neil who works at a Rock and Roll museum. For questions 1–6, choose the best answer (A, B or C).

1 Why did Danny decide to become a tour guide?
  A The salary was higher.
  B He wanted to meet well-known musicians.
  C A friend offered him the job.

2 The part of the job that Danny likes most is
  A telling visitors about new exhibitions.
  B learning more about rock and roll.
  C meeting people from around the world.

3 What does Danny say about famous musicians?
  A They prefer talking to other famous people.
  B They are shyer than people think.
  C It's hard to think of the right thing to say to them.

4 Danny thinks being a tour guide has taught him to
  A be comfortable speaking in public.
  B remember things better.
  C admit when he is wrong.

5 What advice does Danny have for visitors to the museum?
  A try on rock star clothing
  B look at historical documents
  C play musical instruments

6 How does Danny feel about his new job?
  A aware of his lack of experience
  B anxious about new responsibilities
  C frustrated with his workmates

3 SPEAK **Would you like to visit the Rock and Roll Hall of Fame? Why/Why not?**

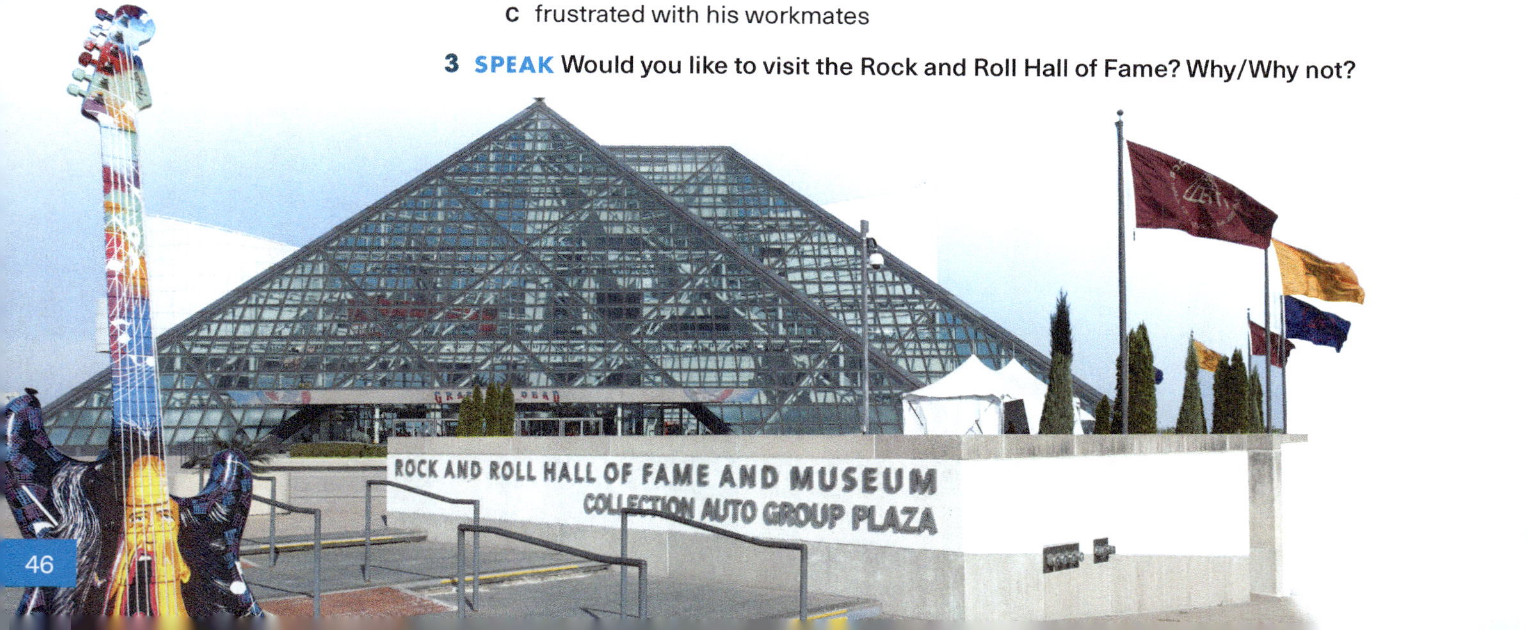

Language focus Present perfect simple

1 These extracts from the listening contain examples of the present perfect simple in bold. Look at the extracts and choose the correct alternatives in the rule below.

1 *I **have met** lots of famous people in my lifetime.*
2 *I **have** just **started** a new job and I'm feeling a bit stressed out.*
3 *The museum **has collected** lots of artefacts since 1995, when it opened.*

To form the present perfect simple, we use the appropriate form of *to have* / *to be* with the *past simple* / *past participle* form of the verb.

2 We use the present perfect to show a connection between the past and the present. Match each extract (1–3) in Exercise 1 to the specific uses (a–c) below.

a to talk about a recent past event with a result we can see in the present.
b to talk about an action or situation that started in the past and continues into the present.
c to talk in general about past experiences, without saying exactly when they happened

3 Match each sentence (1–6) to a use (a–c) in Exercise 2.

1 Have you ever seen your favourite group live in concert?
2 He's lost his key and now he can't get into his flat.
3 We've visited Bali twice, but we've never been to Lombok.
4 We've had this car since 2022.
5 I've just seen a text from Ivana – she wants to come to the film with us.
6 I haven't played cricket for 10 years.

4 Look at sentences 4 and 6 in Exercise 3. Complete sentences 1–2 below with *for* or *since*.

1 ____________ introduces the point when a time period started.
2 ____________ introduces the length of a time period.

5 Go to Ready for Grammar on page 210 for rules, explanations and further practice.

6 Complete each gap using the present perfect simple so the second sentence has the same meaning as the first. Use the word in brackets. You may need to use a different verb to the one in the first sentence.

Danny began working here ten years ago.
Danny has *worked here for 10 years.* (*for*)

1 This talented musician started playing the piano when she was a child.
This talented musician has ______________________________. (*since*)
2 I stopped studying Italian 10 years ago.
I haven't ______________________________. (*for*)
3 Laura still needs to buy a new phone charger.
Laura hasn't ______________________________. (*yet*)
4 Is this your first time making this dish?
Have ______________________________ before? (*ever*)
5 The last time I heard from him was last Wednesday.
I haven't ______________________________. (*since*)
6 Are the children still asleep?
Have ______________________________? (*yet*)

7 SPEAK Complete sentences 1–5 so they are true for you. Discuss your sentences with a partner.

1 For a long time, I've wanted to ...
2 Personally, I've never liked ...
3 Since I was a child, I've always loved ...
4 I've never had the opportunity to try ... but hopefully one day I will.
5 I haven't visited ... yet, but I'd like to one day.

Reading Part 4 Gapped text

1 SPEAK Work in pairs. Look at the photograph of people cycling in the mountains. What do you think they are enjoying about this activity?

2 Read the blog post, ignoring the gaps for now. Does the writer mention any of your ideas from Exercise 1?

How to go about it

- In Part 4, the text describes a series of events, so it's good to read the whole text first to understand what happens in the narrative.
- Then look at sentences A–H. Carefully choose the one that fits into each gap. The missing sentence needs to fit the context of the paragraph. Pay particular attention to pronouns (*it, these*) and linkers (*however, also, for this reason*). To help you, linking words and expressions appear in bold in this Part 4 task. (They are not in bold in the official exam.)
- Before you finish, read the whole text again to check that your answers make sense.

3 Five sentences have been removed from the blog post. Choose from the sentences A–H the one which fits each gap (1–5). There are three extra sentences which you do not need to use.

A And, so far, it has been quite enjoyable.
B **Because of this**, I didn't know exactly what to expect.
C It was **also** made of soft dirt.
D I haven't been able to post any of these pictures on social media.
E **But** I've never been on one like this before.
F **Even with these**, it was a challenging ride.
G This meant we had to carry extra weight.
H The road was mostly flat.

4 Linking words and expressions often help you choose the correct missing sentence. In each sentence (1–6), complete the expression in bold with the correct word from the box.

course despite fact spite way why

1 She is a natural runner. ____________ **this**, she finds it boring and prefers cycling.
2 My old bike seat was a bit uncomfortable. **That's** ____________ I bought this new one.
3 They love these organised bike trips. **In** ____________, they're doing another one this spring.
4 Let's stop here. **That** ____________, we can look at the map and decide which route to take.
5 I always carry lots of water. And **of** ____________, I remind the other riders to do the same.
6 They arrived in winter. **In** ____________ **of this**, the weather was surprisingly mild.

FROM COAST TO COAST BY BIKE

NEW POST

Hello from Mendoza, Argentina. I've just finished another amazing day of cycling. In total, my fellow cyclists and I are going to ride 1,600 kilometres, starting in Valparaíso, Chile, and finishing in Buenos Aires, Argentina. Over the years, I've participated in a number of organised bike tours. **1** ___ Imagine crossing an entire continent by bike!

Our tour started three days ago in the historic centre of Valparaíso in Chile, a five-minute walk from the Pacific Ocean. For the first 20 km, we followed the coast. **2** ___ We then turned away from the sea and started climbing up and up through the Central Valley, a beautiful wine-growing region of Chile. By the early evening, we had reached 1,300 metres above sea level.

Yesterday morning, we woke up early. After a big breakfast, we got back on our bikes. The mountain road was steep, consisting of turn after turn. **3** ___ This meant we had to put special tyres on our bicycles the night before.

It was a long day. Thankfully, the cycling company arranged breaks every couple of hours, setting up a table with all the food and water we would need. **4** ___ By sunset, we had climbed high in the Andes mountains: over 3,800 metres above sea level. From our hotel, there were views of Aconcagua, the highest mountain in South America.

We're now on day three. **5** ___ All this morning, we rode down from the mountains, pausing from time to time to enjoy the views, finally finishing here in the lovely city of Mendoza. We still have many kilometres left to ride – there is still the Pampas region of Argentina to cross before we reach Buenos Aires. But the most difficult part of the trip is now behind us.

Language focus Present perfect simple and past simple

1 **Read sentences 1 and 2 and choose the correct alternative in rules a and b below.**

1 I've been to Argentina twice.

2 I went to Argentina in 2012 and 2018.

When talking about past events,

a we use the *past simple / present perfect* if we say when they happened. The time, or time period, in which they happened has finished.

b we use the *past simple / present perfect* if they happened at some point between the past and now. When they happened is not mentioned and/or not important.

2 **Choose the correct alternative.**

1 They *lived / have lived* in Toronto **from 2010 to 2015**.

2 Claudia is away on business in France again, so that means she *worked / has worked there* on three occasions **in the last month**!

3 *Did Simon visit / Has Simon visited* his father **yesterday afternoon**?

4 **In recent months**, many people *suggested / have suggested* that I buy a flat, but I prefer to rent.

5 I *didn't eat / haven't eaten* any ice cream **these last few weeks** and I'm starting to miss it.

3 **Put the time expressions from the box in the correct columns of the table.**

all my life ~~at the weekend~~ for the last 24 hours in September last night/week these last few weeks two days ago until now / so far when I was a child

Finished time expressions (past simple)	Unfinished time expressions (present perfect)
at the weekend	

4 **Now add the time expressions in bold from Exercise 2 to the table in Exercise 3.**

5 **SPEAK Work with a partner. Read the pairs of sentences and answer the questions.**

a Joe has lived in London for 10 years.

b Chris lived in London for 10 years.

1 Who still lives in London, Joe or Chris?

a 'I've had two coffees this morning,' said Lucy.

b 'I had two coffees this morning,' said Eva.

2 Which of these two people is speaking in the morning, Lucy or Eva?

6 **Go to Ready for Grammar on page 210 for rules, explanations and further practice.**

7 **Imagine you have recently started doing one of these outdoor activities. Write a blog post about your experience so far. Use both the past simple and present perfect.**

- climbing
- fishing
- kayaking
- mountain biking
- scuba diving
- snowboarding
- surfing
- trekking

I've been scuba diving three times recently and I love it! We had our first couple of lessons in a pool, but after that we went to a nearby lake. So far, ...

8 **SPEAK Work in small groups. Share your posts with your classmates. Discuss who has had the most interesting experience so far.**

Vocabulary Social media

1 **SPEAK** **Work in pairs. Describe the photographs below. What activities related to social media do they show? How often do you do these activities? Use the words below to help you.**

chat click follow like post react reply share tag watch

2 **There is ONE adjective in each group that we do not normally use before the nouns in capital letters. Cross out the word which does not fit.**

1	fashion	latest	open	global	**TREND**
2	personal	flat	strong	public	**OPINION**
3	funny	short	viral	proud	**VIDEO**
4	talented	smart	steep	important	**PEOPLE**
5	large	quick	online	international	**COMMUNITY**

3 **Choose the correct options to complete the sentences.**

1 The best thing about social media is the opportunity to *join* / *associate* an online **community** of people with similar interests.

2 You should always ask people's permission before *hanging* / *posting* **pictures** of them on social media.

3 It's important to regularly *inform* / *update* your **profile**, adding new pictures or information.

4 I don't like it when friends *tag* / *mark* me in **photos** because it creates a link that anybody can follow to my profile.

5 To get lots of 'likes,' it's better to *register* / *record* a short **video** of yourself discussing a topic, rather than just writing a post about it.

6 Let's be honest; most social media activities like *observing* / *commenting* on **posts** are a complete waste of time.

7 Social media companies *enter* / *influence* public **opinion**, changing people's minds on a range of issues, but they want us to believe this isn't true.

8 Social media users only seem to *share* / *participate* good, instead of bad, **news**, which creates the false impression that they live a perfect life.

9 One of the best ways to *attend* / *notice* **trends** in your profession is to use social media to *follow* / *accompany*, or connect with, important **people** in your field.

4 **SPEAK** **Work in small groups. Do you agree or disagree with the statements in Exercise 3? Explain why.**

Writing Part 1 Email

1 Read the Writing Part 1 task below. Which four points do you have to include in your answer?

Read this email from your English-speaking friend Stella and the notes you have made.

From: Stella

Subject: Your visit!

Hi,

It's great that you're coming to visit me next week. <u>I'm really looking forward to it!</u> — *Me too!*

I know you enjoy music. I've just seen an advert for a hip-hop concert in a nearby park. There is also a musical show at the local theatre. <u>Which would you prefer?</u> — *I prefer …*

It would be nice to invite some other friends to come with us. <u>Do you agree?</u> — *Tell Stella …*

During your visit, are there any <u>other activities</u> you want to do together? — *Suggest …*

Reply soon!

Stella

Reply to Stella using **all the notes**. Write your **email** in about **100 words**.

What to expect in the exam

In Writing Part 1, you start by reading an email from somebody you know, e.g. a friend, classmate or teacher. The email includes notes. These notes tell you the four points you must include in your reply to the email.

2 Using a mind map helps you organise your ideas before you write. Look at the example below and add your own ideas for points 3 and 4.

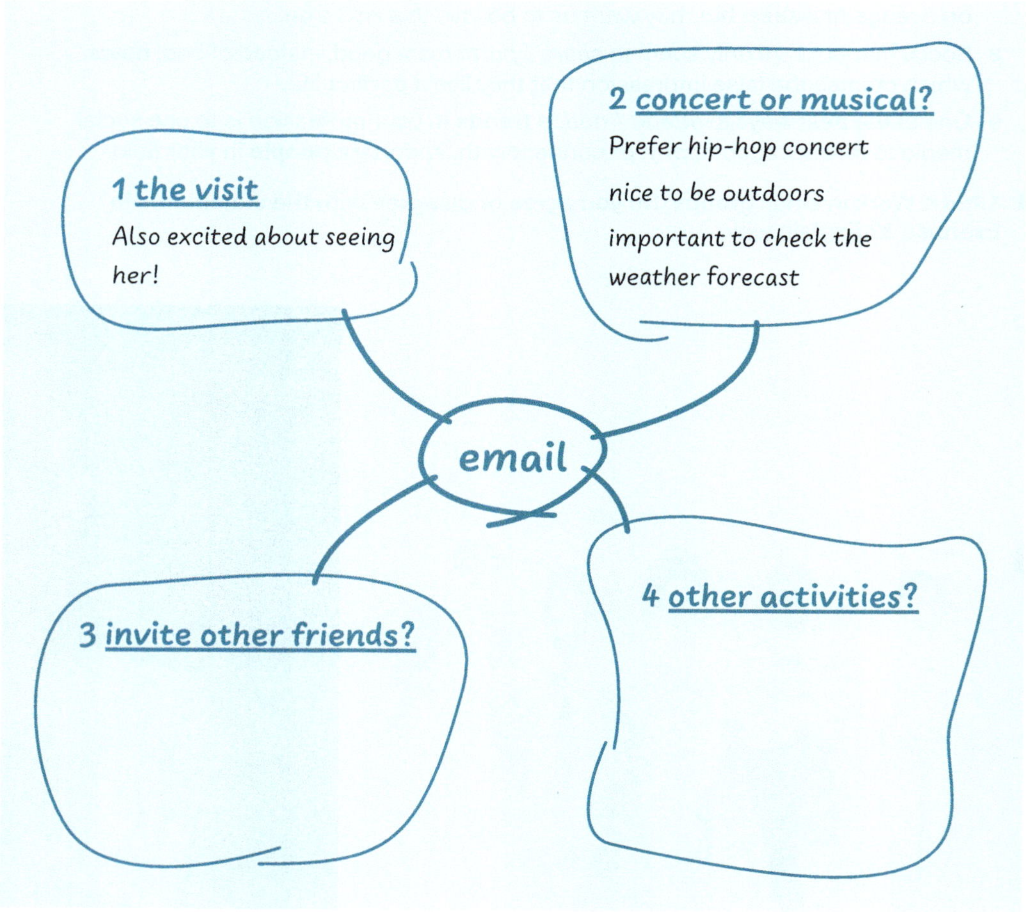

3 **Now read a model answer to the Part 1 task in Exercise 1, ignoring the gaps for now. Did the writer use any of your ideas?**

> Hi Stella,
>
> Thanks for your email. I'm really excited about my visit, **(1)** ____________!
>
> The musical sounds nice, **(2)** ____________ I think I prefer the hip-hop concert. I love listening to music outdoors, so a concert in the park would be fantastic. I've just checked the weather forecast **(3)** ____________ it's supposed to be warm and sunny. Yes, let's invite some of your friends. Are Mario and Aria available?
>
> During my visit, I'd like to go to the modern art museum **(4)** ____________ we didn't have the chance to go there last time I came. What do you think?
>
> Talk to you soon,
>
> Jennifer

4 **Complete the gaps (1–4) in the model answer with the linking words in the box.**

too and because but

5 **Do the following Writing Part 1 task. Use a mind map to organise your ideas before you write.**

Read this email from your English-speaking classmate Guy and the notes you have made.

> From: Guy
>
> Subject: Film night!
>
> Hi everyone,
>
> As you know, I'm organising a film night for students at our language school. I've spoken to the head of the school and she said that we can do it once a month, <u>starting next week</u>. ← Great!
>
> There are two available days for the film night: Wednesday or Thursday evening. <u>Which do you think is better?</u> ← I think …
>
> <u>Shall we all bring some snacks?</u> ← Yes, …
>
> <u>Do you have any film recommendations?</u> The film has to be in English! ← Suggest …
>
> See you in class.
>
> Guy

Reply to Guy using **all the notes**. Write your **email** in about **100** words.

For more information on writing emails, see pages 192–193.

4 REVIEW

Language focus Present perfect simple

Read Maureen's to-do list for starting a new video channel on social media. Write sentences with *already* and *yet* about what she has and has not done.

To do

- ★ register for an account ✓
- ★ order a new microphone ×
- ★ download video editing software ✓
- ★ buy special lights ✓
- ★ create a timetable for posting videos ×

1 *Maureen has already registered for an account.*
2 ____________
3 ____________
4 ____________
5 ____________

Language focus Present perfect simple and past simple

Complete the time expressions in 1–6 with a word from the box. Use the verb tenses to help you. The first one is done for you.

~~at~~ eight in so these when

1 ___*At*___ **the weekend**, we had lunch with an old friend.
2 ________ **June**, Ali and Sakina moved into their new flat.
3 ________ **far**, Chad hasn't explained why he got so upset.
4 ________ **I was seven**, I started taking art lessons.
5 ________ **hours ago**, this street was completely full of water.
6 ________ **last few weeks**, it's been hard to find time for fun hobbies.

Vocabulary Social media

Complete each sentence with a word from the box.

community photo profile trend video

1 Take a selfie in front of our shop and **tag** the ________ with #Englishbookshop.
2 You should really **update** your ________ picture on LinkedIn – it doesn't look very professional.
3 Many companies now ask potential candidates to **record** a ________ CV as part of the application process.
4 Lately I've **noticed** a new ________ in the world of memes: questions with multiple-choice answers.
5 It's an online ________ that lots of parents are **joining** to share tips on raising young children.

Reading Part 6 Open cloze

How to go about it

In Reading Part 6, first read the text quickly, ignoring the gaps, to get a general idea of what it is about. The second time you read it, fill in the missing words. Then read the text a third time to check that all of your answers make sense.

1 Read the text, ignoring the gaps for now. What is Neil's podcast about?

Hi Gloria,

How are you? I hope you don't mind, but I'm writing in order **(1)** .... ask you for a favour. Could you help me create a website?

You see, a few weeks ago, my best friend and I started a new podcast and it's become surprisingly popular. The number of listeners **(2)** .... gone up with each new episode and it continues to grow. Believe it **(3)** .... not, after just five shows, 10,000 people follow us!

The idea of the podcast is very simple: in each episode, we choose one album by The Beatles and discuss **(4)** .... for an hour. We are both huge fans of the group, so we're never short **(5)** .... things to talk about! The problem is that we don't have a way of sharing pictures, videos or music with our fans. That's **(6)** .... we want a website. So, what do you think? Could you help us out?

Let me know!

Neil

2 Now read the email again. For each question (1–6), write the correct answer. Write **one word** for each gap.

Writing Part 2 Article

You see this advertisement on an English-language website.

Articles wanted!

Live Music

- What kind of music do you like?
- What are the good and bad things about live music concerts?

Write an article answering these questions and we'll publish the best ones on our website.

Write your **article** in about **100 words**.

For more information on writing articles, see page 195.

Pronunciation Suffixes *-sion* and *-tion*

1 4.2 These words ending with *-sion* and *-tion* appear in the Listening Part 4 task on page 46. Listen and choose the correct alternative in the sentences (1–3) below.

decision, passion

exhibition, information

1 In words ending with the suffixes *-sion* and *-tion*, the word stress falls on the *last syllable* / *second-to-last syllable* in the word.

2 The letters 's' and 't' in these suffixes are pronounced with *the* /s/ *and* /t/ *sounds* / *the* /ʃ/ *sound in 'show.'*

3 The letters 'io' in *-sion* and *-tion* are pronounced with *the* /ə/ *sound ('open')* / *the* /əʊ/ *sound ('phone').*

2 Using *-sion* and *-tion*, write noun forms for the following verbs. Sometimes you have to make further spelling changes, e.g. *apply/application*. The first one is done for you.

1	organise	*organisation*	7	connect	______
2	explain	______	8	discuss	______
3	express	______	9	operate	______
4	celebrate	______	10	decide	______
5	define	______	11	react	______
6	produce	______	12	describe	______

3 4.3 Listen and check your answers. Note that the word stress in the verb and noun forms is sometimes different (*organise*, *organisation*), but the noun form always follows the pronunciation rules in Exercise 1.

4 **SPEAK** Work in pairs and do the quiz. The answers are words ending in *-sion* or *-tion.* There is an example at the beginning. Can you say the words correctly?

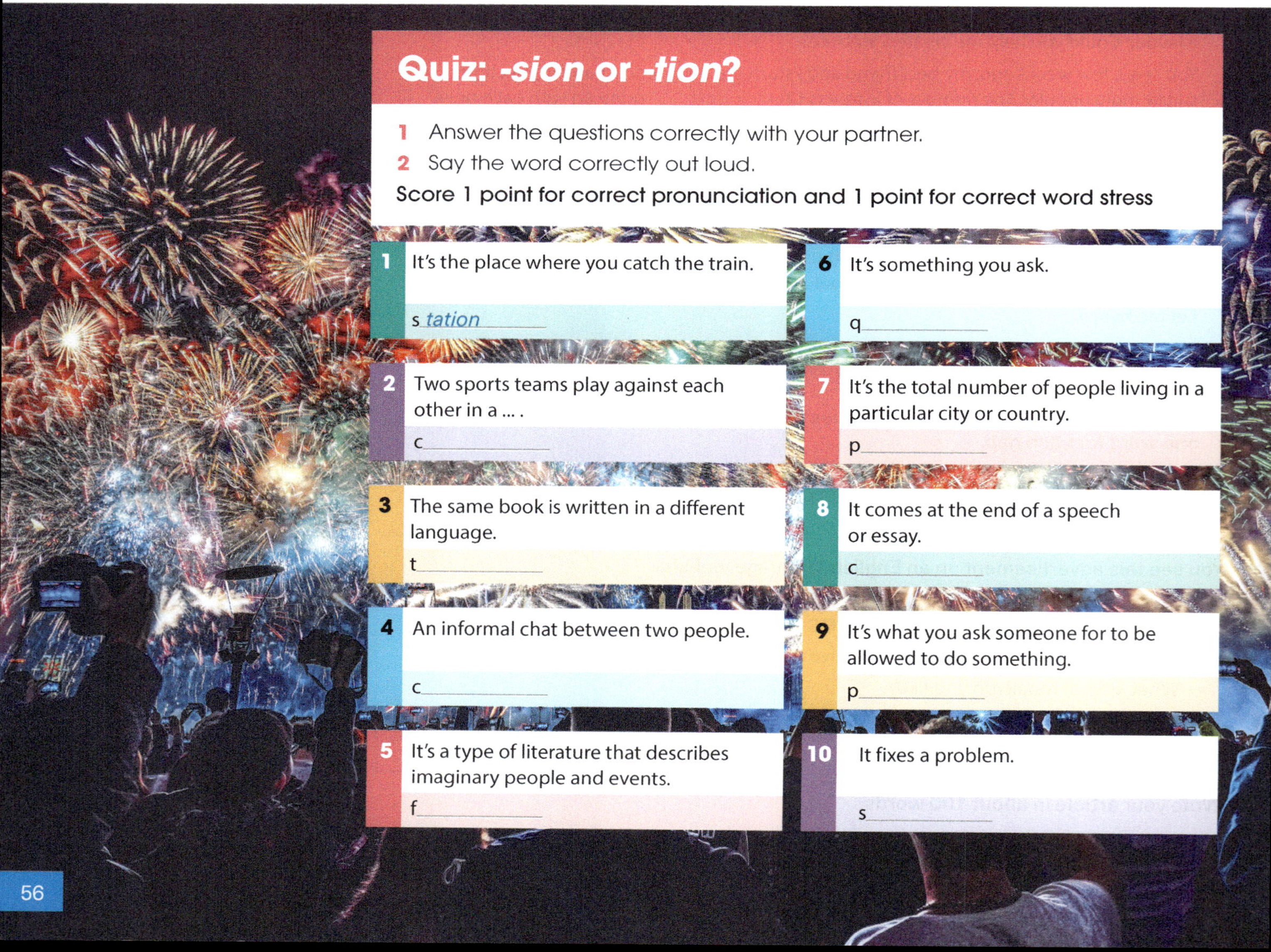

Quiz: *-sion* or *-tion*?

1 Answer the questions correctly with your partner.

2 Say the word correctly out loud.

Score 1 point for correct pronunciation and 1 point for correct word stress

1 It's the place where you catch the train.
s *tation*

2 Two sports teams play against each other in a ... .
c______

3 The same book is written in a different language.
t______

4 An informal chat between two people.
c______

5 It's a type of literature that describes imaginary people and events.
f______

6 It's something you ask.
q______

7 It's the total number of people living in a particular city or country.
p______

8 It comes at the end of a speech or essay.
c______

9 It's what you ask someone for to be allowed to do something.
p______

10 It fixes a problem.
s______

READY FOR READING

Introduction

The Reading paper has six parts and you have 45 minutes to complete all the questions. You will read various types of texts to answer the questions, including brochures, emails, leaflets, magazines, newspapers, notes, notices, signs, text messages and websites.

What to expect in the exam

Read the following sentences and decide which are true **(T)** and which are false **(F)**. Correct any false sentences.

1 You should use a pen to complete the answer sheet. **T / F**

2 You have an additional five minutes to write your answers on the answer sheet. **T / F**

3 There are 32 questions in total. Each question is worth one point. **T / F**

4 You can complete each part of the exam in any order. **T / F**

5 You can make notes on your exam paper. **T / F**

1 Complete each gap (1–6) with the correct phrase (a–f).

a one word **b** five sentences **c** six gaps **d** five short texts **e** four options **f** eight short texts

Part	Description	Tests an understanding of ...
Part 1 Multiple choice	Read **(1)** ______, which can be notices, signs or text messages. Each question has three options to choose from.	The main message of a text.
Part 2 Matching	There are descriptions of five people and **(2)** ______ about a particular topic. You need to match each person with the most appropriate text.	Detailed comprehension of several short texts.
Part 3 Multiple choice	Read a longer text and answer five multiple-choice questions. Each question has **(3)** ______.	Global meaning as well as a detailed comprehension of a text, including an understanding of the writer's attitude and opinion.
Part 4 Gapped text	**(4)** ______ are removed from a longer text, and there are eight sentence options. You need to decide which of the options best fits each gap.	How a coherent, well-structured text is formed.
Part 5 Multiple-choice cloze	Read a shorter text with **(5)** ______. Choose from one of four words to complete each gap.	The correct vocabulary that fits each gap.
Part 6 Open cloze	There is a shorter text with six gaps. You must write **(6)** ______ for each gap.	The correct grammatical word, phrasal verb or fixed phrase that fits each gap.

2 **Linking words and phrases connect ideas within a sentence, paragraph or longer piece of writing. Read the following text and decide which sentence (A–C) fits the gap.**

A JOURNEY OF A LIFETIME

Last year, I decided to follow my dream of travelling to northern Canada to see polar bears. I spent ages researching which tour to go on and when I should go. **(1)** ______ I was relieved when I managed to get a few weeks off work last autumn to make the two-day journey to Churchill, which is located just south of the Arctic Circle.

A I was greeted by my guide Binesi, an elderly Ojibwe man, who told me his name meant *thunderbird*.

B I soon discovered that the best time to observe these magnificent creatures is from October to early November.

C I was so convinced I needed to go on this Canadian adventure that I permanently left my full-time job.

3 **SPEAK** **Discuss in pairs which sentence fits the gap and why the other two sentences don't.**

How to go about it

- Develop good habits for recording and learning new vocabulary by keeping a vocabulary notebook throughout your learning journey.
- Organise your notebook by topic, note the part of speech of new words, include a definition and write an example sentence for each new word.
- Pay special attention to any words that collocate with a new word, and don't forget that words can collocate *before* and/or *after* another word.

Reading Part 1 Multiple choice

In Part 1, you will read a range of short texts, which represent the types of messages you see in your everyday life. This part of the exam tests your understanding of these types of messages.

1 **SPEAK** **In pairs, read the message below and discuss the questions.**

1 What type of message is it?
2 Who is it for?
3 Who is it from?
4 What is the purpose of the message?

2 **Read the question and answer options (A–C). If an option is wrong, explain why. Write notes next to each option. The first one has been done for you.**

What does Jemma want Mateo to do?

Hi Mateo
My cousin's just given me his ticket for the concert tonight, and he doesn't want anything for it. I know how much you want to go, so let me know what you think!
Jemma

A offer to buy her cousin's ticket	*Jemma says her cousin doesn't want anything for it, which means the ticket is free.*
B confirm if he would like a ticket	
C arrange to meet her cousin to get a ticket	

3 **Match each Part 1 question (1–5) on** **page 59** **with the type of text in the box. Decide if the texts are personal or public messages.**

a public sign **b** email **c** text message **d** advert **e** review

4 Read texts 1–5 and choose the correct option (A, B or C).

1

Zoe
Did you manage to go to the National Gallery to see the latest paintings on display? I'm curious to know if you were as impressed as I was.
Ashley

Why did Ashley send this message?

A to find out Zoe's opinion about an art exhibition
B to arrange with Zoe a suitable time to visit an art exhibition
C to ask Zoe whether an art exhibition is worth seeing

2

REVIEWS | APPS

What2Read app offers brilliant fiction and non-fiction recommendations that I almost always read. However, the thumbs-up and thumbs-down option for reviewing these titles is too limited.

Julius, Madrid

What is Julius saying about the app?

A Users occasionally receive book suggestions that are suitable.
B There should be a wider range of books for users to choose from.
C The way users provide feedback about books could be improved.

3

ATTENTION!

When hiking on trails in Banff National Park, be aware of your surroundings and avoid approaching or following bears.

This notice is telling visitors

A where they can go to see some wildlife.
B how to behave if they come across any wildlife.
C what to do to make dangerous wildlife go away.

4

FROM: Mr Yuan
TO: Geography students

I should have mentioned earlier that you need to focus on how pollution is affecting the ocean region that you have decided to research this term.

What does Mr Yuan want his students to do?

A confirm which ocean region they would like to study for their project
B consider including a broad range of information for their project
C concentrate on a particular issue for their project

5

Explore Australia's Daintree Rainforest!

Adult-only guided walking tours

Through thick jungle and deep water-crossings

High level of fitness required

Limited spaces

A People of any age may join the tour.
B People must be in good shape to go on the tour.
C People can expect a boat journey as part of the tour.

Don't forget!

Don't choose an option just because it has the same word or phrase as the text. It's important to compare each option with the meaning of the text.

5 Go to the Additional materials on page 197.

Reading Part 2 Matching

In Part 2, you will read descriptions of five people and eight short texts about a particular topic. You need to find the text that matches each person's needs.

1 SPEAK In small groups, look at the photograph on page 61 and discuss the questions.

1. Do you enjoy baking cakes?
2. Do you enjoy watching programmes about baking?
3. What you think of when you hear the term 'extreme cake making'.
4. Would you like to go on an extreme cake-making course?

How to go about it

- Read the instructions and title to help you understand what the task will be about.
- Read the five descriptions and underline three things each person wants or requires.
- Next, read all eight texts and underline what matches the five people's needs.
- Now compare each person's description with any possible matches.
- Choose which text meets all three of each person's needs.

2 Read the descriptions of people 1–5. For each person, underline three key pieces of information about them and what type of course they are looking for. The first one has been done for you.

1 Mateo is interested in meeting a famous extreme cakemaker. He wants to plan how a cake will look and bake it using unusual flavours on the course.

2 Elena is keen to meet someone who owns a cake business. She would like to learn more about creating cake recipes and stay in contact with other extreme cake makers after the course.

3 Christos would like some advice about his cake designs from someone who creates realistic-looking cake designs. He would prefer to make an extreme cake with other people.

4 Aiko wants to meet someone who writes cookbooks. She would like tips for taking photos of her cakes and how to advertise them.

5 Chima would like to receive advice about entering baking competitions. He hopes to exchange cake ideas with other extreme cake makers and receive information about the science of baking cakes.

3 Read about eight extreme-cake baking courses (A–H). Underline three key pieces of information about each course.

4 SPEAK In pairs, look at the three key points you have for Mateo in Exercise 2. Explain to your partner which course you think is the best option for him and how it matches the key information you underlined in Exercise 3. Does your partner agree?

5 Compare your answers for the other people.

6 Now, for each person (1–5), decide which course (A–H) would be the most suitable.

Extreme CAKE-MAKING COURSES

Learn how to turn delicious cakes into works of art!

A Advanced Cake Art

If you've heard of Christy Moore, it's probably from the extreme cake-making programme, *Over-the-top Cakes*. Her course teaches you how to make an incredible-looking cake that tastes delicious. With a background in photography, she offers tips and advice so your extreme cake-making skills get noticed on social media platforms.

B UNBELIEVABLE *Cakes!*

Parker Jones has a shop that only sells extreme cakes, and it's just as successful as his latest cookbook. His course teaches you that making your own cooking instructions for the perfect cake is possible. Once the course is finished, you join a private social media group to stay in touch with other talented bakers whose cakes look like pieces of art.

C HOW SWEET!

Nila Michelsen is well-known for her simple recipes for creating the most amazing extreme cakes. On the course, students experiment with some of her recipes before they try to make their own. Nila will judge teams of students to see who can create a realistic-looking cake design that tastes great.

D CAKE CRAFTING

After creating life-sized cake designs on the reality series *Extraordinary Cakes*, Bella Douglas became a celebrity almost overnight. She'll give you step-by-step instructions so the cake of your dreams becomes a reality! And you won't be following traditional recipes either. You'll experiment with a variety of ingredients no one expects in a cake, like wildflower honey and gold.

E CAKE DECORATING

Lilli Becker is well-known for making cakes that look so true to life that you wouldn't know they're actually cakes! If you want to improve the way your cakes look, then sign up for Lilli's extreme cake-making course. You'll also face the challenge of working in a team to make a huge dragon cake.

F Designing Cakes

Winning first place in an extreme cake-making contest isn't easy, and Chizoba Olutola will tell you why, and how to do well in them. She also goes through the chemistry and laws of physics involved in baking cakes. During Chizoba's course, she encourages her students to share their recipes and extreme cake designs so they get inspired by one another.

G ARTISTIC BAKING

Dawid Adamski is a talented artist and baker whose extreme cakes have won international awards. All he asks his students to do is show up with some ideas for a cake design. Then he gives you the skills to make it into a reality. Dawid also explains the scientific process of making a cake in his course.

H Sweet Sculpting

Jordi García is a bestselling author who has a new recipe book out. On his course, you'll do more than improve your baking skills. He'll show you tricks for making extreme cakes look incredible on social media posts – all you need is a phone. Not only that, he'll explain ways to promote your work so people will rush to buy your cakes!

Don't forget!

Remember that there are eight short texts to choose from. Only one text will match each person, so there are three extra texts that you won't need to use.

7 SPEAK Discuss the questions.

1 What events or occasions do you think extreme cakes are most suitable for?
2 Are art or baking skills more important for extreme-cake makers?

Reading Part 3 Multiple choice

What to expect in the exam

- Part 3 has the longest text in the exam, so make sure you leave enough time to complete it.
- You will answer five multiple-choice questions, each with four options.
- The first four questions follow the order of the text and often test your understanding of the writer's purpose for writing, their opinion, attitude or the opinion of someone else quoted by the writer.
- The final question often tests your understanding of the global meaning of the text and the answer can be found anywhere in the text.

How to go about it

- First, read the instructions and title to find out the topic of the text.
- Next, quickly skim through the text to get a general understanding of what it is about.
- Then read the questions and underline any key information in the questions and four options.
- Now carefully read the text again to answer each question. Compare each option with the text before choosing an answer. Think about why an option is correct or incorrect.
- Finally, check your answers again to ensure you have answered all questions correctly.

1 SPEAK In pairs, discuss the questions.

1 What do you know about the Balearic Islands?
2 Have you ever visited any of the islands?

2 Read the text on page 63. For questions 1–5, choose the correct answer (A, B, C or D).

1 Why did Piper sail to the Balearic Islands on her own?
  A She could travel to various destinations faster.
  B She was unable to find anyone to go with her.
  C She bought a boat suitable for the journey.
  D She wanted to have a new challenge.

2 According to the second paragraph, Piper felt
  A exhausted at the start of the journey.
  B lonely for some of the journey.
  C satisfied for most of the journey.
  D confident by the end of the journey.

3 What was Piper's favourite activity when she wasn't on her sailing boat?
  A relaxing on beaches
  B going deep-sea diving
  C seeing historical sites
  D visiting towns and villages

4 What advice does Piper give about sailing around the Balearic Islands?
  A Set practical goals to achieve.
  B Try to enjoy the whole experience.
  C Decide which route to take in advance.
  D Have enough money in case of an emergency.

5 What might Piper write in her journal about sailing to the Balearic Islands?
  A I knew exactly which route I wanted to take. I wanted to visit Ibiza first before it became full of tourists over the summer.
  B I avoided going to coastal towns that were crowded unless I really had to. I wanted to have a peaceful time enjoying nature.
  C It wasn't easy trying to convince my parents I could do the journey by myself. After some time, they said I could borrow *Silver Lining*.
  D I loved going on a long sailing journey by myself. Spending time alone was great, but it's more enjoyable sailing with a crew.

3 SPEAK Work in pairs. Discuss the questions.

1 Have you been been travelling by yourself?
2 What are the advantages and disadvantages of travelling on your own?

Sailing solo

25-year-old Piper Kuran talks about sailing on her own to the Balearic Islands in the Mediterranean Sea off Spain's eastern coast

I had the most incredible childhood sailing around the world with my parents. We've always had a flat in London, but now I live on *Silver Lining*, our 40-foot sailing boat. I started going on short journeys on my own, but never overnight. When I asked if I could take our boat to the Balearic Islands for the summer, my mum and dad were worried, but agreed. They knew I had the skills and experience necessary for the journey, but I needed to be extra careful sailing without a crew.

I wanted to sail to each of the four main islands, Formentera, Ibiza, Majorca and Menorca, which are all popular tourist destinations – particularly Ibiza. I was pretty nervous when I first set out, but once I realised I'd be fine, I began to relax and take my time sailing around these beautiful islands. It took just over a week to reach the Balearic Islands from London. The whole journey took great strength and concentration, so I'm glad I'm fit and didn't have anyone bothering me while I was at sea. When I returned home three months later, I knew without a doubt that I would continue sailing alone.

I wasn't always on *Silver Lining* because there was so much to see and do on the Balearic Islands. I enjoyed exploring ancient ruins more than anything else, so I did that whenever I could. And spending time on white sandy beaches after a day of diving in the Mediterranean Sea was really fun too – especially when I saw some seahorses and loggerhead turtles. I only went to populated areas along the coast when I needed more supplies, like food and fuel, because many of these locations are crowded, popular tourist destinations.

I'd highly recommend sailing to the Balearic Islands, but there are a few things to consider. For instance, be realistic about how far you can sail each day. I had a rough idea of the route I wanted to take, but when there was terrible weather, I had to change my plan; otherwise, sailing would be really dangerous. The last thing I wanted to do was damage *Silver Lining* on some rocks and pay for repairs. Take care, and you'll have the most amazing time sailing around this spectacular location, just like I did.

Reading Part 4 Gapped text

How to go about it

- First, read the instructions and title to understand the context.
- Next, quickly skim-read the text for a general idea of what it's about.
- Now carefully read around each gap to help you find the sentence that fits the gap.
- Finally, read the whole text again to make sure it makes sense.

In Part 4, you need to read a longer text with five sentences that have been removed. There are eight sentences to choose from. This part tests whether you can follow how the text is organised and understand the attitudes and opinions that are expressed in it.

1 SPEAK In pairs, look at the photographs and discuss whether you would like to visit this place.

2 You are going to read an article about a man who visited a Canadian wilderness resort. Five sentences have been removed from the article. Choose from the sentences A–H the one which best fits each gap (1–5). There are three extra sentences which you do not need to use.

TRAVEL JOURNALIST *Abioye Sowande* VISITS A RESORT IN THE CANADIAN WILD

This summer, I travelled to the other side of the world to visit Klahoose Wilderness Resort off the coast of western Canada. As the sun began rising, Randy, a member of the Klahoose First Nations people and guide at the resort, took me to my cabin overlooking the Pacific Ocean. **1** ____ A group of whales were swimming in the harbour. Randy joked, saying he'd timed that with Mother Nature.

It was a dreamlike start to my first morning at the resort, 160 kilometres north of Vancouver. It opened in 2008 and was purchased by the Klahoose First Nation's Economic Development Corporation in 2020. **2** ____ This includes Randy, who welcomes me with a song in the Salish language while beating a painted drum.

You can only arrive here by boat or private seaplane, but once you do, there is no schedule. The resort is a large wooden house with comfortable common areas and three additional cabins. **3** ____ Everything about Klahoose makes the middle of the Canadian wilderness feel incredibly cosy.

The Great Bear Rainforest is one of the main reasons people visit the resort – to see grizzly bears in the wild. **4** ____ On the way there, we passed waterfalls and ancient pictographs (rock art) until we reached an area densely populated with grizzly bears.

Randy and I hiked to a platform to view grizzly bears in their natural habitat and didn't have to wait very long to see some. **5** ____ I wanted a closer look, but Randy insisted that we remain hidden, as females with their young can be incredibly dangerous. On my final night, Randy shared stories about the land, his family and their traditional ceremonies, making the world around me seem even more alive. The following morning, just as I was leaving Klahoose, I saw more whales as Randy played his drums to say goodbye.

A As I floated in the chilly water, I saw some eagles flying high above.
B A baby cub was running behind its mother, trying to keep up.
C We made sure we followed two important rules for viewing bears: no food or noise.
D It isn't over-the-top luxury, but it's certainly charming.
E It took about an hour by boat to reach a viewing area.
F I noticed something moving in the distance as we stood on the balcony.
G These huge creatures attract visitors from all over the world.
H Since then, it's been almost entirely run by traditional landowners from the region.

3 SPEAK Compare your answers with a partner. Explain why you chose each answer and how it fits the information surrounding each gap.

4 SPEAK Work in pairs. Discuss the questions.

1. How different do you think an indigenous resort might be from other resorts?
2. Do you think it's important for travellers to learn about local and indigenous cultures?

Reading Part 5 Multiple-choice cloze

What to expect in the exam

- In Part 5, you need to read a short factual text with six gaps. This part of the test mainly tests vocabulary.
- Each question has four options, each of which is the same type of word and/or has a similar meaning. These are usually verbs, nouns, adjectives and adverbs.

1 **SPEAK** In pairs, look at the photographs and discuss what you know about Japan's cherry blossom festival. Have you ever experienced or seen cherry blossoms?

2 Read the text and for questions 1–6, choose which answer (A, B, C or D) best fits each gap.

Cherry Blossom Festival

Japan is known around the world for its cherry blossom festival. In Japanese, the term *hanami* means *flower viewing*, which is an ancient **(1)** .... that is over 1000 years old. *Hanami* takes **(2)** .... every spring when cherry blossom trees bloom, producing beautiful light pink-to-white flowers. People go to parks to have picnics and parties under the flowering trees to celebrate their beauty with family, friends and colleagues. The parties often **(3)** .... on into the night, when paper lanterns are lit.

The cherry blossom festival is a unique celebration because no one can predict when exactly the trees will start to bloom. **(4)** .... this, Japanese news stations keep an eye on the cherry trees and regularly **(5)** .... on the progress of the blossoms in what is called 'The Blossom Forecast'. Once the cherry blossoms are in flower, the festival begins. Since the flowers only live approximately two weeks, they **(6)** .... people that nothing lasts forever.

	A	B	C	D
1	system	routine	custom	attitude
2	place	advantage	part	control
3	remain	keep	hold	carry
4	Instead of	Due to	According to	Out of
5	report	announce	communicate	inform
6	advise	say	signal	remind

3 **SPEAK** Work in groups. Does your region have any festivals that celebrate nature or natural events? Why do you think people celebrate natural events by having festivals?

How to go about it

- Read the whole text quickly, ignoring the gaps, so you understand the general meaning of the whole text.
- Next, carefully read each sentence to decide which option fits.
- Eliminate options that are definitely wrong before choosing the answer.
- Once you complete all the questions, read the text to make sure it makes sense.

Don't forget!

Pay special attention to how words collocate with each other, as this can be tested in this part of the exam.

Reading Part 6 Open cloze

What to expect in the exam

- In Part 6, you need to read a short text with six words removed.
- You need to write **one word** in each gap.
- This part of the test mainly focuses on grammatical knowledge, but some questions can test phrasal verbs and fixed phrases.

1 **SPEAK** Work in pairs. Discuss the questions.

1 How often do you take selfies?

2 Do you think it's important to take selfies when you visit attractions?

2 Read the review below. For each question (1–6), write the word which best fits each gap. Write **one** word for each gap.

Don't forget!

› Make sure your handwriting is clear on the answer sheet so the examiner can read your writing.

› It's important to check your spelling as you won't receive a mark if your spelling is incorrect.

How to go about it

- Quickly read the title and text to understand the topic and general meaning.
- Don't worry about the gapped words when you first read the text.
- Next, read around each gap and think of the single word that fits in each gap.
- Once you complete each gap, read the text again to make sure it makes sense and to check your spelling.

TrustReviews News Reviews Buy More ›

★★★★☆ Mei Goh review of 29Rooms

A picture-perfect art exhibition

I'm glad I visited 29Rooms while this travelling art exhibition was in Singapore. The American artists who created the travelling exhibition made it look (1) .... an adult playground. They achieve this (2) .... designing twenty-nine zones, each with its own theme, sounds and even scents. (3) .... of the incredible photo opportunities at the exhibition, 29Rooms became a popular destination for taking selfies.

The central attraction was Merry-Go-Round, an interactive area created in order (4) .... show where the average Singaporean is seated throughout the day: on public transport, in office chairs, at coffee shops, in living rooms, on toilets, and in bedrooms. It made me think about how I share the same daily routine with millions of other people. (5) .... of my favourite rooms was called Long-Lost-Friend, where I wrote a postcard to myself that will be sent to me a year from now. On the (6) ...., the exhibition was well worth a visit.

3 Look back at the gaps in Exercise 2. Which of the parts of speech below is being tested in each gap? You will need to use one of the options more than once. The first one has been done for you.

1 phrasal verb

determiner idiom infinitive phrasal verb preposition

5

THE GREAT OUTDOORS

KEY LANGUAGE

Present perfect continuous
Relative clauses
Nature
Environmental issues

PRONUNCIATION

Intonation in questions

EXAM SKILLS

Reading Parts 3 & 6
Writing Parts 1 & 2
Listening Parts 2 & 3
Speaking Parts 1, 2 & 4

Speaking Part 1 Interview

Work with a partner. Discuss the questions.

1 What is your favourite outdoor activity?
2 Describe a natural area that you have visited.
3 Do you enjoy watching documentaries about nature?
4 What was your favourite animal when you were young?
5 How important are environmental issues to you?

Speaking Part 2 Extended turn

Which of these words could you use to talk about the weather in the photograph? Describe the picture.

cloudy cold cool hot foggy humid icy mild sunny rainy warm wet windy

5 THE GREAT OUTDOORS

Vocabulary Nature

1 Match the words 1–12 to the pictures a–l.

1 cave ____	**5** forest ____	**9** hill ____
2 cliff ____	**6** island ____	**10** stream ____
3 desert ____	**7** jungle ____	**11** valley ____
4 field ____	**8** lake ____	**12** waterfall ____

a

b

c

d

e

f

g

h

i

j

k

l

2 Cover the words in Exercise 1 and look at the pictures. Can you remember the words?

3 What's the difference between a *hill* and a *mountain*, and a *stream* and a *river*?

4 **SPEAK** Work in small groups. Talk about natural areas in your region or country. Which would you recommend to foreign visitors? Why?

I would recommend / suggest going to … because …

Have you ever been to …? There are lots of beautiful lakes/waterfalls/mountains there.

Speaking Part 4 General conversation

Useful language

Add at least three words to lists 1–2.

1 Camping activities: hiking / fishing / bird watching / ________ / ________ / ________

2 Camping supplies: tent / sleeping bag / torch / ________ / ________ / ________

How to go about it

- Listen carefully to the questions.
- Talk about your opinions and personal experiences.
- Give reasons or examples to support your ideas.
- Ask your partner questions and respond to what they say.
- Use a variety of vocabulary and grammar.

SPEAK Work in groups of three. Read the instructions and do the speaking task.

Students A and B: you are candidates. Close your books. Answer the questions Student C asks you.

Student C: you are the examiner. Keep your book open and ask questions 1–5. Use at least three of the follow-up questions below.

1 Do you like camping?
2 What is the best time of year to go camping?
3 What do you need to take with you on a camping trip?
4 Would you prefer to go camping with your friends or family?
5 Why do people enjoy spending time in nature?

Follow-up questions

- Why?/Why not?
- Do you agree?
- How/What about you?
- What do you think?

Reading Part 6 Open cloze

1 SPEAK Work in pairs. Are there any good places to go hiking close to where you live?

2 For questions 1–6, read the text below and think of the word which best fits each gap. Write one word for each gap.

Don't forget!

› Look carefully at the words before and after the gap.
› Complete each gap with only ONE word.

It was my friend Kate's idea to go on a hiking trip together. To **(1)** .... honest, I was a bit nervous at first, but Kate is a very experienced hiker and she promised to take good **(2)** .... of me.

It took us quite **(3)** .... while to choose where to go. **(4)** .... were so many interesting routes to choose from! But, in the end, we decided on the *Carros de Foc*, a seven-day route in the Pyrenees.

Packing was difficult. Everything had to fit into two backpacks, including extra clothing, sleeping bags, food and water. We also brought waterproof jackets and trousers in case **(5)** .... rain.

It was an amazing trip. We saw forests, waterfalls and snow-covered mountains. The trip was full of nice moments, but one of my favourites **(6)** .... the incredibly beautiful view of the lake called Estany Major de Colomèrs at sunset. I remember watching the landscape slowly change from orange to purple. It was spectacular.

Listening Part 2 Multiple choice

1 5.1 You will hear people talking in six different situations. For questions 1–6, choose the best answer (A, B or C).

How to go about it

- As you listen, put a mark next to wrong answers.
- Check your answers the second time you listen.

1 You will hear two people talking about ice skating.
The man is worried that
A the skates will not fit.
B he will get injured.
C people will laugh at him.

2 You will hear a man and woman talking about a documentary they saw.
What do they agree about?
A The information was interesting.
B The music was excellent.
C The photography was beautiful.

3 You will hear two people talking about gardening.
What does the man like most about gardening now?
A It's a good form of exercise.
B It's a good way to relax.
C It's a good reason to be outside.

4 You will hear a woman telling her friend about her plans for the guest bedroom in her house.
What does she decide to do in the guest bedroom?
A add new, modern furniture
B fix furniture that is broken
C move furniture to a new place

5 You will hear two friends talking about a rock-climbing lesson.
How did the woman feel about it?
A happy with the price she paid
B surprised by the progress she made
C impressed by the size of the gym

6 You will hear two students talking about a German course.
They both complain that
A the teacher is hard to understand.
B there are too few speaking activities.
C the course materials are difficult.

Language focus Present perfect continuous

1 Look at the extracts from the listening and answer questions a–c below.

1 **A:** How long **have you been** ice skating?
B: Since I was a kid – my dad taught me.

2 **A:** Look at your clothes – they're so dirty!
B: I**'ve been working** outside in the garden.

3 **A:** You **haven't been going** to our German course recently.
B: I got a bit tired of it, to be honest.

a In positive sentences, we form the present perfect continuous with *has/have* + *been* + the *-ing* form of the main verb. How do we form the present perfect continuous in questions and negative sentences?

b In which example(s) does the action start in the past and continue into the present?

c In which example(s) has the action just stopped, but it has a present result?

2 Complete the sentences using the present perfect continuous form of the verb in brackets.

1 I'm starting to lose my patience with this bus. We ______'ve been waiting______ (*wait*) for over half an hour!

2 This strategy clearly ______________ (*not work*) for quite a while now. It's time to think of a new one.

3 Deborah ______________ (*run*) Lights Out Camping Inc. for the last five years and it's become quite successful.

4 How long ________ your son ______________ (*study*) music? He's very talented.

5 **A:** You look tired.
B: Yes, I ______________ (*cycle*).

6 You look exhausted. ________ you ______________ (*get*) enough sleep?

7 Lately, I ______________ (*eat*) more fruit and vegetables and I feel much healthier.

8 For the last decade, we ______________ (*not do*) enough to protect our national forests.

3 Go to **Ready for Grammar** on **page 212** for rules, explanations and further practice.

4 SPEAK Work in pairs.

Student A: Turn to the **Additional materials** on **page 197** and follow the instructions.

Student B: Turn to the **Additional materials** on **page 198** and follow the instructions.

Reading Part 3 Multiple choice

1 SPEAK Work in pairs. One of these eight facts about giraffes is false. Which one is it?

1 Giraffes are the tallest land animals on Earth.
2 Giraffes have the same number of neck bones as humans.
3 Giraffes don't communicate with sounds.
4 Giraffes can run up to 60 km per hour.
5 Giraffes' necks are too short to reach the ground.
6 Giraffes only need between five and thirty minutes of sleep a day.
7 Giraffes only need to drink water once every few days.
8 Giraffes can stand up 30 minutes after they are born.

2 Read the following article about a man who studies giraffes in Tanzania. What problems do giraffes currently face?

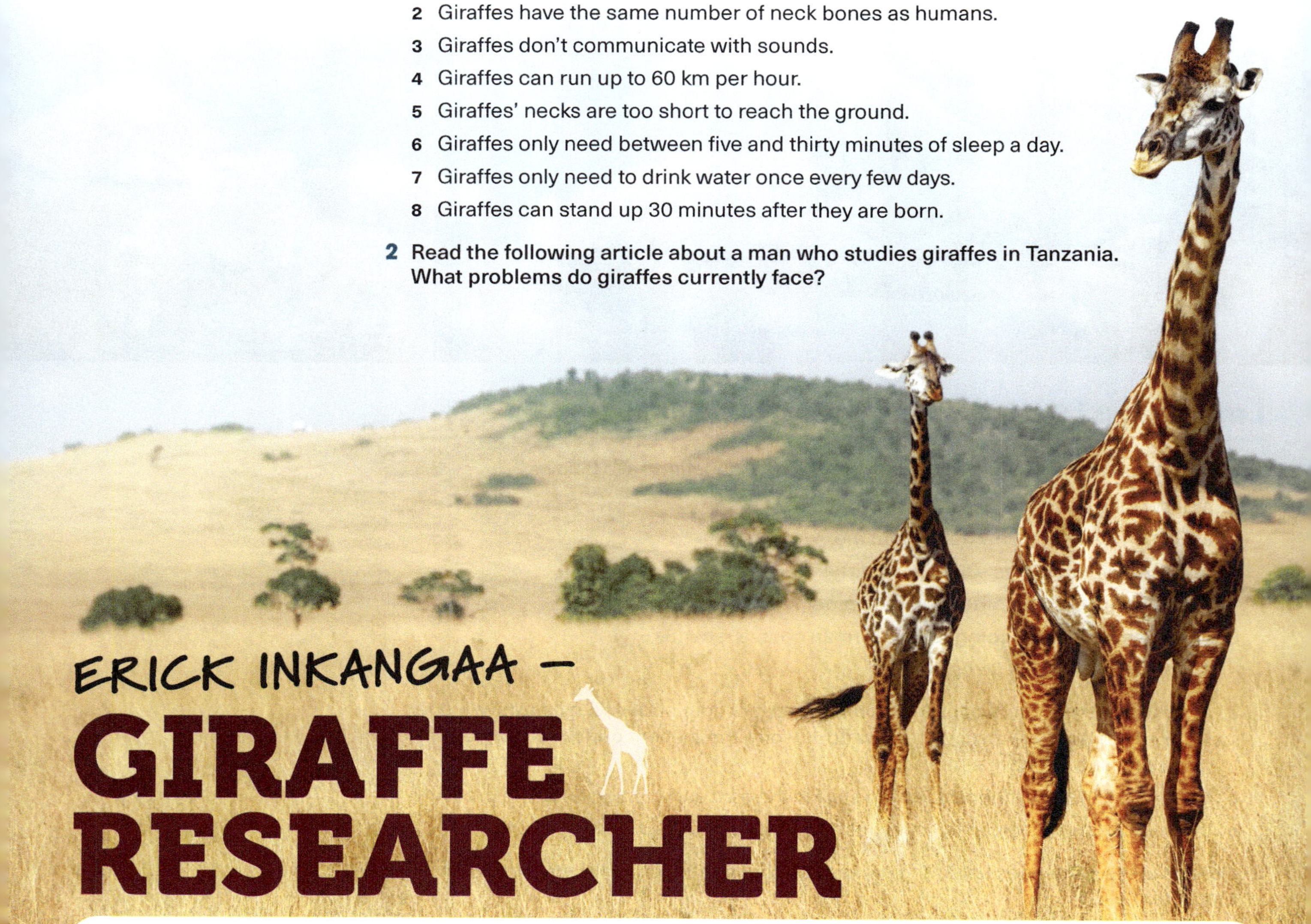

ERICK INKANGAA – GIRAFFE RESEARCHER

How did I start studying giraffes? It all started 10 years ago when I attended a conference shortly after finishing my degree in Wildlife Science at the University of Dar es Salaam. There I met a friendly group of researchers, who offered me a paid job studying giraffes. I accepted immediately. At the time, I didn't feel the same passion for these animals that I do now, but I couldn't say no to working in the beautiful savannah in the north of my country, Tanzania, photographing Masai giraffes in their natural habitat. As part of our research, we use these pictures to study the social lives of giraffes.

This research has led to some exciting discoveries. For example, giraffes form strong social networks, which we call 'communities'. Female giraffes tend to stay in the same community they are born into, while male giraffes usually leave for a new one at the age of four. Interestingly, two females often live in the same area but never spend time together because they belong to different social groups. These communities are also important for giraffes' health. Our research also shows that female giraffes whose social connections are strong live longer than those who live mostly on their own.

People all over the world love giraffes, but these animals are in serious trouble. Hunters kill them and the trees they eat are cut down. But that's not all. Due to rising temperatures, it now rains more heavily in the African savannah, and this spreads diseases among giraffes. However, there is still hope. We have seen that when governments pass laws that protect giraffes and their habitats, and when police ensure people follow these laws, it makes a big difference. A hotter climate, though, is still a problem with no clear solution.

For giraffes, time is running out. To make a difference, I believe that scientists like me need to share our work with the public. If we don't do it, who will? That's why I've started organising short courses in primary schools. I taught my first one a few weeks ago. I knew that over 200 pupils would attend, so I was sure I would spend the whole hour feeling anxious. Thankfully, I relaxed after a few minutes. And, luckily for me, it isn't hard to make giraffes interesting. The children loved looking at the pictures of giraffes which I took with me on my visit, and they loved learning facts about giraffes – for example, that they only sleep 30 minutes or less a day and can run up to 60 km an hour.

My hope is that experiences like these will encourage young people to value – and help protect – the amazing wildlife we have here in Tanzania.

What to expect in the exam

- In Part 3 you have to answer five multiple-choice questions. For each question, there are four options (A–D).
- To get the right answers, you have to understand specific details, as well as the writer's attitude and opinion.
- For the first four questions, information in the text is in the same order as the questions. However, the last question tests general understanding, so the correct information could be in any part of the text.

How to go about it

- First, read the text quickly to get a general idea of what it is about.
- For each question, find the part of the text that relates to the question. Then check to see what information in options A–D is correct.
- Put a cross (×) next to answers that are clearly wrong.
- Choose the best option. If you are not sure, guess. In the B1 Preliminary exam, you don't lose points for wrong answers.

3 Read the article again. For questions 1–5, choose the correct answer (A, B, C or D).

1 Erick decided to research giraffes because
- A he was interested in becoming a photographer.
- B he was able to study an animal that he loved.
- C he wanted to work in a natural area.
- D he needed to pay for his university studies.

2 What does Erick say about female giraffes?
- A They live longer lives than male giraffes.
- B They live together in groups in order to stay safe.
- C They join new groups as soon as they become adults.
- D They avoid interacting with giraffes they don't know.

3 According to Erick the most difficult part about saving giraffes is
- A slowing down global warming.
- B protecting their natural habitat.
- C stopping hunters from killing them.
- D passing environmental laws.

4 How did Erick feel before teaching his first course in a primary school?
- A glad that the school had asked him to do it
- B convinced that he wasn't going to enjoy it
- C surprised at how many pupils signed up
- D worried that he wouldn't have enough time.

5 What would be a good way to introduce this article?

A **Erick Inkangaa describes how his love of giraffes developed into a career.**

B **Erick Inkangaa talks about what he has learned from a decade of studying giraffes.**

C **Erick Inkangaa explains why giraffes are so difficult to study in the wild.**

D **Erick Inkangaa tells us what happened when he moved to Tanzania to study giraffes.**

4 **SPEAK** Work in small groups. Are there any endangered animals in your country?

Language focus Relative clauses

Defining relative clauses

1 **A defining relative clause defines, or makes it clear, which person or thing we are talking about. Look at these examples:**

The children loved looking at the pictures.

(It is not clear which pictures the writer is talking about.)

The children loved looking at the pictures of giraffes which I took with me on my visit.

(The underlined relative clause makes it clear which pictures the writer is talking about.)

2 **Underline the defining relative clauses in these sentences.**

1 People who know more than one language make better researchers.
2 It's an organisation whose members are dedicated to saving the environment.
3 The café where I met my wife is just around the corner.

3 **In defining relative clauses, we can replace both the relative pronouns *who* and *which* with *that*. Look at these examples:**

The children loved looking at the pictures ***which/that*** *I took on my visit.*

People ***who/that*** *know more than one language make better researchers.*

4 **In the first sentence in Exercise 3, we can leave out the relative pronoun, but in the second sentence we cannot. Why?**

5 **Go to Ready for Grammar on page 214 to check your answers to Exercise 4 and for further rules, explanations and practice.**

6 **SPEAK Work in pairs. Tell your partner about topics 1–4. Ask follow-up questions for more information.**

1 A place where you played as a child
2 A sport which you would like to try
3 An actor whose films you enjoy
4 A person in your family who you admire

Non-defining relative clauses

1 **A non-defining relative clause does not define which person or thing we are talking about, but instead adds extra information about them. Look at these examples:**

The person who we pay to clean our windows is always very cheerful.

(Defining – the relative clause makes it clear which person we are talking about.)

My dad, who you'll meet tomorrow, has a great sense of humour.

(Non-defining – with the words '*My dad*', it is already clear which person we are talking about.)

2 **Complete the rules for non-defining relative clauses.**

In non-defining relative clauses

a we *can* / *cannot* replace *who* or *which* with *that*.
b we *can* / *cannot* leave out the relative pronoun.
c we *have to* / *do not have to* use commas to separate the relative clause from the rest of the sentence.

3 **Go to Ready for Grammar on page 214 to check your answers to Exercise 2 and for further rules, explanations and practice.**

4 **In sentences 1–4, use your imagination to add extra information to the words in bold using non-defining relative clauses. There is an example at the beginning.**

The hikers looked down on the **valley**.

The hikers looked down on the valley, which was full of beautiful white flowers.

1 The **flat** is worth a lot of money.
2 **Roberto** was home for the holidays.
3 Lisa and Tom are in **Scotland**.
4 We all ate ice cream except for **Julio**.

5 **SPEAK Work in pairs. Compare your ideas. Who wrote the most interesting sentences?**

Listening Part 3 Gap fill

1 **SPEAK** For one minute, write down words you associate with Iceland, e.g. *glaciers*, *long winters*. Compare your words with a partner.

How to go about it

- Read the sentences with gaps before you listen. Predict what type of word is missing in each gap, e.g. a name, number or date.
- Don't write down the first word you hear. There are usually distractors – words that make sense in the sentence, but are wrong.
- Check your answers the second time you listen.

2 5.2 You will hear a tour guide talking about arrangements for a day trip in Iceland. For questions 1–6, write the correct answer in the gap. Write **one** or **two words**, or a **number** or a **date** or a **time**.

A DAY TRIP IN ICELAND

1 Date of tour: ....
2 Bus leaves at: .... am
3 First stop: the Skógafoss ....
4 Lunch: next to a ....
5 Bring: ....
6 Last stop: the .... beach

3 **SPEAK** Would you like to visit Iceland? Why/Why not?

Vocabulary Environmental issues

1 SPEAK Do you think people do enough to protect the environment? Why/Why not?

2 Read the following quotes from people talking about environmental issues. Complete each gap with a word or phrase in the box.

climate change fast fashion food waste litter noise pollution
public transport recycling saving energy

1 ________________ is so easy – you just have to separate your rubbish into plastics, metal, paper and so on. So why don't more people do it?

2 I work in a restaurant and ________________ is a big problem there. When customers don't finish their meals, we throw away everything left on their plates.

3 I wish there was better ________________ in my town. People here rely on their cars for everything, from getting to work to doing the shopping.

4 At home, ________________ is something I've started thinking more about – for example, switching off lights and electronic devices when I'm not using them.

5 The weather in my country is changing. It's hotter than it used to be. ________________ is real and if we keep on ignoring it, it's only going to get worse.

6 Levels of ________________ are going up, and studies show that the constant noise of traffic or planes flying overhead damages your health. Plus, it scares away birds and other wildlife.

7 I reject ________________. Instead of buying loads of trendy clothes at low prices, I buy a few pieces of simple but high-quality clothing that will last a long time.

8 One big problem in my neighbourhood is ________________. Everywhere I look there are empty cans and bottles on the ground. I pick up as much as I can, but people keep dropping more.

3 Look at the phrasal verbs which are underlined in the texts in Exercise 2. Write the phrasal verbs next to their meanings below. Use the infinitive without *to* form. The first one has been done for you.

1 *pick up* to collect
2 ________________ to continue
3 ________________ to need or depend on somebody/something
4 ________________ to stop electricity from reaching a machine
5 ________________ increase

4 SPEAK Work in small groups. Discuss some of the environmental issues facing your country or region, using either the issues from Exercise 2 or your own ideas. Which issue is the most serious?

Writing Part 2 Story

1 SPEAK Work in pairs. Read the following Writing Part 2 instructions and think about a story you could write. Discuss questions 1–4.

Your English teacher has asked you to write a story. Your story must start with this sentence:

Rob and I walked down the hill and stopped at the side of the river.

Write your **story** in around **100 words.**

1 What did they see at the river?
2 What did they talk about at the river?
3 What surprising thing happened at the river?
4 What happened afterwards?

2 Now read the model answer to the task in Exercise 1. Are your ideas similar or different?

A CLOSE CALL

Rob and I walked down the hill and stopped at the side of the river.

'Look!' said Rob.

There were hundreds of fish. Maybe thousands. We **(1)** <u>were looking at</u> this beautiful and unexpected scene, when suddenly a rock under my foot moved and I started to fall. Rob quickly **(2)** <u>took</u> my arm.

'Thanks,' I said. 'That was close.'

'No worries,' he **(3)** <u>said</u>. 'Hey, is that your phone in the water?'

Rob got my mobile phone from the water and **(4)** <u>gave</u> it to me. To my surprise, it still worked perfectly.

'Today is my lucky day!' I said.

Don't forget!

- In your story, use the same names or pronouns (*she*, *we*, *they*) as the sentence from the task instructions.
- Use a good variety of vocabulary and grammar.
- Before you finish, check your story for spelling errors and other small mistakes.

3 Strong verbs make writing more interesting. Replace verbs 1–4 in the model answer with the correct form of the stronger verbs in the box.

admire grab hand reply

4 Read the following tips for writing interesting stories. Which tips (1–4) did the writer follow in the story about the river?

1 Describe what the characters see, hear, touch, feel or smell.
2 Use dialogue, e.g. 'What's wrong?'
3 Use a mixture of long and short sentences.
4 Give your story a title that makes people want to read it.

5 Now do the following Part 2 task. Follow the tips in Exercise 4.

Your English teacher has asked you to write a story. Your story must start with this sentence:

When the two friends arrived, the field was full of people.

Write your **story** in about **100 words.**

For more information on writing stories, see page 194.

5 REVIEW

Vocabulary Nature

Complete the gaps with words from the Vocabulary section on page 68. You may need to use the plural form of the words.

TOP FIVE NATURAL WONDERS OF BRAZIL

1 Fernando De Noronha

Enjoy the wildlife and amazing beaches of Fernando de Noronha Marine National Park, a group of 21 **(1) i**__________ located 350 km off the coast of Brazil in the Atlantic ocean.

2 The Meeting of Waters

When the Amazon and the Rio Negro meet, their waters don't mix. For 6 km, the two rivers flow side by side through the **(2) j**__________, separated by a huge difference in temperature and speed.

3 Serra Dos Órgãos

Hikers will love the Serra Dos Órgãos mountain range. Some of the peaks are so high you can see them from Rio de Janeiro, 50 km away. In this area, a wide variety of tropical birds and other animals live in the dense **(3) f**__________.

4 Iguazú Falls

This 2.7 km long **(4) w**__________ is located at the intersection of three countries: Brazil, Argentina and Paraguay. In places, the water can fall from a height of 80 metres.

5 Abismo Guy Collet

Abismo Guy Collet is the deepest **(5) c**__________ in South America. At the bottom, 671 metres below the surface of the Earth, explorers have discovered an underground body of water, or **(6) l**__________.

Vocabulary Environmental issues

Match the sentence beginnings 1–6 to the endings a–f to make complete sentences.

1 One problem for whales and dolphins is **noise**
2 The *New York Times* invented the term **fast**
3 Fish, meat and fruit can be sources of **food**
4 When you compare it to driving alone, **public**
5 We really must do something to slow **climate**
6 Many modern cities have found ways of **saving**

a **change**: storms are getting stronger as temperatures increase.
b **transport** reduces air pollution in cities by as much as 45%.
c **energy**, such as using LED technology for street lighting.
d **pollution** in the ocean because they use sound to navigate.
e **fashion** to describe the trend of cheap, trendy clothing.
f **waste**, because they typically go off in just a few days.

Language focus Present perfect continuous

Write the words in the correct order to complete the conversations. There is an example at the beginning.

A: Why are your hands so dirty?
B: bike. / been / I've / my / mending
I've been mending my bike.

1
A: Are the kids hungry?
B: they've / no, / snacks. / eating / been

2
A: Is she good at programming?
B: it / she's / studying / years. / for / been / yes,

3
A: Do you know what's happening with the presidential election?
B: paying / haven't / no, / attention. / been / I

4
A: has / how / raining? / long / been / it

B: Since yesterday evening – it just won't stop!

5
A: Are your friends excited about the trip?
B: been / week. / they've / yes, / about / talking / it / all

6
A: long / Copenhagen? / been / have / in / how / you / living

B: Since 2015. I love it here.

Writing Part 1 Email

Read this email from your English-speaking friend Bruna and the notes you have made.

From: Bruna
Subject: Bike ride!
Hi
I'm looking forward to going mountain biking with you. Shall we go on Saturday or Sunday? ← Say which …
There are two routes near where I live. One goes along a river and the other goes round a lake. Which would be better? ← Tell Bruna …
On the way home, we could have lunch at a restaurant. There are lots of options. What kind of food should we eat? ← Suggest …
If you want, I can drive us in my car. Let me know what time to pick you up. ← Thanks, …
Bruna

Reply to Bruna using all the notes. Write your email in about 100 words.

For more information on writing emails, see pages 192–193.

Pronunciation Intonation in questions

1 5.3 Listen to these sentences from Speaking Part 4 on page 69. Does the voice rise (↗) or fall (↘) at the end of the question? Underline the correct intonation pattern.

1 Do you agree? ↗ / ↘
2 Do you like camping? ↗ / ↘
3 What is the best time of year to go camping? ↗ / ↘
4 Why do people enjoy spending time in nature? ↗ / ↘

2 Look at Exercise 1 and answer the questions.

Do we use a *rising* (↗) or *falling* (↘) intonation pattern at the end of

1 questions that you can answer "yes" or "no"?
2 questions that start with questions words like *who*, *what*, *why*, *when* or *how*?

3 **SPEAK** Work in small groups. Read the rules and play the board game.

HEADS OR TAILS

1 Toss a coin. Move two spaces for heads and one space for tails.
2 Ask the question in the space, using the correct intonation. Discuss the question in your group for one minute.
3 The first player to reach the finish is the winner.

START	How often do you spend time in nature?	Do you like winter sports? Why/ Why not?	MISS A TURN
			Have you ever visited a national park?
In your town or city, are there enough green spaces?	MOVE FORWARD ONE SPACE	Would you like to live in the middle of the countryside? Why/Why not?	When was the last time you went cycling?
What is the most beautiful beach you have ever visited?			
Did you play outdoors as a child? Why/Why not?	GO BACK ONE SPACE	Do you enjoy gardening? Why/ Why not?	When you want to spend time outdoors, where do you go?
			Do you find it relaxing to spend time in nature? Why/Why not?
FINISH	Is it important for children to spend time outdoors? Why/Why not?	GO BACK TWO SPACES	What can we do to protect forests and other natural areas?

6 AWAY WE GO

KEY LANGUAGE

Comparatives and superlatives
Future forms
So, such, too and *enough*
Adjectives
Travel compound nouns

PRONUNCIATION

Word stress

EXAM SKILLS

Reading Parts 2 & 5
Writing Parts 1 & 2
Listening Parts 1 & 4
Speaking Parts 1, 2 & 3

Speaking Part 1 Interview

Work with a partner. Discuss the questions.

1 What activities do you enjoy doing on holiday?
2 What did you do on your last holiday?
3 Which do you prefer, summer holidays or winter holidays?
4 What countries would you like to visit?
5 Do you enjoy travelling by train? Why/ Why not?

Speaking Part 2 Extended turn

Describe how the person in the photo is feeling. Use the words below to help you.

disappointed excited miserable
relaxed surprised tired upset worried

6 AWAY WE GO

Reading Part 2 Matching

1 **SPEAK** Do you like watching travel shows or reading travel books? Why/Why not?

2 The people below all want to find a travel book to read. On the opposite page there are eight book reviews. For each person (1–5), decide which book (A–H) would be the most suitable.

1 Laila likes reading books about the natural world. She wants to read a modern story about somebody who goes on a long journey and describes the problems they have to deal with.

2 Jakob likes learning about extraordinary things that people did in the past. He would like to read about somebody who made discoveries and explored new places.

3 Vasiliki likes books that make her laugh. She wants a book where the author goes on a strange journey and talks to lots of interesting people along the way.

4 Valeria would like a travel book that is set in one country. She is looking for a personal story where the author learns about their family.

5 Karl likes reading books about history. He wants a book by a famous writer who travelled to other countries to report on important events.

3 **SPEAK** Work in pairs. Which book would you be most interested in reading? Why?

TRAVEL BOOK *Reviews*

My books | Browse | **Reviews** | Community

A UNDERLAND
by Robert Macfarlane

After reading this fascinating book, you will never look at the natural world the same way again. In *Underland*, we follow the author as he travels the world trying to understand the relationship between humans and the environment. In this book, you will learn about everything from caves to ancient myths to nuclear waste.

B LOOKING FOR TRANSWONDERLAND: *Travels in Nigeria*
by Noo Saro-Wiwa

The author spent time in Nigeria as a child and, in this book, she returns after many years away, in the hope of better understanding her father and the country he loved. She takes the reader from busy cities to peaceful mountains, from museums to dog shows, painting a funny and honest picture of an extraordinary nation.

C XU XIAKE (1586–1641): *The Art of Travel Writing*
by Julian Ward

This book tells the story of one of the world's first backpackers, Xu Xiake, who walked thousands of kilometres across China during the 15th century. Xiake was a true explorer, fascinated not by money but by a sense of adventure. During his travels, he found the sources of important rivers and he was the first person to visit certain remote areas.

D THE RINGS OF SATURN
by W. G. Sebald

Is this a novel or a travel book? It's not always clear. As we follow the main character on a walking tour of Southern England, he describes local places he visits and explains how these places are connected to important historical events in Europe, North America and China. This unusual book is worth reading at least twice.

E ROUND IRELAND WITH A FRIDGE
by Tony Hawks

Why would someone choose to hitchhike with an old refrigerator? To write a hilarious book about it! In order to reach his goal of crossing Ireland with a fridge, the author relies on help from dozens of strangers, each with their own story to tell. This book proves that travel writing doesn't need to be serious to be good.

F THE GREAT RAILWAY BAZAAR: *By Train Through Asia*
by Paul Theroux

In his first book, now a classic, this famous travel writer takes a long journey from London to Tokyo – mainly by train. The heart of the book is the passengers he meets. It's a perfect travel book, beautifully written with a wide range of landscapes and people.

G FERAL: *Losing myself and finding my way in America's National Parks*
by Emily Pennington

In this book, the author tells the story of how she quits her job as a Hollywood executive and decides to change her life. She buys a small van and sets out on a year-long trip around the USA to visit 63 national parks. Along the way, she admires magnificent views, makes new friends, faces extreme weather events, and slowly discovers the new person she wants to become.

H THE WORLD: *Travels 1950–2000*
by Jan Morris

From the fall of the Berlin Wall to the first trip to the top of Mount Everest, this book collects fifty years of articles from one of Britain's most well-known travel writers. Written in a very descriptive style, this is both a travel book and one writer's personal view of the 20th century.

Vocabulary Adjectives

1 **Find words with a similar meaning to 1–6 below in the relevant sections of the reading text on page 83.**

1 very interesting (section A) ________
2 very old (section A) ________
3 calm (section B) ________
4 very funny (section E) ________
5 beautiful (section G) ________
6 famous (section H) ________

2 **In sentences 1–7, complete the two gaps with words from the box that have a similar meaning to the word that has been underlined.**

challenging dull essential glad hard incredible necessary
odd pleased typical uninteresting unusual usual wonderful

1 Personally, I was very happy with the museum tour. Are you ________ / ________ you came?
2 On a normal day, I wake up at 7 am, but on holiday my ________ / ________ routine involves sleeping late.
3 When scuba diving, it's important to know how to clear water from your mask. It's a/an ________ / ________ skill.
4 Jane found it very difficult to cancel her hotel reservation. Getting a refund for the rental car was ________ / ________ too.
5 We had an amazing tour of Lithuania. The whole journey was ________ / ________.
6 At the planetarium, the long lecture on Jupiter was boring, and the exhibition on moon rocks was just as ________ / ________.
7 It's a bit strange they decided on Greenland for their honeymoon. What a/an ________ / ________ choice!

3 **Go to the Additional materials on page 197 for further practice.**

Language focus Comparatives and superlatives

1 **SPEAK** **Do the quiz in pairs.**

1	Australia is **wider** than the moon.	T / F
2	China is the country with **the largest** population.	T / F
3	Switzerland has **the most expensive** public transport in the world.	T / F
4	Montreal is **further** south than Paris.	T / F
5	London is a **more popular** tourist destination than New York.	T / F
6	Tokyo has **the busiest** train station in the world.	T / F
7	Greenland is **the least populated** country in the world.	T / F

2 **Look at the words in bold in Exercise 1 and answer questions 1–5.**

1 Which are comparative forms of adjectives?
2 Which are superlative forms of adjectives?
3 When do we use *-er* or *-est* to create these forms?
4 When do we use *more* or *most* to create these forms?
5 Which comparative form is irregular?

3 **Now read the sentences and answer questions 1–2.**

*Kazakhstan is **as** big **as** Argentina.* *Australia is **not as** big **as** Brazil.*

1 Which phrase means we are comparing two things that
a) are the same? b) not the same?
2 Do we use the comparative form of adjectives with (*not*) *as … as …*?

4 Go to Ready for Grammar on page 216 for rules, explanations and further practice.

5 **SPEAK** Look at the chart and compare the cities using the comparative or superlative forms of adjectives. Use (*not*) *as* ... *as* ... to make comparisons too.

The Great Wall of China is by far the most visited landmark.

The Tower of London is not as popular as the Eiffel Tower.

Landmark	Country	Approximate number of visitors per year (millions)
1 Great Wall of China	China	10
2 Taj Mahal	India	7.5
3 Eiffel Tower	France	7
4 The Colosseum	Italy	6
5 Statue of Liberty	USA	4.3
6 Tower of London	UK	3

6 Go to the Additional materials on page 197 for further practice.

Speaking Part 3 Discussion

1 **SPEAK** Work in pairs. Do you enjoy going on holiday to places that are hot and sunny? Why/Why not?

2 **SPEAK** A family is going on holiday to a place that is hot and sunny. Here are some things they could take with them. Talk together about the different things they could take on their holiday and decide which one is the most important.

Vocabulary Travel compound nouns

1 **SPEAK** Work in pairs. Do you prefer travelling by plane or car? Why?

2 Read chats A and B below, ignoring the gaps for now. Were their travel experiences good or bad? Why?

3 Now complete the chats with the compound nouns in the box. Use the words in bold to help you.

airlines car park check-in desk driving licence hand luggage motorway return ticket speed limit traffic jam window seat

Chat A

Julia

Hey, how was your trip?

Great! You know, everybody complains about these **low-cost (1)** ________, saying the companies don't care about passengers, but I had a good experience.

Miracles do happen!

I'm being serious! The staff were super friendly and they even let me **sit in** a **(2)** ________ when I asked. It was cool to look down at the city while we were landing.

Did you **carry** any **(3)** ________? They're always so strict about what you can bring on the plane.

Just a small backpack, so it wasn't an issue. Honestly, the whole trip was great, except for one thing: I had **bought** a **(4)** ________ for Sunday, but the flight back got cancelled.

Oh no.

There was **a long queue at the (5)** ________, but once it was my turn, the man was really helpful. He got me on the next flight back and I only arrived a few hours later than scheduled.

Lucky you!

Chat B

Tom

Are you back? How was your holiday?

It was a bit of a nightmare, actually.

Really? What happened?

It all started when we picked up the hire car in an **underground (6)** ________ at the airport. While we were leaving, I hit a pillar and damaged the passenger door.

That's very unlucky.

But that was only the beginning. We got on a **busy (7)** ________, which was the only available road to the coast, and immediately **got caught in a (8)** ________. For hours, we were either completely stopped or moving very slowly. I wanted to cry!

I bet.

Then, once the traffic cleared, I was very impatient and started **driving above the (9)** ________, but I got stopped by the police almost immediately! If that wasn't bad enough, I didn't have a **valid (10)** ________. I had forgotten to renew it.

Uh-oh.

Thankfully, the police officer only gave me a warning, but my friend had to drive for the rest of the trip.

4 There are no consistent spelling rules for compound nouns: we write some as one word and others as two. Choose the correct alternative in sentences 1–6.

1 For short trips, do you carry your things in a *backpack* / *back pack* or a small *suitcase* / *suit case*?

2 At museums, do you like walking around by yourself or following a *tourguide* / *tour guide* who explains things?

3 Which is more relaxing, spending the day at the *seaside* / *sea side* or in the *countryside* / *country side*?

4 When the sun is bright, do you prefer wearing a *sunhat*/*sun hat* or *sunglasses* / *sun glasses*?

5 Do you ever take a *guidebook* / *guide book* on holiday or do you rely on the internet to find information about a new place?

6 While travelling abroad, is it better to pay in cash or with a *creditcard* / *credit card*?

5 **SPEAK** Work in pairs. Discuss the questions in Exercise 4.

Listening Part 4 Multiple choice

How to go about it

- Read the questions carefully before you listen. Underline key words.
- While you listen, put a mark next to answers that are wrong. Choose the option that is most similar to what the speakers say.
- Check your answers the second time you listen.

1 **SPEAK** Do you think it would be nice to work on a cruise ship? Why/Why not?

2 **6.1** You will hear an interview with a woman called Zoe, who works on a cruise ship. For questions 1–6, choose the best answer (A, B or C).

1 Zoe decided to work on a cruise ship after
  - A watching online videos.
  - B quitting her first job.
  - C talking to an old friend.

2 How did she feel working as a cleaner?
  - A grateful to have helpful colleagues
  - B surprised by the amount of work
  - C upset by comments people made

3 The part of her current job that Zoe likes most is
  - A meeting new people.
  - B saving money.
  - C travelling abroad.

4 Every day, she makes sure to
  - A check social media.
  - B get some exercise.
  - C talk to her family.

5 What is Zoe's favourite cruise destination?
  - A New Zealand
  - B Jordan
  - C the Bahamas

6 What does Zoe say she wants to do next?
  - A change professions
  - B work in a different country
  - C get a better position

Language focus Future forms

1 **Look at the sentences from the Listening Part 4 task on page 87. Then complete rules 1–3 below with the words in the box.**

*A friend ... was telling me about working on cruise ships, and I thought, "I think I'**ll apply**. Why not?"*

*For now, though, I'**m going to focus** on my career here at sea.*

*I'**m meeting** my boss tomorrow morning to talk about a new job.*

going to the present continuous will

1 We use ______________________ for arrangements or plans we make with someone else to do something in the future.

2 We use ______________________ for personal plans and intentions to do something in the future.

3 We use ______________________ to talk about decisions which are made at the moment of speaking.

2 **Read sentences 1–5. In each case, underline the sentence (A or B) that is the most similar in meaning to each sentence 1–5.**

1 My mum and I have arranged a surprise birthday party for my sister tonight.
  A My mum and I will throw a surprise birthday party for my sister tonight.
  B My mum and I are throwing a surprise birthday party for my sister tonight.

2 She's got a doctor's appointment this afternoon.
  A She's seeing the doctor this afternoon.
  B She'll see the doctor this afternoon.

3 What time did we agree to meet at the station?
  A What time will we meet at the station?
  B What time are we meeting at the station?

4 Chris has made the decision to book his ticket.
  A Chris will book his ticket.
  B Chris is going to book his ticket.

5 Hmm, I can't decide what to order; the salad, I think.
  A Hmm, I think I'll order the salad.
  B Hmm, I think I'm ordering the salad.

3 **Go to Ready for Grammar on page 218 for further rules, explanations and practice.**

4 **SPEAK** **Work in groups. Take turns to talk about prompts 1–6 below. Ask follow-up questions. Use a dice to decide which prompt to discuss.**

1 Tell your classmates about two arrangements you have in the next few weeks.

2 Guess your classmates' plans for this evening.

3 Talk about two ambitions you have related to your job or studies.

4 Imagine you have planned a trip for this weekend. Give your classmates as many details as you can about the trip, where you are going, when you're leaving, etc.

5 Tell your classmates about two good intentions you have for this year.

6 Imagine you are in the following situations. Use *I think I'll* to make a decision in the moment:
  a You're on a plane and the flight attendant gives you two meal options: pasta or roast chicken.
  b You look out of the window of your flat and see that the weather is really nice.
  c You get home after a long day at work or school and you feel exhausted.

Writing Part 1 Email

1 Read the following Writing Part 1 instructions and input email. In your notebook, write down interesting vocabulary you could include in your reply.

Read this email from your English-speaking friend Oli and the notes you have made.

From: Oli
Subject: Our trip
Hi,
It's great that you are going to come with me on the trip that I won as first prize in a travel writing competition. ← Thank Oli…
I have more information now. For two days, we're going to the mountains to try adventure sports. Would you prefer to go rock-climbing or explore a cave? ← Tell Oli …
We can decide when to go. Are you free for a weekend next month (May)? ← No, because …
Do you have any questions about our trip? ← Ask …
Reply soon!
Oli

Reply to Oli using **all the notes**. Write your **email** in about **100 words**.

2 Now read Enzo's reply. Does he use any of the vocabulary you wrote down in Exercise 1?

Hi Oli,
Nice to hear from you. Thanks again for inviting me on this trip.
Unfortunately, I have to say no to rock climbing. I'm afraid of heights, so I don't think I would enjoy **(1) it**. I do like the idea of exploring a cave though. I've never done **(2) that** before.
Sorry, but I'm not available in May. I'm going to be very busy **(3) then** because I have to study for my university exams. How about in June?
What mountains are we going to? How are we going to get **(4) there**?
Talk to you soon,
Enzo

3 Reference words help you connect sentences and avoid repeating words. Look at the reference words 1–4 in the model answer. What do they refer to?

4 Go to the Additional materials on page 198 and do the Writing Part 1 task.

For more information about writing emails, see pages 192–193.

Don't forget!

- Identify the four points in the input email.
- Plan your email before you write it.
- Connect your sentences using linkers (*so*, *but*, etc).

Listening Part 1 Multiple choice

Don't forget!

The speaker(s) mention all three of the pictures, but only one correctly answers the question.

6.2. You will hear people talking in seven different situations. For questions 1–7, choose the best answer (A, B or C).

1 What did the man do this morning?

A

B

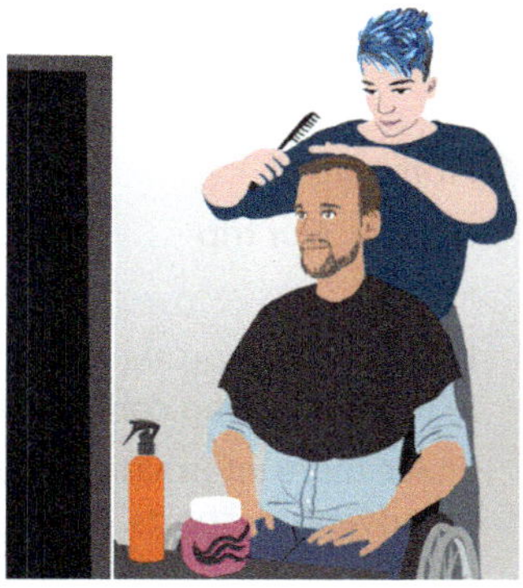

C

2 What is the weather forecast for this afternoon?

A

B

C

3 Where does the woman think she left her purse?

A

B

C

4 Which plate do the man and woman decide to buy?

A

B

C

5 What time is the train expected to leave?

A

B

C

6 What book does the man recommend to the woman?

A

B

C

7 Who was the woman's French teacher?

A

B

C

Language focus *So, such, too* and *enough*

1 Complete these sentences from the listening with *so*, *such*, *too* or *enough*.

1 Do we have ______________ time to go back there before our train leaves?

2 It has ______________ a beautiful design.

3 There is ______________ much snow for trains to pass safely.

4 I learnt ______________ much from him about music.

2 Go to Ready for Grammar on page 216 for rules, explanations and further pract ce.

3 SPEAK Work in pairs. Think of five complaints a tourist would make about a hotel. Use *so*, *such*, *too* or *enough*.

It was too expensive.

It was so cold in my room that I couldn't sleep.

6 REVIEW

Reading Part 5 Multiple-choice cloze

Don't forget!

Read the whole sentence before you choose the correct option.

Read the text and for questions 1–6, choose which answer (A, B, C or D) best fits each gap.

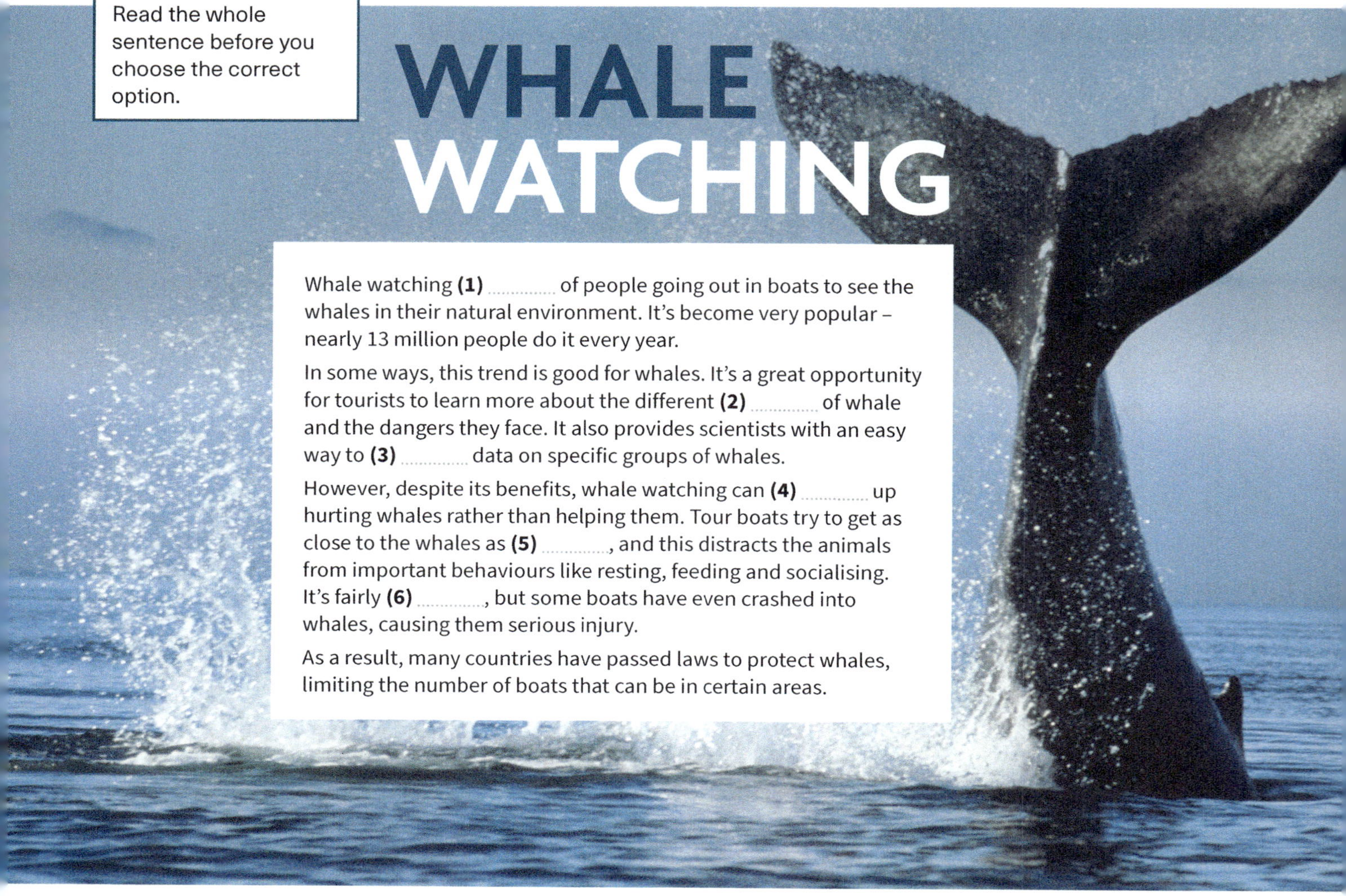

WHALE WATCHING

Whale watching **(1)** .... of people going out in boats to see the whales in their natural environment. It's become very popular – nearly 13 million people do it every year.

In some ways, this trend is good for whales. It's a great opportunity for tourists to learn more about the different **(2)** .... of whale and the dangers they face. It also provides scientists with an easy way to **(3)** .... data on specific groups of whales.

However, despite its benefits, whale watching can **(4)** .... up hurting whales rather than helping them. Tour boats try to get as close to the whales as **(5)** ...., and this distracts the animals from important behaviours like resting, feeding and socialising. It's fairly **(6)** ...., but some boats have even crashed into whales, causing them serious injury.

As a result, many countries have passed laws to protect whales, limiting the number of boats that can be in certain areas.

1	**A** contains	**B** involves	**C** consists	**D** includes
2	**A** names	**B** species	**C** ranges	**D** forms
3	**A** transfer	**B** enter	**C** collect	**D** display
4	**A** hold	**B** set	**C** bring	**D** end
5	**A** possible	**B** appropriate	**C** likely	**D** reasonable
6	**A** irregular	**B** careless	**C** opposite	**D** unusual

Language focus Comparatives and superlatives

Complete each sentence with one word.

1 I think Singapore is ______________ most expensive city I've ever visited.
2 The Forbidden City in Beijing is ______________ as crowded in winter as in summer.
3 The Eiffel Tower is three times taller ______________ the Statue of Liberty.
4 The high-speed trains in China are faster ______________ the ones in Europe.
5 Tokyo is one of the ______________ modern cities in the world.
6 The weather in Sardinia was not ______________ nice as I expected.
7 ______________ highest mountain in South America is Aconcagua.

Vocabulary Adjectives

Complete the sentences using a word from the box which has a similar meaning to the word in brackets.

challenging dull essential odd pleased usual wonderful

1 The castle has some ____________ (*incredible*) views of the countryside.
2 He blamed his ____________ (*unusual*) behaviour on a lack of sleep the night before.
3 I found this problem just as ____________ (*hard*) to solve as the last one.
4 Why didn't she write this article in her ____________ (*typical*) informal style?
5 Rylan is going to be very ____________ (*glad*) to hear that you got the job!
6 Design and testing are two ____________ (*necessary*) parts of the process.
7 The plot and the characters were so ____________ (*uninteresting*) that I almost fell asleep.

Language focus *So, such, too, enough*

Read the comments (1–4) that tourists wrote on a travel website. Choose the correct alternative.

TRAVELReviews News **Reviews** About More ›

★★★★★
1 We had *so / such* a good time! In just one morning, we saw all the most important sites in Rome. And the tour guide knew *so much / so many* about the history of the city! I was really impressed.

★★★☆☆
2 There were *too much / too many* people in our tour group. The tour guide was great, but most of the time she was *so / too* far away for me to hear her properly.

★★★★☆
3 My only complaint is that we had *too little / too few* time at the Colosseum. It's *so / such* a fascinating place.

★★☆☆☆
4 It was *so / too* cold on the bus that I asked the driver to turn down the air conditioning. Plus, the wi-fi wasn't *fast enough / enough fast*, so I couldn't send any pictures to my family and friends.

Writing Part 2 Article

You see this announcement on an English-language website.

> **Articles wanted!**
>
> **History and travel**
>
> - What kinds of places can you visit to know more about the history of a city?
> - How important is it to learn about the history of the places you visit?
>
> Write an article answering these questions, and we'll publish the best ones on our website.

Write your article in about 100 words.

For more information on writing articles, see page 195.

Pronunciation Word stress

1 6.3 Listen to and repeat these compound nouns from the vocabulary section on page 86.

1 airline
2 hand luggage
3 car park
4 motorway
5 speed limit
6 window seat

2 Choose the correct alternative to complete the rule about word stress in compound nouns:

If a compound consists of two nouns, the word stress usually falls on the *first / second* noun.

3 **SPEAK** Work in pairs. Read the rules and play the game.

WHAT'S IN YOUR BACKPACK?

1 Imagine you are going on a beach holiday to an island. You will only take a small backpack. Decide which six items you would like to bring.

2 Try to guess what is in your partner's backpack. Take turns to ask questions. Remember to use the correct word stress! The person who guesses the six items first is the winner!

A: Have you got sunglasses in your backpack? B: No, I haven't.

7 WORK LIFE

KEY LANGUAGE

Will, *may* and *might*
Zero and first conditional
Jobs
Work life

PRONUNCIATION

/ɪ/ and /iː/

EXAM PRACTICE

Reading Parts 3 & 6
Writing Parts 1 & 2
Listening Parts 1 & 3
Speaking Parts 1, 2, 3 & 4

Speaking Part 1 Interview

Work with a partner. Discuss the questions.

1 What kind of job would you like to do? Why?
2 Do you like working with other people?
3 What did you want to be when you were a child?
4 What kinds of jobs do you think are difficult?
5 Which jobs do you think are the most essential?

Speaking Part 2 Extended turn

Work with a partner. Decide which adjectives in the box are positive and which are negative. Describe the picture using some of the words in the box.

dull exciting fun hard incredible stressful tiring unusual

7 WORK LIFE

Don't forget!

You may hear more than one word that could go in the space, but only one will be correct. Listen carefully and make sure your word fits the meaning of the sentence AND what you hear.

Listening Part 3 Gap fill

1 SPEAK Work in pairs. Discuss the questions.

1 What kinds of jobs do people do in Antarctica?
2 What do you think the most difficult thing about working there is?
3 Would you like to work there? Why/Why not?

2 SPEAK Work in pairs. Read the questions in Exercise 3. Which gaps are connected to time and which gaps need nouns?

3 7.1 You will hear a scientist called Jessica Thomson talking about her experience working in Antarctica. For questions 1–6, write the correct answer in each gap. Write one or two words or a number or a date or a time.

Working in Antarctica

Jessica worked in the Antarctic for **(1)** ....

Jessica worked with the penguins in the **(2)** ....

To check she had counted the penguins correctly, Jessica used some **(3)** ....

When she went to Antarctica, Jessica was surprised that there was **(4)** ....

Jessica found life difficult because there was no **(5)** ....

Jessica is going to return to Antarctica next **(6)** ....

4 SPEAK Work in pairs. Look at the places in the box and discuss the questions.

in a cave	in space	in the desert	in the jungle	in the mountains	on an island

1 What do you think is difficult about working in these places?
2 What do you think is exciting about working in these places?
3 Which places would you like to work in? Why?

Vocabulary Jobs

1 Label the pictures of jobs (a–g) with the words in the box.

businessperson chef cleaner dentist engineer nurse receptionist

a

b

c
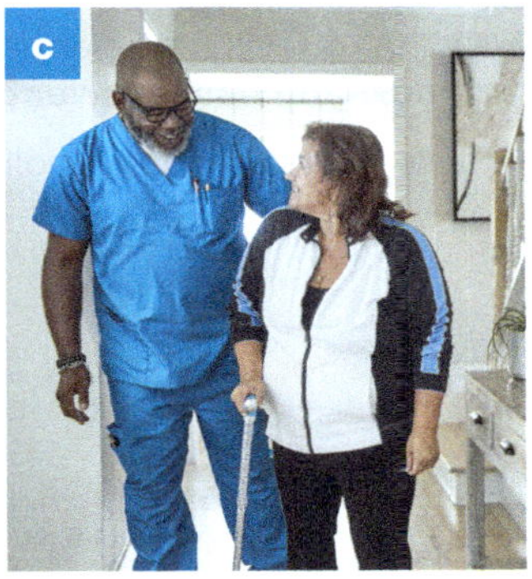

d

e

f
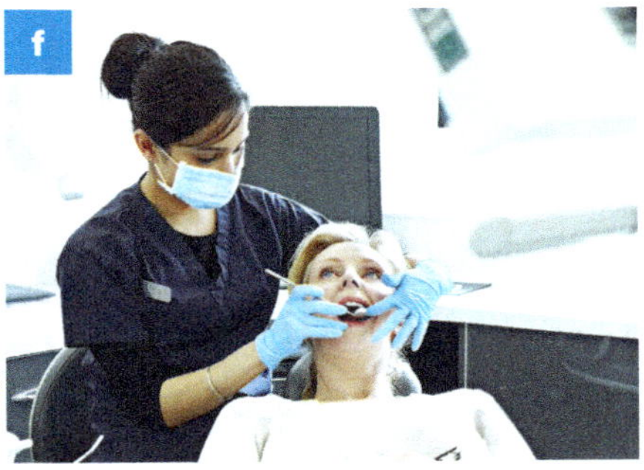

g

2 Choose the correct alternative to complete each job description.

1 *An actor / A builder* **reads a script** and **acts on the stage** or **in films** or TV programmes.
2 *A photographer / A reporter* **interviews people** and **asks questions**. They **write articles**.
3 *A director / An architect* **designs buildings**. They **make plans** of houses and offices.
4 *A police officer / A scientist* **helps people**. They make sure people **follow the law**.
5 *A farmer / A lawyer* **gives** people **advice** about the law. They **help people** in a court.

3 **SPEAK** Work in pairs. Describe what the people in Exercise 1 do in their jobs. Use the verbs in the box to help you.

check cook design fix help manage prepare speak wash

4 Write the jobs from this page that end in *-er*, *-ist* or *-or* in the table below.

-ER	-IST	-OR
reporter	*receptionist*	*actor*

5 **SPEAK** Work in pairs. Can you think of any more jobs with the same suffixes?

6 **SPEAK** Work in pairs. Look at the jobs in the table in Exercise 4 again and discuss the following questions.

In your opinion, which job is ...

- the most stressful?
- the dullest?
- the easiest?
- the most interesting?

Listening Part 1 Multiple choice

1 **SPEAK** **Work in pairs. Look at questions 1 and 2 in Exercise 2.**

Student A: Look at the pictures in Question 1 and describe them to your partner.

Student B: Look at the pictures in Question 2 and describe them to your partner.

2 **7.2 You will hear people talking in seven different situations. For questions 1–7, choose the best answer (A, B or C).**

1 What is the woman going to do after work?

A

B

C

2 What job does the man's son do?

A

B

C

3 What has the woman lost?

A

B

C

4 Why did the man miss his flight?

A

B

C

5 Where will the people have the meeting?

A

B

C

6 What did the man forget to order?

A

B

C

7 How does the woman travel to work?

A

B

C

Language focus *Will*, *may* and *might*

1 Complete the sentences from the listening with *will*, *won't* or *might*.

1 **A:** Excuse me ... are you okay?
B: Oh, sorry ... I think I dropped my keys in here. They __________ be on the floor.

2 It probably __________ be any quicker, but the journey __________ be more comfortable!

2 7.3 Now listen to the audio and check your answers to Exercise 1.

3 Match the rules (1–2) to the correct words below.

1 Possibilities in the present or future.
2 Predictions about the future.

will (not) ______ *may/might (not)* ______

4 Underline the correct alternative to complete the sentences.

1 Victoria *may / will* come to the cinema with us on Friday. She hasn't decided yet.
2 We *will / won't* have enough time to see everything in the museum. It's so big and we've only got an hour to see everything.
3 Who do you think *will / might not* get the job – Tim or Clara? They are both excellent.
4 She *won't / might not* come to the meeting this afternoon, but she doesn't know yet.
5 They *might / might not* buy a new sofa for the living room. They are going to look at some on Saturday.
6 Cooking for ten people *will / won't* be easy, but I'm going to ask my friend to help me.

5 Go to Ready for Grammar on page 218 for rules, explanations and further practice.

6 SPEAK Work in pairs. Finish the sentences about your partner. Use *will*, *may* or *might* and some of the ideas from the box.

be a manager | become an actor | go to the beach | go shopping | have lots of money | travel around the world | win a competition

1 Next year, you ...
2 In your future job, you ...
3 On your next holiday, you ...
4 At the weekend, you ...

Writing Part 2 Story

1 **SPEAK** Read the following Writing Part 2 task. Discuss with a partner what kinds of things you could include in your answer.

Your English teacher has asked you to write a story. Your story must begin with this sentence.

> **It was only a summer job, but I will never forget my first day.**

Write your **story** in about **100 words.**

2 Read the model answer below. Are the ideas in the story the same as yours or different? What do you like about the story?

A SUMMER SURPRISE

It was only a summer job, but I will never forget my first day.

It was a wet day when I walked into the gorgeous hotel. I felt a little anxious. I'd never had a job before, so I didn't know what to expect.

In the morning, I learnt how receptionists should be polite to guests and how to use the booking system. It seemed simple, and I felt relaxed and calm. Suddenly, I heard my manager make a strange noise like she was shocked. I looked up and I couldn't believe it. The captain of the national football team was standing in front of me! "Hello," she said, "I'd like to check in."

3 Look at the underlined words in the model answer. Answer the questions.

1 Are the underlined words nouns, adjectives or verbs?
2 What does *wet* describe?
3 Which word describes a place?
4 Which word is about the job?
5 Which words describe people?

Useful language

Adjectives

You can use adjectives in your writing to be descriptive and add details.

Put the adjectives in the correct category. Some adjectives go in more than one category.

bright clever confident enjoyable friendly helpful
honest modern professional spectacular stressful strict

JOB	PEOPLE	PLACE

4 Now write your answer to the Writing Part 2 task in Exercise 1. Remember to use some adjectives.

For more information on writing stories, see page 194.

Vocabulary Work life

1 SPEAK Work in pairs. Read the email. What other things can Marcos do to get a job?

Hi Marcos

Thanks for your email. It was good to hear from you.

I can't believe you've quit your job and you're moving to the city in June. How exciting! Don't worry about looking for a job here. There are lots of jobs and I'm sure you'll find one quickly. With your business degree, I think you can earn a lot of money.

You could apply for a job with my employer. It's a great place to work. We have lots of temporary jobs in the summer, but also a few people are retiring soon – they're almost at the retirement age – so you might get a permanent job. You could send in your CV to the manager. He might ask you to fill in an application form as well, but don't worry, I can help you with that.

Speak soon,

Sonia

2 Complete each sentence with one of the underlined verbs in the email in Exercise 1. You may need to change the form of the verb.

1 Doctors usually ________ more money than nurses.
2 Before you ________ for this job, please read the job description carefully.
3 Andres ________ his job because he didn't like the new manager.
4 You can ________ in your CV by email or by post.
5 I'm so happy for Jan – she's ________ a new job and she really loves it.
6 Please ________ an application form and email it to the manager.
7 Peter ________ from his job after 50 years with the same company.
8 More people ________ jobs online now than in newspapers.

3 Choose the correct options to complete the sentences.

I work for a company called Mirez Travel.

I'm a **(1)** *colleague / manager* in the sales **(2)** *department / career*. I think I'm a good boss. There are ten members of **(3)** *staff / employers* on my team and they are very happy.

We have some staff who are **(4)** *permanent / temporary*, and they only work during the summer. All the other **(5)** *employees / colleagues have worked here for years.*

4 SPEAK Work in pairs. What are the differences between the pairs of words below?

1 employee/employer
2 quit/retire
3 earn/win
4 apply/ask
5 temporary/permanent

5 Complete the questions with the words in the box.

career employee manager temporary

1 What kind of ________ are you interested in?
2 What are the advantages and disadvantages of permanent and ________ jobs?
3 Would you like to work as a ________? Why/Why not?
4 Is it better to be an ________ or an employer? Why?

6 SPEAK Work in groups and answer the questions in Exercise 5.

Reading Part 3 Multiple choice

Don't forget!

Read the questions before you read the text. The questions will give you an idea of what the text is about, the organisation of the text and what information you need to look for.

1 SPEAK Work in pairs. Discuss the questions.

1 Do you read or watch the news? Why/Why not?
2 What kinds of news stories are most popular in your country?
3 What is the best way to find out about news?

2 Read the article. For questions 1–5, choose the correct answer (A, B, C or D).

1 Daniel first became interested in being a reporter
  A when he was at school.
  B when his friends gave him some advice.
  C when he started working on a newspaper.
  D when he realised he couldn't be a vet.
2 What was the hardest part of his training?
  A trying to take notes for articles
  B trying to get more important jobs
  C trying to find stories to write about
  D trying to make the stories interesting
3 What kinds of news does he report on now?
  A sports stories
  B funny stories
  C political stories
  D local stories
4 How does he feel about news stories on the internet?
  A They are badly written.
  B They are too short.
  C They aren't interesting.
  D They aren't always correct.
5 What is Daniel's general opinion about being a reporter?
  A It's very difficult to succeed at.
  B It is worse than it used to be.
  C It can have a lot of variety.
  D It will change with the internet.

3 SPEAK Work in pairs. Do the roleplay below.

Student A

You are the editor for a local newspaper. You are going to interview a candidate to be a reporter for your newspaper. Prepare your questions for the interview. Ask about:

1 **Career:** e.g. *Tell me about your previous job.*
2 **Studies:** e.g. *What did you study at university?*
3 **Reasons for applying:** e.g. *Why have you applied for this job?*
4 **Interests:** e.g. *Do you enjoy playing sports?*

Student B

You have applied for a job at a local newspaper. You are going to attend an interview. Prepare some answers for the interview. Talk about:

1 **Career:** e.g. *In my last job, I wrote short articles for a magazine.*
2 **Studies:** e.g. *I did a degree in journalism.*
3 **Reasons for applying:** e.g. *I would like this job because ...*
4 **Interests:** e.g. *I enjoy watching and writing about sports.*

Now roleplay the interview.

LIFE AS A REPORTER

by Daniel Hill

Being a reporter is an exciting job, and I love doing it, but I didn't always want to be a reporter. When I was a child, I loved animals and wanted to become a vet, but I didn't do very well in science at school. That's when I knew I had to choose something else. We received some careers advice at school about different types of jobs. One of them was being a reporter, but I wasn't interested in that job then. Later, at university, my friends worked on the university newspaper, and I joined the team just to spend time with them, but it was so much fun. This is when I decided that I wanted to do it as a job.

I got some proper training with a local newspaper, and I did all kinds of things. Some things were boring, like bringing my managers coffee or making photocopies, but I also got to write short articles. My stories weren't important ones. They were usually just things like local news reports about a cat being stuck up a tree! I often forgot to write down the details when I was asking questions. It wasn't easy to listen and write at the same time, but I soon learnt to do it!

I've been in the job now for about 20 years, and I still enjoy it. I spent a long time working on sports stories, but it really wasn't my area of interest. If I could report on anything, I'd prefer to report on politics. I hope one day to work on national TV, doing that. At the moment, I work for a TV channel and report on stories just in my area, of any kind, but the funny cat stories now go to someone else!

Some of my colleagues write articles for our website. They often want our TV reports to be put online. Our web reporters are generally pretty good. They write the stories well and always try to check the information. The problem is that they usually can't write too much in the article. When people read more than three paragraphs online, they often lose interest. Well, that's what the people working on the internet tell me.

I know that internet news is so popular these days, but I don't want to change. I love doing TV news. If my job stays the same, I'll continue working as a reporter until I retire. Even if I have to look my best every day for the camera!

Language focus Zero and first conditional

1 Read the sentences from the text on page 103. In what tenses are the underlined verbs?

A When people read more than three paragraphs online, they often lose interest.

B If my job stays the same, I'll continue working as a reporter until I retire.

2 Answer the questions about the sentences in Exercise 1.

1 Which sentence is about a **future possibility**?

2 Which sentence is about something **generally true**?

3 Go to Ready for Grammar on page 220 for rules, explanations and further practice.

4 Underline the correct alternative to complete the sentences.

1 If we *finish* / *will finish* work early today, we *go* / *will go* for a walk.

2 When my parents *visit* / *will visit*, we always *have* / *will have* a big dinner.

3 I *have* / *won't have* enough money for my holiday if I *start* / *don't start* saving soon.

4 If she *doesn't arrive* / *won't arrive* soon, she *misses* / *will miss* the start of the film.

5 If you *want* / *will want* some help with the cleaning, *ask* / *will ask* Anita.

5 Complete the sentences so that they are true for you.

1 If I feel tired, I ...

2 If it's sunny this weekend, I ...

3 When I have free time, I ...

4 If I become rich, I ...

6 SPEAK Work in pairs. Compare your answers to Exercise 5.

Speaking Part 3 Discussion

1 Look at the Speaking Part 3 task on page 105. Which job would you prefer? Why? Before you do the Speaking task, look at the Useful language box below.

Useful language

In the exam, it's important to give reasons for your answers. In addition to '*I think working with children would be the most enjoyable*', say why.

Giving reasons

Being a firefighter is an important job ***because*** *they save lives.*

Being a firefighter is a difficult job ***because of*** *the danger.*

Being a firefighter is an exciting job. ***The reason why is that*** *it involves lots of different tasks.*

Adding reasons

Also*, firefighters earn lots of money.*

Another thing *is firefighters retire early.*

They keep fit, ***too****.*

Find and correct the mistake in each of the examples below.

1 Working with old people is good because of it's important.

2 Working with animals is fun. Too the animals are very sweet.

3 Helping people get fit is the most enjoyable. Reason why is you change their lives.

4 Being a police officer is fun why you can meet lots of people.

2 Now do the Speaking task. A young man wants to get a job where he can help others. Here are some of the jobs he could get. Talk together about the different jobs, and decide which one you think would be the best for him to help others. Use some of the expressions from the Useful language box.

Don't forget!

You don't need to discuss all the options. It's fine to talk about just three or four.

Jobs a man can do to help others

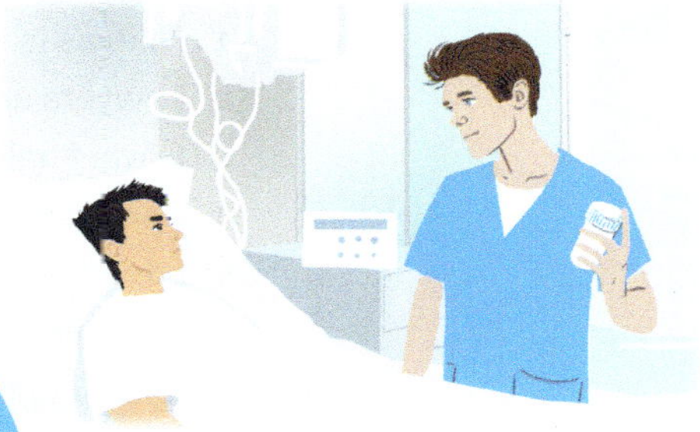

Speaking Part 4 General conversation

Work in pairs. Discuss the questions below.

1 What do you think the best jobs are?
2 What jobs are the most difficult to do?
3 Is it important to have a job you enjoy? Why/Why not?
4 Is it important to earn a lot of money? Why/Why not?
5 Do you think people work too much these days? Why/Why not?

7 REVIEW

Vocabulary Work life

Match the sentence beginnings 1–8 to the ending a–h to make complete sentences.

1 Nikolas is finally going to **retire** ...
2 Lawyers and accountants often **earn** ...
3 Olivia finally **found** ...
4 Remember to **send** ...
5 I decided to **quit** ...
6 To **fill in** ...
7 Jake decided to **look** ...
8 Sandra has **applied** ...

a your CV to the manager by email.
b a job as a receptionist at a hotel.
c the job because the salary was so low.
d at the age of 75!
e the application form, go to the website.
f a good salary but work long hours.
g for a new job but hasn't got a reply yet.
h for a new job that pays more money.

Reading Part 6 Open cloze

For questions 1–6, read the text below and think of the word which best fits each gap. Use only one word in each gap.

STARTING A NEW JOB

I started a new job last week, and I've **(1)** .... so busy! I think starting a new job is **(2)** .... of the most stressful things a person can do. I've been very nervous about it. For a start, I need to learn how to do everything because I've never done it before. Also, I'm meeting all the people who work there and I can't remember all **(3)** .... names!

The job is much better **(4)** .... I expected, though. The people are quite nice, and my boss is lovely. I think the work will **(5)** .... very interesting, and the salary is good, too. I'm lucky to have a job like this. **(6)** .... I try hard, it will all be fine – I'm sure! People always get nervous when they start new jobs.

Language focus Zero and first conditional

Complete the conversations with the verbs and modal verbs in the box. There is one extra verb in each box.

do email go have don't want will

A: What do I **(1)** __________ when I want to **(2)** __________ on holiday?

B: If you **(3)** __________ to request a holiday, please **(4)** __________ your manager or use the holiday booking system on the computer.

A: Okay, thanks. If I **(5)** __________ any problems, I **(6)** __________ ask you!

B: Of course!

don't gets isn't look send will won't

A: If I **(7)** __________ get the job, I **(8)** __________ be very disappointed. I really want it!

B: Well, if someone else **(9)** __________ the job, it **(10)** __________ be a disaster because there are lots of other jobs.

A: Yes, I suppose you're right.

B: When I **(11)** __________ for jobs, I always **(12)** __________ my CV to lots of companies to improve my chances!

Writing Part 1 Email

Read this email from your old work colleague and the notes you have made.

From: Paula

Subject: New job!

Hi!

I'm so excited that I am coming to work with you again. I loved working with you before, and I am so happy that I have got a job at your new company. ← Me too!

I've never worked at such a big company before. Can you tell me what it is like? I hope the people are nice. ← Tell Paula …

Also, I'm not sure how to travel to the office. Do you think it's best to drive or take public transport? ← Explain which …

Shall we meet for lunch on my first day? Where shall we go? ← Yes! Suggest …

See you soon,

Paula

Reply to Paula using all the notes. Write your email in about 100 words.

For more information on writing emails, see pages 192–193.

Pronunciation /ɪ/ and /iː/

1 7.4 Listen and complete the words.

1 th ___ ___ ___
2 pol ___ ___ ___
3 bu ___ ___ ___
4 ch ___ ___ ___
5 l ___ ___ ___
6 bel ___ ___ ___ ___
7 s ___ ___ tem
8 ___ ___ ___ ning
9 p ___ ___ ___ le
10 bisc ___ ___ ___
11 k ___ ___
12 vill ___ ___ ___

2 Put the words in Exercise 1 in the correct columns in the table.

/ɪ/ like *chip*	/iː/ like *cheap*

3 Underline the /ɪ/ sounds and circle the /iː/ sounds in the sentences.

1 Leave these biscuits in the tin.
2 Many people built this bridge.
3 This evening we'll leave the village.
4 She keeps fit in the gym every evening.

4 7.5 Listen and check your answers.

5 Now practise saying the sentences in Exercise 3.

6 **SPEAK** Work in pairs and play the game.

ROLL THE DICE

How to play: Student A chooses a square by rolling a dice twice – first for the top row and second for the down column. For example if you roll a 2 and then a 4, the word is *women*.

To score points, Student A must say the word correctly. If not, Student B has a chance to say the word and score the points. Continue until all the words are crossed out.

purple squares = 1 point **blue squares = 2 points** **green squares = 3 points**

The student who crosses out the most words wins.

	1	2	3	4	5	6
1	pretty	recover	activity	minute	between	lettuce
2	imagine	mystery	receipt	give	insect	fix
3	deep	city	manage	beauty	cream	depart
4	thick	women	beach	disagree	thief	maybe
5	busy	neither	symbol	receive	even	quickly
6	ceiling	meet	million	recipe	quit	luggage

READY FOR LISTENING

Introduction

There are four parts in the Listening paper. You will hear people talking in a variety of situations – for example, radio announcements, interactions in a shop, a conversation between friends or colleagues, interviews with someone on the radio or a podcast.

How to go about it

You will hear each recording twice. Check your answers the second time you listen to the recording.

1 Complete each sentence with a number from the box.

1 4 6 20 25 30 45

1 There are __4__ parts in the Listening paper.
2 There are ______ questions in total.
3 The Listening lasts for approximately ______ minutes.
4 You receive ______ point for each question you answer correctly.
5 You have ______ seconds to read the Part 3 questions before the recording starts.
6 You have ______ seconds to read the Part 4 questions before the recording starts.
7 You have exactly ______ minutes at the end of the exam to transfer your answers to the answer sheet.

2 Each part of the Listening paper tests your listening skills in a different way. Match the words 1–5 to their definitions a–e.

1 gist
2 monologue
3 dialogue
4 detailed understanding of attitudes or opinions
5 specific information

a a conversation between two or more people
b a long speech by just one person
c understanding the general meaning of something, rather than specific details
d listening for and identifying certain words or phrases
e being able to identify what the speakers think and feel from what you hear

3 Complete the table below about each part of the exam using the words from the box.

multiple choice detailed understanding of attitudes or opinions
dialogue specific information

Parts	Type of Listening	Testing focus	Task
1	*dialogue* or *monologue*	Listen for *specific information*	*multiple choice*
2	*dialogue*	Listen for *gist*	
3	*monologue*	Listen for	*gap fill*
4		Listen for	*multiple choice*

Don't forget!

- For each part of the exam, you should try to predict the type of information you will hear before you listen.
- When you first listen, try to identify the correct answer. Then, check your answer when you hear the recording the second time.

Listening Part 1 Multiple choice

In Part 1, there are seven short listening tasks. Each question has three pictures. You need to decide which picture (A, B or C) correctly answers the question.

How to go about it

- Read each question and look at the images. Try to predict what words and phrases you might hear in each question.
- If you have time, quickly write these words by each image to help you focus on the topic and context. Predicting encourages active listening, which can improve your listening skills.

1 **SPEAK** Work in pairs. Look at the Part 1 question below and discuss the questions.

1 What type of book does each image represent? Choose from *horror*, *crime fiction* or *science fiction*.

2 What sort of words might you hear for each image? Can you think of any other words or phrases the speakers might use in their discussion.

For horror, we might hear 'frightening', 'scary', etc.

What type of novel does the man most enjoy reading?

A

B

C

2 Read the Audioscript for the question in Exercise 1 on page 247 and follow the instructions 1–2 below.

1 Underline the information that answers the question.

2 Underline the information that makes the other two options incorrect.

3 0.1 Now listen and check your answers.

Don't forget!

Pay attention to how many speakers there are for each question. Some questions ask for information from a specific speaker
(i.e. *What does the woman ...?*). Alternatively, two speakers may need to agree (i.e. both like something) or come to an agreement. Underline this type of information in the question to help you stay focused.

4 Look at the Part 1 questions 1–7 in Exercise 6 and underline the key information in each question.

5 Go to the Additional materials on page 199.

What to expect in the exam

You will hear a range of accents in the audio scripts. These include North American, British and Australian accents. This means that some of the language the speakers use will vary according to the accent (i.e., *sneakers* (US), *trainers* (UK), *runners* (AUS), etc.).

6 0.2 You will hear people talking in seven different situations. For questions 1–7, choose the best answer (A, B or C).

1 What's the woman's favourite souvenir from her last trip?

A

B

C

2 What will the weather be like tomorrow?

A

B

C

3 Where do the friends decide to go to first?

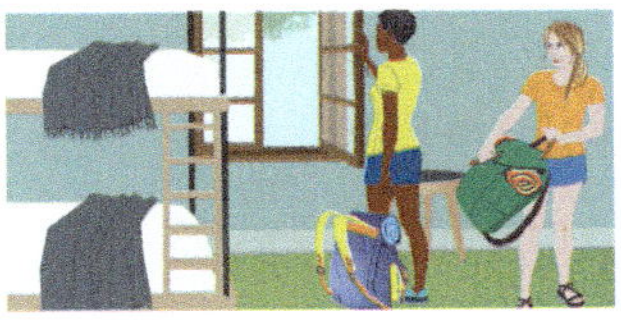

A

B

C

4 What animal will the university student study for his research project?

A

B

C

5 What documentary series would the woman like to watch?

A

B

C

6 What did the man injure while on holiday?

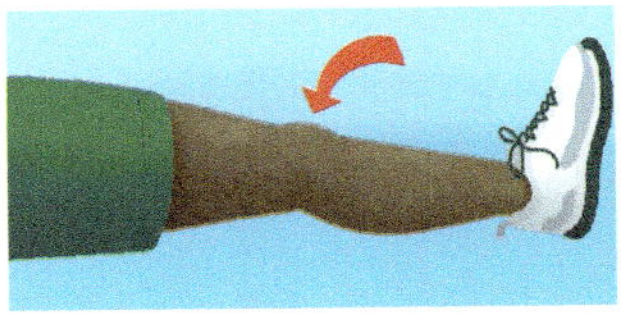

A

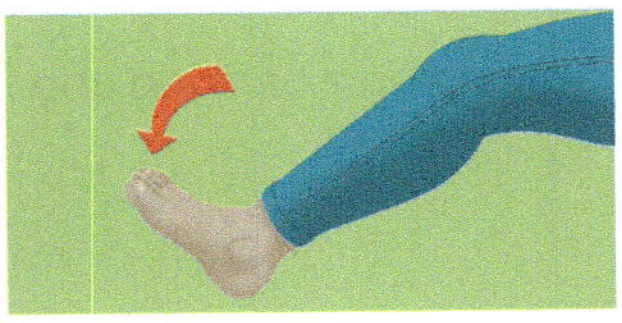

B

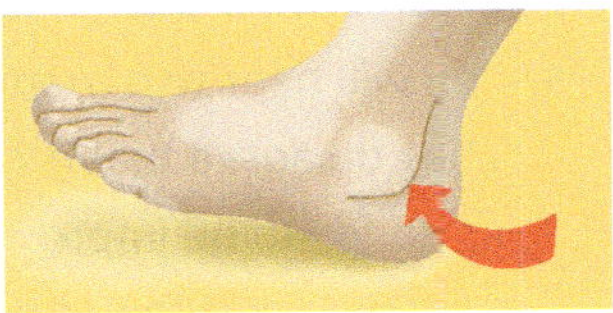

C

7 What activity did the woman do last night?

A

B

C

7 **SPEAK** In pairs, discuss which Part 1 questions you found most difficult. Look at the Audioscripts on page 248 and underline the information that answers the question.

What to expect in the exam

- You will hear each recording twice. The second time you listen, you can check your answers and see if you missed any important information.
- Remember there will be words included to distract you, so you need to listen carefully to what they are saying.

Listening Part 2 Multiple choice

In Part 2, there are six short conversations. Each question has a context sentence and a question with three options.

1 **SPEAK** Work in pairs. Look at the questions 1–6 in Exercise 2 below and decide who will give the answer: *both speakers*, *the man* or *the woman*.

What to expect in the exam

Each question will focus on a conversation between two people about different contexts. The context sentence helps you understand their relationship (i.e. friends, colleagues, classmates, etc). The question tells you what information listen for.

Don't forget!

Answer every question even if you aren't sure about the answer. You might have understood more than you thought! Importantly, you won't lose marks if you answer a question incorrectly.

2 **0.3** You will hear people talking in six different situations. For questions 1–6, choose the best answer (A, B or C).

1 You will hear two friends talking about a music festival.
What do they agree about it?
A It was very crowded.
B It was well-organised.
C It was worth the entrance fee.

2 You will hear a woman talking about visiting Machu Picchu in Peru.
What does she say about it?
A She needed to stop and rest on the path.
B She enjoyed seeing the whole site.
C She wanted to spend more time there.

3 You will hear two colleagues talking about an invention.
What advice does the woman give to the man?
A complete an important document
B discuss his idea with experts
C do some more research

4 You will hear two friends talking about doing an escape-room experience.
What did they find most challenging to complete?
A maths puzzles
B physical puzzles
C word puzzles

5 You will hear two friends talking about a reality talent show.
The man says that anyone who wants to enter must
A pay a small fee.
B make a short video.
C write their own music.

6 You will hear two friends discussing a banking app.
They disagree that it
A needs to be improved.
B makes saving money easy.
C is better than other banking apps.

3 **SPEAK** Work in pairs. Which of the recordings did you find easy or difficult? Do you ever talk about these topics with your friends or colleagues?

Listening Part 3 Gap fill

In Part 3, there are some notes with six pieces of information removed. Listen to the recording and fill in the numbered gaps with the exact words you hear in the monologue to complete the missing information.

How to go about it

- Read the instructions to help you understand who will be speaking and what the topic is.
- You have 20 seconds to read the notes on the question paper. Use this time to help you find what type of information you need to listen for (i.e. a kind of food, a number, a website address, etc).
- The words you write in each gap must be the exact word or noun phrase you hear in the tapescript. You must not change the word or noun phrase in any way (e.g. make a singular noun plural).
- When you listen the second time, check your answers, including your spelling.

1 SPEAK Work in pairs. Discuss the following questions.

1 What plants or flowers are most typical in your region?

2 In your country, do people give flowers on special occassions? Which?

3 Do you have a favourite flower or plant? What is it?

2 0.4 You will hear a tour guide called Lars talking about visiting attractions with tulips, a type of flower popular in the Netherlands. For questions 1–6, write the correct answer in each gap. Write one or two words or a number or a date or a time.

Lars' guided

tulip tour

in the Netherlands

Morning

At a museum, visitors learn how tulips affected the Dutch **(1)** .... in the 17th century.

Visit a farm in Bollenstreek to see approximately **(2)** .... varieties of tulips.

Afternoon

Eat some **(3)** .... made of tulip bulbs at a 5-star restaurant.

The best place to see Keukenhof Gardens is from a **(4)** ....

Visitors will go on **(5)** .... to see where tulips have been sold since 1862.

To take tulip bulbs abroad, tourists must show a **(6)** .... at customs.

3 SPEAK Work in pairs. Discuss the questions.

1 Have you ever been on a guided tour? Did you enjoy it? Why/Why not?

2 Are there any tours you would like to go on in the future?

Listening Part 4 Multiple Choice

In Part 4, you listen to a longer recording, which will be an interview with someone on a particular topic. There are six multiple-choice questions, each with three options.

What to expect in the exam

Part 4 is the longest recording. Each question follows the order of the information you will hear. The interviewer will say at least one keyword or a close paraphrase of each question, so you know which question is being discussed.

1 SPEAK Work in small groups. Discuss some advantages and disadvantages of doing a six-month working holiday.

2 Read the questions in Exercise 3. What type of information (a–f) do you need to find out for each question? Write the question numbers 1–6.

a an explanation about a task ____
b a frequent activity ____
c a difficulty ____
d providing a suggestion ____
e an unexpected benefit ____
f a reason for doing something ____

Don't forget!

You have six minutes to write your answers on the answer sheet after you hear the final recording. This is an excellent opportunity to check your answers one last time.

3 0.5 You will hear an interview with a woman called Zara Cross, who went on a six-month working holiday to manage a bookshop in Ireland. For questions 1–6, choose the best answer (A, B or C).

1 Zara wanted to run a bookstore because
A she was unhappy in her career.
B she decided to follow a lifelong dream.
C she wanted to open her own business one day.

2 What surprised Zara about her working holiday at *Bookends*?
A how many interesting people she met
B how many new skills she developed
C how many books she got to read

3 What did Zara find most challenging about running *Bookends*?
A serving unpleasant customers
B completing the paperwork
C predicting which books would sell

4 Which became a regular event at *Bookends*?
A author talks
B musical performances
C creative writing classes

5 Zara says her window displays
A took a lot of time and effort.
B became more and more creative.
C were an important way to attract customers.

6 What advice does Zara give about going on a working holiday in a bookshop?
A Learn from your mistakes.
B Make sure you are in good shape.
C Enjoy every minute of your experience.

4 SPEAK Work in pairs. Discuss the questions.

1 Would you like to go on a working holiday? Why/Why not?
2 If you could go on any working holiday, what would you do and where would you go?

8

GET SET, GO!

KEY LANGUAGE

Second conditional
Modals of permission, advice, obligation and prohibition
Types of sports
Sports collocations

PRONUNCIATION

Silent letters

EXAM PRACTICE

Reading Parts 1, 4 & 5
Writing Part 2
Listening Parts 2 & 4
Speaking Parts 1 & 2

Speaking Part 1 Interview

Work with a partner. Discuss the questions.

1 Do you prefer watching or playing sports?
2 What are your favourite sports?
3 Do you support a sports team?
4 How do you feel after you do sport?
5 When was the last time you did exercise?

Speaking Part 2 Extended turn

Describe the picture and say:

- where the people are.
- how the people are feeling.
- what the people are wearing.

8 GET SET, GO!

Vocabulary Types of sports

1 Label the pictures (a–l) with the sports in the box.

athletics   basketball   handball   ice hockey   karate   mountain biking
rock climbing   rugby   skateboarding   skiing   table tennis   windsurfing

a

b

c

d

e

f

g

h

i

j

k

l

2 SPEAK Work in pairs. Discuss the questions.

1. Which of the sports in Exercise 1 have you tried? Do you think you would enjoy the sports you haven't tried? Why/Why not?
2. What other sports have you played?
3. What sports are most popular in your country?

3 Write the names of the sports from Exercise 1 next to where they take place.

Track: ________ Pitch: ________ Court: ________, ________
Rink: ________

4 Complete the rules (a–c) with the sports from Exercise 1.

a The verb *play* is commonly used with games and ball sports, e.g. *football,* ________, ________, ________, ________ and ________.

b The verb *go* is commonly used with sports that end in *-ing*, e.g. *swimming,* ________, ________, ________, ________ and ________.

c The verb *do* is commonly used with individual or non-ball sports, e.g. *gymnastics,* ________ and ________.

Vocabulary Sports collocations

1 **Complete the sentences with the correct form of the verbs in the box. Use the words in bold to help you.**

accept achieve bring deal enter score treat take part

1 I love watching sport with other fans. We hug each other, or even cry, when our team ____________ the winning **point**.

2 I don't understand why some athletes believe that following specific routines, such as getting dressed in a certain way, will ____________ them **luck**.

3 I want to be the best at the **sports** I ____________ **in**, and I think practising often is the best way to ____________ this **goal**.

4 When I ____________ **a competition**, I always want to win. And, if I lose, it's hard for me to ____________ **defeat**.

5 Young people can learn a lot from sport, for example how to ____________ with the **disappointment** of losing a match and how to always ____________ your opponent with **respect**.

2 **SPEAK** **Work in pairs. Are the sentences in Exercise 1 true for you? Why/Why not?**

Reading Part 4 Gapped text

1 **SPEAK** **Work in pairs. What do you know about paddleboarding? Would you like to try it? Why/Why not?**

2 **You are going to read an article about a man who took up paddleboarding. Five sentences have been removed from the article. Choose from the sentences A–H the one which fits each gap (1–5). There are three extra sentences which you do not need to use.**

Don't forget!

Read the sentences before and after the gaps carefully. Look for linking words and pronouns. They can help you find the correct sentence.

BATTLING MY FEARS

I had always been scared of the sea when I was a child. My family thought it was strange, because we lived in a town on the coast and went to the beach most afternoons. [1] I never thought I would ever become a fan of a water sport.

One day on holiday in Spain, my girlfriend wanted me to try paddleboarding. We noticed a school on the beach and decided to have lessons. [2] But then I saw some children having lessons and I thought to myself, if I listen to the instructor, I'll learn how to do it. After all, I was nearly 25 years old! The instructor gave me a life jacket, which made me feel much safer, but just trying to get on the board was difficult.

[3] This was quite easy. However, the instructor then wanted us to stand up. At this point, I was really shaking. The thought of falling into the sea was scary, and I wasn't sure if I could balance on the board. I realised I had to try though. My girlfriend said it would be a great way to deal with my fear. So, slowly, I got up. [4] Soon, I was going up and down the coast on it, enjoying the sights.

Now, I feel like I've lost my fear of the sea and I love paddleboarding. I always do it when I have the chance. I have fallen in a few times, but I quickly get up and back on the board. I'd like to do it more often. [5] The sea is much colder here though. If I lived in a warmer country, I would go paddleboarding every day!

A I went out to sea sitting down on the board.

B We often went swimming quite far out at sea.

C I am actually thinking of buying a board and doing it in my home country.

D However, just the thought of all the creatures under the water scared me!

E At first, I was afraid and didn't want to go into the water.

F I thought her idea was perfect.

G To my surprise, I didn't find it difficult at all.

H It's always nice to do it in a warm country because the sea is nicer.

3 **SPEAK** **Work in pairs. Think of a time you tried a new sport. Tell your partner what happened.**

Language focus Second conditional

1 Read the sentence from the Reading text on page 117 and underline the verb forms.

If I lived in a warmer country, I would go paddleboarding every day!

2 Choose the correct options to complete the rules (1–2). Use the example in Exercise 1 to help you.

1. We use the second conditional to talk about *likely* / *imaginary* situations.
2. We form the second conditional with the *present* / *past* tense and *would* + infinitive without *to*.

3 Complete the sentences in the second conditional with the correct form of the verbs in brackets.

1. If you ________ (*go*) to university in France to study for a year, you ________ (*need*) to speak French.
2. If Erika ________ (*not work*) so much, she ________ (*have*) more free time.
3. He ________ (*not be*) late for work if he ________ (*wake up*) on time.
4. You ________ (*be*) delighted if they ________ (*invite*) you to the party.
5. If I ________ (*have*) more money, I ________ (*buy*) a new car and go on holiday.
6. We ________ (*go*) to the beach if it ________ (*not be*) raining.
7. If we ________ (*live*) in a city, it ________ (*be*) noisier than living here.
8. If Tom ________ (*do*) more exercise, he ________ (*feel*) healthier and fitter.

4 Go to Ready for Grammar on page 222 for rules, explanations and further practice.

5 Make questions in the second conditional from the prompts. There is an example at the beginning (0).

0. If / become / famous / what / job / choose
   If you became famous, what job would you choose?
1. If / move / another country / where / go
   ____
2. If / find / money / street / what / do
   ____
3. Who / ask / if / need / help
   ____
4. What / buy / if / have / more money
   ____
5. Who / choose / if / can / meet / anyone from history
   ____

6 **SPEAK** Work in groups. Ask and answer the questions in Exercise 5.

Listening Part 4 Multiple choice

1 SPEAK Work in pairs. Look at the photograph and answer the questions.

1 What is the woman doing?
2 Do you think she earns money for this? Why/Why not?

2 8.1 You will hear an interview with a woman called Hannah Chapman, a coach for a teenage football team. For questions 1–6, choose the best answer (A, B or C).

1 Hannah became an assistant coach
  A to encourage parents to help in the community.
  B because her daughter's team needed coaches.
  C so she could get to know her daughter's friends.
2 What did Hannah learn on her training course?
  A how to teach a certain age group
  B ways to explain the rules of football
  C techniques for teaching large groups
3 It's difficult for the team to find more coaches because
  A most parents are too busy.
  B training sessions are too long.
  C a lot of parents live far away.
4 The football team receives money from
  A a popular clothing brand.
  B local businesses.
  C players' families.
5 How do the players travel to matches?
  A by minibus
  B by train
  C by car
6 What does Hannah say about the team's results?
  A They are always good.
  B They've been disappointing.
  C They've improved recently.

3 SPEAK Work in pairs. Discuss the questions.

1 Do you think you would be good at working with teenagers? Why/Why not?
2 If you worked with teenagers, what activities would you like to help them with? Why?

Language focus Modals of permission, advice, obligation and prohibition

1 **Choose the correct options to complete these sentences from the listening.**

1. I think all the assistant coaches *should* / *must* do it.
2. At the moment, parents *ought to* / *have to* drive their daughters.

2 **Read the sentences in Exercise 1 again and choose the correct options.**

1. Sentence 1 is about *permission* / *advice*.
2. Sentence 2 is about *obligation* / *prohibition*.
3. The infinitive *with 'to'* / *without 'to'* comes after the modal verb.

3 **Match the sentences 1–5 to the situations a–e.**

1. All staff have to arrive at 9 am for a meeting tomorrow.
2. Children can play in this area with their parents.
3. You should do some more exercise at the weekends.
4. People must not cross the street when the light is red.
5. Patients don't have to wear a mask if they don't want to.

a This is advice.
b This is a choice.
c This is an obligation.
d This is permitted.
e This is prohibited.

4 **Go to Ready for Grammar on page 224 for rules, explanations and further practice.**

5 **SPEAK Work in pairs. Think of your favourite sport or game and describe it to your partner by answering the questions.**

1. What must you do to win?
2. What equipment do you need to use?
3. What should you do to play it well?
4. What are you not allowed to do?

Speaking Part 2 Extended turn

1 **Read the information in the Useful language box below and complete the sentences.**

Useful language

Modal verbs for speculation

We can use modal verbs to speculate about what is happening.

For things we think are **true**, we use ***must be***.

For things we think are **possible**, we use ***may/might/could be***.

For things we think are **not true**, we use ***can't be***.

Look at Picture 3 on page 121. Use *must*, *might* or *can't* to complete the sentences.

1. They ____________ be boxers. They are dressed for judo or something.
2. Some of the people ____________ be feeling disappointed because they didn't win.
3. The man in the centre ____________ be the winner. I can see his gold medal!

2 **SPEAK** Work in pairs. Look at photographs 1 and 2 and decide whether you agree with the sentences about each picture. Give reasons for your answers.

1

1 He could be lost.
2 He can't be tired.
3 He might be scared.
4 He must be in a race.
5 He might be cold.

2

1 They must be tired.
2 They can't be in a professional race.
3 They might be brother and sister.
4 They must enjoy running.
5 The woman could win the race.

3 **SPEAK** Work in pairs. Look at photographs 3 and 4. They show people taking part in sports events.

Student A: Look at photograph 3. Tell your partner what you can see in the photograph.

Student B: Look at photograph 4. Tell your partner what you can see in the photograph.

4 Now change roles.

3

4

Reading Part 1 Multiple choice

1 Work in pairs. Read the text below and answer the questions.

1

Hi Ollie,

Who likes Greece? → I'm having a great time in Greece!

We've been to the beach every day.

Does Chad's sister like hot weather? → It's a bit too hot for my sister, but for me it's perfect. I've been swimming,

Who can swim? Who can't swim? → and I'm teaching her to swim too!

See you soon!

Chad

Ollie Walters
51 Grange Close
Bedford
MK40 1BD
United Kingdom

Don't forget!

You might see words from all the options A, B and C in the text, but only one is correct. Do not just match words from the answer options. Make sure that the whole sentence agrees with the information in the text.

2 **SPEAK** Work in pairs. Read the answer options (A–C) below. Which answer is correct? Why?

A Chad's sister doesn't like Greece.
B Chad's sister loves hot weather.
C Chad's sister can't swim.

3 Read texts 2–5 and choose the correct option (A, B or C).

2

SUMMER CAMP!

Interested in games, football and art? Pinnacle Summer Camp will take place in August for people between the ages of 10 and 16. You must reserve a place by emailing info@pinsc.info, with your contact information.

A The camp is not for younger teenagers.
B You should be good at sports to go to the camp.
C It's essential to book the camp in advance.

3

THIS JUICE IS MADE WITH REAL FRUIT.

Once opened, keep in the fridge and use within 48 hours.

Best served with ice.

A You must consume the drink quickly.
B You must keep the drink cool.
C You must add ice to the drink.

4

TO: Sarah
FROM: Tess
SUBJECT: Later

Sarah,
I forgot to book the tennis court for tonight. Can you do it? I'm in a meeting all day, so I can't call.
Tess

A Tess is too busy to book the court.
B Tess can't play tennis tonight.
C Tess will call Sarah after her meeting.

5

ALL VISITORS

You must report to reception and get a badge before you enter the building. Please give the name of the person you are visiting.

A Visitors can wait in reception.
B Visitors need to wear a badge.
C Visitors should say their names.

Writing Part 2 Article

1 SPEAK Work in groups. Read the Writing Part 2 task below and answer the questions.

1 What sport would you choose to write about? Why?
2 What type of vocabulary would you include?

> **Articles wanted!**
> - What is your favourite sport? Why do you like it?
> - Do you prefer doing it or watching it? Why?
>
> The best articles answering these questions will be published next month.

Write your **article** in about **100 words.**

2 Read the model answer below and answer the questions.

1 What sport did the student write about?
2 What do they like about it?

A great sport for everyone

The sport that I like the most is swimming. There are many **amazing** outdoor places where people can go swimming such as **pools**, **lakes**, **rivers** and the **sea**. You only need a **swimsuit** or **trunks**, but some people like to wear **goggles** to **protect** their eyes. For me, swimming is a **fantastic** way to **exercise**, and I also like to be **outside** in the **sunshine**.

I enjoy watching swimming **competitions** on TV because the **swimmers** are **professionals**. However, in my opinion, it's better to **play** sports than **watch** them. If you only watch sports, you won't get any health **benefits**.

3 Put the vocabulary in bold from the model answer in Exercise 2 in the table.

Places:	*pools*	Equipment:	
People:		Other nouns:	
Verbs:		Adjectives:	

Useful language

Topic vocabulary

1 Underline the word in each group that is NOT usually associated with the sport in **bold**.

1 **tennis**: net, stick, racket
2 **swimming**: gloves, goggles, cap
3 **cycling**: bike, helmet, match
4 **skateboarding**: knee pads, ramp, boots
5 **basketball**: court, pitch, hoop

2 Complete the sentences with words from Exercise 1.

1 Don't forget to wear a ____________ when you go cycling.
2 To score points in basketball, the ball must go through the ____________.
3 Saltwater can hurt your eyes so wear ____________.
4 At the start of the match, my new tennis ____________ fell on the ground and broke.
5 Beginner skateboarders should wear helmets and ____________.
6 A tennis court has a ____________ in the middle.

4 You are going to write your own answer to the task in Exercise 1. Before you begin, make a list of some vocabulary you can include from the useful language box and the table in Exercise 3.

5 Now write your **article** in about **100 words.**

For more information about writing articles, see page 195.

Listening Part 2 Multiple choice

1 8.2 **You will hear people talking in six different situations. For questions 1–6, choose the best answer (A, B or C).**

1 You will hear two friends talking about a sports event.
They agree that it was
A in a great location.
B good value for money.
C more exciting than last time.

2 You will hear a man telling a friend about a shopping experience.
How did he feel about it?
A satisfied with the customer service
B shocked at the poor quality of the products
C confused by the design of the shop

3 You will hear a man telling a friend about a new exercise class.
He thinks the instructor
A communicated well with the students.
B did not have enough experience.
C made the class too difficult.

4 You will hear two friends discussing a cycling trip.
What does the woman say about it?
A They have to book some hotels.
B They only need a little equipment.
C They should camp along the route.

5 You will hear a man telling a friend about a competition he is going to enter.
He thinks that it would be better if
A it was closer to home.
B the tickets were cheaper.
C there were more competitors.

6 You will hear two friends talking about a walking holiday.
What problem did they have?
A taking the wrong clothes
B not using technology
C following the right route

8 REVIEW

Language focus Modals

Choose the correct alternatives to complete the text.

It is difficult for adults to know how to play games with their young children. It's important for children to experience losing, so their parents **(1)** *shouldn't / have to* lose all the games to make their children feel good. Children **(2)** *have to / don't have to* learn that they **(3)** *can't / mustn't* always win. However, parents **(4)** *must / can't* be patient as well. Children learn at different speeds.

When young children lose games and get upset, older brothers and sisters **(5)** *mustn't / can* be helpful because they have already learnt about winning and losing. The most important thing for all children in the family to learn is that they **(6)** *don't have to / mustn't* win to have fun.

Vocabulary Sports

Choose the correct alternatives to complete the texts.

Kristina has **(1)** *done / played* a lot of team sports such as basketball, football and **(2)** *handball / athletics*, but last year she tried something different. She went on a trip to Canada to learn to **(3)** *play / go* ice hockey. On the first day she skated on to the **(4)** *ice rink / pitch* and fell over immediately! She thought it would be like **(5)** *going / doing* skiing, but it was more difficult.

Yoshi **(6)** *plays / does* karate twice a week. He is quite good and last month he entered a **(7)** *competition / game*. He didn't win but he managed to **(8)** *deal / treat* with his disappointment by going to watch his friend play rugby. Standing on the edge of the **(9)** *court / pitch* cheering made him feel much better and his friend **(10)** *scored / accepted* twice, helping his team to win!

Reading Part 5 Multiple-choice cloze

Read the text. For questions 1–6, choose which answer (A, B, C or D) best fits each gap.

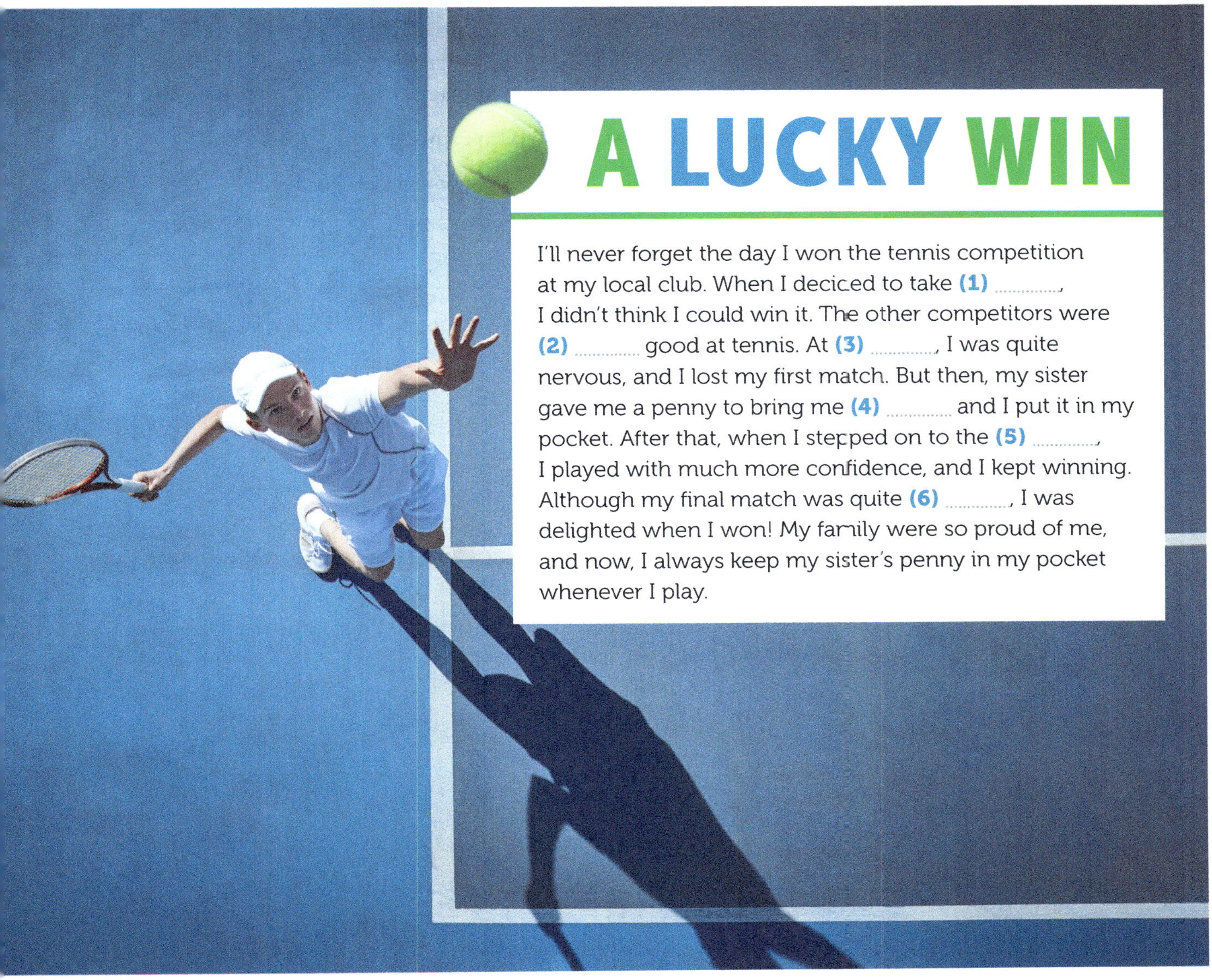

A LUCKY WIN

I'll never forget the day I won the tennis competition at my local club. When I decided to take **(1)** ...., I didn't think I could win it. The other competitors were **(2)** .... good at tennis. At **(3)** ...., I was quite nervous, and I lost my first match. But then, my sister gave me a penny to bring me **(4)** .... and I put it in my pocket. After that, when I stepped on to the **(5)** ...., I played with much more confidence, and I kept winning. Although my final match was quite **(6)** ...., I was delighted when I won! My family were so proud of me, and now, I always keep my sister's penny in my pocket whenever I play.

1 **A** place	**B** away	**C** part	**D** care
2 **A** so	**B** such	**C** too	**D** enough
3 **A** once	**B** first	**C** least	**D** last
4 **A** chance	**B** respect	**C** defeat	**D** luck
5 **A** pitch	**B** court	**C** track	**D** rink
6 **A** wonderful	**B** odd	**C** dull	**D** challenging

Writing Part 2 Story

Your English teacher has asked you to write a story. Your story must begin with this sentence:

It was a great day for mountain biking, but as we set off, we had no idea what was going to happen.

Write your **story** in about **100** words.

For more information on writing stories, see page 194.

Pronunciation Silent letters

1 Underline the silent letters in the words below.

1 column 2 comb 3 knee 4 wrote 5 scenery 6 doubt 7 muscle
8 climber 9 science 10 hour 11 where 12 autumn 13 sign 14 honour

2 8.3 Listen and look at the Audioscript on page 243 to check your answers.

3 8.3 Listen again and repeat the words in Exercise 1.

4 Put the words from Exercise 1 in the correct columns in the table.

Silent b	Silent c	Silent g	Silent h	Silent k	Silent n	Silent w

5 8.4 Listen and complete the sentences. Go to the Audioscript on page 243 to check your answers.

1 ____________ don't always ____________ all the ____________.
2 The ____________ was ____________ about his mistake.
3 In the ____________, it's nice to ____________ for many ____________.
4 I spent a ____________ ____________ ____________ to the ____________.

6 SPEAK Work in pairs. Play the game.

GUESS THE SILENT LETTER

Student A: Point to one of the pictures.
Student B: Say the word you see. How do you spell it? What is the silent letter?
Take turns until you have used all the images.
Score 1 point for the word and one point for the silent letter.

1

2
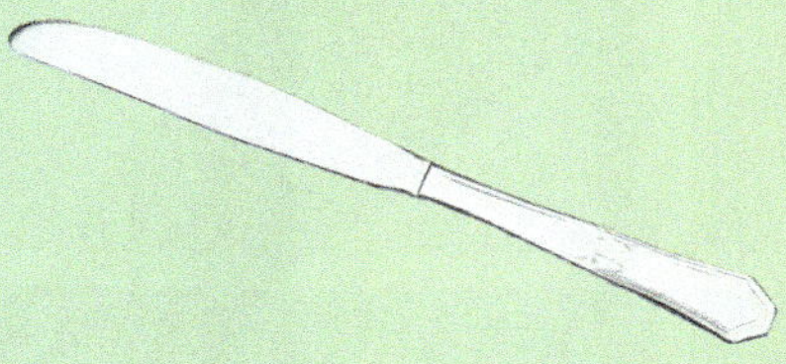

3

4

5
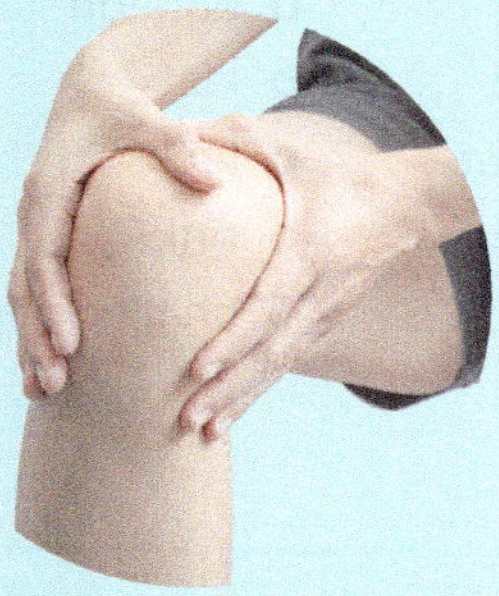

6

7
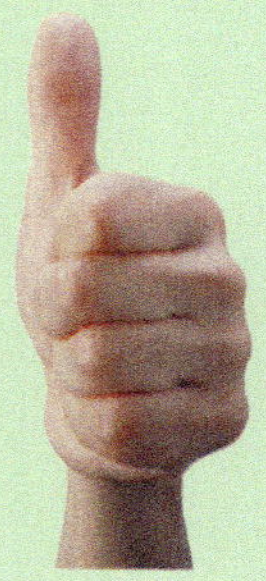

8
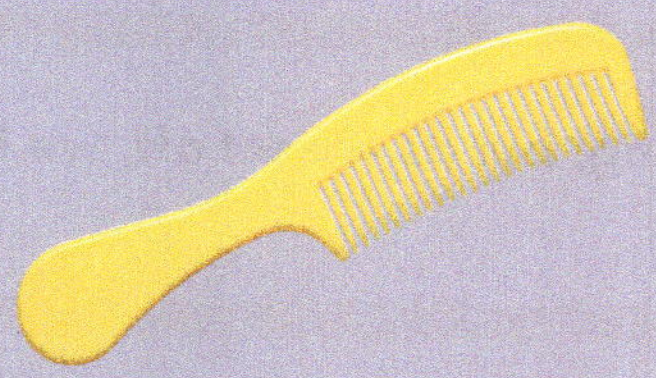

9

9

LIFELONG LEARNING

KEY LANGUAGE

Past perfect simple and continuous
Gerunds and infinitives
Student life
Different types of study

PRONUNCIATION

/ɜː/, /eə/ and /ɪə/

EXAM PRACTICE

Reading Parts 1 & 6
Writing Parts 1 & 2
Listening Parts 1 & 4
Speaking Parts 1, 2, 3 & 4

Speaking Part 1 Interview

Work with a partner. Discuss the questions.

1 What was the last course you studied?
2 Do you enjoy learning new things? Why/ Why not?
3 Do you prefer practical subjects or more academic subjects?
4 If you could study any subject, what would you choose to learn?
5 What are you planning to learn in the future?

Speaking Part 2 Extended turn

Work with a partner. Describe what you see in the picture. Use the phrases in the box to help you.

It looks like ... *They might/could be ...*
Perhaps/Maybe they're... *They seem ...*

9 LIFELONG LEARNING

Vocabulary Student life

1 Look at the questionnaire below. Complete the questions with the words in the box.

essays exam homework instructions marks projects

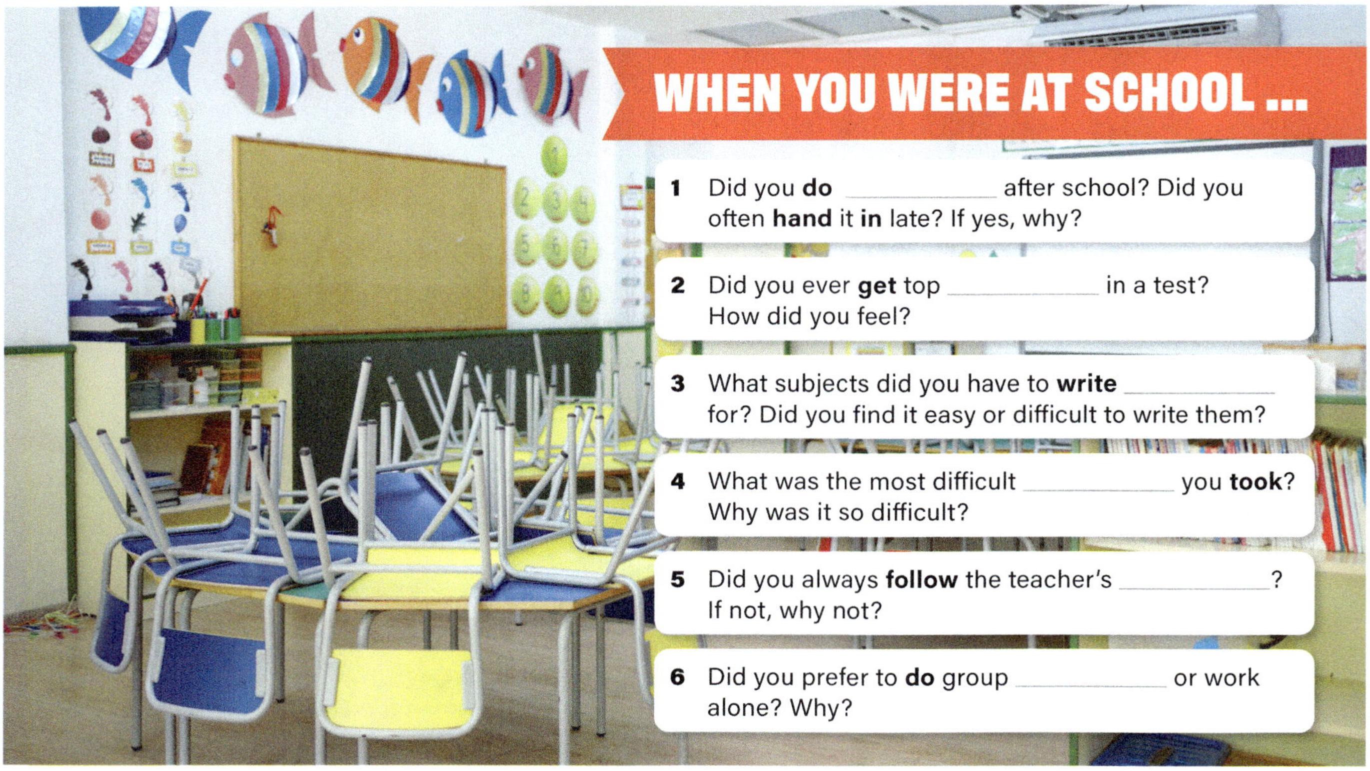

WHEN YOU WERE AT SCHOOL ...

1 Did you **do** ________ after school? Did you often **hand** it **in** late? If yes, why?

2 Did you ever **get** top ________ in a test? How did you feel?

3 What subjects did you have to **write** ________ for? Did you find it easy or difficult to write them?

4 What was the most difficult ________ you **took**? Why was it so difficult?

5 Did you always **follow** the teacher's ________? If not, why not?

6 Did you prefer to **do** group ________ or work alone? Why?

2 **SPEAK** Work in pairs. Do the questionnaire in Exercise 1.

3 Look at the people talking about education. Choose the correct verbs to complete the speech bubbles.

I always listened to the teacher and **(1)** *took / did* notes in class. It helped me remember what I learnt.

I've only **(2)** *failed / tested* one exam in my life, and that was a maths exam. It was too hard!

I want to **(3)** *get / make* a master's degree in chemistry, so I can work as a scientist.

I always forgot to bring my pencil case, and I had to **(4)** *lend / borrow* a pen from someone.

I always **(5)** *study / have* English lessons in the evenings, because I work during the day.

4 **SPEAK** Look at the speech bubbles in Exercise 3. How true are the sentences for you?

Speaking Part 3 Discussion

SPEAK Look at the pictures below. A language teacher wants to organise an end-of-year activity for her adult advanced-level class. She wants it to be fun and educational, and easy to organise. Here are some of the activities she could choose. Talk together about the different activities she could do and say which would be the best. Use the phrases in the Useful language box to help you.

End-of-year activities for an adult class

Useful language

Making suggestions

How/What about ...?

Do you think ... is a good idea?

She could ... What do you think?

I think ... is a good idea.

Agreeing

Yes, that sounds good.

That's a good idea.

I agree (with you).

Disagreeing

I'm not so sure.

I don't think that's a good idea.

Hmm ... I think ... is better.

Don't forget!

You have to speak to your partner. Try to ask questions, make suggestions and respond to your partner's questions and ideas.

Speaking Part 4 General conversation

SPEAK Work in pairs. Discuss the questions.

1 Why do people learn English as adults?
2 What other things do people learn as adults? Why?
3 Is it important to have fun when you learn? Why/Why not?
4 Why do you think some people prefer to study online?

Reading Part 1 Multiple choice

1 **SPEAK** Work in pairs. Discuss the questions.

1 What kinds of things do people sell?
2 Where do you see things for sale?
3 What information do 'for sale' advertisements include?

2 Look at question 1 in Exercise 3 below. Does the advert include the kind of information you talked about in Exercise 1?

3 Read texts 1–5 and choose the correct answer (A, B or C).

Don't forget!

You will see lots of different text types in this part. Think about the purpose of each text, e.g. is it a note to someone or a sign giving an instruction?

1

Piano for sale £140

- Electric piano for sale.
- Works perfectly.
- Please call to see it.
- No deliveries.
- Buyer must collect.
- Headphones and pedal (worth £60) also included.

A People must pay separately for headphones and pedal.
B People must come to the owner to get the piano.
C People must order the piano by phone.

2

RESERVATIONS

We do not take reservations.

If you want a table, please go to the bar.

The waiter will assist you and find you a table.

A Customers can choose where they sit.
B Customers have to reserve a table.
C Customers should speak to a member of staff.

3

Jen. I've forgotten my student card! I've just checked and it's not in my pocket. I thought I had put it in there, but maybe it's on the table. Can you look for it and bring it to me, please? I'm at the bus stop. Olly

Olly is asking Jen to
A wait for him at the bus stop.
B find his student card.
C bring him a coat.

4

ALL STUDENTS

The library is shut this weekend.
If you want to study, the classrooms will be open for this weekend only.

A Students can study in a different place.
B Students must wait to return books to the library.
C Students' classrooms are always open.

5

Kyle,

The children won't be home for dinner tonight. They have extra classes. Don't cook anything for us. How about we eat out?

Hannah

Hannah
A doesn't want to cook dinner.
B wants to eat dinner with the children.
C wants to have dinner at a restaurant.

Language focus Past perfect simple and continuous

1 Read the sentences and circle the action that happened first.

*The rain **had stopped** by the time I **left** the house.*

1 By the time we **arrived**, he **had** already **prepared** the dinner.
2 We **hadn't studied** all of the topics before we **took** the exam.
3 I **went** back to visit my old school and it **had changed** a lot.
4 **Had** you **studied** any English before you **started** this course?
5 Miss Greene **gave** the best lecture I'**d** ever **attended**.

2 Complete the following rule about the past perfect. Use the example sentence in Exercise 1 to help you.

We use the past perfect to talk about an action that happened *before* / *after* another past action.

3 Go to Ready for Grammar on page 226 for rules, explanations and further practice.

4 Complete the text using the past perfect simple, past perfect continuous or past simple form of the verbs in brackets.

HOME NEWS BLOG ABOUT

THE WORLD'S TOUGHEST COURSE?

Most people choose to study a language or cookery course when they are older, but not me. I wanted to learn how to survive in the wild! I **(1)** ______ **(think)** about doing a survival course for ages and I had some free time, so I **(2)** ______ **(decide)** to book one in the jungle. I thought it was perfect for me as as I loved watching survival programmes on TV. When I **(3)** ______ **(arrive)** in the jungle, the trainer **(4)** ______ **(already / set up)** lots of different tasks to do. We had to build a place to sleep, start a fire and learn to collect water and food. Unfortunately, I **(5)** ______ **(not /manage)** to light a fire by the time it **(6)** ______ **(get)** dark. It was far more difficult than I thought. But I loved the course! Now, I can definitely survive in the wild – for a few days at least!

5 Complete the following sentences using the past simple and past perfect simple or past perfect continuous.

Event 1: get the job offer *Event 2: finish my degree*

I had got the job offer before I finished my degree.

1 Event 1: buy a car Event 2: pass her driving test
She ______ before ______.
2 Event 1: practise the piano Event 2: decide to take a break
He ______ all day, so ______.
3 Event 1: not arrive at the bus stop Event 2: bus come
She ______ by the time ______.
4 Event 1: try to fix his PC Event 2: start working
He ______ all day, when suddenly it ______.

6 **SPEAK** Work in groups. Tell your group all the things you had done before 9 am this morning. Who did the most?

By 9 am, I'd already gone shopping / cleaned my teeth / got dressed / called my best friend ...

Writing Part 2 Story

1 **SPEAK** Work in pairs. Read the following Writing Part 2 instructions. Talk to your partner about what your story could be about.

Your English teacher has asked you to write a story. Your story must begin with this sentence:

> **As I opened the envelope, I was terrified to look at the results.**

Write your **story** in about **100 words**.

2 Read the model answer below and answer the questions.

1 Does it have any similarities to your own ideas from Exercise 1?
2 Do you think it is a good answer? Why/Why not?

As I opened the envelope, I was terrified to look at the results. I had been studying every day for the exams, and I really wanted to do well. My dream was to study law at university, but I couldn't do that without getting top marks.

I slowly looked down at the paper and when I saw the grades, I couldn't believe it. I had failed nearly all my subjects! This was terrible news. But then, I suddenly realized the name on the envelope wasn't mine! I had picked up another person's results!

I quickly put the envelope back and picked up the correct one. In the end, I got the marks I wanted. I felt really bad for that other person, though!

3 **SPEAK** Work in pairs. Compare your answers to Exercise 2.

4 The underlined words in the story are adverbs. We use adverbs to give more information about a verb. Use the underlined words in the model answer to complete the descriptions below.

1 an adverb that means **very**: ____________
2 an adverb that means **almost**: ____________
3 three adverbs that tell us **how** something happened: ____________, ____________, ____________

5 Now do the following Writing Part 2 task. Use adverbs in your answer.

Your English teacher has asked you to write a story. Your story must begin with this sentence:

> **I'll never forget how embarrassed I felt on my first day of the course.**

Write your **story** in about **100 words**.

For more information on writing stories, see page 194.

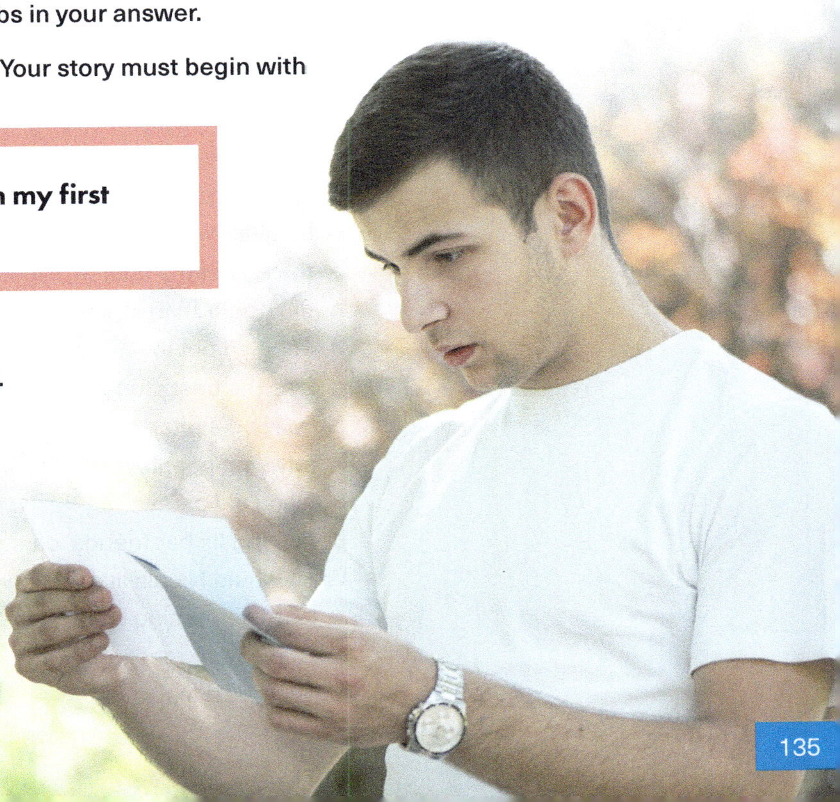

Listening Part 4 Multiple choice

1 **SPEAK** Look at the picture. What is the woman learning? Where can people learn this?

2 9.1 You will hear an interview with a woman called Nicola Martin, who is learning how to fix cars. For questions 1–6, choose the best answer (A, B or C).

1 Nicola wanted to take a car mechanic course because
  A her car had lots of problems.
  B she wanted to change jobs.
  C she thought it would be interesting.

2 When did Nicola decide to study?
  A in the mornings
  B in the evenings
  C at the weekends

3 What did Nicola find hard at first?
  A remembering new vocabulary
  B learning practical skills
  C dealing with other students

4 At the end of the course, Nicola
  A did better than she had expected.
  B decided not to take the exams.
  C was the best student in the class.

5 Now, Nicola often spends time
  A advising people on what cars to buy.
  B fixing old cars.
  C helping fix her friends' cars.

6 What would Nicola like to do next?
  A learn something else
  B study more mechanics
  C become a teacher

Vocabulary Different types of study

1 **Read the following statements and complete definitions 1–5 with the words in bold.**

I'm studying Chinese at **evening classes** at the local college. It's difficult but really interesting!

Mario

I'm learning to drive, and my **instructor** is so calm. She thinks I'll pass my test next week!

Suzanne

I'm a **full-time** student at university. I'm doing a master's **degree** in geography. My **professor** knows so much about the subject.

Katy

My company is paying for me to do a **part-time** course in customer service. It's a **distance learning** qualification and I study online. My **trainer** is very professional, and I like the course too.

Ahmed

1 A ______________________ course means students study at home or online.
2 A ______________________ student studies for twenty or thirty hours a week, but a ______________________ student only studies for about ten hours per week.
3 Somebody who studies at the end of the day is taking ______________________.
4 A ______________________ works at a university and teaches students who are studying for a ______________________.
5 A ______________________ or an ______________________ teaches skills related to work, practical activities or sports.

2 **Go to the Additional materials on page 199 for further vocabulary practice.**

Language focus Gerunds and infinitives

1 **Read the extracts from the listening on page 136 and choose the correct alternatives.**

1 I didn't have a full-time job and the children were at school, so I decided *to do* / *doing* a course!
2 I also don't mind *to give* / *giving advice* to people who want it.

2 **9.2 Listen and check your answers to Exercise 1.**

3 **Go to Ready for Grammar on page 228 for rules, explanations and further practice.**

4 **Complete the following interview using the correct form of the words in brackets.**

NEXT STEPS: Interview with Noelia Sanchez

1 What did you enjoy ______________ (*study*) at school?
Well, my favourite subject was maths. In fact, I did a degree in it when I finished school!
2 Were any subjects difficult ______________ (*do*) at school?
Yes! I was very bad at art! I can't draw or paint!
3 Why did you decide ______________ (*learn*) English?
Everybody does in my country. Most people start English classes when they are five years old.
4 Do you prefer ______________ (*study*) practical or academic things?
I like studying both. In my school, most subjects were academic, but I love learning practical things like how to build or fix something.
5 Are you thinking about ______________ (*develop*) any new skills?
I'd like to learn to cook. I love cooking but I don't have much time to do it now, and I'm not very good at it!

5 **SPEAK** **Work in pairs. Interview your partner. Use the questions in Exercise 4.**

Listing Part 1 Multiple choice

Don't forget!

Think of the differences between the pictures and how to describe them before you listen.

1 **SPEAK** **Work in pairs. Look at the three pictures in question 1 in Exercise 2 below. Describe what you see in each picture. Use the vocabulary in the box.**

behind near next to on the left on the other side opposite

2 **9.3 You will hear people talking in seven different situations. For questions 1–7, choose the best answer (A, B or C).**

1 Where is the Newton Building?

A

B

C

2 What subject did the woman do best in?

A

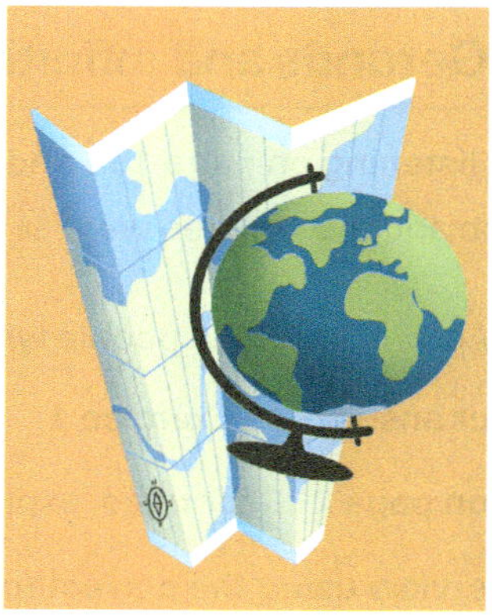

B

C

3 How will students receive a student card?

A

B

C

4 What was the noise?

A

B

C

5 What does the woman plan to study?

A

B

C

6 What does the man want?

A

B

C

7 How does the woman prefer to learn?

A

B

C

Language focus Gerunds and infinitives

Complete the text with the correct form of the verbs in the box (infinitive with *to* or *-ing*).

apply be find fix help play study

PINNACLE ONLINE COLLEGE

More than just a college!

Is it hard (1) ______________ the right course for you?
Does your local college not offer the variety of courses you need?
Why not try Pinnacle Online College.

With over 1000 courses, we promise **(2)** ______________ you find your perfect course! Perhaps you love **(3)** ______________ a musical instrument and want to take an exam in it? Or perhaps you want to learn **(4)** ______________ cars. Whatever your interest, we have something for you.

(5) ______________ even just one or two subjects can take up a lot of your time, so it's important you can learn when you want: full-time, part-time, evenings or weekends. We have designed our courses **(6)** ______________ flexible too. You can study when you want!

If you're thinking about **(7)** ______________ for a course, please get in touch at info@pincoll.coll

Vocabulary Student life

Match the sentence beginnings 1–8 to the endings a–h to make complete sentences.

1 I always find it easy to **follow**
2 I'm sorry I couldn't **hand in**
3 Do you mind if I **borrow**
4 We need to **do a group**
5 If you want to **get good**
6 Jim's dad is very clever, he's **got**
7 Can I **do** my
8 Remember to **take**

a **project** this week. Let's work together!
b **notes** during the class. You can look at them at home.
c **your book** please? I left mine at home this morning.
d **instructions** because I listen carefully to the teacher.
e two master's **degrees** from a top university!
f **my work** on time. I've been ill this week.
g **homework** after dinner, please?
h **marks,** you need to study hard!

Reading Part 6 Open cloze

For questions 1–6, read the biography below and think of the word which best fits each gap. Use only **one** word in each gap.

The Amazing Ada Lovelace

Ada Lovelace was born in 1815, at a time when it was unusual for a girl to have an education. Ada had more opportunities than most girls. Firstly, (1) .... mother found her teachers who taught her at home. She also knew and talked to famous scientists and writers such (2) .... Michael Faraday and Charles Dickens.

By the time she was 18, she (3) .... already studied a lot of maths and science. It was at this time that she started working with Charles Babbage. Babbage is known as 'The Father of Computers'. She used her language skills (4) .... translate information from other languages into English, and designed a language that computers could use. Because of this, she became famous for being (5) .... first female computer programmer. It is very different to the complicated languages computers use now, but it is perhaps the first example of (6) .... computer languages work.

Writing Part 1 Email

Read this email from your English-speaking friend Jake and the notes you have made.

From: Jake
Subject: Starting college
Hi,
I'm so excited that I am going to go to the same college as you! I'm also a little nervous too. ← Me too!
I don't know much about the college. What is it like? ← Tell Jake ...
What advice can you give me for my first day? I don't know what do bring or where to go! ← Suggest ...
Also, what was your first day like? Did you feel nervous too? ← No, because ...
I am so happy that I will see you there.
See you soon!
Jake

Reply to Jake using **all the notes**. Write your email in about **100 words**.

For more information on writing emails, see pages 192–193.

Pronunciation /ɜː/, /eə/ and /ɪə/

1 9.4 Listen and number the words in the order you hear them.

here ______ her ______ hair ______

2 Underline the word with the different sound in each group.

1	serve	here	term
2	work	wear	word
3	clear	learn	heard
4	nurse	hurt	wear
5	there	bird	shirt

3 9.5 Listen and check your answers.

4 Put the words in the box in the correct columns in the table. There is an example in the table.

~~fair~~ ~~fear~~ pear pier rarely really stare steer we're where

/ɪə/	/eə/
fear	*fair*

5 9.6 Now listen and check your answers to Exercise 4.

6 **SPEAK** Work in groups. Play snakes and ladders.

SNAKES AND LADDERS

Take turns to roll the dice and move across the board. If you land on a space with a word, you must say the word correctly. If you pronounce it incorrectly, go back 1 space. You go UP the ladders and DOWN the snakes.

10 GETTING BETTER

KEY LANGUAGE

Reported speech: statements
Reported speech: questions
Health
Strong and weak adjectives

PRONUNCIATION

Word endings

EXAM PRACTICE

Reading Parts 3 & 6
Writing Parts 1 & 2
Listening Parts 3 & 4
Speaking Parts 1 & 2

Speaking Part 1 Interview

Work with a partner. Discuss the questions.

1 Do you try to be active and eat healthily?
2 In what ways do you try to stay healthy?
3 What do you do when you feel ill?
4 What bad habits do you have?
5 Do you always follow the doctor's advice?

Speaking Part 2 Extended turn

Work with a partner. Describe what you see in the picture. Say:

- where the person is
- what the person is doing
- how the person is feeling

10 GETTING BETTER

Reading Part 3 Multiple choice

1 SPEAK Work in pairs. Look at the photograph and discuss the questions.

1. What is the doctor doing?
2. What do you think is difficult about her job?
3. Why do some people work helping people in other countries?

2 Quickly read the article about a doctor who worked in a different country. Did she enjoy her experience?

My Year with DOCTORS WITHOUT BORDERS

My name is Chloe Bell, and I got my medical degree six years ago. I always wanted to help people and that's the reason I decided to become a doctor. I didn't always enjoy studying, but I loved all the practical work that we did, like working with patients. When I finished, I worked in a local hospital in the UK for four years, but then **another student from my course told me that he had worked for Doctors without Borders.** It's a charity that sends doctors to places that need help. He applied after he had seen an advert on TV about it. He said it was an amazing experience.

I thought the idea of taking some time off from my job and helping people in another country was really exciting, so I did some research on the internet about the organisation. I found out that the doctors often make a big difference to the areas they work in, so I decided to apply. **When I told my parents what I wanted to do, they said that I was crazy!** I think they couldn't understand why I wanted to leave my great job. I was worried too, at first. When I got on the plane to Madagascar, I didn't know if I had made the right decision, and for the first few months, it was very difficult. I didn't speak the local language, and I didn't have access to all the things I had at my hospital back home – people couldn't always get a prescription for medicine. Medicine was hard to find. And sometimes there weren't enough beds for patients.

I soon realised what a big difference my skills made. After the first few months, I felt much better, and by the time I had to leave, I didn't want to go! The experience changed my life. I didn't realise how easy life is at home, and how lucky we are to have lots of medicine and doctors. When I came back home, I returned to my old job, but the work doesn't make me as happy. I would like to go and work with Doctors without Borders again one day. I made lots of friends in Madagascar and I think about them every day. We are still in contact, and I hope to see them again soon – this time just for a holiday!

3 **Read the article again. For questions 1–5, choose the correct answer (A, B, C or D).**

1 How did Chloe find out about Doctors without Borders?
   A from a person she knew
   B on the internet
   C from her workplace
   D on the television
2 How did Chloe's parents feel about her decision?
   A They were surprised.
   B They supported her decision.
   C They disliked the idea.
   D They thought it was interesting.
3 When Chloe arrived in Madagascar
   A it was difficult to find a place to stay.
   B she started learning to speak a new language.
   C it was very different to how she had worked before.
   D she thought she had made a bad decision.
4 What does Chloe say about Madagascar now?
   A She aims to go back and work there again.
   B She would like to visit the people she met.
   C She is a better doctor because of the experience.
   D She has arranged to go on holiday there soon.
5 What would be a good introduction to this article?
   A Chloe Bell explains why everyone should do a year with Doctors without Borders.
   B In this article, Chloe Bell tells us how doctors can help overseas.
   C Doctor Chloe Bell tells us about her experience volunteering at home and overseas.
   D For Chloe Bell, a year working overseas was one she will never forget.

Don't forget!

If you are not sure about a question, guess. You do not lose points for a wrong answer.

4 **SPEAK** **In groups, think of other jobs that people volunteer to do. Decide what each person in the group would be best at.**

I think Juan would like to work on a farm, maybe helping with the fruit or the animals because he loves being outdoors.

Vocabulary Health

1 Look at the article on page 144 again. Which verbs do we use before these words?

1 __________ some time off
2 __________ a prescription

2 Match the sentence beginnings 1–8 to the endings a–h to make complete sentences.

1 When I'm ill, I don't usually **take**
2 In an emergency, you should **call**
3 My uncle is going to hospital to **have**
4 If you want to see the doctor, **make**
5 You look exhausted! You should **get**
6 If you want to lose weight, you should **go**
7 My brother isn't at school today. He **broke**
8 Don't come near me if you **have**

a **an ambulance** to give you urgent help.
b **a cough** – I don't want to get ill!
c **an appointment** at reception.
d **any pills**; I prefer natural cures.
e **some rest** and try to relax!
f **an operation** on his knee.
g **on a diet**. Exercise is not enough.
h **his arm** playing football.

3 Choose the word that does *not* usually go with each verb.

1 **take** a fever, time off, your temperature
2 **have** an accident, sick, the flu
3 **go to** the chemist's, the doctor, medicine

4 Read the health problems below and complete the replies. Use vocabulary from Exercises 2 and 3.

1 I need to get to the hospital urgently. — I'll __________ an __________.
2 I've had this cough for two weeks. — Try to __________ an __________ with your doctor.
3 I feel very hot. What do you think? — Let me __________ your __________.
4 I'm so tired. I've been working a lot. — Why don't you __________ some __________? You're always so busy.
5 I'm overweight. I'm sure it's the food I'm eating. — If I were you, I'd __________ on a __________ and eat less fast food.
6 I shut my finger in the door, and it really hurts. — Maybe you've __________ it.
7 I've got a headache. — You should __________ a __________. I've got some in my bag.

5 **SPEAK** Work in pairs. You each have a health problem and would like some advice.

Student A: Describe a health problem to your partner.
Student B: Give some advice.

When you have finished, change roles.

Language focus Reported speech: statements

1 Read the sentences in **bold** in the text on page 144. What is the difference between the sentences in the text and the speech below?

I've worked for Doctors without Borders.

I want to work overseas.

You're crazy!

2 Choose the correct alternatives to complete the sentences.

1 Jessica *said* / *told* that she was going to study chemistry at university.
2 Roberto *said* / *told* me that he didn't feel very well.
3 My manager said *that* / *if* we had sold a lot of products that month.

3 Complete the rules for reported speech.

1 The verb ________ does NOT have a pronoun after it.
2 We use a pronoun after the verb ________.
3 We can use the word ________ after the verbs *say* and *tell*.

4 Go to Ready for Grammar on page 230 for rules, explanations and further practice.

5 Correct the underlined words in the following sentences.

1 'Oh no, it's raining outside,' <u>say</u> Mina.
2 My father <u>told</u> that he was too tired to go shopping.
3 The players said they <u>are</u> practising a lot for the match.
4 Jana told <u>we</u> that she had been to the cinema.
5 Leon said that he <u>wants</u> to play the drums.
6 My friend told me she <u>has</u> a cough last week.

6 Write the direct speech in reported speech using the verbs and pronouns in brackets.

1 Ivan: "I need to buy a new jacket for winter."
Ivan (say) ________
2 Amir: "I'm going to the doctor tomorrow."
Amir (say) ________
3 The children: "We haven't cleaned the kitchen yet."
The children (tell / their mother) ________
4 Ella and Harry: "We didn't go to the concert last week."
Ella and Harry (tell / us) ________
5 Oliver: "My friend Jana plays tennis really well."
Oliver (say) ________

7 SPEAK Work in pairs. Tell your partner what someone said to you about these topics.

- foods that are good for your health.
- the best type of exercise.
- what to do if you have a headache.
- how to improve your English.

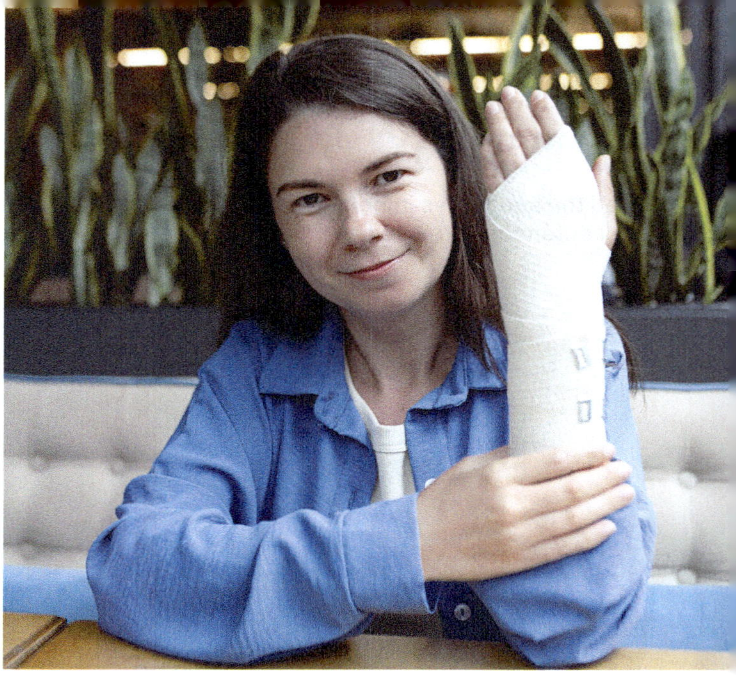

Listening Part 4 Multiple choice

1 SPEAK What can you see in the photos? What do you think has happened to the woman? Use the prompts below.

She's hurt her ... | *I think she might ...*
She's holding her ... | *She must ...*

2 10.1 You will hear an interview with a woman called Marsha Jones about an accident that she had on a skiing holiday. For questions 1–6, choose the best answer (A, B or C).

1 Marsha decided to go skiing because
 A her family don't like cultural holidays.
 B she wanted a new experience.
 C she enjoys learning different sports.

2 What did the ski instructor do in the class?
 A reminded them of the basics
 B helped them when they fell over
 C taught them some new skills

3 Why did Marsha have an accident?
 A She wasn't skiing fast enough.
 B She wasn't careful of other skiers.
 C She wasn't prepared properly.

4 After the accident, Marsha
 A took some medicine.
 B had an operation.
 C stayed in the hotel.

5 What did Marsha do for the rest of the holiday?
 A stayed in the hotel
 B read some books
 C visited local places

6 Marsha would like to
 A take up a different sport.
 B continue to learn to ski.
 C have a different instructor.

3 SPEAK Work in pairs. Ask and answer the questions.

1 Do you think skiing is dangerous? Why/Why not?
2 Have you ever hurt yourself when you were playing a sport?

Vocabulary Strong and weak adjectives

1 Which adjectives in the box mean extremely good and which mean extremely bad?

awful brilliant fantastic terrible

Strong and weak adjectives

Hot is a weak adjective, and ***boiling*** is the strong adjective.

We use words like *a little*, *a bit*, *quite*, *really*, *very* and *extremely* with **weak adjectives**.

We use words like *really* and *absolutely* with **strong adjectives**.

We can say:	
a little	*hot*
a bit	
quite	
really	
very	
extremely	

× We can't say:	
absolutely	*hot*

✓ We can say:	
absolutely	boiling
really	

× We can't say:	
a little	*boiling*
a bit	
quite	
very	
extremely	

2 Choose the correct alternative to complete the sentences.

1. The hospital was *absolutely* / *very* good. The doctors were friendly, and we didn't have to wait long.
2. I've got the flu and I've been in bed for a week. I feel *absolutely* / *a bit* awful.
3. I've been on a new diet for a month, and I feel *really* / *very* fantastic.
4. I felt *quite* / *absolutely* bad yesterday, so I didn't go to work.
5. Those pills are *really* / *absolutely* strong, so you should take them with food.

3 Find a strong adjective in the box which has a similar meaning to the weak adjectives (1–8). ONE word has TWO strong adjectives.

beautiful delighted enormous exhausted
freezing huge miserable shocked tiny

1 happy ______ 4 sad ______ 7 tired ______
2 surprised ______ 5 small ______ 8 pretty ______
3 cold ______ 6 big ______, ______

4 Complete the sentences using a strong adjective from Exercise 3.

1. It's ______ here in winter. You should wear a big coat when you go out.
2. Sam had to get up at 4 am to catch a flight, so now he's ______.
3. The children were absolutely ______ when their mother shouted at them. She'd never done that before, and certainly never in the middle of a shop like that!
4. The views on the journey were ______ – the mountains were so pretty!
5. I was absolutely ______ that all my family could come to lunch to celebrate my birthday with me. I couldn't stop smiling.
6. Our new house is really small, but the garden is ______ and I love it. There's lots of space for barbecue parties!

5 Go to the Additional materials on page 199.

Speaking Part 2 Extended turn

1 **SPEAK** Look at the photographs below. They show people with different health problems. Match the words in the box to the photographs.

appointment cold dentist off work pain sneeze tissues toothache

1

2
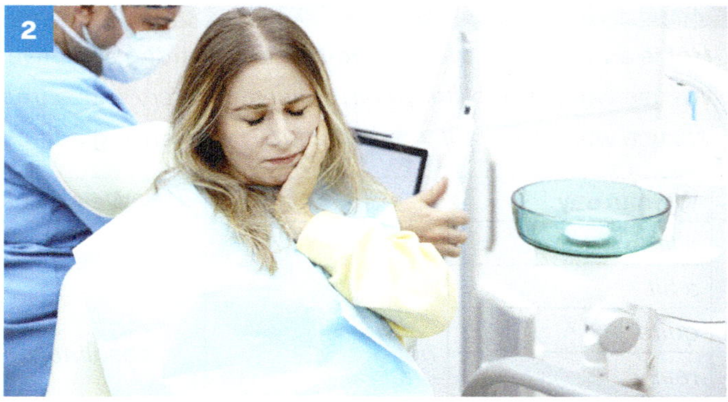

2 **SPEAK** Describe the photographs.

Student A: Look at photograph 1. Tell your partner what you can see in the photograph.

Student B: Look at photograph 2. Tell your partner what you can see in the photograph.

3 **SPEAK** Now change roles.

Listening Part 3 Gap fill

1 **SPEAK** Look at the photograph. Is this kind of activity something you would like to do?

2 10.2 You will hear a yoga instructor called David talking to new guests on a yoga weekend. For questions 1–6, write the correct answer in each gap. Write **one** or **two words** or a **number** or a **date** or **time**.

TALLTREES YOGA WEEKEND

For yoga classes: Wear **(1)** ....

Morning classes: **(2)** .... am in the garden

Breakfast: bread, yoghurt, fruit and **(3)** ....

Second yoga class: 11.30 am

Lunch: guests will **(4)** .... together

Activities: Saturday – walk through the forest
Sunday – go to the **(5)** .... for a painting class

Final class: 8 pm then have a **(6)** .... before bed

Bedtime: 10 pm

3 **SPEAK** Work in pairs. How can these things help people's health?

gardening going to museums spending time with friends walking holidays

Language focus Reported speech: questions

1 **Look at the extracts from the listening on page 150. Decide which is correct, a or b.**

1 a Amira asked me what you had any free time in the morning.
  b Amira asked me if you had any free time in the morning.

2 a The chef here has offered to teach us some vegetarian dishes.
  b The chef here has offered teach us some vegetarian dishes.

3 a Some of you also asked that we were doing in the afternoons.
  b Some of you also asked what we were doing in the afternoons.

2 **10.3 Listen and check your answers.**

3 **Match the extracts from Exercise 1 (1–3) to the direct questions below (a–c).**

a "What are we doing in the afternoons?"
b "Do we have any free time in the morning?"
c "Do you want me to teach you some vegetarian dishes?"

4 **Look at the examples in Exercise 1 again. Match each reported speech structure below (1–3) to a rule (a–c).**

1 *yes/no* questions
2 *wh-* questions
3 offers/requests

a reporting verb + *wh-* question word + clause
b reporting verb + *to* infinitive
c reporting verb + *if* + clause

5 **Go to Ready for Grammar on page 230 for rules, explanations and further practice.**

6 **Put the words in brackets in the correct order to make complete sentences.**

1 My father (**drive / to / offered**) ________________ me to the airport.
2 Jack (**if / asked / had / she / read / her**) ________________ all the Harry Potter books.
3 Mr Jones (**what / us / learnt / asked / had / we**) ________________ in class the day before.
4 The shop assistant (**needed / if / asked / we**) ________________ any help choosing some clothes.
5 The tour guide (**where / asked / were/ the tourists / they**) ________________ from.

7 **Rewrite the questions in reported speech using the information in brackets.**

1 Do you eat healthy food? (Your doctor asked you)
____
2 Can you buy some more coffee, please? (You asked your flatmate Lina).
____
3 Where do you go running? (Your friend Amanda asked you)
____
4 What are you listening to? (Daniel asked you and your friends)
____
5 Would you like me to help you? (Your English teacher asked your class)
____

8 **SPEAK Work in groups of three.**

Student A: Ask Student B a question about Student C.
Student B: Change the question to reported speech.
Student C: Answer the question. Then change roles and repeat.

Student A to Student B: "Has Emma ever eaten octopus?"
Student B to Student C: "Vanessa asked if you had ever eaten octopus?"
Student C: "No, I haven't."

Writing Part 2 Article

1 **SPEAK** Work in groups. Make a list of things that keep you healthy. Then, tell the group which ones you do and which ones you don't do, and why.

2 Read the Writing Part 2 task and the plan below. Answer the questions.

1 Does the plan answer all the questions?

2 Is there any extra information that should not be there?

You see this notice on an English-language website.

> **Articles wanted!**
>
> **Staying healthy**
>
> How healthy do you think you are?
>
> What do people tell you about how to stay healthy?
>
> Do you follow this advice? Why/Why not?
>
> The best articles will be published on our website next month.

Write your article in about 100 words.

How healthy? – Very healthy. Why? Because I don't drink fizzy drinks. Just water and juice. I play football twice a week and I walk to work and back.

What someone said – Doctor: "Eat vegetables or salad with every meal." "Don't drink too much coffee."

Do I follow advice? – Some, – don't like eating vegetables or salad. But, follow advice to not drink coffee.
Plus – I exercise every day.

3 Read the following article. Does it follow the plan in Exercise 2?

HEALTHY HABITS HEALTHY LIFE!

Have you ever watched TV and eaten pizza all day? It's fun, but it isn't good for your body. To stay fit, it's very important to move around and eat healthy food.

I'm very fit because I love playing football and I play twice a week. I walk to work and back too! I also drink a lot of water and I don't drink fizzy drinks. They're very bad for you.

Recently, my doctor told me to eat vegetables with every meal and not to drink too much coffee. For me, it's easy to drink less coffee, but I don't like eating vegetables. I do some exercise every day though, and that is good for me!

4 Read the model answer in Exercise 3 again. Find examples of the following things:

1 title
2 direct question
3 reasons for answers
4 reported speech

5 To develop your ideas, it is important to give reasons for your answers. Choose the correct answers for you and give reasons.

1 I *do* / *don't do* a lot of exercise because ...
2 I *eat* / *don't eat* vegetables because ...
3 I *drink* / *don't drink* fizzy drinks because ...
4 I *try* / *don't try* to ... because ...
5 I *follow* / *don't follow* advice about staying healthy because ...

6 Write your own answer to the Writing Part 2 task in Exercise 2.

For more information about writing articles, see page 195.

Don't forget!

Try to think of an interesting title that will make the reader want to read your article.

10 REVIEW

Language focus Reported speech

In each sentence there are ONE or TWO mistakes. Find the mistakes and correct them.

1 Jona told me that he seen Pavel and his family at the cinema the day previous.
2 She asked that I wanted tea or coffee for breakfast.
3 I called Richard and he said me that he is walking home from work.
4 My teacher offered give me some extra worksheets to prepare for the exam.
5 My friend told we that she will come to visit next summer.
6 My parents told to me no to open the presents before my birthday.
7 She told that she didn't want to come to my party.
8 My brother asked me go to the chemist's to buy him some pills.

Vocabulary Health

Complete each gap with one word. The first letter has been given.

HOME BLOG ARCHIVE ABOUT

Feeling sick?

Winter is the time for people to get colds and the flu.

If you notice that you **(1) h**__________ a temperature or a cough, don't worry. You don't need to **(2) m**__________ an appointment with your doctor unless you feel very bad. Just **(3) t**__________ a pill to lower your temperature, **(4) g**__________ some rest at home and drink lots of water.

If you think you have the flu, try to **(5) t**__________ some time off work to recover. If you are worried, **(6) g**__________ to the chemist's. They can recommend something to help you feel better.

Reading Part 6 Open cloze

For questions 1–6, read the diary entry below and think of the word which best fits each gap. Use only one word in each gap.

The CAMINO de SANTIAGO

The Camino de Santiago in northern Spain is probably one of the (1) .... famous walks in the world. Many people from many different countries come to Spain to do it. Just last year I decided (2) .... walk the path. I had always wanted to, and I thought it would be a great way to get fit too. I've (3) .... training for the journey ever since, and I'm fitter (4) .... ever.

I am writing this from the start (5) .... the route now. Tomorrow will be my first day of walking the Camino de Santiago. The path is around 800 kilometres long and it is not easy. It will take me around 30 days. (6) .... I can finish this walk, I'll be so happy! This is the start of a great adventure!

Writing Part 1 Email

Read this email from your English-speaking friend Emily and the notes you have made.

From: Emily
Subject: Next weekend
Hi,
I'm really looking forward to seeing you next weekend. ← Me too!
We had planned to go to the beach, but as you know, I've broken my arm, so I can't swim. What other things can we do? ← Suggest …
I hope it won't be too difficult for you, but could you pick me up from the station please? My train arrives at 10 am on Saturday morning. ← Of course!
Also, what would you like me to bring? ← Tell Emily.
See you soon!
Emily

Reply to Emily using **all the notes**. Write your **email** in about **100 words**.

For more information on writing emails, see pages 192–193.

Pronunciation Word endings

1 10.4 Listen to the pairs of words and write the missing final letters. Write one or two letters.

1 pain / pain___
2 neck / nex___
3 feel / fiel___
4 lie / li___ ___
5 goal / go___ ___
6 may / ma___ ___
7 fine / fin___

2 10.4 Listen again. Repeat the words.

3 10.5 Listen to some of the words from Exercise 1 again. Circle the words you hear.

4 SPEAK Work in pairs. Play Battleships.

BATTLESHIPS

Draw YOUR ships on the grid. Put 4 small ships (1 square for each), 3 medium ships (2 squares for each) and 1 large ship (3 squares).

HOW TO PLAY:

Student A: Say a square to Student B, for example *field – pain*.

Student B: Say *hit*, *miss* or *sunk* (if it is the whole ship).

Student A: Mark the grid with 'x' for hit and 'o' for miss.

YOUR SHIPS

	fiel___	nex___	li___	fin___	mai___	gol___	pain___
neck							
pain							
lie							
feel							
may							
goal							
fine							

YOUR PARTNER'S SHIPS

	fiel___	nex___	li___	fin___	mai___	gol___	pain___
neck							
pain							
lie							
feel							
may							
goal							
fine							

READY FOR SPEAKING

Introduction

There are four parts to the B1 Preliminary Speaking paper. The test is normally done in pairs and lasts 12 minutes. Sometimes the test is done in a group of three, which lasts 17 minutes. There are always two examiners: the interlocutor, who asks you questions and gives you instructions, and the assessor, who just listens.

Speaking Part 1 Interview — Total time: 2 minutes

Part 1 is an opportunity to talk about yourself. The interlocutor asks you questions about everyday topics – your likes and dislikes, your friends and family, your work/studies and daily routine. In Part 1, you speak to the interlocutor, not to your partner.

1 Match the sentence beginnings 1–5 to the endings a–e to make Part 1 Speaking questions.

1 Do you work	a do last weekend?
2 What did you	b go on your next holiday?
3 What kind of shows	c or are you a student?
4 Where do you think you will	d favourite kind of music?
5 What is your	e do you enjoy watching on TV?

2 Use the following prompts to write your own Part 1 questions.

- Which do you prefer: ... or ...?
- What's your favourite type of ...?
- What did you do last ...?
- How often do you ...?
- Tell us about ...

Which do you prefer: summer or winter?

Tell us about a TV series you like.

3 Work in pairs. Choose a total of five questions from Exercises 1 and 2, and then discuss them with a partner. If your partner doesn't give full answers, ask them *Why/ Why not*? This will encourage them to extend their answers.

4 0.6 Watch or listen to two students, Pilar and Carlos, doing Part 1 of the Speaking test and answer the following questions.

1 Does the interlocutor ask any of the same questions that you prepared in Exercise 2?
2 What does Carlos do when he doesn't understand one of the questions?
3 What advice would you give Pilar to help her improve her performance?

Don't forget!

- It's okay to be nervous! This is normal. The questions in this part of the test are designed to be simple, giving you the opportunity to relax and get comfortable.
- If you don't understand a question, it's okay to ask the examiner to repeat it. You don't lose marks for this.
- Show the examiners how good your English is by extending your answers. Provide relevant reasons and examples. The examiners can only assess the English they hear!
- If you're not quite sure how to answer a question, start by saying *Well* ... or *That's a good question*. This gives you a little more time to think.
- Don't memorise answers, but be prepared to talk about yourself – what you study or do for work, where you live and so on.

Speaking Part 2 Extended turn — Total time: 3 minutes

In Part 2, you have one minute to describe a photograph. You and your partner each describe a different photograph. In general, the photographs show people doing everyday activities in familiar situations.

1 **Student A: Look at photograph 1. It shows people in a supermarket. Tell your partner what you can see in the photograph.**

2 **Student B: Look at photograph 2. It shows people at the beach. Tell your partner what you can see in the photograph.**

3 **0.7 Watch or listen to Pilar and Carlos doing the Part 2 task and answer the following questions.**

1. Do they talk about the same things you mentioned? Do they talk about anything you didn't mention?
2. What happens when Pilar can't think of anything else to say?
3. What do Pilar and Carlos do well?
4. What could they do to improve their marks?

1

2

What to expect in the exam

- In this part of the test, you talk to the examiner, not your partner.
- You have one minute to describe your picture.
- The examiner will stop you when a minute has passed.

How to go about it

- First, listen carefully to the instructions.
- Don't join in while your partner describes their photograph. Just listen quietly.
- When it is your turn, describe everything you can see in the picture. Imagine you are describing the photograph to somebody who can't see it. Don't worry about the time – just keep talking until the examiner stops you.
- Summarise what you can see in general and then go into more detail about the people and place. That way your description is clear and organised.

4 **While describing the pictures in Part 2, it's important to use a good range of vocabulary. Write the words in the box in the correct category.**

adult ~~autumn~~ bookshelf child cloudy dining room kitchen living room skirt sofa spring summer stormy sunny table teenager T-shirt trousers

1 seasons	*autumn*
2 weather	
3 furniture	
4 types of room	
5 age	
6 clothing	

5 **Work in pairs. Add at least one more word to categories 1–6 in Exercise 4.**

Useful language

Saying what you can see

In the picture, I can see ...

There is/are ...

She/He has ... / They have ...

Saying where things are

At the top/bottom ...

On the right/left ...

In the middle ...

Behind / Opposite / Next to ...

Paraphrasing

I don't remember how to say it but ...

It's a kind/type/sort of ...

It's a thing you use to ...

It's a place where you ...

It's a person who ...

6 **Go to the Additional materials on page 201 and do the Speaking Part 2 task. Use the different categories in Exercise 4 and the phrases in the Useful language box to help you describe the photographs.**

Speaking Part 3 Discussion   Total time: 4 minutes

In Part 3, the interlocutor gives you some images and you and your partner have three minutes to discuss a situation. In this part of the test, you talk to your partner, not the examiner.

How to go about it

- Listen carefully to the instructions. It's important to understand the situation before you start discussing it.
- Discuss the options and work together with your partner to decide which option is best. Give reasons to support your points.
- During the task, discuss at least three of the options and be careful not to reach a decision too fast. You have 3–4 minutes for this part. Keep talking until the interlocutor stops you.
- In this part of the test, you are in charge of the interaction. The interlocutor will not help you unless communication completely breaks down, so it's important to help your partner if they start to struggle and don't know what to say.
- Don't worry if you don't agree on one of the options by the end of the task. This won't affect your mark. You just have to show that you made an effort to reach a decision or find a solution.

1 **SPEAK** What ways of exercising are popular in your country?

2 Look at the pictures on page 161. A young man wants to get fit and healthy. He is looking for a new way to exercise before or after he goes to work. In pairs, discuss the activities using some of the adjectives in the box below.

cheap   convenient   expensive   fun   healthy   relaxing   sociable

3 Now do the exercise in the Useful language box below.

Useful language

Write the correct heading (a–c) in each section (1–3).

a asking your partner a question   **b** making a decision   **c** making suggestions

1 ______________________

I think ... would be a good option.
I think he/she/they should ...
If I were him/her/them, I would ...

2 ______________________

What do you think?
What/How about ...?
Why/Why not?

3 ______________________

So, it seems like we agree that ... is the best option.
So, what do you think? Shall we go with ...?
Let's go for ... then.

4 **SPEAK** Now do the speaking task on page 161. A young man wants to get fit and healthy. He is looking for a new way to exercise before or after he goes to work. Here are some activities he could try. Talk together about the different ways to exercise, and say which would be best. Use the expressions in the Useful language box to help you.

Activities to help the man get fit and healthy

5 **Discuss the questions below with your partner. Give specific examples from your conversation.**

Did you and your partner:

- keep speaking for 3–4 minutes without stopping?
- discuss at least three of the options?
- ask each other questions?
- take turns, giving each other the same opportunities to speak?
- make a sincere effort to reach a decision?

6 **0.8 Now watch or listen to Pilar and Carlos doing Part 3 and answer the questions.**

1 How does Carlos help Pilar during Part 3?
2 How many of the options do they discuss?
3 Do Pilar and Carlos reach a decision at the end of the task?

Speaking Part 4 General conversation Total time: 3 minutes

In Part 4, the interlocutor asks you questions related to the topic of the Part 3 task. For some questions, you answer individually; for other questions, you have to talk together with your partner.

Don't forget!

It's important to give full answers to the questions. Provide reasons or examples to support your points.

1 Discuss the questions below with your partner.

1 Do you enjoy doing exercise?
2 Is there a way of doing exercise you would like to try?
3 What ways of doing exercise are popular in your country?
4 Is it better to do exercise alone or with friends?
5 Is it important to do exercise every day?

2 0.9 Watch or listen to Pilar and Carlos doing Part 4 and answer the following questions.

1 What does the interlocutor do when Carlos does not give full answers to the questions?
2 How well do Pilar and Carlos interact with each other?

3 Pilar and Carlos agree and disagree with each other's ideas. This is a good way to improve your mark for *interactive communication.* With a partner, practise agreeing and disagreeing with statements 1–5 below. Use some of the expressions in the useful language box.

1 Cycling in the city is dangerous.
2 Going to the gym is boring.
3 Doing exercise makes you feel happy.
4 After a stressful day, doing exercise is good way to relax.
5 If you eat a healthy diet, you don't need to do exercise.

Useful language

Agreeing and disagreeing

I agree/disagree.
You're right.
I'm not sure if I agree with you about that.

Giving opinions

For me ...
In my opinion ...
I think / don't think ...

Talking about likes and dislikes

I prefer to ...
I really like ...
To be honest, I'm not very keen on ...

Giving reasons support your points

Because ...
That way ...
If he/she/they ... then he/she/they will ...

11

HOUSE AND HOME

KEY LANGUAGE

Passive
Have/Get something done
Buildings
Household objects
Chores

PRONUNCIATION

The schwa /ə/

EXAM PRACTICE

Reading Parts 2 & 5
Writing Parts 1 & 2
Listening Parts 1 & 2
Speaking Parts 1, 2 & 4

Speaking Part 1 Interview

Work with a partner. Discuss the questions.

1 Do you prefer living in a city or in the countryside? Why?
2 Would you prefer to live on your own or with others? Why?
3 How important is it for you to like your neighbours?
4 Which is your favourite room in your house? Why?
5 How long have you lived in your current home?

Speaking Part 2 Extended turn

Describe the picture. Use the phrases in the box to help you.

fantastic view(s)	enormous room
brilliant location	beautiful furniture

11 HOUSE AND HOME

Vocabulary Buildings

1 Label the images of buildings (1–8) with the words in the box.

apartment/flat   block of flats   cottage   monument
office block   palace   skyscraper   tower

1

2

3

4

5

6

7

8

2 SPEAK **Work in pairs. Discuss the questions below.**

1 Which of these buildings
   - do people usually live in? Which would you like to live in? Why?
   - do people work in? What types of buildings do you / your family members work in?
   - do people often visit when sightseeing? What kinds of buildings do you like to visit?

2 Who lives in a palace? What would be good and bad about living in a palace?

3 Where can you usually see a cottage? Would you like to live in this type of home? Why/Why not?

Writing Part 1 Email

1 SPEAK Work in pairs. Discuss the questions.

1 How would you describe the area you live in?
2 What do you like most about your home and the area, and what do you like least?

2 Read the following Writing Part 1 task and the model answer. How is Sofia's description similar to your area? How is it different?

Read this email from your English-speaking friend Arnie and the notes you have made.

From: Arnie
Subject: Your new home
Hi,
I know you have moved to a new town. Do you like your new home? ← Yes!
I'm so excited for you! What is the area like? And what is your new flat like? ← Tell Arnie.
Do you prefer it to where you used to live? ← Yes, because …
I'd love to come and visit you soon. Let me know if you would like me to come and stay. ← Yes.
Write soon!
Arnie

Write your email in about 100 words.

Hi Arnie!
Thanks for your email. How are you?
I really love my new flat and the neighbourhood where I live. There are lots of skyscrapers and so many cars **(1)** . / , people and shops. My flat has two bedrooms and it is on the 20th floor of a building in the city centre. It's fantastic **(2)** ? / !
I prefer it here to my village in France **(3)** , / . It was a bit quiet there and I enjoy having lots of things to do. New York is perfect for that.
You can visit me soon. Can you come next month **(4)** . / ? I'll show you the best places to go.
Speak soon,
Sofia

3 Look at the model answer in Exercise 2. For 1–4, choose the correct punctuation mark.

4 In the B1 Preliminary exam, you must write about all the points in the input email. Underline where the email reply in Exercise 2 does this.

5 Write your own answer to the task in Exercise 1. Write your email in about 100 words.

Useful language

Adding details

You can add details by using quantifiers and intensifiers e.g.

a lot of skyscrapers — *a bit quiet*
so many cars — *really love*
lots of things to do

Complete the sentences so they are true about where you live.

1 In my area, there are lots of ___________.
2 There aren't many ___________.
3 I really love the ___________ in my area.
4 I think my home is a bit ___________.

Don't forget!

Correct punctuation is important in writing. It helps your reader understand when a statement ends, and when you are asking a question.

For more information about writing emails, see pages 192–193.

Don't forget!

Remember that you need to match ALL the information in 1–5 to the descriptions A–H. Some of the distractors may have SOME information that matches but not ALL the information.

Reading Part 2 Matching

1 **SPEAK** Work in pairs. Quickly read the descriptions of places to live on page 167 and tell your partner which place you would most like to live in and why.

2 Read the eight descriptions of homes to rent (A–H). For the people 1–5, decide which place would be the most suitable.

1 **Chris and Katie** have just got married and they want a cheap, small flat as their first home. They love going out and having fun, and they also have a puppy.

2 **Deborah** has retired and wants to sell her large four-bedroom home and rent something smaller without a garden. She enjoys history and countryside walks, but also wants to have easy access to the city.

3 **Hannah and Daryl** are looking for a family home for themselves and their three children. They'd like a place with plenty of space for the children to play, but that is also near the local facilities.

4 **Raúl** wants to rent a place near his office in the city so that he doesn't have to travel so far to work every day. He wants a small place that he can use during the week, and then spend weekends at his larger home with his family.

5 **Naveen** is looking for a place for him and his father. His father has difficulty walking, but loves to sit and relax in the garden, while Naveen needs easy access to the city centre for his work.

Dream Homes

A MILLGATE TOWER

Brand new building! This huge penthouse apartment is located in the city centre with great views of the city and just minutes away from the river. The apartment has four bedrooms, one large family bathroom and a second shower room, and a garage. A gym will be opened on the ground floor next month. Pets allowed.

£2500 per month

B 12 LANDSDOWNE ROAD

This is a beautiful house just 20 minutes' walk from the centre of town. The house has a large kitchen and living room, as well as a good-sized garden. There are six bedrooms and two bathrooms. In a quiet location, this house is also a short walk away from shops and schools.

£1700 per month

C 12A PITCHFORD COURT

This is a truly wonderful two-bedroom ground-floor flat in a quiet part of town. It is just minutes away from the train station with many direct trains to the city. It has a garden and a large open-plan kitchen and living room. The flat is being decorated at the moment. No pets allowed.

£900 per month

D FLAT 10A PORTLAND PLACE

This is a stylish one-bedroom apartment in the city centre. The flat has one bathroom and a small balcony. The kitchen and bathroom are new, and the building is very modern. The building is cleaned once a week (included in the rent). It is five minutes' walk from a main train station and has great transport links.

£1050 per month

E DAYTON MANOR

The best house in the area! This is a large country house, and it was built in 1800. The house has seven bedrooms, three bathrooms and a large garden with swimming pool. The property is in the countryside with views of the hills and sea. The nearest town is a thirty-minute drive away. Pets allowed.

£2800 per month

F 6C ADDINGTON WAY

A lovely, one-bedroom flat in the town centre. The flat is above a shop and near all the bars and restaurants in town. There is a small, shared garden at the back of the building which is perfect for relaxing or barbecues! Pets allowed.

£700 per month

G FLAT 11 CHESTERFIELD COURT

This is a great one-bedroom, one-bathroom second-floor flat with a balcony. The building has a lift to all floors. The flat is located on the edge of a quiet village, with great views of the countryside. The town has a few shops and a café, and there are buses and trains to the city.

£675 per month

H 27 PEMBERTON ROAD

Lovely ground-floor flat with a garden in a small, historic village. It has one bedroom, one bathroom and a large lounge. There is a train station in the next village, which is a 16-minute drive away. Pets allowed. Ideal for elderly people or people looking for a quiet life in the countryside.

£1000 per month

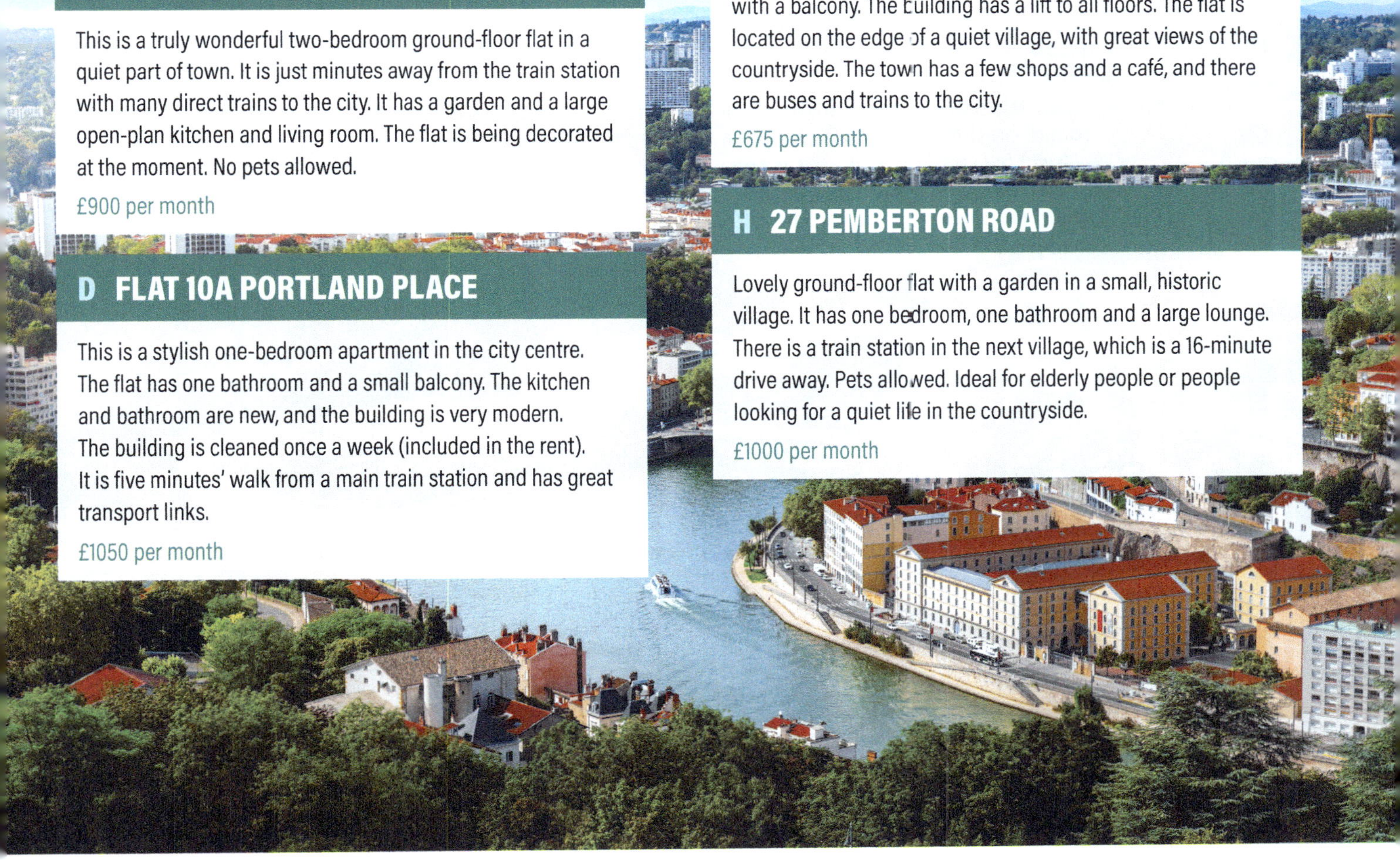

3 SPEAK Work in groups. What would you dream home be like?

My dream home would be a house. It would have two bedrooms and an office. It would have a big, bright kitchen and a small garden.

Language focus Passive

1 **Choose the correct options to complete the sentences from the reading text.**

1 A gym *opens* / *will be opened* on the ground floor next month.
2 The building *cleans* / *is cleaned* once a week.
3 This is a large country house, and it *built* / *was built* in 1800.

2 **Now check your answers in the texts on page 167.**

3 **Complete the rules on how to form the passive in the table below.**

Present simple passive	*is*/*are* + past participle
Past simple passive	**(1)** ____________/*were* + past participle
Future simple passive	**(2)** ____________ + *be* + past participle

4 **Read the sentences in Exercise 1 again and answer the questions.**

1 Do we know who does the actions? yes / no
2 Is it important to know who does the action? yes / no

5 **Go to Ready for Grammar on page 232 for further rules, explanations and practice.**

6 **Complete the text with the present simple passive or past simple passive form of the verbs in brackets.**

WOULD YOU LIVE HERE?

On social media, the Lodge on Ellidaey Island, Iceland **(1)** ____________ (*know*) as the world's loneliest house. This is because it's the only building on the island and miles away from other places. The Lodge **(2)** ____________ (*build*) on the island in 1953. Today, it **(3)** ____________ (*use*) for tourism, but as it is the only house there, not many people go! The island **(4)** ____________ (*visit*) by people interested in wildlife and who want some peace and quiet.

Places like this **(5)** ____________ (*talk*) about a lot online, and the Lodge is no different. Many people believe it **(6)** ____________ (*give*) to Björk, a famous Icelandic singer, but that isn't true. However, there is one mystery. Why **(7)** ____________ the Lodge ____________ (*surround*) by a fence? Who, or what, do they want to keep out when there are no neighbours on the whole island?

7 **Complete the quiz questions with the past participle form of the verbs in the box.**

born build film use watch

CAN YOU THINK OF...

1 a famous building that was ____________ more than 500 years ago?
2 movies that were ____________ in your country?
3 sports that are ____________ on TV by thousands of people every week?
4 famous people that were ____________ in your country?
5 modern technological inventions that are ____________ by lots of people every day?

8 **SPEAK** **Work in pairs. Answer the questions in the quiz in Exercise 7.**

Vocabulary Household objects

1 SPEAK Look at the pictures. Match the words in the box (a–q) with objects in the pictures. Are there any objects that can go in more than one room?

a air conditioner / heater **b** armchair **c** bath **d** cupboard
e dishwasher **f** drawers **g** fridge **h** lamp **i** microwave **j** mirror
k oven **l** sink **m** shower **n** sofa **o** taps **p** toilet **q** wardrobe

1
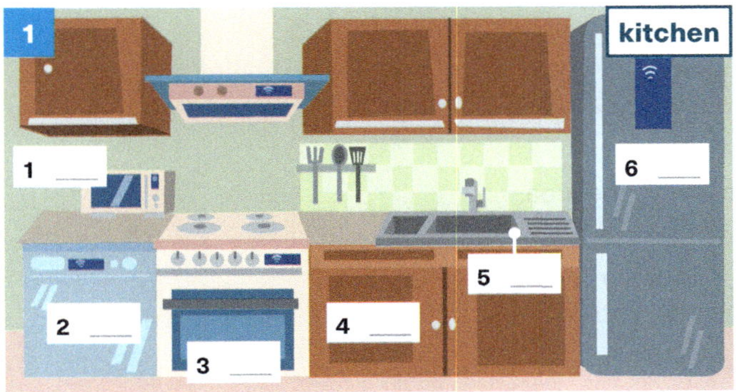

2

3

4

2 SPEAK Choose one of the rooms in your house or apartment. In pairs, tell your partner which items it has in it.

In my kitchen, there's an oven, a fridge, a sink, a dishwasher, some cupboards and drawers, but we haven't got a microwave.

Vocabulary Chores

1 Choose the correct options to complete the blog.

Since I've been at university, I've realised how many chores there are to do in my new apartment. I (1) ***make* / *do* the bed** every morning and in the evening, I make sure I (2) ***put* / *make*** all my clothes **away**. My flatmate, Carl is great. He loves cooking and always (3) ***gives* / *makes* dinner** for both of us, but he usually (4) ***makes* / *puts*** quite a big **mess** in the kitchen. I always (5) ***tidy* / *arrange* up** the kitchen after dinner and (6) ***do* / *clean* the washing up**. I also (7) ***collect* / *throw* away** the **rubbish**. We (8) ***do* / *make* the shopping** together every weekend, and we try to spend just £30 a week on food. We also make sure we (9) ***switch* / *cut* things off** like the TV or the computer. We don't want to waste money! We don't like (10) ***doing* / *tidying* the washing** though, and often leave it until we have no clean clothes left!

2 Complete the quiz with the correct verbs from Exercise 1.

3 SPEAK Work in pairs. Ask and answer the quiz questions.

4 SPEAK Work in pairs. Ask and answer the questions.

1 Which chores do you prefer to do?
2 Which chores do you dislike the most?
3 Do you keep your house tidy?
4 When do you usually do the housework?

In your house, who

1 *tidies* up the bathroom?
2 ______ breakfast?
3 ______ the shopping?
4 ______ the washing up?
5 ______ away clean clothes?

Listening Part 2 Multiple choice

11.1 You will hear people talking in six different situations. For questions 1–6, choose the best answer (A, B or C).

1 You will hear two flatmates talking about a washing machine.
What do they agree about?

A They should try to fix the old one.

B They will need to spend a lot of money.

C They should look online for a new one.

2 You will hear part of a town meeting.
How does the mayor feel about the new office building?

A It will be good for employment.

B It might hurt family businesses in the area.

C They should change the location.

3 You will hear a man asking for directions.
The woman suggests that the man should

A call for help.

B go another day.

C get a taxi.

4 You will hear two friends discussing their neighbours.
What is the problem?

A They are unfriendly.

B They are loud.

C They are messy.

5 You will hear a tour guide talking about a castle.
The location for the castle was chosen because

A it was safe.

B it was near a town.

C it was a special place.

6 You will hear two people talking about cleaning their houses.
They both think that

A it's a boring job.

B it's worth paying someone.

C it's better to do it daily.

Speaking Part 4 General conversation

1 SPEAK Work in pairs. Take it in turns to ask and answer the questions.

1 Do you prefer to spend your free time at home or outside the house?

2 Would you prefer to live in a modern house or one that was built over 100 years ago?

3 What is important to you when choosing a town or city to live in? Why?

4 Would you rather live in a house or a flat?

5 What do you think houses will be like in the future?

Useful language

Phrases to give yourself time to think

That's a good/interesting question.

Let me think ...

Give me a moment to think about that.

Let me give you an example ...

I'm not sure, but ...

Well, some people think that ...

2 SPEAK Work in pairs. Go to the Additional materials on page 200.

Language focus *Have/Get* something done

1 **Look at the sentences below. In each sentence, does the speaker want to repair the machine themself or ask someone else to repair it?**

1 *... maybe we should try to* ***have it repaired*** *before we buy a new one.*
2 *... maybe we should try to* ***repair it*** *before we buy a new one.*

2 **Match sentences (1–4) to the person doing the action (a–b).**

1 I had the car cleaned yesterday.
2 I cleaned the car yesterday.
3 We painted the garage.
4 We got the garage painted.

a The speaker did the action.
b Another person did the action.

3 **Choose the correct options to complete the rule for *have/get something done*.**

We use the verbs *get* or **(1)** ***be*** / ***have*** + (something) + **(2) past participle** / **past simple** to talk about something that another person does for us.

4 **Write the words in the correct order to make sentences or questions.**

1 pizza / last / get / night. / delivered / didn't / We
We didn't get pizza delivered last night.
2 decorated? / has / Amanda / her / had / kitchen
____
3 professional. / had / taken / photo / they / by / a / their
____
4 you / cleaned? / did / your / jacket / where / get
____
5 alarm / are / their / having / our / an / neighbours / installed / in / house.
______________________________.
6 get / going / tomorrow. / David / his / tested / eyes / is / to
______________________________.

5 **Go to Ready for Grammar on page 232 for rules, explanations and further practice.**

6 **Use the prompts to make sentences that they are true for you or someone you know.**

house / clean: My parents have their house cleaned once a week.

1 hair / cut
2 mobile phone / steal
3 car / fix
4 food / deliver / house
5 nails / paint

7 **SPEAK Work in pairs. Tell your partner your sentences from Exercise 6. Ask each other follow-up questions.**

A: I get my hair cut once a month.
B: Do you always go to the same hairdresser's?

Listening Part 1 Multiple choice

1 11.2 You will hear people talking in seven different situations. For questions 1–7, choose the best answer (A, B or C).

Don't forget

- There will be words to distract you, so listen carefully to the whole dialogue before you choose the answer.
- You will hear each recording twice. The second time you listen, check your answers.

1 Which hotel room does the woman choose?

A

B

C

2 What does the car need?

A

B

C

3 Where is the saucepan?

A

B

C

4 Where is the man's new flat located?

A

B

C

5 How much does the company charge per hour?

A

B

C

6 Where do they decide to put the lamp?

A

B

C

7 Who does the building belong to?

A

B

C

2 SPEAK Work in pairs. Discuss the questions.

1 How often do you stay in a hotel?
2 Do you like staying in hotels? Why/why not?
3 What would you like to have in your room if you stayed in a hotel?

11 REVIEW

Language focus Passive

Complete the sentences with a passive form of the verb in brackets.

1 Starting next week, the rubbish ________________ (*collect*) on Wednesday mornings.
2 My brother ________________ (*take*) to hospital yesterday because he broke his arm.
3 The bathroom ________________ (*not clean*) before you arrived, so I'll do it now.
4 The packages ________________ (*send*) last week, but Ali didn't receive them.
5 A new cinema ________________ (*build*) in the city centre at the moment.
6 The contract ________________ (*sign*) tomorrow morning in our office.

Vocabulary Chores

Complete the texts with the correct form of the verbs in the box.

do (x 3) make (x 3) switch throw tidy

Tom is very organised. Every morning he **(1)** ____________ his bed before going to work. In the evening he **(2)** ____________ his room and puts his clothes in the wardrobe. He never **(3)** ____________ a mess in his flat!

Oleana enjoys cooking. She **(4)** ____________ dinner every day, but she doesn't **(5)** ____________ the washing up because she has a dishwasher. On Saturday mornings, she **(6)** ____________ the shopping in a market near her house.

Kai likes to save money. He doesn't **(7)** ____________ any food away and he always remembers to **(8)** ____________ off the lights in his house. He **(9)** ____________ the washing once a week and only washes the clothes that are dirty.

Reading Part 5 Multiple-choice cloze

Read the text and for questions 1–6, choose which answer (A, B, C or D) best fits each gap.

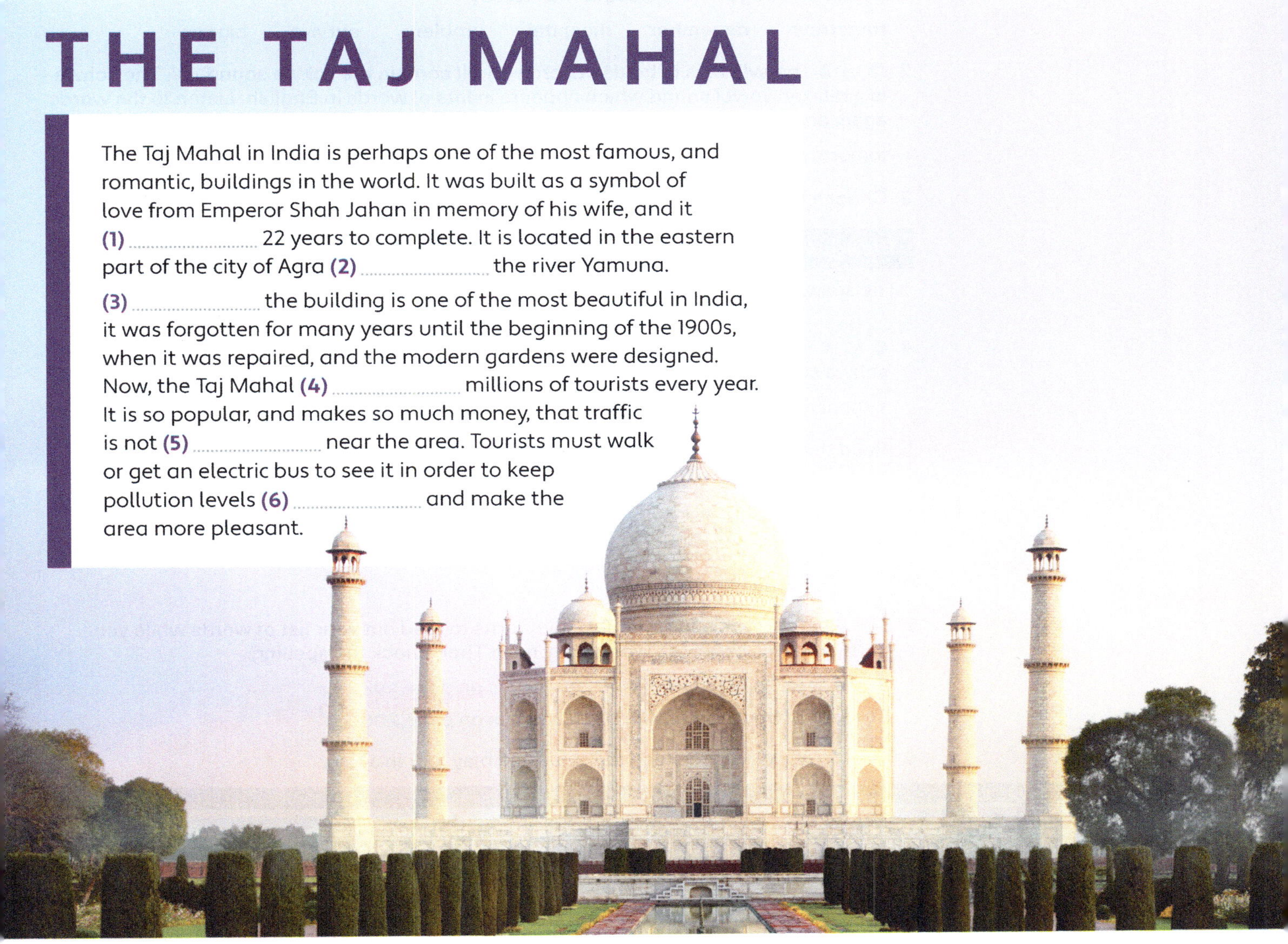

THE TAJ MAHAL

The Taj Mahal in India is perhaps one of the most famous, and romantic, buildings in the world. It was built as a symbol of love from Emperor Shah Jahan in memory of his wife, and it **(1)** .... 22 years to complete. It is located in the eastern part of the city of Agra **(2)** .... the river Yamuna.

(3) .... the building is one of the most beautiful in India, it was forgotten for many years until the beginning of the 1900s, when it was repaired, and the modern gardens were designed. Now, the Taj Mahal **(4)** .... millions of tourists every year. It is so popular, and makes so much money, that traffic is not **(5)** .... near the area. Tourists must walk or get an electric bus to see it in order to keep pollution levels **(6)** .... and make the area more pleasant.

1	**A** passed	**B** ran	**C** took	**D** had
2	**A** about	**B** along	**C** among	**D** against
3	**A** Because	**B** After	**C** Unless	**D** Although
4	**A** assists	**B** attends	**C** attracts	**D** admires
5	**A** supported	**B** allowed	**C** driven	**D** involved
6	**A** low	**B** pure	**C** last	**D** close

Writing Part 2 Article

You see this notice on an English-language website.

Articles wanted!

Your dream house

- What kind of house or apartment would you like to live in?
- Where would you like to live?
- How would you decorate it?

Write an article answering these questions and we will put it in our online magazine.

Write your article in about 100 words.

For more information about writing articles, see page 195.

Pronunciation The schwa /ə/

1 11.3 Listen and repeat the words. Pay attention to the sound of the syllables in bold. What do you notice about the words?

tomorrow remem**ber** hospi**tal** prob**lem** **sur**vive big**ger**

2 11.3 The syllables in bold in Exercise 1 all contain the schwa sound /ə/. The schwa is a relaxed vowel sound which appears in lots of words in English. Listen to the words again and underline the stress in each word.

tomorrow remember hospital problem survive bigger

3 Choose the best word to complete the rule about the schwa.

The schwa

The schwa only appears in ***stressed / unstressed*** syllables.

4 11.4 Some words have more than one schwa sound. Listen and underline the schwa sounds.

1 banana 2 comfortable 3 America 4 accurate 5 possible

5 Read the text aloud and underline where you think the 20 schwa sounds are.

Yesterday I went to London because I wanted to buy a present for my brother. I visited a lot of shops, but I couldn't find anything suitable. Finally, I saw an amazing pair of trainers, so I bought them.

6 11.5 Now listen and check.

7 SPEAK Work with a partner. Take it in turns to read out your list of words while your partner writes down the words they hear. Then check the spelling.

Student A: Go to the Additional materials on page 198.

Student B: Go to the Additional materials on page 200.

8 SPEAK Work in pairs. Read the rules and play four in a row.

FOUR IN A ROW

If you pronounce a word correctly, you win the space and you can cross it out on the board.
You must get FOUR spaces in a row to win.
Remember, you need to stop your partner winning four spaces in a row.

extra	magazine	banana	computer	cousin
leisure	tonight	correct	survive	disagree
stadium	happen	together	stomach	alone
remember	enormous	communicate	exercise	given
again	machine	arrive	condition	problem

12 TECHNOLOGY TODAY

KEY LANGUAGE

Third conditional
Future continuous
Computers and devices
Changes and amounts
Knowledge and invention

PRONUNCIATION

Connected speech: linking

EXAM PRACTICE

Reading Parts 4 & 5
Writing Part 2
Listening Parts 2 & 3
Speaking Parts 1 & 2

Speaking Part 1 Interview

Work with a partner. Discuss the questions.

1 How does technology help you with your daily life?
2 How has travel changed in the past 100 years?
3 How do science and engineering improve our lives?
4 Would you like to explore space? Why/ Why not?
5 What invention do you think has changed our lives the most?

Speaking Part 2 Extended turn

Work in pairs. Describe what you see in the picture. Say

- where the people in the photo are.
- how they are feeling.
- what they might be doing.

12 TECHNOLOGY TODAY

Reading Part 4 Gapped text

1 SPEAK Work in pairs. Discuss the questions.

1 Are you good with technology?
2 Is there anyone you know who is a technophobe? Who?
3 Have you ever had any problems with technology? What happened?

2 Read the article quickly, ignoring the gaps for now. Complete the summary of the text with the correct option (a, b or c).

The text describes

a what was difficult about the writer's job.
b how the writer got her first job in an office.
c why the writer dislikes working with technology.

Don't forget!

Read the whole text before answering the questions. This will give you an idea of the topic and what happens in the text.

3 Five sentences have been removed from the article below. Choose from the sentences (A–H) the one which best fits each gap (1–5). There are three extra sentences which you do not need to use.

A BAD START

I grew up in the 1980s, when hardly anybody sent emails, and I got my first job in 1996. It was as an assistant in a big office in London. When I arrived for my first day, I remember sitting down at my desk and seeing the huge computer in front of me. 1 ___

To be honest, I was a little scared. I think that was normal. 2 ___ I thought the only kind of program was on TV! My manager was very kind to me though, and he explained how to use the computer. However, it was a lot of information! I did try to write some of it down, but I didn't get all of it.

In the first week of the job, I forgot my password for my computer, deleted an important document, and broke the printer! 3 ___ My boss had complained about one of our customers, and I mixed up the 'subject' box and the 'to' box on the email – and sent the complaint to the customer! My boss was furious with me. In fact, he was so angry that I lost my job!

4 ___ I was not the best student in the class, but I was determined to learn. If I hadn't done that, I would never have been brave enough to go back into an office. 5 ___ Computers don't scare me now. In fact, I'm probably better with computers than most of my friends, and maybe even my kids!

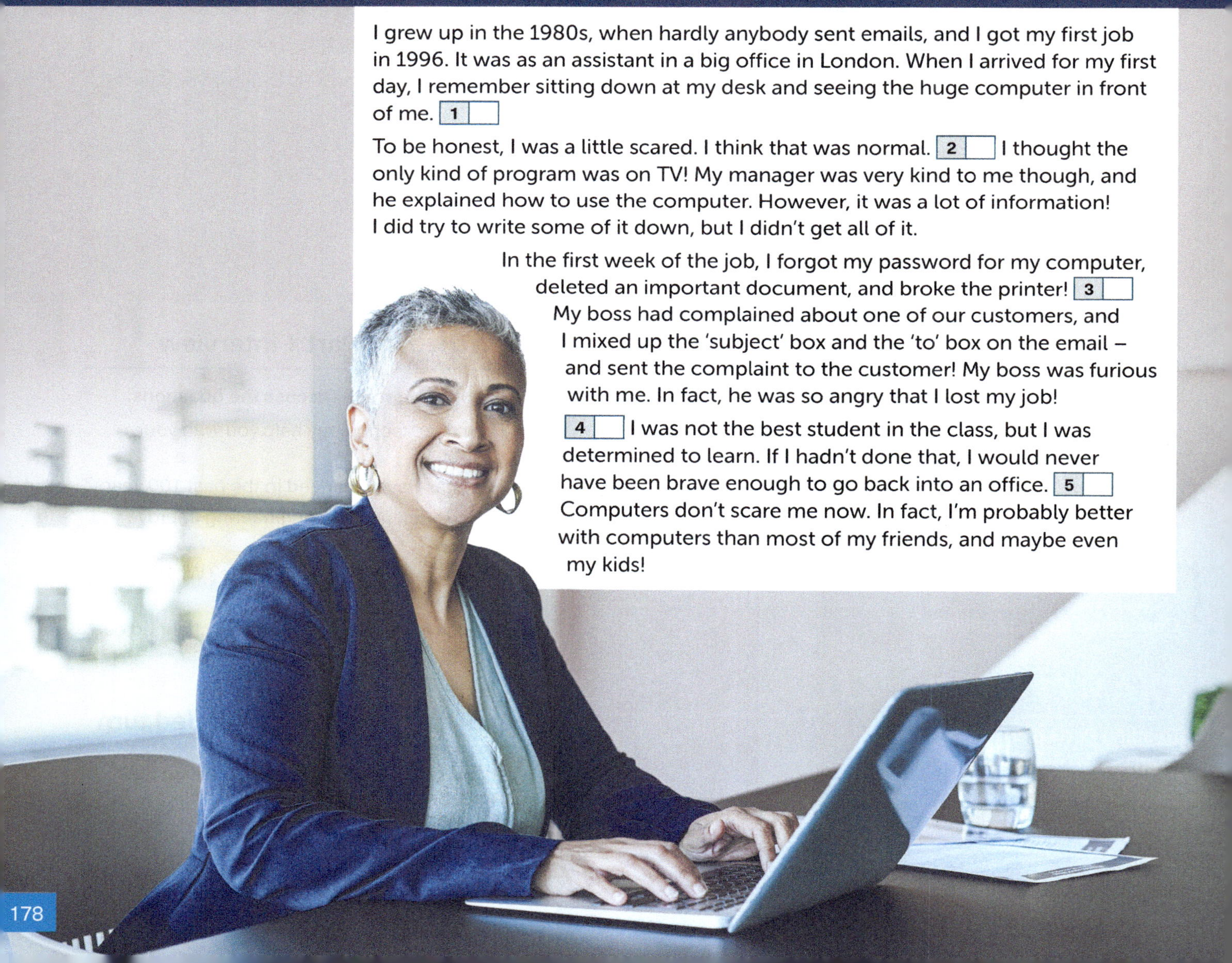

A I got another job a year later, and I stayed at the company for 20 years.
B However, the worst thing happened the week after.
C There were lots of new employees like me in the company.
D In those days, the screens looked like big boxes!
E After that experience, I decided to go on a computer course.
F So, I asked a friend to help me understand computers.
G In the second week, I realised using the computer was quite easy.
H After all, it was my first day in my first job, and I had no idea how to use a computer!

4 SPEAK Work in pairs. Discuss the questions.

1 When did you learn how to use a computer?
2 How would you feel if you made the same mistakes as the writer?

Vocabulary Computers and devices

1 Cross out the verb which does *not* usually collocate with the nouns in bold.

1	save	switch on	delete	a **file** or **document**
2	get	collect	send	an **email** or **message**
3	install	print	uninstall	a **program** or **app**
4	enter	remember	connect	your **username** or **password**
5	restart	shut down	begin	a **computer** or **laptop**

2 Complete each sentence with the correct form of an appropriate verb from Exercise 1.

56% of workers say they've accidentally **(1)** ________ a **file** at work!

33% of people don't **(2)** ________ their **computers** at night – what a waste of electricity!

Many people choose **passwords** that are easy to **(3)** ________. The most common? **123456**

Adults under 45 years old **(4)** ________ and receive around **85** text **messages** a day!

Around **80 apps** are **(5)** ________ on the average smartphone.

3 SPEAK Work in pairs. Discuss the facts in Exercise 2. Are any of them true for you?

Language focus Third conditional

1 Look at the sentence from the reading on page 178 and choose the correct options.

If I hadn't done that, I would never have been brave enough to go back into an office.

1 The writer *did* / *did not* go into an office again.
2 The sentence talks about alternatives in *the future* / *the past*.
3 The underlined tense is the *past perfect* / *present perfect*.
4 The structure after the comma is *past simple* / *would* + *have* + *past participle*.

2 Match the sentences 1–4 to the types of conditionals a–d.

1 If we had the money, we would buy a new TV.
2 If you practise playing the game, you'll get better.
3 If you had switched your computer off, it wouldn't have got too hot.
4 If you book online, you get a discount.

a zero conditional
b first conditional
c second conditional
d third conditional

3 SPEAK In pairs, answer the questions about the types of conditionals in Exercise 2.

Which conditional ...

1 describes things that are generally true?
2 is used for possible or probable situations?
3 is used for imaginary or unreal situations?
4 imagines a different past situation or result?

4 Go to Ready for Grammar on page 234 for rules, explanations and further practice.

5 Complete each third conditional sentence with a word from the box.

had hadn't have wouldn't

1 If I had known you needed help, I would ______ texted you.
2 If you ______ sent your application in, you wouldn't have got the job.
3 If I had known this computer was so slow, I ______ have bought it.
4 You'd have remembered your password if you ______ written it down.

6 Complete the text using the correct form of the verbs in brackets. Use zero, first, second or third conditionals.

www.theWorldwideWeb.com

History of the Worldwide web

Nowadays, the World Wide Web is an important part of all our lives. **(1)** If we ______ (*want*) to order a pizza, we **(2)** ______ (*order*) one on our phones, and we don't need to go to the library to find out information – it's all there on our web browser! What **(3)** ______ (*our lives* / *be*) like at school and work if we **(4)** ______ (*not have*) the World Wide Web? Certainly, more difficult than they are now.

The man who invented it was Tim Berners Lee, and he did something very special with his creation – he gave it to the world for free. If he **(5)** ______ (*not do*) this, it probably **(6)** ______ (*not grow*) so quickly. The World Wide Web is now huge, and has no owner, so it belongs to all of us.

This means we can put anything on the web. This can be good and bad, but if we **(7)** ______ (*use*) the internet with care, it **(8)** ______ (*continue*) to be a great help to us all in the future.

7 SPEAK Work in pairs. Think of past events in your life. Use the third conditional to talk about how the situation could have been different. Here are some ideas for you to talk about.

- friends/family
- work
- school/university
- home
- money
- travel/holidays

If I hadn't gone to my university, I wouldn't have met my best friend.

Vocabulary Changes and amounts

1 **Write the words from the box next to the phrase (1–4) which has a similar mean ng.**

decrease decline drop grow improve increase

1 get better ____________
2 get worse ____________
3 go up ____________, ____________
4 go down ____________, ____________

MOBILE PHONE USE

WORLD STATISTICS

Sales of smartphones increased from **122 million** phones in 2007 to **1339 million** phones in 2023.

Perhaps because of smartphone use, sales of personal computers dropped by **16%** in that time.

YOUNG PEOPLE IN THE UK – MOBILE PHONE USE

20% of 5–7 year-olds have a smartphone, compared to over **95%** of 12–17 year-olds.

YOUNG PEOPLE IN THE USA – MOBILE PHONE USE

WHEN?

(1) 93% use their phones when travelling by bus, train or car.

(2) 50% often use their phones in bed before falling asleep!

WHAT?

Just **(3) 3%** usually read books on their phones.

(4) 25% listen to podcasts on their phones.

2 **Read the infographic about mobile phone use. Match the numbers in the infographic (1–4) to the descriptions (a–d).**

a half ______
b almost every(one) ______
c a quarter ______
d almost no (one) ______

3 **SPEAK** **In pairs, summarise the information in the infographic using the expressions from Exercises 1 and 2.**

4 **Go to the** **Additional materials** **on** **page 200.**

Listening Part 3 Gap fill

1 **SPEAK** **Work in pairs. Read the task in Exercise 2 below and discuss the type of information (e.g. a date, a verb, etc.) you might need to write in the gaps (1–6).**

2 **12.1** **You will hear a radio presenter called Steven Porter talking about a robot show. For questions 1–6, write the correct answer in each gap. Write one or two words or a number or a date or a time.**

JAPAN ROBOT SHOW

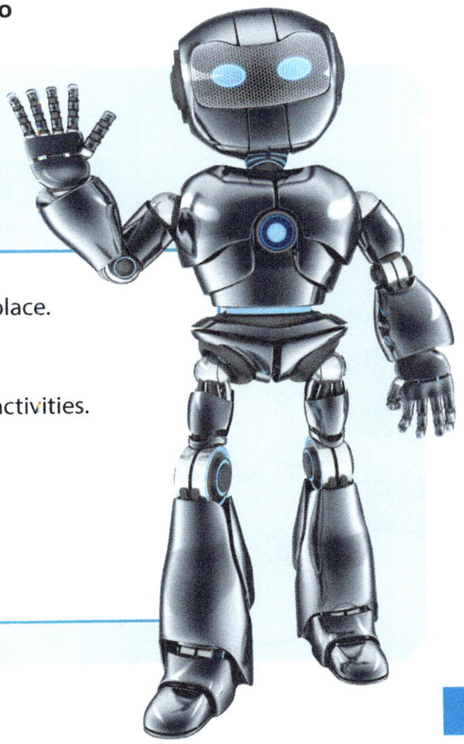

ROBEAR:	This robot moves **(1)** .... people from place to place.
	It will soon be used in **(2)** ....
SPOT:	A working robot that is useful for more **(3)** .... activities.
CAFÉ X:	A café which functions without **(4)** ....
GEMINOID HI-1:	This is a robot that **(5)** .... its inventor.

Next robot show starts on **(6)** .... in London.

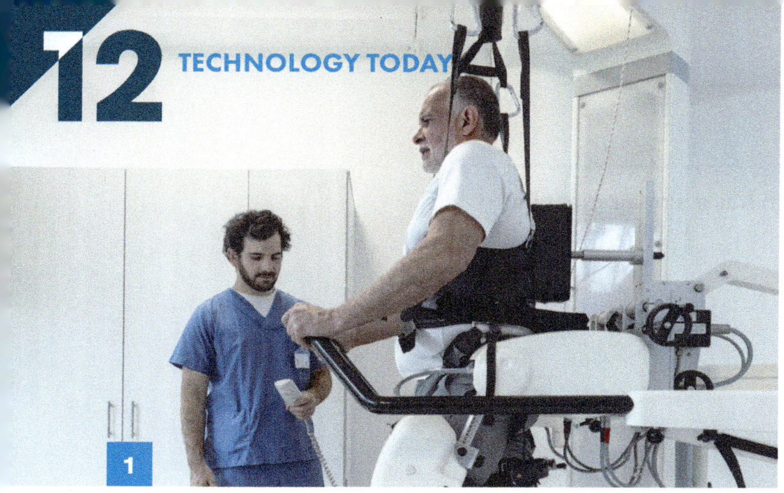

1

2

Speaking Part 2 Extended turn

1 Look at photographs 1 and 2. They show how technology helps people.

Student A: Tell your partner what you can see in photograph 1.

Student B: Tell your partner what you can see in photograph 2.

2 Now look at photographs 3 and 4. They show people using technology. Before you do the speaking task, read the information in the box below.

Student A: Look at photograph 3. Tell your partner what you can see in the photograph. Use the questions in the How to go about it box to help you.

Student B: Listen to your partner's answer. Did they talk about all the information included in the How to go about it box?

Don't forget!

Remember to describe the photo in general first and then add some specific information and details.

How to go about it

Organise your answer into the following areas to help you structure your response and think about what you can say.

Subject

What can you see?

What might be happening?

Place

Where are they?

What does it look like?

People

Who is there? Who might they be?

What do they look like? What are they wearing?

What are they doing? How might they be feeling?

Items

What can you see? What colour is it? Where is it in the photo?

3 Now change roles.

Student B: Look at photograph 4. Tell your partner what you can see in the photograph. Use the questions in the How to go about it box to help you.

Student A: Listen to your partner's answer. Did they talk about all the information included in the How to go about it box?

3

4

Vocabulary Knowledge and invention

1 Match the sentence beginnings 1–8 to the endings a–h to make complete sentences.

1 If you don't understand how it works, I can **draw**
2 In order to test how polluted the water was, the scientists **collected**
3 Before Nicola started writing her historical novel, she had to **do**
4 It's hard working with Mauricio because he never wants to **share**
5 The local government met to try and **find** a
6 To learn about science, children can **do** simple
7 Every scientist wants to **make a**
8 In order to leave the cat in the house all day, my mother **built** a

a **data** from the rivers in the local area.
b his **ideas** or help anyone else.
c **machine** that gives it food every six hours.
d big **discovery** in their career, but only a few manage to do this.
e **a diagram** to explain it more clearly to you.
f some **research** into what life was like in the 1920s.
g **solution** to the traffic problems in the area.
h **experiments** using objects in the home.

2 SPEAK Read the text in Exercise 3 below, ignoring the gaps, and discuss the following questions with a partner.

1 Do you think you would be a good scientist or engineer? Why/Why not?
2 Do you think scientists' jobs are interesting? Why/Why not?

3 Complete the text with the correct form of the nouns in bold in Exercise 1.

WORKING IN SCIENCE AND ENGINEERING – WHAT IS IT LIKE?

There are many different people who work in science and engineering, from people who **make (1)** __________ like x-rays, to others that **build (2)** __________ like computers or engines. And almost all of these people have made our lives much easier. However, their jobs aren't easy. They have to try to **find** the right **(3)** __________ to each problem. Because this is sometimes complicated, engineers and scientists often **draw (4)** __________ to help make the information easier to see.

Scientists and engineers have to do things step by step. First, they **do** some **(5)** __________, like reading other scientists' work. Then they have an idea, which they need to test. They **do** different **(6)** __________ in a laboratory to test their ideas. They **collect (7)** __________ from their tests to find out if their ideas work or not. The final stage is **sharing** their **(8)** __________ and conclusions with others, whether they work or not. This is the basis of the scientific method, which is a way of making progress in science and engineering.

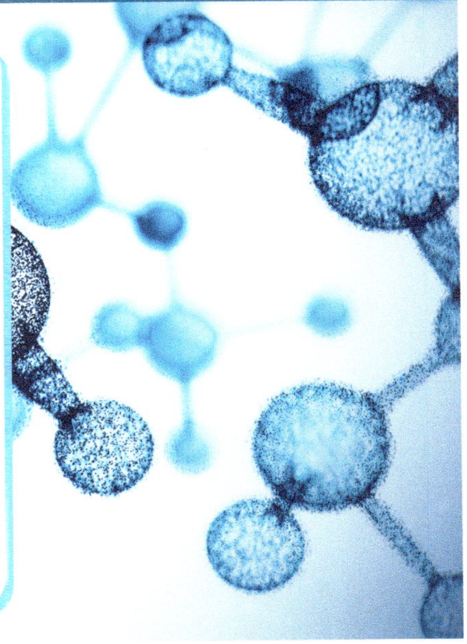

4 SPEAK Work in pairs. Ask and answer the questions.

1 Can you think of an important invention from the last 20 years?
2 What do you think will be invented in the next ten years? Think about the following areas:

- health and medicine
- education
- communication
- environment
- homes
- travel

Listening Part 2 Multiple choice

1 **Read the Listening Part 2 question below. Match phrases 1–6 to options A–C from the question. There are two phrases for each option. The first one has been done for you.**

1 You will hear two friends talking about buying a mobile phone.
The man says that
A he needs to talk to an expert before buying one. ___2___ + ______
B it would be easier to buy one online. ______ + ______
C he doesn't like going to phone shops. ______ + ______

1 It's difficult for me to get to a shop.

2 I think I should speak to someone.

3 I'd like some assistance.

4 I think those places are awful.

5 Buying from the website is more convenient.

6 I'd rather not go into one of those shops.

Don't forget!

Remember you will not hear all the same words from the options A–C in the audio.

2 **12.2 You will hear people talking in six different situations. For questions 1–6, choose the best answer (A, B or C).**

1 You will hear two friends talking about buying a mobile phone.
The man says that
A he needs to talk to an expert before buying one.
B it would be easier to buy one online.
C he doesn't like going to phone shops.

2 You will hear a man telling a friend about a technology problem.
What is the problem with?
A a printer
B a document
C an email

3 You will hear two friends discussing electric cars.
They both agree that
A more people should buy them.
B they are too expensive.
C the technology is extraordinary.

4 You will hear two friends talking about a robot cleaner.
The man says he
A bought a cheap one first.
B asked friends for advice.
C researched different products.

5 You will hear two colleagues talking about a conference.
What does the man say about it?
A He's looking forward to it.
B He won't be attending it.
C He isn't interested in it.

6 You will hear two friends talking about a mobile phone app.
What does the man think about the app?
A He's delighted by the design.
B He's amazed at the price.
C He's pleased with the content.

Language focus Future continuous

1 SPEAK Look at these predictions for the year 2100. Which do you think are most likely to come true?

1 Paper money won't exist.
2 People will be living on other planets.
3 We will be able to control the weather.
4 Robots will be doing most of the work.

2 Look at the two forms of the future in Exercise 1 and complete the rules.

Future simple: *will/won't* + infinitive without *to*

Future continuous: *will/won't* + ____________ + ____________

3 Go to Ready for Grammar on page 234 to check your answers and for rules, explanations and further practice.

4 Look at the predictions. Complete the sentences with the future continuous.

futurepredictions.com

WHAT WILL I BE DOING IN 50 YEARS?

- You **(1)** ____________ (*live*) in a beautiful apartment in New York.
- You **(2)** ____________ (*learn*) Chinese in the evenings.
- You **(3)** ____________ (*run*) your own fashion business.
- You **(4)** ____________ (*not drive*) a car – you ____________ (*fly*) a car.

5 SPEAK Work in pairs. Make predictions about the future.

Student A: Choose a time in the future. Ask your partner to predict your future.

Student B: Make some predictions for your partner about the topics below or think of your own topics. Use the future simple or continuous.

- house and home
- work life
- travel
- family and friends

Now change roles.

Writing Part 2 Article

1 SPEAK Work in pairs. Choose one of the areas below and make some notes about how you use technology in that situation.

- at school/work/home
- for shopping and entertainment
- for giving/getting directions
- for communication

2 SPEAK Share your answers to Exercise 1 with another pair. Do you use technology in the same way or differently? Why/Why not?

3 Read the Part 2 Writing task and tick the topics you should include in your answer.

- how technology helps the world in general ____
- what technology you prefer ____
- how technology makes your daily life better ____
- why technology is bad ____
- reasons why you like using some technologies ____
- what technology people should use ____

You see this announcement in an English-language magazine.

Articles wanted!

Technology

- What technology do you like using? Why?
- How does technology help you in your everyday life?

Write an article answering these questions and we will put it in our magazine.

4 Read the model answer below. Does it mention the topics you ticked in Exercise 3?

Smartphone apps make smart lives

(1) What do you think about when you think about technology? For me, it's mobile phone apps **(2)** and kitchen technology **(3)** because they are so convenient.

These inventions have really improved my life. **(4)** Firstly, a weather app helps me choose the best clothes to put on in the morning. **(5)** Then, I can just press a button to get a delicious coffee from my amazing coffee machine. A travel app tells me if my train will arrive on time. **(6)** Finally, at lunch and dinner, I can make meals quickly using a microwave when I'm in a hurry.

(7) Imagine how much more challenging our lives would be without these things!

Don't forget!

Answer all the questions in the task.

5 Look at the model answer on page 186. Does the writer answer each of the questions from the task in Exercise 3?

6 Read the model answer again and match the numbered sections (1–7) to the organisation features below (a–e).

a a word to introduce a reason ______
b a question to make the reader interested in the article ______
c a word to connect two ideas in a sentence ______
d words to show the order of information ______, ______, ______
e a sentence to make the reader think ______

Useful language

Making articles more interesting

1 Add the words in the box to the examples below:

exciting   like   quickly   what

There are many ways that you can make articles more interesting.
Add adjectives: *I play* **(1)** ______ *games on my computer.*
Add adverbs: *My scooter helps me get to work* **(2)** ______.
Giving examples: *I love shopping apps* **(3)** ______ *Etsy.*
Asking questions: **(4)** ______ *would our lives be like without technology?*

7 Write your answer to the task below. Write about **100 words.**

You see this announcement in an English language magazine.

> **Articles wanted!**
> **Inventions**
> - What do you think is the most important invention in the last 100 years? Why?
> - How is this invention important for you in your daily life?
>
> Write an article answering these questions and we will put it in our magazine.

For more information about writing articles, see page 195.

12 REVIEW

Language focus Third conditional

Complete the email with the correct form of the verbs in brackets.

Dear Lynne,

I hope you are well. I went for a job interview yesterday, and it didn't go well. The job was to work in a laboratory at the university. First, I woke up late and missed the bus. If I **(1)** ________________ (*leave*) home just ten minutes earlier, I **(2)** ________________ (*catch*) it! So, I arrived late to the interview. Then, the interviewer told me his name and I immediately forgot it! I'm sure, I **(3)** ________________ (*remember*) it if I **(4)** ________________ (*be*) so nervous.

Next, he asked me for a copy of my CV, but I had left it on the bus! I'm not sure if the person next to me saw it. If they **(5)** ________________ (*see*) it, I'm sure they **(6)** ________________ (*say*) something to me.

So, anyway, I tried my best, but I don't think I've got the job. It's a shame. Next time, I will set two alarms!

Speak soon,

Pete

Vocabulary Computers and devices

Match the sentence beginnings 1–6 to the endings a–f to make complete sentences.

1 Is the report finished? We must **send**
2 I've been trying all morning to **install**
3 If you have any problems, try **restarting**
4 Click on this link if you have **forgotten**
5 When I paid for the room, I **received**
6 I worked on my essay for eight hours and then **deleted**

a **this program** onto my computer, but it just won't work.
b **your password** and we'll send you an email.
c **the document** by accident!
d **the file** by the end of the day.
e **an email** confirming my booking.
f **your computer**; that normally works.

Reading Part 5 Multiple-choice cloze

Read the text and for questions 1–6, choose which answer (A, B, C or D) best fits each gap.

WHY GAMING IS GOOD

Most people have played a video game once or twice in their lives, but not everybody (1) .... this into a hobby. In fact, some people even see it as a (2) .... of time. However, gaming can help our ability to think and solve problems and react quickly to what is happening. These are also great (3) .... to develop in life, and they aren't the only ones that video games can help us with.

People who play video games can also learn to do many things at (4) .... They develop this from gaming, where they may be looking for dangers, moving their character around, and looking at their scores. They can also help improve our social (5) .... Nowadays, many games (6) .... communicating with other people in some way. This could be typing or speaking during the game or talking about these games with others around them.

1	A brings	B turns	C passes	D puts
2	A block	B hole	C waste	D loss
3	A ways	B manners	C forms	D skills
4	A same	B once	C time	D sudden
5	A worlds	B parts	C times	D lives
6	A involve	B display	C attach	D experience

Writing Part 2 Story

Your English teacher has asked you to write a story.

Your story must begin with this sentence:

As I entered the laboratory, I knew my life would never be the same.

Write your **story** in about **100** words.

For more information on writing stories, see page 194.

Pronunciation Connected speech: linking

1 12.3 **Listen and complete the sentences with the words you hear.**

1 Have you ______________________ your computer?
2 I always ______________________ from my phone.
3 We do lots ______________________ in science class.
4 Please ______________________ copies of your work.

2 Read the sentences below. Which two sentences are true about speech in English?

Words sound like they are joined when

a the first word ends in a consonant sound and the following word starts with a vowel sound.
b the first word ends in a consonant sound and the following words starts with a consonant sound.
c the first word ends in a vowel sound and the following word starts with a vowel sound.
d the two words end and begin in the same sound.

3 Using the rules above, make a mark where you think the words will be joined in speech. There is an example at the beginning.

Almost‿everyone owns a mobile phone these days. These can be as cheap as 40 pounds or cost hundreds of pounds, but the most expensive mobile phone in the world is an enormous 40 million pounds. It is made of gold and diamonds, and it belongs to the wife of the richest man in Asia.

4 12.4 **Listen and check your answers.**

5 Look at the wordsearch below with a partner.

WORD SEARCH

1 Find the 8 pairs of words. The first word for each pair is in the coloured box.
2 Decide which pairs of words are connected, 2 pairs are not connected.
3 Make a sentence with each connected word pair.

Find these words and their pair:
SWITCH
VIDEO
CATCH
TV
WEB
SHARE
LOST
ALMOST

S	Z	A	S	K	T	W	A	N	M	A	O
L	L	V	H	O	V	E	T	O	K	E	R
O	S	O	A	Z	S	B	T	L	S	J	W
S	O	E	R	P	C	B	B	S	N	L	R
T	P	A	E	R	R	R	V	C	L	R	I
E	Z	V	I	D	E	O	G	A	M	E	L
M	S	R	D	J	E	W	T	T	N	L	Z
A	S	S	E	P	N	S	V	C	J	A	D
I	O	E	A	R	O	E	W	H	L	M	D
L	R	Y	S	M	V	R	C	U	S	S	V
T	T	A	L	O	N	P	R	P	D	R	H
L	B	A	S	W	I	T	C	H	O	N	L

COLLOCATION REVISION UNITS 1–12

In each of the spaces below, write one word which collocates with *all* three of the other words. You will need to write nouns in the left-hand column and verbs in the right-hand column. The numbers in brackets refer to the relevant units of the book where the words you require first appeared.

Adjective + noun

1	comfortable trendy smart	______	(1)
2	an online a short a part-time	______	(2)
3	takeaway traditional fast	______	(3)
4	well-known talented famous	______	(4)
5	an organised a one-way a day	______	(4)
6	a natural a remote local	______	(5)
7	a stressful an essential a temporary	______	(7)
8	a business a master's a medical	______	(7)
9	advanced English evening	______	(9)
10	a brand new a modern an office	______	(11)

Verb + noun

1	______	a prize a competition first place	(1)
2	______	a musical instrument a game a sport	(2)
3	______	exercise a course a degree	(2)
4	______	success baking the sights	(4)
5	______	a show a talk a conference	(4)
6	______	time in nature money weekends	(5)
7	______	a job a fine top marks	(7)
8	______	notes a pill time off work	(9)
9	______	a cough a temperature the flu	(10)
10	______	the bed dinner a mess	(11)

READY FOR WRITING

How to go about it

You should spend about 20 minutes on each part. This includes time to plan and check your writing. Think about timing yourself when you practise doing Writing exam tasks, but don't worry if you take longer than 20 minutes. With enough practice, you should be able to complete both parts within 45 minutes.

Introduction

For the **Writing** paper, you must complete two tasks in 45 minutes. For each Writing task, you have to write about **100 words**.

Writing Part 1

For Part 1, you have to reply to an email on a particular topic. There are four notes on the email that you need to respond to.

Writing Part 2

For Part 2, you can choose between either an article or a story.

Marking

There are four main areas that examiners consider when they assess writing, and each area can score a mark out of five. Match each assessment area (a–d) to the general advice and information (1–4).

a Content **b** Communicative Achievement **c** Organisation **d** Language

(1) ______ Think about the order of ideas in your writing. This includes using paragraphs and linking words (e.g. *because, also, then*).	/5
(2) ______ Try to include a wide range of vocabulary and grammar and check this carefully for mistakes.	/5
(3) ______ Make sure your writing is in the appropriate register (i.e. informal, semi-informal, formal) and in the correct format (e.g. an email is formatted like an email).	/5
(4) ______ Make sure you read the instructions carefully and include all the necessary information (i.e. your email must include all the points).	/5

Writing Part 1 Email

Read this email from your English-speaking teacher Ms Gómez and the notes you have made.

Write your email to Ms Gómez using all the notes.

From: Ms Gómez

Subject: National Photography Competition

Dear Class,

The National Photography Competition is coming soon and I think you should enter. [Good idea!]

The topic of this year's competition is 'Someone Special'. You need to enter a photo of someone important in your life, so please let me know who this will be. [Explain.]

You also need to think of the best place to take the photo. [Suggest a place.]

You should use a good-quality camera for the competition. Let me know if you need to borrow one from the photography department at college. [No thanks, because …]

Best wishes,

Ms Gómez

Write about **100 words**.

What to expect in the exam

- Part 1 is always an email with some notes. You have to reply to the email in about 100 words. You must include the information in the notes.

Model answer

an appropriate greeting →	Dear Ms Gómez,	
response to the first note →	Thank you for informing me about the National Photography Competition. I am looking forward to this exciting creative opportunity.	
response to the second note →	After some careful thought, I have decided to photograph my grandmother, <u>who</u> has always been a positive influence in my life. <u>Ever since</u> I was little, she has taught me to respect and value nature, <u>so</u> we often spend time in the countryside together.	← appropriate formal style
response to the third note →	I am planning on taking my grandmother's photo at Garibaldi Lake, <u>where</u> she loves to go hiking and swimming.	← use of linking words
response to the fourth note →	I won't need to use any equipment from the college's photography department <u>as</u> I already own a high-quality camera.	
appropriate ending →	Best regards,	
	Jules	

Task

Read this email from your English-speaking friend Jerry and the notes you have made.

Write your email to Jerry using all the notes.

Hi!

Do you remember talking about going to the weekend music festival in July? I've won two free tickets! <u>Would you like to have one?</u> ← Of course!

We'll need to camp at the festival, and I have some extra camping equipment. <u>Do you need to borrow anything?</u> ← No, because …

What do you think we should do about food? There'll be loads of food stalls, <u>or we could cook</u> our meals in the camping area. ← I prefer …

There are several stages with all kinds of performances. <u>Do you think we should plan what acts we'll see?</u> ← Tell Jerry …

Write back soon!

Jerry

Write about 100 words.

Useful language

You need to think about who the email is for to help you decide whether to use formal or informal language. Here are some formal and informal ways to greet and say goodbye in an email.

Informal greetings:

Hey [Name]! / Hi [Name]! /Hello [Name],

Informal endings:

Cheers,

See you soon,

Bye for now,

Formal greetings:

Dear Mr/Mrs/Ms [Last name],

Formal endings:

Sincerely,

Yours faithfully,

Kind regards,

Writing Part 2 Story

What to expect in the exam

In Part 2, you can choose between an article or a story. Read each task and decide which you prefer.

Your English teacher has asked you to write a story.

Your story must begin with this sentence:

The friends were hiking in the woods when they heard a thunderstorm.

Write your **story** in about **100 words.**

Model answer

starts with opening sentence, as instructed → The friends were hiking in the woods when they heard a
beginning → thunderstorm. They started to run as the rain began to pour.

It wasn't long before they stood at the entrance of a well-hidden cave. Inside, they were relieved to find somewhere dry. As they looked around, they saw ancient drawings all over the walls and took a closer look. ← range of vocabulary and past verb forms

middle →

Suddenly, the cave shook as if it was angry and wanted them to leave. But that's when they noticed a pile of gold coins all over the ground. The friends no longer cared about the storm or the strange cave. They were too busy filling their pockets with gold. ← use of linking words and phrases

ending →

How to go about it

- Look at the opening sentence and note what tense(s), names and pronouns are used in the opening sentence. Make sure your story follows the same pattern.
- Include a range of tenses in your story (e.g., past simple, past continuous and past perfect). You want to show the examiner that you can accurately use a good range of grammatical structures and vocabulary.

Task

Your English teacher has asked you to write a story.

Your story must begin with this sentence.

The flatmates weren't expecting anyone when they heard someone knock on their door.

Write your **story** in about **100 words.**

Useful language

Time linkers

You want your story to have a clear beginning, middle and end and be interesting to read. To achieve this, you can use time linkers to connect your writing.

All of a sudden ...	*While ...*	*It wasn't long before ...*
Out of nowhere ...	*When ...*	*Just at that moment ...*
As soon as ...	*As ...*	*That's when ...*
Suddenly ...	*After a while ...*	

Writing Part 2 Article

You see this announcement in an online English-language magazine.

> **Articles wanted!**
>
> **Traditional festival**
>
> - Do you think traditional festivals are important? Why?
> - Describe a festival that takes place in your region. What is special about it?
>
> The best articles answering these questions will be published next month.

Write your **article** in about **100 words**.

Model answer

LA TOMATINA

introduction → beginning →

In my opinion, traditional festivals are very important because they help keep cultures alive. Not only that, but celebrations also make local communities stronger by bringing people with different backgrounds together. ← use of linking words and phrases

Answer all parts of the question and include your opinion. →

In Spain, there's an annual festival called *La Tomatina* in a town called Buñol. It's quite unusual because it's all about a huge tomato fight! People throw tomatoes at each other; therefore, the festival is very messy. What makes it so special, however, is how many locals and visitors join in to have a great time. In addition to this, ← use a lively, informal style

a closing comment → *La Tomatina* shows the fun side of Spain's culture. It's a festival you won't forget!

Task

You see this announcement in an English-language website.

> **Articles wanted!**
>
> **Setting goals**
>
> - Do you have an important goal that you would like to achieve? What is it? Why?
> - How will you achieve this goal?
>
> We will put the best articles on our website next month!

Write your **article** in **100 words**.

How to go about it

- Organise your ideas into clear paragraphs and answer each part of the question.
- Include a variety of linking words to connect your ideas.

Useful language

Linking words

Put the following linkers in the correct category. Each word or phrase can only be used once.

Also ... As a result of ... As well as ... Because ... Besides ... Despite ... Due to ... During ... Finally ... For example ... For instance ... For this reason ... However ... In addition ... Including ... Like ... Meanwhile ... Next ... Not only that ... Previously ...Still ... Such as ... Therefore ... While ... Yet ...

Giving examples	Contrasting ideas	Showing cause and effect	Expressing time	Adding information
For example ...				

ADDITIONAL MATERIALS

UNIT 1

Reading Part 1 Multiple choice

In Reading Part 1, the correct option repeats the same main message of the text, but using different words. Fill each gap with a word from the box. The second sentence should have the same meaning as the first.

arrangements discounts fine fortnight lift maximum

1 Do you want me to drive you to the city centre?
Would you like me to give you a ____________ to the city centre?

2 They've given us three tests in the last two weeks.
We've had three tests in the last ____________.

3 If the police catch you driving too fast, you could pay €200.
Speeding could lead to a ____________ of €200.

4 Tickets are cheaper when you present a student card.
____________ are available on tickets when you show a student card.

5 After you open the bottle, drink the milk within a week.
Drink the milk within a ____________ of one week of opening the bottle.

6 I can't drive you to the office. Can you find a different way of getting to work?
I can't drive you to the office. Can you make other ____________?

Go back to page 5.

Writing Part 1 Email

Read this email from your English-speaking classmate Clara and the notes you have made.

Write your email to Clara using all the notes. Write your answer in about 100 words.

From: Clara

Subject: Party for Laura

Hi everyone,

As you know, our English teacher, Laura, is leaving the language school where we study. She has worked there for 12 years! Laura is an excellent teacher, so we should organise a party for her. ← Great idea!

We could have the party at the language school or at a park. Which would be better? ← Tell Clara

Shall we all bring food to the party? ← Yes, …

I think it would be nice to get Laura a special gift. What can we give her? I know her favourite colour is green. ← Suggest …

I look forward to hearing your suggestions!

Clara

Go back to page 11.

READY FOR READING

Reading Introduction

Read some words taken from the Part 1 questions on page 59. Match each word (1–5) to the correct definition (a–f).

1 arrange	**a** to think carefully about something you are doing and nothing else
2 consider	**b** to make an arrangement definite often by phone or in writing
3 find out	**c** to think or believe something will happen
4 confirm	**d** to think carefully about something
5 expect	**e** to make the necessary plans for something to happen
6 concentrate	**f** to get information about something

UNIT 5

Language focus Present perfect continuous

Student A

Choose one of the prompts below and say it to your partner. Your partner has to discover the reason for your prompt by asking questions with the present perfect continuous, e.g. *Have you been ...?* When your partner guesses correctly, they will say one of their prompts.

My trainers are dirty. (Reason: I've been walking in the countryside.)

I'm really tired. (Reason: I've been working hard all week.)

My eyes hurt. (Reason: I've been watching TV for hours.)

I'm stressed. (Reason: I've been studying hard for a test but I don't think I will pass it.)

Go back to page 71.

UNIT 6

Vocabulary Adjectives

1 Prepare to use the adjectives in Exercise 2 on page 84 to describe one of your own travel experiences. Make notes on each of the ideas in the box to help you.

accommodation food places transport

2 **SPEAK** Work in pairs. Take turns to talk about your travel experiences. Ask follow-up questions.

Go back to page 84.

Language focus Comparatives and superlatives

1 You are going to tell a classmate about three towns or cities that you know well. Think about how they are similar or different. Use the words below to help you.

big small | good bad | hot cold | rich poor | busy quiet

cloudy sunny | boring interesting | historic modern | ugly beautiful | cheap expensive

2 **SPEAK** Work in pairs. Take turns to talk about your towns or cities. Ask follow-up questions for more information.

A: I think Budapest is more interesting than Prague.

B: Really? What makes you say that?

Go back to page 85.

UNIT 5

Language focus Present perfect continuous

Student B

Your partner is going to tell you a prompt, e.g. *My hair is wet.* You have to discover the reason for the prompt by asking questions with the present perfect continuous, e.g. *Have you been ...?* When you guess correctly, it's your turn to say a prompt.

- My back hurts. (Reason: I've been carrying heavy boxes.)
- I'm feeling frustrated. (Reason: My friend hasn't been responding to my messages.)
- Sorry I'm late. (Reason: I've been sitting in a traffic.)
- I feel satisfied. (Reason: I've been getting good marks in my course.)

Go back to page 71.

UNIT 6

Writing Part 1 Email

Read this email from your English-speaking friend Boris and the notes you have made.

From: Boris

Subject: Weekend trip?

Hi,

Next Friday we're going to have a day off because it's a holiday. We could go away for the weekend. Do you think it's a good idea? ← Yes!

We could go to a small village or a city. Which would be better? ← I think ...

I've never been very good at finding cheap prices for hotels. Do you know any good websites to look at? ← Suggest ...

Oh, one more question: can we take your car? ← No, because ...

Let me know!

Boris

Write your **email** to Boris using all the notes. Use reference words when appropriate.

Go back to page 89.

UNIT 11

Pronunciation

Student A

- cupboard
- similar
- finger
- agree
- neighbour
- university

Go back to page 176.

READY FOR LISTENING

Listening Part 1 Multiple choice

Some words are different in American English and British English. Match the words in British English to the equivalent in American English.

British English	American English
trousers	soccer
lift	movie
football	college
crisps	pants
film	French fries
pavement	elevator
university	potato chips
chips	sidewalk

Go back to page 110.

UNIT 9

Vocabulary Different types of study

SPEAK Work in pairs. Talk about the following topics using some of the vocabulary in Exercises 1–3 on page 137.

- how you study now
- good ways for people with jobs to study
- the teachers you have had
- what you would like to study in the future

I'd quite like to study art in my free time. Perhaps in the evenings.

My driving instructor was great. He was so kind.

I don't really enjoy distance learning. I prefer classes in a college.

Go back to page 137.

UNIT 10

Vocabulary Strong and weak adjectives

SPEAK Work in pairs. Change the weak adjective in the questions for a strong adjective, then ask and answer the questions.

1 When were you last **surprised**? Why?
2 What things do you think are **pretty**?
3 What do you do when it's **cold** outside?
4 When do you feel **sad**?
5 What experiences make you feel **happy**?
6 What situations make you **tired**?

Go back to page 149.

UNIT 11

Speaking Part 4 General conversation

Student A: Ask Student B the questions in Box A.

Student B: Ask Student A the questions in Box B.

Try to use phrases from the Useful language box on page 170.

Box A	Box B
• Would you like to build your own house? (Why/Why not?) • What characteristics make a city a good place to live? • What is your favourite appliance or piece of furniture in your house?	• Where in the world would you most like to live? (Why?) • What is the nicest house or flat that you've lived in? Why? • Do you think it's important to have a garden/balcony? (Why/Why not?)

Go back to page 170.

Pronunciation

Student B

- sofa
- important
- doctor
- appliance
- station
- theatre

Go back to page 176.

UNIT 12

Vocabulary Changes and amounts

1 **SPEAK** Work in groups. Ask your classmates the questions in both questionnaires.

WHEN DO YOU USE YOUR SMARTPHONE?

a ... mostly in the morning
b ... before bed
c ... on the bus/train
d ... in class

WHAT DO YOU USE YOUR SMARTPHONE FOR?

a ... watching videos
b ... messaging / video calling friends and family
c ... checking the weather
d ... learning English

2 **SPEAK** Work in pairs. Use the information from Exercise 4 to describe how the people in your group use smartphones. Use the phrases from Exercise 3 on page 181.

Half of the group use their smartphones on the bus.

Go back to page 181.

READY FOR SPEAKING

Speaking Part 2 Extended turn

1 Student A: Look at photograph 1. It shows people on an underground train. Tell your partner what you can see in the photograph.

2 Student B: Look at photograph 2. It shows people on a river. Tell your partner what you can see in the photograph.

Go back to page 159.

READY FOR GRAMMAR

1 Present simple and present continuous

1 Present simple

- To form the present simple of regular verbs, we use the infinitive without *to*. In the third person singular (*he, she, it*), we add *-s* to the end of the verb.

  *She **sings** in a choir.*
  *We **drive** to work.*

- To form negative statements, use *do not / doesn't* and the infinitive without *to*.

  *They **don't understand** the question.*
  *He **doesn't drive** a car.*

- To form questions, we use *Do (not)* or *Does (not)* and the infinitive without *to*.

  ***Does** the computer **work**?*
  ***Don't** I **know** you?*

- To give short answers, we use *do (not)* or *does (not)*.

  *Yes, I/you/we/they **do**.* *No, I/you/we/they **don't**.*
  *Yes, he/she/it **does**.* *No, he/she/it **doesn't**.*

- Some verbs have irregular forms in the present simple, e.g. *be, have, try, do*.

Use

The present simple is used:

- to talk about facts or things that are always true.

  *Water **boils** at 100 degrees Celsius.*

- to describe permanent or long-term situations in the present.

  *She **lives** in Brighton and **works** in London.*

- to talk about actions that happen regularly, such as routines and habits.

  *I **get up** early on Saturdays and **run** by the river.*

- to express thoughts or feelings at the present moment.

  *I really **want** to buy these shoes, but they cost too much.*

2 Present continuous

- To form the present continuous, we use the verb *to be + -ing*.

  *I'**m working** from home.*
  *She'**s playing** tennis with a friend.*

- To form negative statements, we use the verb *to be + not + -ing.*

  *He **isn't working** today.*
  *They **aren't listening** to music.*

- To form questions, we use the verb *to be + -ing*. The subject comes after the verb *to be*.

  ***Am** I **doing** this right?*
  ***Is** it **raining**?*

- To give short answers, we use *to be + not*.

  *Yes, I **am**.* *No, I'**m not***
  *Yes, he/she/it **is**.* *No, he/she/it **isn't**.*
  *Yes, you/they/we **are**.* *No, you/they/we **aren't**.*

Use

The present continuous is used:

- to talk about actions in progress when speaking.

  A: Where's Sara?
  *B: She'**s taking** the dog for a walk.*

- to describe temporary activities or situations in the present, including ones not taking place at the moment of speaking.

  *I'**m learning** Chinese.*
  *She'**s spending** the summer in Milan.*

  NB An 'action' is when something happens, while a 'state' is when something stays the same. The present continuous is **not** used to describe states, with verbs such as *believe, belong, know, matter, prefer* or *seem*.

  *Who **does** this scarf **belong to**?*
  ~~*Who is this scarf belonging to?*~~

1 Adverbs of frequency

We use adverbs of frequency (*always, usually, often, sometimes, hardly ever, never*) with the present simple to describe how often an action takes place.

1 never	**2** hardly ever	**3** sometimes	**4** often	**5** usually	**6** always
0%		50%			100%

We put adverbs of frequency:

- after auxiliaries.

  *I don't **usually** watch the evening news.*

- before the main verb.

  *At the weekend, we **often** eat out with friends.*

- **after** the verb *to be*.

  *This type of product is **hardly ever** on sale.*

We can also put *usually* and *sometimes* at the beginning of a clause when we want to emphasise the frequency.

***Sometimes** I read the news on the train to work.*

Longer adverbial phrases (*all the time, once in a while, once a day/month/week/year, every day/week/month/year*) are also used to talk about how often something happens. We put these at the end of a clause.

*I have trouble sleeping and I feel tired **all the time**.* (always)

*The host interviews a new guest **every week**.* (all the weeks of the month/year)

*I like to walk home from work **once in a while**.* (sometimes, but not often)

1 Present simple and present continuous

1 Five of the following sentences contain mistakes with the present simple or present continuous. Find the mistakes and correct them.

1 Even when it's hot, they're liking to wear long trousers rather than shorts.
2 Perfume is getting very expensive at the moment.
3 It's getting dark in here. Can you turn on the lights?
4 Can you answer the phone? I can't. I cook dinner.
5 It's not mattering what I say. He never listens.
6 Keep your voice down, please. The kids are having a nap.
7 Quick – the thief escapes through the back door. Stop him!
8 I don't know what it is, but something is seeming wrong about this situation.

2 Read the answers and then complete the questions. There is an example at the beginning (0).

0 Do *you want to go to the cinema?* ____________
To the cinema? No, I want to go to the disco.
1 How ____________
Molly? She's playing very badly.
2 What ____________
To work? Megan takes the number 49 bus.
3 Where ____________
Marek and Anna? They're spending their summer holidays in Grenoble.
4 Do ____________
High heels? No, I don't like them at all.
5 Where ____________
Robert? He's working in a department store.

Go back to page 7.

1 Adverbs of frequency

1 Read the inspirational quotes and underline the correct alternative.

1 To keep the doctor away, eat healthy food *usually* / *every day*.

2 Fashion is like food – *always* / *sometimes* it's good to try something new.

3 Work *always* / *all the time* comes before success – except in the dictionary.

4 In life, the journey is *often* / *once a week* more important than the destination.

5 Someone comes into your life *never* / *once in a while* and you can't live without them – that's love.

6 To truly relax, take a long walk *usually* / *every week*.

2 Complete sentences 1–8 by writing the adverb or adverbial phrase in brackets in the correct gap. In two of the sentences, both gaps are possible.

1 We ________ wash ________ coloured and white clothing together in the washing machine. (*never*)
2 ________ she/She ________ arrives on time. (*always*)
3 ________ he/He ________ wears a scarf in winter. (*sometimes*)
4 Do you ________ check your email ________? (*every day*)
5 I am ________ home in the morning ________. (*hardly ever*)
6 At school, they are ________ in trouble ________. (*all the time*)
7 ________ the/The shop doesn't ________ allow customers to return sale items. (*usually*)
8 My company ________ lets me work from home ________. (*twice a week*)

Go back to page 10.

2 Past simple and *used to*

1 Past simple

- To form the past simple, we add *-ed* to regular verbs in positive statements.
  *She **waited** for the bus in the rain.*
- In negative statements, we add *didn't / did not* to the infinitive without *to*.
  *They **didn't come** to the party.*
- In questions, we put *did* before the subject.
  ***Did** you **see** Elena yesterday?*
- Some verbs have irregular past forms, e.g. *begin/began, swim/swam, know/knew, say/said*.
- To give a short answer, we use *did* or *didn't*.
  *Yes, I **did**.* *No, she **didn't**.*

For the past simple, we add *-ed* to the end of most regular verbs, e.g. *clean/cleaned, play/played*. For some verbs, however, we have to follow these spelling rules:

decide, arrive	→	*decide**d**, arrive**d***
hug, stop	→	*hu**gged**, sto**pped***
carry, spy	→	*carr**ied**, sp**ied***

Use

We use the past simple:

- to talk about completed actions and situations in the past.
  *He **visited** his relatives in Prague last week.*
  ***Did** he really **work** there for 20 years?*
- to talk about past actions that happened consecutively.
  *I **opened** my laptop and **checked** my email.*
- to talk about past states.
  *You **were** in a really good mood yesterday.*
- to talk about past habits (often with an adverb of frequency).
  *We always **met up** for a coffee before class.*

2 Used to

- To form sentences with *used to*, we add *used to* before the infinitive without *to* in positive statements.
  *I **used to dance** when I was a child.*
- In negative statements we use *didn't* with *use to*.
  *I **didn't use to exercise,** but now I go to the gym.*
- In questions, we use *Did/Didn't* with *use to*.
  ***Did** you **use to play** chess?*
  ***Didn't** he **use to** work with you?*

Use

We use *used to* when we talk about repeated past actions, habits or situations, in particular when they are no longer true. We can also use the past simple for this.

*We **used to go / went** to the beach every summer.*
*That town **used to be / was** small, but now it's very big.*
*I never **used to listen / listened** to the radio.*

NB We use the past simple, not *used to*, to describe single, completed actions in the past.

*I ~~used to see~~ **saw** him for the first time yesterday.*

---

2 Past simple and past continuous

- To form the past continuous, we use the past form of the verb *to be* + *-ing* in positive statements.
  *She **was swimming** in the lake.*
  *We **were reading** a magazine.*
- In negative statements, we use *was not / wasn't* or *weren't / were not*.
  *I **wasn't listening** to the teacher.*
  *You **weren't watching** TV.*
- In questions, we put the verb *to be* before the subject.
  ***Was** it **snowing**?*
  ***Were** they **talking** to John?*
- To give short answers, we use *was (not) / were (not)*.
  *Yes, she **was**.* *No, she **wasn't**.*
  *Yes, they **were**.* *No, they **weren't**.*

Use

We use the past continuous:

- to talk about temporary activities or situations in progress at a specific time in the past.
  A: Where was the boss yesterday afternoon?
  *B: I think he **was meeting** some new clients.*
- to talk about an action in progress in the past that is interrupted by a completed action. In this context, *when* is often used before the past simple and *while* before the past continuous.
  *While I **was walking** to work, a tourist **stopped** me to ask for directions.*
  *Giulia **was playing** football when she **injured** her leg.*
- to give background or context to another event in the past simple.
  ***Was** it still **raining** when you **left** work?*
  *We **were camping** by a lake, so we **went** for a swim!*

  NB We use the past simple, not the past continuous, to describe past states.

  ~~I wasn't minding the noise.~~
  *I **didn't mind** the noise.*

2 Past simple and *used to*

1 Complete dialogues 1–6 using the past simple form of the verbs in brackets.

1 **A:** What ______ (*you/do*) yesterday morning?
B: I ______ (*get up*) early and I ______ (*go*) for a long walk.

2 **A:** What ______ (*you/have*) for breakfast today?
B: I ______ (*have*) a coffee and a piece of toast with olive oil.

3 **A:** ______ (*you/enjoy*) the last film you watched?
B: It was okay, but I ______ (*not like*) the ending. It was so easy to predict!

4 **A:** What part of the country ______ (*you/grow up*) in?
B: In the north. I ______ (*live*) in Gdańsk until I was 12.

5 **A:** At school, what subjects ______ (*you/be*) you good at?
B: Maths was definitely my best subject. I always ______ (*get*) high marks.

6 **A:** When you were young, ______ (*your parents/teach*) you how to cook?
B: Yes, they did. I ______ (*learn*) to make many of the traditional dishes from my region.

2 SPEAK Work in pairs. Take turns to ask and answer the questions from Exercise 1.

3 Put the words in the correct order to create sentences with *used to*. There is an example at the beginning (0).

0 in / I / live / centre. / city / used / the / to — *I used to live in the city centre.*
1 used / I / very / to / long / work / hours. ______
2 own / I / to / use / car. / didn't / a ______
3 becoming / of / I / to / used / star. / dream / rock / a ______
4 did / to / ballet? / do / use / you ______
5 live? / use / did / where / you / to ______
6 software. / we / this / to / use / use / didn't ______

Go back to page 17.

2 Past simple and past continuous

1 Match each question (1–6) to the correct response (a–f).

1 Where was Paula when the dog bit her?
2 Ava was away last week, wasn't she?
3 Who were you texting?
4 How did Maja and Julia get home?
5 Were you sleeping when I called?
6 Why did you leave the party?

a Yes, I was. But I had to wake up soon anyway.
b My mum – she wanted to know where I was.
c Yes, she was windsurfing down at the coast.
d Everybody was shouting and the music was too loud.
e They got a lift from a friend because it was raining.
f In the park near our house – she was taking her morning walk.

2 For questions 1–5, complete the second sentence so it has a similar meaning to the two above it, using either the past simple or past continuous. There is an example at the beginning (0).

0 Mario studied classical music in Hungary all year. He met his best friend there.
When Mario met *his best friend, he was studying classical music in Hungary.*

1 Sakura went climbing. She injured her finger.
Sakura injured ______

2 The internet stopped working this morning. They played video games all morning.
This morning, they were playing ______

3 I had coffee with Clara during my break. My boss called to tell me the news.
While I was having ______

4 She sat on a bench in the main square. Somebody stole her purse.
Somebody stole ______

5 This afternoon I made lunch. That's when the postwoman delivered the package.
This afternoon, the postwoman delivered ______

Go back to page 21.

3 Countable and uncountable nouns

Nouns can be either countable or uncountable. Nouns like *bin*, *plate*, *note*, *airline*, *location* and *committee* are countable. Nouns like *air*, *rain*, *fame*, *magic*, *happiness* and *corruption* are uncountable.

- Countable nouns can be singular or plural. You can put *a/an* or a number before these nouns.

  *They have a **dog** and three **cats**.*

- Uncountable nouns are always singular. *A/An* is not used before uncountable nouns.

  ***Money** isn't everything.*

- Uncountable nouns either can't be counted (*help*, *anger*, *smoke*, *pollution*, *importance*, *progress*, *knowledge*) or they are not usually counted (*rice*, *sand*, *salt*, *pasta*).

  *The children came home with **sand** in their shoes.*

- Some uncountable nouns in English are countable in other languages, e.g. *advice*, *equipment*, *furniture*, *graffiti*, *homework*, *housework*, *money*, *news*, *information*, *research*.

  *I have a lot of **housework** to do – the flat is an absolute mess.*

- We can sometimes use uncountable nouns in a countable way to describe the quantity or type of something, e.g. *cake*, *cheese*, *coffee*, *detergent*, *juice*, *paint*, *plastic*, *sauce*, *soap*.

  *He loves **coffee**.* (substance)

  *She ordered a croissant and two small **coffees**.* (= cups of coffee)

  *Have we got any **cheese**?* (substance)

  *As a starter, they served a selection of Spanish **cheeses**.* (= types of cheese)

coffee

a coffee

- Some nouns can be countable or uncountable and there is a difference in meaning, e.g. *time*, *iron*, *light*, *room*, *work*.

  *I've been there many **times**.*

  *What **time** is it?*

Quantifiers

Quantifiers are words or phrases that express quantity – for example, *some*, *many*, *a lot of*.

We can use some quantifiers with both countable and uncountable nouns, including:

- *a lot of*. We use *a lot of* in positive sentences.

  *I had **a lot of** emails to write this morning.*

  *Being a parent takes **a lot of** patience.*

- *some* and *any*. *Some* is common in positive sentences; *any* is common in negative sentences and questions.

  *I like **some** types of fish.*

  *Do you have **any** questions?*

  *We don't have **any** milk.*

  NB We can also use *some* in a question if it is an offer or request.

  *Do you need **some** help?*

There are some quantifiers that we only use with countable nouns, including:

- *many*, which is common in questions and negatives.

  *How **many** eggs do I have to add to this pancake mix?*

  *There aren't **many** potatoes.*

- *a few*, which we use to talk about small quantities.

  *At the end of the talk, she answered **a few** questions from the audience.*

There are some quantifiers that we only use with uncountable nouns, including:

- *much*, which is common in questions and negatives.

  *I don't have **much** experience with this program.*

  *How **much** rice did they eat?*

- *a little*, which we use to talk about small amounts.

  *It's okay to eat **a little** junk food sometimes.*

3 Countable and uncountable nouns

1 In each group, ONE of the four words is uncountable. Circle the uncountable nouns.

1	result	weather	generation	queue
2	suitcase	handbag	box	luggage
3	rubbish	freezer	kettle	cupboard
4	ingredient	sausage	flavour	spaghetti
5	popcorn	burger	grape	refreshment
6	position	attitude	research	strategy
7	bean	chip	toast	peanut
8	advice	suggestion	tip	recommendation

2 Five of the following sentences contain mistakes with countable/uncountable nouns. Find the mistakes and correct them.

1 I have an exciting news: I'm getting married!
2 For dessert? I think I'll have the strawberries and cream.
3 All the new office furnitures have arrived.
4 Can you cut up some carrots for the soup?
5 William normally eats a toast for breakfast.
6 We stopped buying this juice because it contains a lot of sugars.
7 The wall is covered with graffitis.
8 Anja has homework to do for both maths and social studies.

3 Underline the correct alternatives to complete the sentences.

1 Not *many* / *much* students came to class this morning.
2 There isn't *any* / *some* juice in the fridge.
3 I don't have *many* / *much* time.
4 I didn't finish the pasta – there is still *a few* / *a little* left.
5 We haven't got *any* / *some* plans for the weekend.
6 If you like these oranges, I can give you *a few* / *a little* to take home.
7 There weren't *many* / *much* empty seats.
8 We can lend you *a few* / *a little* money, if you really need it.
9 There are *any* / *some* photos on the shelf.
10 Not *many* / *much* information is available.

Go back to page 33.

3 Articles

We use **the definite article** *the*:

- to refer to a person, place or thing that you have talked about before.

  I packed an apple and some crisps. I'll eat ***the apple*** *now and* ***the crisps*** *later.*
- when it's clear which one you're referring to.

  Do you want me to get anything from ***the supermarket****?* (the one you always go to)

  (You gave me a book). ***The book*** *was very interesting, thank you.*
- when there is only one of something, e.g. *the ground*, *the Earth*, *the sky, the sun*.

  We looked up at ***the full moon****.*

  Is that your purse on ***the ground****?*
- in many time expressions, e.g. *at the moment*, *in the past*, *in the near future*.

  He always has to work ***at the weekend****.*

  He isn't here ***at the moment****. He's at school.*

We use **the indefinite article** *a/an*:

- to mention a singular countable noun for the first time.

  I bought ***an avocado*** *and* ***a pineapple****. We can have the avocado for lunch and the pineapple for dessert.*
- before a noun that is one of many.

  Is there ***a café*** *near here?*

  Do you have ***a pencil****?*
- in descriptions.

  They live in ***a small flat****.*

  He's from ***a beautiful village*** *in the mountains.*
- to talk about someone's job.

  My mum is ***a software designer****.*

  His sister is ***a dentist****.*
- with *day*, *week*, *month* or *year* to talk about frequency.

  We look after our grandchildren once or twice ***a week****.*

  I brush my teeth three times ***a day****.*

We use **no article**:

- to talk in general about plural or uncountable nouns.

  I love ***cars****.*

  Life *isn't always easy.*
- before *next* or *last* when talking about days, weeks, months and years.

  I ate lunch with my cousins ***last Saturday****.*

  We're going to London ***next week****.*
- with common expressions with *work*, *school* and *home*, and after the prepositions *at*, *to* and *from*.

  Is Laura still ***at school****?*

  I'm on my way home ***from work****.*
- with languages and most countries.

  He speaks good ***English****.*

  She is from ***India****.*

NB We use the definite article with countries that contain a common noun like *Kingdom*, *Republic*, *State* or *Union* in their name, e.g. *The United Kingdom*, *The Dominican Republic*. We also use it with countries with plural names, e.g. *The Netherlands*, *The Philippines.*

3 Articles

1 For each pair of sentences, complete one gap with *the* and leave one gap blank. The first one has been done for you.

1a The world's largest airport terminal is located in ___*the*___ United Arab Emirates.

1b In ____________ modern China, it's possible to pay for almost everything with the WeChat app.

2a It's actually true that ____________ carrots are good for your eyes – they're an excellent source of beta carotene.

2b Dinner is almost ready. I think ____________ carrots only need to cook for another 10 or 15 minutes.

3a Over the years, ____________ computer science has become more and more important in school curricula.

3b Our guest this evening is a leading expert on ____________ science of food and cooking.

4a ____________ mobile phones that are on special offer today include Apple, Huawei, Samsung and Lenovo.

4b People use ____________ mobile phones for everything nowadays.

5a I can't believe you're still at ____________ work! It's 8 pm.

5b I find happiness in ____________ volunteer work I do for various charities.

6a The neighbour's dog woke me up in the middle of ____________ night and I couldn't get back to sleep.

6b I went to the most incredible reggaeton concert ____________ last night.

2 Choose the correct alternatives to complete the sentences.

1 Lina is *pilot / a pilot*. She flies all the way to Brazil twice *a week / the week*!

2 My friends and I are big fans of *sushi / the sushi*. *Next Saturday / The next Saturday* we've got a reservation at a new sushi bar in the city centre.

3 Yesterday, I got to *work / the work* really late again and my manager wasn't happy. She said, "I hope this is *a last time / the last time*."

4 It's important to plan for *future / the future*. That's why I set up *a new retirement account / the new retirement account* that I told you about.

5 How about seeing the film in *English / the English*? I think there is *a cinema / the cinema* in the centre that shows films in the original version.

6 To be a good cook, hard work is more important than *talent / the talent*. That's true of most things in *life / the life*, don't you think?

Go back to page 36.

4 Present perfect simple

- To form the present perfect simple, we use *have/has* + past participle.

  *We**'ve agreed** to help her.*

  *She**'s invited** us to the party.*
- To form negative statements we use *haven't/hasn't* + past participle.

  *They **haven't watched** TV today.*

  *He **hasn't grown** any vegetables.*
- To form questions, we put *Have/Has* before the subject.

  ***Have** you **visited** your cousin?*

  ***Has** it **happened**?*
- To give short answers, we use *have (not) / has (not)*.

  *Yes, I/you/we/they **have**.* *No, I/you/we/they **haven't**.*

  *Yes, she/he/it **has**.* *No, she/he/it **hasn't**.*
- For regular verbs, the past participle is the same as the past simple. For irregular verbs, the past participle can be different: *swim, swam, swum / drive, drove, driven.*

Use

We use the present perfect simple to show a connection between the past and the present. We use it:

- to talk in general about past actions or experiences.

  *I**'ve read** that book.*

  *Have you **ever** been to Norway?*
- to talk about recent past events with a present result

  *I can't play in the football match. I**'ve hurt** my knee.*
- to talk about an action or situation that started in the past and continues into the present.

  *I**'ve been** a fan of punk music since I was a teenager.*

NB We do not use the present simple to talk about something that started in the past and continues now.

~~*He lives in Dublin for many years.*~~ ×

*He**'s lived** in Dublin for many years.* ✓

Time expressions

- To talk about how long something has continued for, we use *since* and *for*. *Since* introduces the time period's starting point; *for* introduces the length of the period.

  *Susan **has been** in Hungary **since** November.*

  *Susan **has been** in Hungary **for** three months.*

Since	For
November, last month, (last) Thursday, 1982, the 25th of March, etc	*a week, six months, years, half an hour, 15 minutes, a long time*, etc

- We use *never* in negative statements and *ever* in questions. Both are placed before the main verb.

  *I've **never** seen any of the Batman movies.* (up to now)

  *Have you **ever** tried kimchi?* (at any time in your life)
- We also use *ever* with superlatives.

  *This is the best book I have **ever** read.*
- We ask questions with *How long* + present perfect to find out the length of time something has continued.

  ***How long** have you had this car?*
- We use *already* before the main verb in sentences to describe an action that happened before now.

  *They've **already** watched this video over a dozen times.*
- We use *yet* in questions to ask if something expected has happened. We put *yet* at the end of the sentence.

  *Have you booked your ticket **yet**? They'll sell out soon.*
- We use *yet* in negative statements to talk about an expected action that has not happened.

  *I ordered a new phone online, but it hasn't arrived **yet**.*
- We use *just* before the main verb in positive statements to say that something happened very recently or a short time ago.

  *You've **just** run 20 kilometres. Of course you're tired!*

4 Present perfect simple and past simple

We use the present perfect to talk about past actions:

- that happened in a time that is not mentioned.

  *I**'ve been** to five different countries in Africa.*
- that happened in an unfinished time period.

  *In the last week, I**'ve watched** too much television.*

We use the past simple to talk about past actions that happened during a finished period of time.

*I **went** skydiving for the first time on my 21st birthday.*

With the past simple, we use time expressions that refer to a finished period of time. With the present prefect simple, we use time expressions that link the past action to the present.

*I attended a new exhibition there **last month**.*

*I haven't met up with my friends **in the last few weeks**.*

Finished time expressions (past simple)	Unfinished time expressions (present perfect)
last night/week/year	these last few weeks/months
two days ago	in the last few days
yesterday morning	over the past year
at the weekend	in recent months/years
in January	

NB Some time expressions are used with either the past simple or the present perfect, e.g. *today, this morning, this week/month/year*. It depends on whether the speaker thinks of the time period as finished or unfinished.

***Have** you **seen** Clara this morning?* (It's still morning.)

***Did** you **see** Clara this morning?* (The morning is finished.)

4 Present perfect simple

1 Write the words in the right order to make sentences with the present perfect simple.

1. your / have / read / message. / I / just ____________________
2. long / you / in / been / Ireland? / how / have ____________________
3. yet? / decision / a / you / made / have / ____________________
4. prize? / ever / a / you / won / have ____________________
5. this / I / read / book. / have / already ____________________
6. our / begun / just / we / journey. / have ____________________
7. received / she / answer / not / an / yet. / has ____________________
8. never / have / accident. / had / we / an ____________________

2 In each sentence 1–8, there is a mistake. Find the mistakes and correct them.

1. We've been married since 20 happy years.
2. How much time have you been involved in the theatre programme?
3. I know my best friend since primary school.
4. He has been a cameraman for five years ago.
5. How long does she work here?
6. I don't know – I've ever thought about it.
7. I just done the washing up.
8. We haven't spoken to him about it already.

Go back to page 47.

4 Present perfect simple and past simple

1 Read the blog post about a whitewater rafting trip and choose the correct alternative. Use the time expressions to help you decide.

A WILD RIDE

Greetings from the Apurímac River in Peru. I **(1)** *lived* / *'ve lived* in Mexico City all my life, so I'm a bit out of my comfort zone here! For the last 48 hours, my husband and I **(2)** *were* / *have been* on a whitewater rafting trip. We **(3)** *arrived* / *has arrived* in Cusco, the nearest city, three days ago. After camping beside the river, we **(4)** *climbed* / *'ve climbed* into our river rafts for the first time yesterday morning. At first, I **(5)** *felt* / *have felt* a bit nervous – and for good reason. My husband and I both **(6)** *fell* / *have fallen* out of the raft almost immediately. But the guides quickly pulled us back in and, at least so far, that **(7)** *didn't happen* / *hasn't happened* again. In these last two days, we **(8)** *travelled* / *'ve travelled* 50 kilometres down the river. Let's see how much further we can get tomorrow!

2 Complete the sentences using the past simple or present perfect simple form of the verbs in brackets.

1. My girlfriend ____________ (*give*) me this book for my birthday a couple of weeks ago. I ____________ (*read*) about half of it so far and it's really good.
2. After she ____________ (*finish*) her university degree last June, Joan ____________ (*get*) a job straight away as a programmer for a new tech start-up.
3. Last month, I ____________ (*try*) *Apex Legends* for the first time and now I'm obsessed! Since then I ____________ (*not play*) any other video games.
4. I ____________ (*never say*) anything until now, but, to be honest, I ____________ (*always think*) Greg is a bit selfish.
5. ____________ (*you find*) time to relax these last few days? You ____________ (*seem*) really stressed out the last time I saw you.
6. I ____________ (*buy*) this computer when I was at university and until now I ____________ (*not have*) a single problem with it.

Go back to page 50.

5 Present perfect continuous

- We form the present perfect continuous with subject + *has/have* + *been* + *-ing*.

  *We**'ve been relaxing** in the garden.*

  *She**'s been painting** the living room.*
- We form negative statements by using *have/has not* + *been* + *-ing*.

  *You **haven't been listening** to me!*

  *My brother **hasn't been working**; he's been sick.*
- To form questions, we put *Have/Has* before the subject.

  ***Have** you **been crying**?*

  ***Has** he **been looking** for me?*
- To give short answers, we use *have (not) / has (not)*.

  *Yes, I/you/we/they **have**.* *No, I/you/we/they **haven't**.*

  *Yes, she/he/it **has**.* *No, she/he/it **hasn't**.*

Use

We use the present perfect continuous:

- to talk about past actions that continue into the present. We often use *recently* or *lately*.

  *I**'ve been travelling** a lot for work **recently**. It would be nice to stay home!*
- to talk about an action that has just stopped, but has a present result.

  A: Your hair is wet.

  *B: I**'ve been swimming**.*
- with actions that have been in progress, or have repeated, for a long period of time. We often use time expressions like *for/since*, *all day/week/month/year*.

  *She**'s been trying** to pass her driving test **for three months**.*

  *I**'ve been looking** forward to this moment **all day**.*
- to emphasise that an action is temporary.

  *He**'s been taking** care of his neighbour's dog.*

  *She**'s been living** with her sister while her house **is being decorated**.*
- to complain about an action that has continued for too long.

  *We**'ve been waiting** in this queue for over an hour!*

  *I**'ve been trying** to call you all morning!*

NB We can't use the present continuous to talk about actions that started in the past but continue into the present.

~~*I'm living here for 10 years.*~~

*I**'ve been living** here for 10 years.*

It is often possible to use either the present perfect simple or the present perfect continuous to talk about an action that started in the past and continues now, or is repeated until now. There is no change in meaning.

*I**'ve listened** to this album a lot since it came out.*

*I**'ve been listening** to this album a lot since it came out.*

However, to say that an action is completed, we use the present perfect simple instead of the present perfect continuous.

*We**'ve fixed** the car. It's working fine now.* (completed)

*We**'ve been fixing** the car, but there is still some work left to do.* (not completed)

*These are all the flowers I**'ve planted**.* (completed)

*I**'ve been planting** flowers all morning.* (not completed)

We use the present perfect simple, NOT the present perfect continuous, to describe states and to give information about 'how many'.

*I**'ve known** her all my life.*

~~*I've been knowing her all my life.*~~

*We**'ve hired** three new employees.*

~~*We've been hiring three new employees.*~~

*I**'ve lost** my wallet a few times.*

~~*I've been losing my wallet a few times.*~~

5 Present perfect continuous

1 Complete the text using the present perfect continuous form of the verbs in brackets.

EARTHWORKS: THE ART OF MICHAEL HEIZER

Recently, the artist Michael Heizer **(1)** ________________ (spend) most of his time in the middle of the desert. Heizer is a 'land artist'. Since the 1960s, he **(2)** ________________ (use) earth-moving machines to create art from natural materials. One piece, called *Levitated Mass*, requires nervous museum visitors to walk underneath a 340-ton rock. Lately, Heizer's work **(3)** ________________ (receive) more and more attention from art critics. In particular, they **(4)** ________________ (talk) about *City*, a collection of enormous triangles and other shapes in the Nevada desert. Heizer started work on *City* in 1970 and he **(5)** ________________ (try) to complete it ever since. The artist has spent 50 years on this ambitious piece of art, but, starting in 2022, people **(6)** ________________ (go) to visit the site in small groups. They say it is a special experience to admire Heizer's art in this harsh, natural landscape.

2 Choose the correct alternative. Sometimes both forms are possible. The first one is done for you.

1 **A:** Do you visit this area often?
B: Yes. In fact, *we've come* / *we've been coming* here at least five or six times this year to go mountain biking.

2 **A:** What app would you recommend?
B: *I've used* / *I've been using* ExpressX for a few years, and so far, I'm happy with it.

3 **A:** This land *has belonged* / *has been belonging* to my family since the 1800s.
B: That's a long time!

4 **A:** *Has he ever stopped* / *Has he ever been stopping* to think about this from her perspective?
B: To be honest, I don't think he has.

5 **A:** Are you having a nice afternoon?
B: Yes, *we've watched* / *we've been watching* a film. We're going to finish it after dinner.

6 **A:** Is she still going to the gym?
B: No, *she's cancelled* / *she's been cancelling* her membership. Now she does indoor rock climbing instead.

7 **A:** How long *have you worked* / *have you been working* here at the national park?
B: For about five years.

8 **A:** *I've tried* / *I've been trying* to connect to the internet all morning, but I still can't get online.
B: That sounds really frustrating.

Go back to page 71.

5 Relative clauses

1 Defining relative clauses

A defining relative clause defines, or makes it clear, which thing or person we are talking about. We use relative pronouns *that*, *where*, *who* and *whose* in relative clauses.

Person	who/that	*Marie is the type of person **who/that** never gets angry.*
Thing	which/that	*I like reading books **that/which** teach me something new.*
Possession	whose	*She is famous writer **whose** books are popular all over the world.*
Place	where	*This is the lake **where** we went camping last year.*

NB When the relative pronoun is the subject of the verb in the relative clause, no further subject is used.

*That's the book **that/which** won the Pulitzer prize.*

~~*That's the book that/which it won the Pulitzer prize.*~~

We can leave out *that*, *which* or *who* if the relative pronoun is the object of the verb in the relative clause, i.e. when the person or thing they refer to is NOT doing the action of the verb. If the relative pronoun is the subject, we cannot leave it out.

*That's the professor (**that/who**) I had last year for geology.*

(subject = *I*, so we can leave out *that/who*.)

*I like trains **that/which** have free wi-fi.*

(subject = *that/which*, so we cannot leave out *that/which*.)

2 Non-defining relative clauses

A non-defining relative clause does not define which person or thing we are talking about, but instead adds extra information about them. This information is not necessary to understand the rest of the sentence.

Badaling is the most visited section of the Great Wall of China. It was built during the Ming Dynasty.

*Badaling, **which was built during the Ming Dynasty**, is the most visited section of the Great Wall of China.*

In non-defining relative clauses:

- we use commas before and after the relative clauses.

  *Cyndy, **who is retired now,** spends a lot of time with her grandchildren.*

  *Tim, **whose brother is a writer,** lives on this street.*

  If the clause comes at the end of a sentence, we only use one comma.

  *He works for Lufthansa, **which is a German airline.***

  *We live in Madrid, **which is the capital of Spain.***

- we cannot use *that* instead of *which* or *who*.

  *Stonehenge, **which** they planned to visit, was closed for repair work.*

  ~~*Stonehenge, that they planned to visit, was closed for repair work.*~~

- we cannot leave out *which* and *who*, even when they are the object of the verb in the relative clause.

  *He lost his favourite watch, **which** his grandfather had given him as a birthday present.*

  (subject = *his grandfather* but we cannot leave out *which*.)

5 Relative clauses

1 Defining relative clauses

1 Complete the sentences using *where*, *which*, *who* or *whose*. Add *that* if it can be used instead.

1 The mechanic ____________ fixed my car was named Roan.
2 The guy ____________ snowboard you bought is a friend of mine.
3 The tent ____________ we've rented is big enough for five people.
4 This is the store ____________ I bought my new hiking boots.
5 The guide ____________ took us up the mountain wasn't very friendly.
6 She's the same ski instructor ____________ I had last year.

2 In which sentences in Exercise 1 can we leave out the relative pronoun?

Go back to page 74.

2 Non-defining relative clauses

1 Combine the two sentences using non-defining relative clauses. The first one has been done for you.

0 Last year, we visited the Bogd Khan Uul Biosphere Reserve. It is one of the oldest national parks in the world.
Last year we visited the Bogd Khan Uul Biosphere Reserve, which is one of the oldest national parks in the world.
1 This national park covers an area of 418 square kilometres. It is located near the capital city of Mongolia.
2 The Bogd Khan Uul mountain is a popular tourist destination. The mountain is 2261 metres high and takes 3–4 hours to hike to the top of.
3 On our walk, we got the chance to see a Siberian musk deer. It is a very rare, endangered animal.
4 Later, we visited the Winter Palace of Bogd Khan. Bogd Khan was a rich and powerful Mongolian leader in the early 20th century.

2 Underline the correct alternative. Sometimes two of the alternatives are possible.

Rachel Carson: a voice for nature

One person **(1)** *who* / *that* / *which* influenced me when I was young is Rachel Carson. She was an American scientist and author **(2)** *that* / *who* / *whose* books inspired a generation of people to care more about the environment.

Carson began her career teaching biology at a university. She then joined the U.S. Fish and Wildlife Service, **(3)** *that* / *which* / *where* she worked as an aquatic biologist. Around this time, Carson started writing science articles for the general public, **(4)** *that* / *which* / *where* were published in the *New Yorker* and other magazines.

Carson had a special talent for writing about scientific ideas in a way **(5)** *that* / *who* / *which* average people could understand. Her books on the environment, **(6)** *that* / *which* / *whose* include *The Sea Around Us* and *The Silent Spring*, were bestsellers and were translated into many languages.

Carson's books, **(7)** *that* / *who* / *which* I've read many times, inspired me to study environmental science. I now work for an environmental engineering company, **(8)** *who* / *whose* / *where* I help develop technology to reduce pollution.

Go back to page 74.

6 Comparatives and superlatives

1 Comparatives

To form the comparative of adjectives:

- we add *-er* to adjectives with one syllable. We add *-r* to adjectives with one syllable ending in *-e*.

  *low → **lower***   *nice → **nicer***
- we double the last consonant of adjectives with one syllable that end in a short vowel sound + consonant, e.g. *big, hot, fat, fit, flat, slim, thin, wet.*

  *big → **bigger***   *flat → **flatter***

  NB Some one-syllable adjectives are irregular.

  *bad → **worse***   *far → **further***
- with adjectives that end in *-y*, we change *-y* to *-i* and add *-er*, e.g. *busy, dry, heavy, happy, lucky, pretty, sunny.*

  *dry → **drier***   *happy → **happier***
- we use *more* or *less* with adjectives that have two or more syllables, e.g. *famous, intelligent, dangerous.*

  *famous – **more** famous / **less** famous*

  NB Some two-syllable adjectives have two forms, e.g. *clever, narrow, quiet, simple.*

  *quiet – **quieter** / **more** quiet*

Use

- Comparative adjectives compare two people or things.

  *His phone is **better** than mine. (comparing two phones)*

  NB We use *than* with comparative adjectives, not *that.*

  *A car is faster ~~that~~ **than** a motorbike.*
- To describe small differences, we use *a bit / a little.* To describe big differences, we use *much / a lot.*

  *This washing machine is **a bit wider** than our old one.*

  *This room is **much better** than mine.*

2 Superlatives

To form the superlative of adjectives:

- we use *the* and add *-est* to adjectives with one syllable and *-st* to adjectives with one syllable ending in *-e.*

  *high → **the highest***   *large → **the largest***
- we double the last consonant of adjectives with one syllable that end in a short vowel sound + consonant, e.g. *big, hot, fat, fit, flat, slim, thin, wet.*

  *fit → **the fittest***   *wet → **the wettest***

  NB Some one-syllable adjectives are irregular:

  *bad → **the worst***   *far → **the furthest***
- with adjectives that end in *-y*, we change *-y* to *-i* and add *-est*, e.g. *dry, heavy, happy, lucky, pretty, sunny.*

  *busy → **the busiest***   *lucky → **the luckiest***
- we use *the most* or *the least* with adjectives that have two or more syllables, e.g. *terrible, amazing, dangerous.*

  *dangerous → **the most** dangerous*

  NB Two forms are possible with some two-syllable adjectives, e.g. *clever, narrow, quiet, simple.*

  *clever → **the cleverest** / **the most** clever*

Use

- Superlative adjectives compare three or more things.

  *It's **the best** car in France. (of all cars in France)*
- To emphasise the difference, we use *by far.*

  *It's **by far the best** camera I've ever owned.*

3 (not) as … as …

- We use *as* + adjective + *as* to say that two things are the same.

  *These pyramids are **as** old **as** the ones in Egypt.*
- We make negative comparisons with *not as* + adjective + *as.*

  *My holiday was definitely **not as** exciting **as** yours.*
- We can qualify comparisons with *as … as …* using *almost/nearly.*

  *In the winter, her flat is **almost as cold as** ours.*
- We can qualify comparisons with *not as* + adjective + *as* using *nearly* (but NOT *almost*).

  *The film was **not nearly as funny as** I expected.*

6 So, such, too and enough

So and such

- Use *so / such* for emphasis, with a similar meaning to *very.* We use *so* + adjectives and *such* + noun phrases.

  *It was **so hot** today. We had **such a nice trip** to Rome.*

  NB Do not use *a/an* with *such* before plural or uncountable nouns.

  *It made me happy to get **such ~~a~~ great feedback**.*
- We can use a *that* clause after *so* + adjective or *such* + noun phrase to talk about a result. *That* can be left out.

  *It was **so hot** today **(that) I couldn't focus on work.***

  *We had **such a nice trip** to Rome **(that) we went back**.*

Too and enough

- *Too* means *more than is necessary or good.* It often suggests difficulty. We put *too* before adjectives.

  *That book was **too long**. (Finishing it was difficult.)*

  NB We cannot use *too* to say how good something is.

  ~~This show is too funny.~~
- We put *too many / too few* before countable nouns. We use *too much / too little* before uncountable nouns.

  ***Too many/few people** signed up for the course.*

  *I think we got **too much/little sleep**.*
- *Enough* means *as much as necessary.* We put *enough* **after** adjectives but **before** nouns.

  *Is there **enough light** in the bedroom?*

  *This internet connection **isn't fast enough**.*

6 Comparatives and superlatives

1 Write the comparative and superlative forms of the three adjectives in each group (1–5).

1 calm — *calmer* / *the calmest*; fresh — ______ / ______; great — ______ / ______

2 surprising — ______ / ______; powerful — ______ / ______; convenient — ______ / ______

3 early — ______ / ______; heavy — ______ / ______; silly — ______ / ______

4 big — ______ / ______; hot — ______ / ______; thin — ______ / ______

5 far — ______ / ______; bad — ______ / ______; good — ______ / ______

2 Write five sentences using comparative and superlative forms of the adjectives from Exercise 1.

*The sea is **calmer** today than it was yesterday.*

3 Complete the second sentence so it has a similar meaning to the first sentence.

1 I'm not as talented as my sister.
My sister is *more talented than me*.

2 The last tour guide wasn't as good as this one.
This tour guide is ______.

3 Dina is the youngest in the family.
Everybody else in the family is ______.

4 The journey was shorter than I expected.
The journey wasn't ______.

5 No student in our school is taller than José.
José is the ______.

6 Ibrahim isn't as interested in studying abroad as Khaled.
Ibrahim is less ______.

Go back to page 85.

6 *So, such, too and enough*

1 For each pair of sentences, match the sentence beginnings (a–b) to the sentence endings (i–ii).

1a Your husband is such — ii a good cook!
1b Your husband is so — i good at cooking!

1a	Your husband is such	i	good at cooking!
1b	Your husband is so	ii	a good cook!
2a	I've spent too much	i	time in the sun. Now I'm very sunburnt.
2b	I've spent too many	ii	days away. I'm starting to miss home.
3a	My son has too much	i	free time. He complains about being bored.
3b	My son has so many	ii	friends. He's very popular at school.
4a	There isn't enough	i	traffic on this road. Let's take another route.
4b	There's too much	ii	space in the car for all our bags.
5a	We've bought too many	i	money on this holiday. Everything is expensive here.
5b	We've spent too much	ii	souvenirs. They won't fit in our bag.

2 Complete the gaps with *so*, *such*, *too* or *enough*.

1 I think we bought *too* many bananas. We'll never eat all of these.
2 I've got ______ much work to do that I'll never finish it all.
3 I don't have ______ money to take the high-speed train, so I'm travelling by bus instead.
4 She was ______ excited about the trip that she couldn't sleep the night before.
5 Labrador retrievers are ______ friendly dogs.
6 It was ______ far to walk to the beach, so we took a bus.
7 It was ______ a nice day that we decided to go for a walk along the lake.
8 Congratulations on your new job – I'm ______ happy for you!

Go back to page 91.

6 Future forms

1 Going to

- We form affirmative statements using *to be* + *going to* + infinitive without *to*.

  *I'**m going to cry**. This film is so sad.*

  *You'**re going to fall**! Be careful!*
- We form negative statements using *to be* + *not going to* + infinitive without *to*.

  *She **isn't going to respond** to you.*

  *We **aren't going to sleep**; it's too early.*
- To form questions, we put *to be* before the subject.

  ***Am** I **going to win**?*

  ***Are** they **going to swim** in the lake?*
- To give a short answer, we use *am/is/are (not)*.

  *Yes, I **am**.* *No, I'**m not**.*

  *Yes, he/she/it **is**.* *No, he/she/it **isn't**.*

  *Yes, we/they/you **are**.* *No, we/they/you **aren't**.*

2 Will

- We form affirmative statements using *will ('ll)* + infinitive without *to*.

  *I like this watch. I'**ll take** it.*
- We form negative statements using *won't (will not)* + infinitive without *to*.

  *They **won't go** to the cinema tonight.*
- To form questions, we put *Will/Won't* before the subject.

  ***Will** you **help** me with my work?*
- To give a short answer, we use *will/won't*.

  *Yes / No, I/you/he/she/they **will / won't**.*

Use

A *Going to* is used to talk about personal plans, intentions or decisions related to the future. This may be in the near future or more distant future.

*I'**m going to finish** work a bit later today.*

*I'**m going to live** abroad after I finish my degree.*

B The present continuous is used for future arrangements or plans that are more fixed, e.g. travel or social arrangements. A specific time and/or location is usually mentioned or implied.

A: Can you meet me at 7 o'clock?

*B: Sorry, I'**m playing** football with Renate then.*

NB It's often possible to use either *going to* or the present continuous to talk about future plans, but the present continuous emphasises that we have made arrangements.

*We'**re going to have** a meeting about this.* (We've decided to have a meeting.)

*We'**re having** a meeting about this at 11 am tomorrow.* (We've decided on the day, time, place; the conference room has been booked, etc.)

C We use *will* for decisions that we make at the moment of speaking. We often use it with *I think*.

*The sun has just come out. I think I'**ll take** the dog for a walk.*

NB We cannot use the present simple for decisions we make at the moment of speaking.

A: Why isn't Paul here? We're going to be late!

~~*B: I call him.*~~

*B: I'**ll call** him.*

7 Will, may and might

1 will

We use *will/won't* + infinitive without *to* to talk about:

- fixed plans, timetabled events or facts.

  *The CEO **will** give a talk next Wednesday at 10.30 am.*

  *We **won't** be able to come to the party next weekend – we'**ll** be on holiday.*

  *Serena **will** be 25 years old in June.*
- offers and promises.

  *I'**ll** drive you to the airport.*

  *We **won't** visit you until the house is ready.*
- decisions that we make as we are speaking.

  *I'**ll** go to the supermarket later.*
- predictions about things we think will happen in the future.

  *More people **will** have electric cars in the next decade.*

Compare the difference between ***will*** for future predictions and ***going to*** for predictions with evidence.

*In ten years, people **won't** travel by plane as much.*

*Look at that grey cloud. It's **going to** rain.*

2 may and might

We use the modal verbs *may* and *might* for possibilities, advice and polite requests. They are always followed by the infinitive without *to*. We can contract the negative form of *might not* (*mightn't*) but we use the full form for *may not*. We use *may/might*:

- to talk about possibility.

  *She **may/might** study business at university, but she's not sure.* (It's possible she will go.)

  *It **may not / might not rain this afternoon** – the sun is shining.* (It's possible it won't rain.)
- we use *may* for polite requests and to give permission in a formal way.

  ***May** I borrow some money?*

  *You **may** go into the exam room now. You **may not** talk during the exam.*
- we use phrases like *as you may/might know* as a way to focus on shared knowledge.

  ***As you may/might know**, Peter is moving house today.*

6 Future forms

1 Choose the correct alternative.

1 **A:** It's freezing in here!
B: *I'll turn / I'm turning* on the heating. Let me just find the thermostat.

2 **A:** What's your brother planning to do for the bank holiday weekend?
B: *He'll visit / He's going to visit* an old friend in Toulouse.

3 **A:** Sorry, I can't meet up on Friday morning. I'm very busy.
B: What about in the afternoon? *Will you do / Are you doing* anything then?

4 **A:** I think this jacket is too small to fit either one of the kids.
B: Okay, *I'll donate / I'm donating* it to a charity shop.

5 **A:** What time does your girlfriend arrive?
B: I spoke to her about it yesterday. *I'm picking / I'll pick* her up from the airport at midnight.

6 **A:** Has Lilian decided what to study?
B: Yes, *she'll do / she's going to do* a degree in physics.

2 Put a tick (✓) next to the sentences that correctly use future forms. If a sentence is incorrect, rewrite it. There is an example at the beginning.

0 I'm buying some vegetables at the market later. Do you want to come? ×
I'm going to buy some vegetables at the market later. Do you want to come?

1 I'm going to tell Scott that I don't like his attitude.
2 **A:** We have to buy decorations for the party. **B:** You go. I stay here and tidy up.
3 I'll go to Leeds at the end of the week. I've already bought the tickets.
4 **A:** Ready to order? **B:** Yes, I'll have the pasta with clams.
5 Have you heard the news? Pedro is going to run for parliament in the next election!
6 When do you meet Samuel for coffee?
7 **A:** There's something wrong with my credit card. **B:** Don't worry, I pay for you.
8 I'm sorry, but I can't meet you tonight. I'm going to my parents' for dinner.

Go back to page 88.

7 *Will, may and might*

1 Match the sentences 1–5 to the different situations A–E.

1 I will tidy the kitchen. ______
2 May I use the wi-fi in your house? ______
3 We may not have enough time to go shopping today. ______
4 The course will begin on Monday 4th September. ______
5 There will be more cures for diseases soon. ______

a a future prediction
b an offer
c a polite request
d a timetabled event
e a possibility

2 Choose the correct options to complete the text.

Hello everyone

On Thursday morning, we definitely **(1)** *won't / might not* have our usual meeting at 9.30 am because Daniel Madison is giving us a presentation about his sales ideas instead. As you **(2)** *won't / might* know, Daniel is the new Sales Manager. Some people **(3)** *may / won't* want to talk to Daniel afterwards and ask him some questions. However, the meeting room **(4)** *won't / might not* be free after 10 am because there is another meeting in there at this time. We **(5)** *will / might* use the café to continue our discussions; I've reserved an area for us.

Kind regards,

Nuriya,

Manager

Go back to page 99.

7 Zero and first conditional

Conditional sentences have two parts. We connect them with a linking word (e.g. *if*). These sentences link together a condition and a result.

1 Zero conditional

- Conditional sentences have two parts: the condition and the result. We use *if* with the condition, and separate the two parts with a comma.

  If** you **heat water,** it **boils.

  ↓ *(condition)* ↓ *(result)*

- We form the zero conditional with *if/when* + present simple, present simple

  ***If** he **doesn't have** any work, he **leaves** the office early.*

  ***When** the weather **is** hot, I **drink** more water.*

- The order of the information can be swapped. In this case, we do NOT use a comma.

  *He **leaves** the office early **if** he **doesn't have** any work.*

  *I **drink** more water **when** the weather **is** hot.*

- We make *yes/no* and *wh-* questions in the zero conditional with *do/does* in the result half of the sentence.

  ***If you don't have** any work, **do you leave** the office early?*

  ***Do you leave** the office early **if you don't have** any work?*

  ***What do you do when** you **have** free time?*

  ***When you have** free time, **what do you do**?*

Use

We use the zero conditional:

- to talk about facts or things that are always or generally true. In this structure, *if* and *when* mean the same thing.

  ***When I drink** coffee in the afternoon, I **don't sleep** well at night.*

  ***If he eats** seafood, he **gets** ill.*

  *Water **turns** to ice **if** you **freeze** it.*

- to give instructions. In this form, we use the imperative structure: *If/When* + present simple, imperative.

  ***If you come** to the meeting, **ask** John for the details.*

  ↓ *(condition)* ↓ *(imperative)*

  or

  ***Ask** John for the details **if you come** to the meeting.*

2 First conditional

- We form the first conditional with *if* + present simple, *will/won't* + infinitive without *to*. We use *if* with the condition.

  ***If the weather is** good, **we'll go** to the beach.*

  ↓ *(condition)* ↓ *(result)*

- The order of information can be switched, as long as the condition is with *if*.

  ***She'll be** very happy **if she gets** the job.*

  ***I won't walk** to the meeting **if it rains** tomorrow.*

  ***We'll go** to the beach **if the weather is** good.*

- To make *yes/no* and *wh-* questions in the first conditional, we put *will/won't* before the subject in the result half of the sentence.

  ***If I go** to the supermarket, **will you come** with me?*

  ***Will you come** with me **if I go** to the supermarket?*

  ***If it rains** tomorrow, what **will you** do?*

  *What **will you do if it rains** tomorrow?*

- We can also use modal verbs instead of *will/won't* in first conditional sentences to talk about possibility and permission.

  ***If the weather is good** at the weekend, **we might go** hiking.*

  *We **might** go hiking if the weather **is** good at the weekend.*

  *If you **come** to Japan, you **can stay** with my family.*

  *The company **may** move to new offices if it **makes** a lot of money.*

  *If you **want** to know more about the city, we **could visit** the museum.*

Use

We use the first conditional to talk about possible or probable situations and their future results.

***If she gets** the job, **she'll be** very happy.*

***If it rains** tomorrow, **I won't walk** to the meeting.*

7 Zero and first conditional

1 **Correct the mistakes in the following sentences.**

1. I don't get hungry if I eat something now.
2. If you don't practise, you will improve your tennis skills.
3. I go to bed when I'll be tired.
4. She'll might be late if she misses the train.
5. If the weather is nice I'll go to the beach later.
6. Will get I the job if I apply for it?

2 **Decide if the sentences should be in the zero or first conditional. Choose the correct options to complete the sentences.**

1. When it rains, she *will take* / *she takes* the car to work.
2. *I'll meet* / *I meet* you later if I finish work early.
3. If I save enough money, *I buy* / *I'll buy* a new car.
4. The company *won't succeed* / *doesn't succeed* if it doesn't sell more products.
5. If you don't want to be here, *you go* / *go* home!
6. I always wear sunscreen when *it is* / *it will be* hot.

3 **Match the sentence beginnings 1–6 to the endings a–f to make complete sentences.**

1. If you want to try a free yoga class,
2. If employees enjoy their jobs,
3. If you don't feel like walking home,
4. If parents read to their children,
5. If a city has good public transport,
6. If we don't stop creating pollution,

a. they will learn to love books.
b. climate change will get worse.
c. people don't drive as much.
d. visit our studio next Tuesday.
e. take the underground instead.
f. they work more efficiently.

4 **Complete the text using the correct form of the verbs in brackets.**

GETTING THE JOB!

When you apply for a job, always **(1)** ____________ (*try*) to do your best. This starts with writing your CV. Make sure it looks good and check it carefully. If your CV is full of mistakes, you **(2)** ____________ (*not get*) an interview. It's a good idea to ask someone to look at it for you.

If you **(3)** ____________ (*be*) lucky enough to get an interview, prepare well. Read about the company and think of some questions to ask them. Plan your route to the interview too. If you arrive late, you **(4)** ____________ (*feel*) stressed. It also isn't a very good start to an interview!

Also remember that the interview is not just about your qualifications - your appearance is also important. The interviewer will think about you in a positive way if you **(5)** ____________ (*dress*) smartly and smile.

Go back to page 104.

8 Second conditional

We use the second conditional to talk about imaginary or unlikely situations and their results in the present or future.

- We form the second conditional with *If* + past simple, *would/wouldn't* + infinitive without *to.* We use *if* with the condition.

  ***If I won** the lottery, **I would leave** my job.* (It is unlikely I will win the lottery.)

  ↓ *(condition)* ↓ *(result)*

  ***If Helen was** the manager, **she wouldn't be** as strict as Mr Smith.* (Helen is not the manager.)

  ***If I had** more money, **I would buy** a new car.*

- The order of information can be switched, as long as the condition is with *if.*

  ***I would leave** my job **if I won** the lottery.*

  ↓ *(result)* ↓ *(condition)*

  ***Helen wouldn't be** as strict as Mr Smith **if she was** the manager.*

  ***I would buy** a new car **if I had** more money.*

  NB There is no comma when the conditional sentence begins with the result.

- To make *yes/no* and *wh-* questions in the second conditional, we put *would/wouldn't* before the subject in the result half of the sentence:

  ***If you had** the opportunity, **would you go** into space?*

  ***Would you go** into space **if you had** the opportunity?*

  ***If you could choose,** what team **would you play** for?*

  *What team **would you play** for **if you could choose?***

NB Notice the difference between the **zero**, **first** and **second** conditionals:

Zero conditional	*If I **go** to the beach, I **read** a book* (always true)
First conditional	*If I **go** to the beach, I **will read** a book.* (possible future situation)
Second conditional	*If I **went** to the beach, I **would read** a book.* (unlikely future situation)

NB We form the second conditional with the past tense, but the meaning is not past. It has an 'alternative present' or future meaning.

- We use *If I were* in the second conditional to give advice to another person. We imagine our actions in the other person's situation.

  ***If I were you, I'd support** a different team!*

  I'd support** a different team if **I were you.

- In the second conditional only, we can use *were* instead of *was* after *I/he/she* and *it*. This is especially common in formal situations.

  *If Daniel **was** older, he could work at the gallery.*

  *If Daniel **were** older, he could work at the gallery. (more formal)*

- For **all** conditionals, we can replace *if* with *unless. Unless* means *if not* or *only if.*

Zero conditional	***If I have** a bit of extra money, **I go** to an expensive restaurant.* ***I go** to an expensive restaurant **if I have** a bit of extra money.*	***Unless I have** a bit of extra money, **I don't go** to an expensive restaurant.* ***I don't go** to an expensive restaurant **unless I have** a bit of extra money.*
First conditional	***If I have** a bit of extra money, **I will go** to an expensive restaurant.* ***I will go** to an expensive restaurant **if I have** a bit of extra money.*	***Unless I have** a bit of extra money, **I won't go** to an expensive restaurant.* ***I won't go** to an expensive restaurant **unless I have** a bit of extra money.*
Second conditional	***If I had** a bit of extra money, **I would go** to an expensive restaurant.* ***I would go** to an expensive restaurant **if I had** a bit of extra money.*	***Unless I had** a bit of extra money, **I wouldn't go** to an expensive restaurant.* ***I wouldn't go** to an expensive restaurant **unless I had** a bit of extra money.*

8 Second conditional

1 In each sentence 1–6, there is a mistake. Find the mistakes and correct them.

1 If I had the time, I'd went to the gym more often.
2 If you could swim, you not worry about travelling by boat.
3 We go and see more matches if we lived nearer the stadium.
4 If Paulo have the money, he'd buy a new car.
5 What will you do if you were a superhero?
6 I wouldn't speak to him again unless you pay me!

2 Complete the second conditional sentences with the correct form of the verbs in the box.

be do go love speak travel

1 If someone was rude to me and didn't apologise, I ____________ to them again!
2 You work so hard. If I ____________ you, I'd ask for more money.
3 I am a big tennis fan. I ____________ to be a world-famous tennis player, if I could play well enough.
4 What ____________ you ____________ if you had more free time?
5 I've always wanted to visit many different countries. If I were rich, I ____________ around the world by bike!
6 I hate the rain. I ____________ out in this weather unless it was for something urgent.

3 Complete the text using the verbs in brackets in the second conditional.

The golfing world

If you could be any professional sports player, what sport **(1)** ____________ you ____________ (*choose*)? I think most people **(2)** ____________ (*play*) football if they could, but it might not be the best sport to play. If you **(3)** ____________ (*be*) a footballer, you would earn a lot of money for sure, but your career would also be short unless you **(4)** ____________ (*become*) a manager.

It **(5)** ____________ (*be*) better to choose a sport that makes money, and that you could do for a long time, if you had the choice. Golf is just this kind of sport. If you **(6)** ____________ (*join*) the golfing world, you would play well into your fifties and could make a fortune at the same time!

Go back to page 118.

8 Modals of permission, advice, obligation and prohibition

- After a modal verb, there is always a main verb in the infinitive without *to*. The modal verb does not change in the third person singular.

  *You **can come** to the party.*

  *He **should eat** more vegetables.*

- We form negatives by adding *not* between the modal verb and main verb.

  *You **cannot/can't** come to the party.*

  *He **should not** / **shouldn't** eat more vegetables.*

- We form questions by putting the modal verb before the subject.

  ***Can** you **come** to the party?*

  ***Should** he **eat** more vegetables?*

Use

1 Modal verbs are often used for rules, regulations, permission and giving advice.

*You **must not speak** in the library.*

*You **can open** the window if you like.*

*You **should get** some rest.*

2 We use *can/can't* + infinitive without *to* to:

- talk about permission.

  You can have my ball. (Yes, it is okay.)

  You can't come into the changing rooms! (No, it is not okay.)

- ask for permission.

  ***Can I come** to the party?*

- talk about ability.

  *John **can** play the saxophone.*

  *Amanda **can't** type very fast.*

NB We use *be able to* when *can/can't* are not possible e.g. in the future.

*I **will be able to** learn Japanese better with this app.*

~~*I **will can** learn Japanese better with this app.*~~

3 We use *could/may* + infinitive without *to* make questions that are more polite.

***Could I come** to the party?*

***May I come** to the party?* (more formal)

NB To answer questions with modal verbs, we can repeat the modal structure.

*Can I come to the party? **Yes, you can. / No, you can't.***

4 We use *should* or *ought to* to give advice or make a suggestion. There is no difference in meaning but *should* is more common.

*You **should play** for the Spanish national team!*

*You **ought to play** for the Spanish national team!* (a good idea)

*You **should practise** every day.*

*You **ought to practise** every day.* (the right thing to do)

5 We use *should not* or *ought not to* to say something is not a good idea or the wrong thing to do.

*You **shouldn't play** with a bad knee.*

*You **oughtn't to play** with a bad knee.*

NB *Ought* uses *to* before the main verb in positive and negative sentences. We do not use *to* in the question form. It is much more common to use *should* in the question.

*He **ought to play** better.*

~~*He **ought play** better.*~~

***Ought I speak** to the manager?*

6 We use *must/mustn't* and *have to / don't have to* to talk about what is essential, not essential or prohibited.

NB *Have to* and *don't have to* are followed by the infinitive without *to*, and they also change in the third person. There is no difference in meaning.

*We **must finish** our homework before we play football.*

*We **have to finish** our homework before we play football.*

*He **must finish** his homework before he plays football.*

*He **has to finish** his homework before he plays football.*

7 In the negative, *mustn't* and *don't have to* have different meanings.

***You mustn't kick** the other footballer!* (Do not do it.)

***She doesn't have to play** today. We have enough players.* (It's not necessary.)

8 We use *must* and *have to* to ask about obligation and prohibition.

***Must we do** our homework now?*

***Do we have to** finish our homework now?*

9 We use *had to / didn't have to* to talk about what was, or was not, essential in the past. We **cannot** use *must / mustn't* in the past.

***I had to leave** the pitch.*

***I didn't have to leave** the pitch.*

***Did you have to leave** the pitch?*

10 We use *not allowed to* to talk about prohibition in the past. The verb *be* changes to the past simple and *allowed* is always followed by *to*.

***I wasn't allowed to** join the team.*

***Were you allowed to** join the team?*

8 Modals of permission, advice, obligation and prohibition

1 Complete the park rules with the words in brackets. Decide if the sentences are positive or negative.

1 You ______________________ (*must / take*) your rubbish with you when you leave. We don't like rubbish!
2 You ______________________ (*must / leave*) your children alone in the park. Please stay together.
3 You ______________________ (*have to / pay*) to use the toilets. They are free.
4 You ______________________ (*can / play*) sports on the pitches, but don't play in the gardens.
5 You ______________________ (*should / feed*) bread to the ducks. It is bad for them.
6 You ______________________ (*can / have*) barbecues in the park. It's too dangerous.

2 Complete the information with the words in the box.

can can't don't have to must mustn't shouldn't

1 You ______________________ buy tickets for children under 12 years old – they can enter for free!
2 Students ______________________ enter the school before 8.15 am if they want to.
3 You ______________________ put your bag there – it might get wet.
4 You ______________________ open the door without a key. It's locked.
5 Visitors ______________________ take photographs in the gallery. It is prohibited.
6 All passengers ______________________ show their passports when checking in.

3 Choose the correct options to complete the sentences. In TWO sentences, both options are possible.

1 You *should / can't* go on to the pitch when the teams are playing. You must watch at the side.
2 You *mustn't / don't have to* join one of the university's sports teams if you don't want to. There are lots of other clubs you can join.
3 If you want to be the best player, you *should / ought to* practise every day!
4 You *should / don't have to* stretch after you do some exercise, so your muscles don't hurt.
5 I wanted to take my son to see the game, but he *wasn't allowed to / didn't have to* go in – he's too young.
6 I *must / have to* get up early every morning because I have basketball practice at 7 am.
7 If you like the water, you *shouldn't / ought to* try surfing – it's great fun!
8 Fans *can't / can* enter the stadium through that door – it's for players only.

Go back to page 120.

9 Past perfect simple and continuous

1 Past perfect simple

- We form the past perfect simple with *had* + past participle.

  *I **had studied** a lot for the test.*

  NB We can contract *had* to *'d*.

  I'd *You'd* *He'd/She'd* *We'd/They'd*

- We form negative statements with *hadn't* + past participle.

  *He **hadn't studied** for the test*

- To form questions, we put *Had* before the subject.

  ***Had** they **studied** for the test?*

Use

We use the past perfect simple to talk about an action or event that happened **before** another action or event in the past.

*I **took** a maths test last week. I **had studied** a lot for the test.*

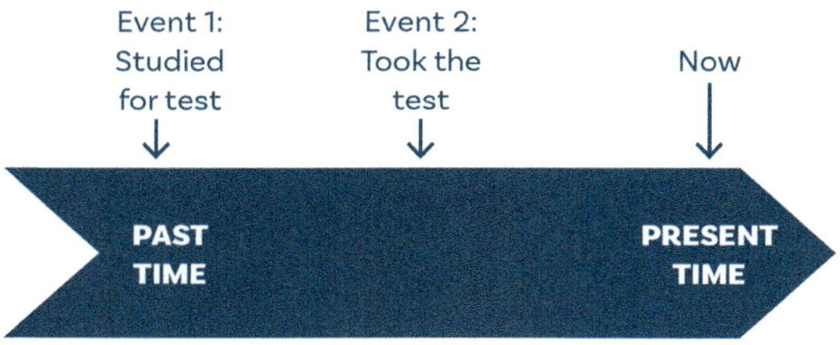

2 Time expressions

1 We can use time expressions like *when, by the time* and *until* to link the two actions in the past in one sentence.

- *when*

  *We decided to go shopping **when** we **had finished** studying.* (Event 1: studied; Event 2: decided to go shopping)

- *until* (up to that point)

  *I **hadn't enjoyed** maths **until** Mr Baker became my teacher.* (Event 1: didn't enjoy maths; Event 2: changed teacher)

- *by the time*

  *The class **had started by the time** we arrived.* (Event 1: the class started; Event 2: we arrived)

2 We often use the past perfect with *before* to show that the first action wasn't finished before the second action happened.

*Jim left school **before** the school year **had finished**.* (Jim did not complete the school year) (Event 1: Jim left school; Event 2: The school year ended)

3 We often use the past perfect with **adverbs**, e.g. *just, already, ever, never* to give more information in the sentence.

- *already* (before a certain time)

  *The teacher wanted to speak to the students, but **they had already left**.* (Event 1: students left; Event 2: teacher wanted to talk to students)

- *just* (a short time before)

  *The lecture **had just started** as I entered the room.* (Event 1: lecture started; Event 2: student entered)

- *ever* (at any time before the past action/event)

  *It was the most interesting subject **I had ever studied**.*

- *never* (at no time before the past action/event)

  ***She'd never studied** German before she went to Germany.*

3 Past perfect continuous

- We form the past perfect continuous with *had* + *been* + *-ing*.

  *She **had been working** on her essay all week.*

  *We **had been cooking** all morning.*

  *They**'d been waiting** for the bus for an hour.*

- We form negative statements with *hadn't* + *been* + *-ing*.

  *She **hadn't been working** on her essay all week.*

  *We **hadn't been cooking** all morning.*

- To form questions, we put *Had* before the subject.

  ***Had** she **been working** on her essay all week?*

  ***Had** you **been cooking** all morning?*

Use

We use the past perfect continuous:

- to talk about an action or event that happened **before** another action or event in the past when we want to focus on the **progress** of the first action. Compare:

  Past Perfect Simple: *I **had studied** a lot for the test, so I thought I would do well.* (focus on finishing studying)

  Past Perfect Continuous: *I **had been studying** a lot for the test, so I didn't have time to do anything else.* (focus on the continuing action)

- to emphasise the length of time something took. In this case, we use a time expression, e.g. *all day, all morning, for hours*, etc.

  *I was tired because I **had been cooking all morning.***

  *The dog **had been crying for hours**, so I took it to the vet.*

9 Past perfect simple and continuous

1 Underline the FOUR examples of the past perfect simple and continuous in the text.

SALSA ACADEMY BLOG HOME | ABOUT | SEARCH

Amira had never danced before she joined the Salsa Academy. She'd always wanted to try it, but she wasn't brave enough. She thought she'd be terrible at it – but actually, she was great! In just a few months, she could dance salsa like a professional! She'd been dancing at the Academy for a year when she decided to enter a competition. She had the chance to win €1000 and to dance on TV! When she was at the competition, she felt nervous – she thought she hadn't practised enough. In the end, she came second. She didn't win the prize, but she had a wonderful day, and she still dances salsa now.

2 In each sentence 1–6, there is a mistake. Find the mistakes and correct them.

1 Carol already knew Chris. She had been met him at a conference last year.
2 By the time I got to the airport, the plane left.
3 When I got out of class, I saw that it had been rained.
4 Leaving home to go to university was the most difficult thing I'd never done.
5 The film had just starting when I came into the room.
6 I been shopping for hours before I found the right present for my mum.

3 Complete the sentences with the past perfect simple or continuous form of the verbs in brackets.

1 Amanda ________ (*not / study*) drama before, and it was clear in her first acting class.
2 David ________ (*learn*) French for five years, but he still couldn't speak it very well.
3 Before she did the marathon, Karla ________ (*run*) 10 kilometres a day.
4 Emma was late. When she arrived at university, her class ________ (*already / start*)
5 The students ________ (*not / finish*) their project before the end of the course.
6 At school, Mr Peters was the best teacher I ________ (*ever / had*).
7 ________ Anna ________ (*leave*) the party by the time you got there?
8 The librarian was annoyed because the students ________ (*talk*) in the library all afternoon.

4 Choose the correct options to complete the sentences.

1 We wanted to get the 10 o'clock train but when we arrived at the station it had *never / already* left.
2 Nobody had *ever / just* won any competitions in my family until I came first in the school poetry competition.
3 I hadn't eaten anything spicy *until / when* I went to Mexico.
4 We had been driving all day, so *by the time / before* we arrived, we were exhausted.
5 When Bob arrived at the cinema, the last tickets for the film had *never / just* sold out.
6 The weather was very bad all morning, so the flight was cancelled *until / before* most people had arrived at the airport.

Go back to page 134.

9 Gerunds and infinitives

Infinitive

We use the infinitive with *to*:

- to show purpose:
  *I'm taking this course **to help** me get a better job.*
  *I need to go to the supermarket **to buy** some eggs.*
- after many adjectives e.g. *difficult, easy, delighted, happy, sad, disappointed, surprised, important*.
  *He found it **difficult to understand** the main points.*
  *My dog was **happy to see** me after my holiday.*

Gerund

We use the gerund (*-ing*):

- at the beginning of a sentence as the subject.
  ***Learning** is easier when we are interested in the subject.*
  ***Swimming** is good for your health.*
- after prepositions (including *look forward to*).
  *We're **thinking about applying** to Cambridge University.*
  *I **look forward to speaking** to you next week.*

Gerund/Infinitive

- When we use two verbs together, the second verb is usually in the infinitive with *to* or the *-ing* form:
  *I **want to study** art.*
  *I **love learning** languages!*
- Some verbs are always followed by the infinitive with *to* and others are always followed by the gerund:

Followed by infinitive with *to*	Followed by *-ing*
want *I **want to buy** a new phone.*	*like/love/hate* *I **love going** to the cinema with friends.*
would like ***Would you like to try** the soup?*	*enjoy* *He **enjoys reading** in his free time.*
learn *My sister is **learning to drive**.*	*mind* *Do you **mind taking** out the rubbish?*
manage *We **managed to finish** the project on time.*	*finish* *Have you **finished tidying** your room?*
offer *They **offered to take** me to the airport.*	*consider* *Have you **considered looking** for a new job?*
promise *I **promised to go** to the concert with her.*	*practise* *I always **practise throwing and catching** before a baseball match.*
decide *We've **decided to go** to France this summer.*	*feel like* *I don't **feel like going** out this afternoon.*
hope *She **hopes to finish** her degree this year.*	*suggest* *The doctor **suggested drinking** more water.*

9 Gerunds and infinitives

1 Match the sentences 1–6 to their uses a–f.

1 I enjoy <u>learning</u> new things.
2 <u>Speaking</u> in class is a lot of fun!
3 He promised <u>to do</u> his homework later.
4 You were clever <u>to get</u> that question right!
5 I went to the shops <u>to buy</u> some pens.
6 He often thinks about <u>taking</u> an evening class.

a to show purpose
b after an adjective
c as a sentence subject
d after a preposition
e infinitive with *to* after certain verbs
f *-ing* after certain verbs

2 Choose the correct alternatives to complete the sentences.

1 *Learn* / *Learning* a second language can help people get a better job.
2 Is it easy *to pass* / *passing* this course?
3 The teacher would like *to talk* / *talking* to you before class.
4 We don't mind *to keep* / *keeping* the library open late for students that want to study.
5 They closed the school over the summer *to build* / *building* a new gym.
6 They are looking forward to *start* / *starting* their university course.

3 Complete the article using the gerund or infinitive of the verb in brackets.

BOAT SCHOOLS

Would you like **(1)** ____________ (*have*) your classes in an unusual classroom? Some children in northern Bangladesh can do just that – they learn on a boat! **(2)** ____________ (*Teach*) children in this area isn't easy. It's difficult **(3)** ____________ (*get*) to a normal school because people live very far away and at some times of the year, there are floods!

The boat schools were created **(4)** ____________ (*help*) bring education to people in these areas. In the morning, the boat schools float along the river, picking the children up. The children enjoy **(5)** ____________ (*learn*) on the boats, and the boats are a mix of classroom and school bus. When they finish **(6)** ____________ (*study*) for the day, the boat takes them home!

Go back to page 137.

10 Reported speech: statements

1 Direct and reported speech

There are two ways we can report what another person says.

- We can use direct speech, which uses the exact words someone said.

  "The doctor gave me some medicine for my cold," ***said*** *Jing. / Jing* ***said****, "The doctor gave me some medicine for my cold."*

- Or we can use reported speech. To use reported speech we have to make changes to the tense and pronouns.

  Jing ***said that*** *the doctor* ***had given her*** *some medicine for* ***her*** *cold.*

2 Tenses

When we report other people's words, we change the tense. The verbs 'move back' one tense except for the past perfect. The past perfect stays the same.

	Direct speech	Reported speech
Present simple	*"I* ***love*** *cooking," she said.*	*She said that she* ***loved*** *cooking.*
Present continuous	*"They* ***are studying****," said Kelly.*	*Kelly said that they* ***were studying****.*
Present perfect	*"We* ***haven't been*** *to Italy," they said.*	*They said that they* ***hadn't been*** *to Italy.*
Past simple	*"The train* ***arrived*** *late," he said.*	*He said that the train* ***had arrived*** *late.*
Past perfect	*"The shop* ***had closed*** *early," he said.*	*He said that the shop* ***had closed*** *early.*
Future	*"I'll* ***help*** *you choose a present," Erik said.*	*Erik said he* ***would*** *help me choose a present.*

3 *that*

We can use *that* after the verbs *say* and *tell*, but it is **not** necessary.

Lea told me ***that*** *she would pick me up at 6 pm.*

Lea told me she would pick me up at 6 pm.

4 Pronouns

We change the pronouns in reported speech.

*"****My*** *brother is arranging a party for* ***you****," said Noah. →*
Noah said that ***his*** *brother was arranging a party for* ***me****.*

*"****I'll*** *help* ***you*** *with* ***your*** *project," said Mr Peterson. →*
Mr Peterson said that ***he*** *would help* ***us*** *with* ***our*** *project.*

*"****We*** *bought a present for* ***our*** *grandmother," said Penny. →*
Penny said that ***they*** *had bought a present for* ***their*** *grandmother.*

5 Time words

In reported speech we change the words that describe **when** something happened.

tomorrow	*the next/following day*
next week/month	*the next/following week/month*
yesterday	*the day before / the previous day*
three days ago	*three days before/earlier*
last week/month	*the week/month before* *the previous week/month*

"I'm going on holiday <u>*tomorrow*</u>*," said Michael. → Michael told me he was going on holiday* <u>*the following day*</u>*.*

6 Reported commands

We report commands with the form *tell* + object + infinitive with *to*.

"Do more exercise," said the doctor. → The doctor ***told me to do*** *more exercise.*

10 Reported speech: questions

1 Yes/No questions

We use *ask* + *if*/*whether* (+ object) + clause to report *yes*/*no* questions. *If* is more common than *whether*.

"Does your sister work for a large company?" → She asked if my sister worked for a large company.

2 Wh- questions

We use *ask* + *wh*- question word + *clause* to report *wh*-questions.

"What film do you want to watch tonight?" → He asked the family what film they wanted to watch that night.

3 Offers and requests

We use *offer*/*ask* + infinitive with *to* to report offers and requests.

"Do you want me to lend you some money?" → Sofia offered to lend me some money.

"Can you tell me when the train will arrive?" → He asked when the train would arrive.

10 Reported speech: statements

1 Choose the correct options to complete the text.

My friend Natalia called me yesterday and she **(1)** *said* / *told* that she **(2)** *wants* / *wanted* to meet me for lunch. We decided to go to a restaurant near the river. As soon as we sat down, she told **(3)** *me* / *my* that she had some amazing news. She said **(4)** *what* / *that* she had got a new job. She'd been looking for a new job for a long time, so I told **(5)** *her* / *she* it was fantastic news and I said that I **(6)** *would* / *will* pay for lunch. She was surprised and said that I **(7)** *don't* / *didn't* have to pay, but I insisted on paying because I really wanted to do something nice to celebrate!

2 For each question, choose the correct option (A, B or C).

1 Our manager ______ early because it was the end of the week.
   A told us to leave   B told us left   C said we leave
2 The weather report ______ this weekend.
   A told us that it isn't raining   B said that it didn't rain   C said it wasn't going to rain
3 Sami ______ at seven in the evening.
   A told that we would meet   B said that he would meet us   C said us to meet
4 Local residents ______ more money on hospitals and health services.
   A said the mayor spending   B said the mayor she spent   C told the mayor to spend
5 Maria ______ to the conference in London last week.
   A said she was going   B said that she goes   C told that she went

Go back to page 147.

10 Reported speech: questions

Rewrite the questions using reported speech.

1 "Would you like me to help you cut the grass in your garden?" asked my neighbour.
   My neighbour ______________________
2 "Have you finished painting your house yet?" he asked me.
   He ______________________
3 "Did you see the accident yesterday?" the police officer asked us.
   The police officer ______________________
4 "Can you call the restaurant and book a table?" my sister asked.
   My sister ______________________
5 "Do you want me to make you some lunch?" Mia asked the children.
   Mia ______________________
6 "Can I borrow your car?" asked my friend.
   My friend ______________________

Go back to page 151.

11 Passive

We form the passive with the verb *to be* + past participle.

Present simple	*am/is/are* + past participle *Our rubbish* ***is collected*** *once a week.*
Present continuous	*am/is/are* + *being* + past participle *The station* ***is being painted*** *this week.*
Past simple	*was/were* + past participle *This book* ***wasn't written*** *by a local author.*
Will **future**	*will* + *be* + past participle *The package* ***won't be delivered*** *next Friday.*
Going to **future**	*am/is/are* + *going to* + *be* + past participle *Our class photo* ***is going to be taken*** *tomorrow.*

To form questions, we change the order of the subject and verb.

Is *our rubbish* ***collected*** *once a week?*

Will *the package* ***be delivered*** *next Friday?*

Use

- In an active sentence, the focus of the sentence is usually on the doer of the action (the agent). We use the passive when the person or thing affected by an action is more important that the agent.

  They ***built*** *that skyscraper in 1950.* (active)

  That skyscraper ***was built*** *in 1950.* (passive)
- We use the passive when we do not know, it isn't important or it is obvious who does the action.

  That skyscraper ***was built*** *in 1950.* (We don't know who by and/or it isn't important.)

  Your hotel room ***will be cleaned*** *in the morning.* (It's obvious that the cleaners will do this.)

  If we want to include the agent who did the action, we use *by*.

  The film was made ***by*** *a young, unknown director.*
- We use the passive in formal writing and in official notices.

  Eating ***is prohibited*** *in the classrooms.*

---

11 *Have/Get* something done

We use the form subject + *have/get* + object + past participle when we ask someone else to do an action for us.

We ***have the house cleaned*** *every week.*

Carrie ***is having her hair cut*** *at the weekend.*

He ***hasn't had his photo taken*** *yet.*

Did you ***get the computer repaired****?*

NB The object goes after *have/get* and before the past participle.

Use

We use *have/get something done* to:

- talk about something that someone else did for us (usually a paid professional).

  Peter and Anika ***painted*** *their living room.* (Peter and Anita did the painting.)

  Peter and Anika ***had their living room painted.*** (Someone else painted their living room for them.)

  Sara ***cut*** *the grass in her garden.* (Sara cut the grass herself.)

  Sara ***got the grass cut*** *in her garden.* (Sara did not cut the grass; someone cut it down for her.)
- describe a negative experience that happened to us. We usually use the verb *have* not *get*.

  We ***had our bags stolen*** *on the train.*

  I ***had my car damaged*** *in the storm.*

11 Passive

1 Choose the correct options to complete the sentences.

1 Most people in Austria *speak* / *are spoken* German as a first language.
2 Antoni Gaudí *designed* / *was designed* Park Güell in the early twentieth century.
3 Why *was* / *did* that train cancelled?
4 This match *is watching* / *is being watched* by millions of people around the world.
5 I wonder if the thieves *will ever be caught* / *will ever catch*.

2 Complete the news article using the active or passive form of the verbs in brackets.

ARTS, CRAFTS AND COFFEE – all under one roof!

In 2013, a group of local artists **(1)** ____________ (*start*) selling their work at a market in south London once a month. They called their group Handmade Palace – it **(2)** ____________ (*name*) after the local area, Crystal Palace. It quickly **(3)** ____________ (*become*) a weekly event and one of the artists, Beth, became the manager. It was very successful, and soon Beth realised that they **(4)** ____________ (*need*) to move to a larger space.

In 2016, a suitable building **(5)** ____________ (*find*), and The Paxton Centre was opened. All the artwork and products on sale **(6)** ____________ (*make*) by local artists. There is so much to choose from, and lots of different prices.

You can find more details on the website, which gives more information about the centre and lists all the upcoming classes and events. However, artworks **(7)** ____________ (*not sell*) online. The centre has grown over the last few years and now **(8)** ____________ (*include*) a café and workspace as well. It's a real local success story!

3 Write passive sentences with the same meaning as the following active sentences. There is one example at the beginning (0).

0 Someone took Imani's magazine out of her room.
Imani's magazine was taken out of her room.
1 We invite a local artist to the studio once a month.
____
2 Will someone finish this report by Friday?
____
3 Lucas gave me this jacket.
____
4 Someone is selling tickets to the concert online.
____
5 Has anyone fed the cat today?
____

Go back to page 168.

11 *Have/Get something done*

1 Complete the sentences with the correct form of *have* or *get* and the past participle of one of the verbs in the box.

deliver fix paint test

1 We usually buy food online and ________ it ________ to our house.
2 Fatima ________ her window ________ yesterday.
3 My daughter is going to ________ her eyes ________ at the optician's tomorrow.
4 Did Alex ________ her nails ________ at the beauty salon?

2 In each sentence 1–4, there is a mistake. Find the mistakes and correct them.

1 Gina had repaired her necklace at a jewellery shop.
2 You can't visit this month because we have the kitchen redecorated.
3 We're going to make the table by a carpenter.
4 The museum will have the objects check by history experts.

Go back to page 171.

12 Third conditional

- We form the third conditional with *if* + past perfect, *would/wouldn't* + *have* (*'ve*) + past participle. We use *if* with the condition.

  If *you* ***had told*** *me about your problem, I* ***would have helped*** *you.*

  ↓ *(condition)* ↓ *(result)*

- To form questions, change the order of the words in the result clause: (question word) + *would* + subject + *have* + past participle.

  If you had known *how it important it was for your career,* ***would you have studied*** *Japanese at university?*

  What would you have done *differently if you had known this was going to happen?*

Use

We use the third conditional to imagine a hypothetical situation or action in the past and its results/effects in the past.

I didn't get tickets to the concerts. (actual situation)

If I ***had got*** *tickets to the concert, I* ***would have had*** *a great time.* (hypothetical situation)

She bought the app and discovered it had a lot of problems. (actual situation)

She ***wouldn't have bought*** *the app if she* ***had known*** *it had so many problems.* (hypothetical situation)

---

12 Future continuous

- We form the future continuous with *will* + *be* + *-ing*.

  *They****'ll be staying*** *at the Grand Hotel.*

  I'll be having *lunch with the directors.*

- For negative sentences, we can use either *will not* or *won't*. Both are correct.

  They ***will not be staying*** *at the Grand Hotel.*

  They ***won't be staying*** *at the Grand Hotel.*

- To form a question, we change the order of *will/won't* and the subject.

  Will *you* ***be staying*** *at the Grand hotel?*

  Won't *you* ***be having*** *lunch with the directors?*

- For short answers, we use *will* and *won't.*

  Yes, I/you/he/she/we/they ***will.***

  No, I/you/he/she/we/they ***won't.***

NB We don't use the future continuous with state verbs. To describe a state, we must use either an active verb or change to the future simple.

*I****'ll*** ~~***be being***~~ *at the cinema.*

*I****'ll be*** *at the cinema.*

*I****'ll be watching*** *a film.*

Use

We use the future continuous to talk about actions or events that we predict will be in progress at a certain time in the future.

*I****'ll be staying*** *at the Grand Hotel next week.* (This action will happen over the week.)

I ***won't be working*** *at the lab tomorrow. I have the day off.* (This action will not happen over the next day.)

12 Third conditional

1 Underline the correct alternatives to make third conditional sentences. There is an example at the beginning (0).

0 The experiment *would have* / *will have* worked if *they design* / *they had designed* it better.
1 They *wouldn't have won* / *won't have won* the prize if they *give up* / *had given up* on the research.
2 If the tickets *have been* / *had been* cheaper, they *would have gone* / *would go* to the museum.
3 They *would have made* / *would made* a better robot if they *had had* / *had* more money.
4 If he *knew* / *had known* about its short battery life, he *wouldn't have* / *have been* chosen that phone.

2 Match sentence beginnings 1–8 to the endings a–h to make sentences in zero, first, second and third conditional.

1 If they had left for the tech conference earlier,
2 When you freeze water,
3 If you win first prize at the science fair,
4 If I had a robot that could do chores,
5 We would have enjoyed the science museum more
6 I'll take the laptop back to the shop
7 He would improve more quickly
8 The battery runs out

a if you don't keep it charged.
b it turns to ice.
c they would have arrived in time for the opening speech.
d if it hadn't been so crowded.
e I would use it all the time.
f if he did his homework every week.
g your teacher will be very proud of you.
h if it suddenly shuts down like that again.

3 Match the sentences in Exercise 2 with the type of conditional sentence.

zero conditional: *2*, ______
first conditional: ______, ______
second conditional: ______, ______
third conditional: ______, ______

Go back to page 180.

12 Future continuous

Monday	10 am – cycling in the mountains
Tuesday	8.30 pm – meet Carmen for dinner at restaurant
Wednesday	3 pm – do homework
Thursday	11 am – take train to airport 4.30 pm – fly to Venice
Friday	11 am – visit museum
Saturday	12 pm – go on boat tour
Sunday	all afternoon – walk around the city

1 Look at Manuela's diary. Answer the questions about her plans using the future continuous.

1 What will she be doing at 10.15 am on Monday morning? ______.
2 What will she be doing at 3.15 pm on Wednesday? ______.
3 What will she be doing at 4 pm on Sunday? ______.

2 Answer the questions about Manuela's plans using the future continuous. There is an example at the beginning (0).

0 Will she be cooking on Tuesday evening?
No, she won't. She'll be meeting Carmen for dinner at a restaurant.
1 Will she be driving to the airport on Thursday morning?
______
2 Will she be studying at 11.30 on Friday?
______
3 Will she be watching a film at 12.15 pm on Saturday?
______

Go back to page 185.

AUDIOSCRIPTS

1.1

W = Woman M = Man

1

What does the woman decide to order?

W: I'm glad we decided to have Italian food. I really like this restaurant.

M: Me too. What do you want to eat? If I know you, it'll be the pizza. That's what you usually have.

W: Yes, this one with mushrooms and peppers looks delicious. But then, well – this pasta with prawns looks really interesting, too. I don't often eat pasta.

M: What about the risotto? You like rice.

W: It's true, but you know what? I think I'll have what I normally order.

M: OK, and I think I'll have that pasta you mentioned.

1.2

M = Man

2

How is the man getting to work today?

M: Hi, it's Mark. Sorry, but I'm going to be a bit late for our meeting this morning. As you know, I drive to work every day, but there's a problem with my car and I don't have time to stop by the mechanic's. I've just called for a taxi, but nobody can come to pick me up until 10 because of the big football match. At this point, I think the best option is to go by bike. According to the app on my phone, it takes 30 minutes to cycle to the office. I'll be there as soon as I can.

3

What has the woman lost?

M: You're still packing? We have to leave for the airport now.

W: I'm almost ready.

M: Oh no, please don't tell me you've lost your passport again.

W: Don't you have it? I remember handing it to you yesterday.

M: Ah! Yes, you're right.

W: It's my mobile phone charger. I can't find it anywhere.

M: I've got an extra one. Let me see if I can find it.

W: Thanks. Okay, now I just have to fit this travel pillow into my suitcase. This one is actually getting a bit old. Maybe I'll buy a new one at the airport.

4

What T-shirt is the woman wearing in the photo?

M: I love this photo you chose for your social media profile. The T-shirt is perfect.

W: Thanks! I didn't plan on wearing that one at first. As you know, I usually wear plain white T-shirts, but I thought that would be a bit boring. So I looked through my clothes for something more interesting. One of my favourites is a T-shirt with stripes, but I've heard that stripes don't look good in this type of photo. That's when I found this one with a picture of my favourite jazz singer and put it on for the photo. I think it says something about me – you know, about my personality.

M: Definitely.

5

What is the price of the newest smartwatch this week?

M: Mark here from Mark's Techshop in the Sun Valley shopping centre. Thinking about buying a new watch? If so, we've got an amazing offer for you. This week – and this week only – the latest smartwatch is just £200. That's right: it's £100 less than the usual £300 pounds. This newest model has it all – it monitors your health and sleep and you can use it to pay in shops. But, if that price is still too high, you'll be happy to know we've also reduced the price of last year's model to just £100. Don't miss this big sale!

6

Which magazine does the man decide to buy?

M: I think I'll buy one of these magazines to read on the train. Which one would you get?

W: I'd go for this one about cinema. There are always interesting film reviews to read. But you should choose the one you want.

M: My friend buys this magazine about cars. He usually gives it to me to read when he's finished, though. Maybe that's not the best one to choose. This food magazine looks really interesting – I love cooking – but it's mostly photos and there isn't much to actually read.

W: Well, there aren't any other options, so it looks like you're going to get the same one I'd buy.

M: Yes.

7

Why are the streets around the main square closed today?

M: Now for some local news. If you're planning to drive into the city centre, avoid all the streets around the main square. Today they're closed, like they were last weekend for the classical music concert, but this time it's for a big farmer's market. Head over there if you're looking to buy fresh fruit and vegetables. Talking of the main square, a political event for the local elections will also be held there next Saturday, so the streets will once again be closed to traffic. Moving on to sports ...

1.3

0 cook
1 good
2 put
3 food
4 move
5 true
6 come
7 sun
8 just

2.1

M = Man W = Woman

1

You will hear two students talking about their local library.

M: This is a great library.

W: I agree. It's more than just a beautiful old building – it's an important part of our community. There's always something happening here – storytelling for children, reading clubs for seniors, and it doesn't cost a thing.

M: Lots of students like us come here to study.

W: Yes, it seems that for most people being in a quiet place helps them concentrate, but not me. I prefer cafés. No, what brings me back here every week or two is the fiction section. I'll never manage to take home and read all the novels here, but it doesn't mean I can't try!

2

You will hear two friends talking about the characters in a TV show they've watched.

W: Have you seen *Broken*?

M: I've just finished the first season. Isn't it exciting?

W: It is. You never know how each episode is going to end. I'm not sure about the characters, though. In general, I prefer shows where the characters develop and change over time, the way people do in real life. That doesn't really happen in *Broken* – or at least not yet. It's a shame there isn't more dialogue. That way we would get to know the characters a bit better.

M: True, they don't talk to each other much, but the conversations they do have make me laugh. There are some great jokes.

3

You will hear a man talking about a tourist apartment.

W: How was the apartment you rented?

M: It was nice. We usually stay in hotels when we go on holiday, so this was a new experience for us. Instead of eating out, my wife and I bought fresh ingredients at local markets and made some really nice meals at home. I did miss being in a hotel sometimes, though. At first, there was no hot water, but when we contacted the owner, she came and fixed the problem immediately.

W: Was it near the beach?

M: Yes, just a five-minute walk away, which was great. Unfortunately, we were in the most popular part of town and the beach was extremely crowded.

4

You will hear two workmates talking on the phone about a report.

W: Hi Paul, this is Stacy. I'm calling about the report you sent.

M: Okay. Is there something wrong with it?

W: Well, it's mostly great. The thing is, I found some small mistakes in it – missing words or words that are spelt wrong. Do you use a spell-checking programme?

M: Of course. But I guess it doesn't find everything ...

W: Do you ever read aloud what you write? That's what I do. Sometimes I can hear mistakes I can't see.

M: Good idea. I never thought of that.

W: It also helps me find sentences that aren't clear or don't sound right.

M: This is great advice. Thanks.

5

You will hear two friends talking about a history museum.

W: I went to the history museum last Saturday.

M: Really? I was there with the kids on Sunday.

W: I'm sure they loved it. I used to take my children to that museum a lot when they were younger, but now they're teenagers and don't find it interesting. Did you eat at the café? I couldn't believe the prices of the salads and sandwiches.

M: Yes, everything costs twice as much. But you can see those huge dinosaurs from the eating area, so that's kind of special. Talking of dinosaurs, they've made some nice improvements to that area of the museum.

W: I don't know. To me, it looks the same as before.

6

You will hear two friends talking about an online course.

M: Did you finish that online course in software development? I've heard it's quite difficult.

W: Yes, I finished it two months ago. In general, the information was pretty easy to understand. The teacher always found creative ways to teach the subject – videos, podcasts, that sort of thing. I thought that it would be difficult to find time to complete all the tasks and projects, but that was hardly ever a problem.

M: So, is the course worth taking?

W: I learnt a lot, for sure. But I'd recommend doing it together with a friend or colleague, like I did, instead of doing it completely on your own.. It's a lot more fun.

2.2

1 started, decided, performed, repeated
2 answered, received, ordered, searched
3 checked, divided, fixed, walked

3.1

W = Woman M = Man

W: So, which one do you want to talk about first? There are a few good options, I think.

M: What about this one? It looks like they are giving people food in front of the school.

W: Yes, free food. It's not a bad idea.

M: It's okay. People like eating nice food – especially when it's free! But it depends ... it depends on how many people, uh, you know, walk down the street.

W: That's true. Maybe nobody comes. Hmm ... I think it's a great idea to put ... a cooking video on social media. Do you agree?

M: Yes, a lot of people will see the video there. You're right. Today everybody, eh, everybody uses social media – maybe too much!

W: Hahahaha ... Yes. Um, what about these other options? In my opinion, it makes sense to give a free cooking class – it's fun!

M: Hmmm ... If you ask me, it's not the best choice. People just go for the free class.

W: All right, so ... shall we talk about the newspaper now?

M: Okay. To be honest, I'm not sure about that one. People, uh, people usually read the news online. I mean, of course some people read the paper, but it's not like ... it's not like it was, in the, in the past, fifty years ago.

W: Yes, I completely agree. I, uh, I still think a cooking video on social media is the best option. What about you?

M: Okay sure, let's go with that one then.

3.2

Hi everyone, my name is Chris Molina. Let me start by telling you a bit about myself. I was born in England, but when I was little my parents and I moved to Greece. A few years later, we moved again, this time to Northern Spain, and that's where I've lived ever since.

3.3

Hi everyone, my name is Chris Molina. Let me start by telling you a bit about myself. I was born in England, but when I was little my parents and I moved to Greece. A few years later, we moved again, this time to Northern Spain, and that's where I've lived ever since.
Although I've become a bit of an expert in biology and forest science since I left university, I actually studied marketing for my degree. But it only took me about a month of working in an office to realise that I wanted to work outdoors. Today, I'm a professional mushroom hunter.

It's autumn, and there are a lot of mushrooms to pick, so my daily routine consists of getting up at seven o'clock in the morning and having a light breakfast. Then I drive up to a pine forest near my town. At eight, the sun is just starting to rise, filling the forest with soft, gentle light. That's when my workday begins.

So, how do you get good at finding mushrooms? Well, to start with, you have to learn about forests, how their ecosystems work, or you won't know where to start looking. But the most important thing is not to give up too easily. Sometimes you can go for hours without finding a single mushroom. If you're not patient, it's easy to get frustrated.

While hunting mushrooms, you don't need to pack much. Some people use plastic bags to collect mushrooms. I use a basket, though. That way spores – little, tiny pieces of mushroom – fall out of the basket while I'm walking, helping the forest grow more mushrooms. At home, I sort all the mushrooms into boxes and get them ready to sell.

Before I finish, I just wanted to mention the trips that I organise. They're great for families in particular. Little kids love searching for mushrooms! To learn more, go to my website, www.rovellon.es. I'll spell that. That's R-O-V-E-double L-O-N.

So, any questions?

3.4

1 heat, whole, ahead, unhappy
2 valley, value, oven, clever, serve, drive
3 whether, waiter, always, takeaway
4 zero, zone, dozen, busy, amaze, cheese

4.1

W = Woman M = Man

W: Welcome to the dream jobs interview. Today I'm here with Danny O'Neil, who works at the Rock and Roll Hall of Fame and Museum in Ohio. So, Danny, how did you start working there?

M: Well, music has always been my passion. I used to be the lead singer in a rock band and it was exciting to travel and spend time with other musicians, but I got tired of that life after a while. I started working at a music store, and then somebody told me about a tour guide job at the museum. The money was good, more than I was making at the time, and that's why I applied, to be honest. It was a great decision, though. I love my job.

W: What's your favourite part of the job?

M: I enjoy so many things, but if I had to choose one, it'd be the opportunity to interact with visitors from Japan, India, Argentina – every country you can think of. I've also gained so much knowledge about music. That comes in as a close second. One thing I do get tired of, though, is talking about certain topics again and again. Some exhibitions haven't changed for years!

W: So, have you ever met anyone famous?

M: Yes, I have. In fact, I have met *lots* of famous people in my lifetime. At our events, I've been in the same room as members of The Rolling Stones and many other bands. That said, I've never had a long conversation with any of them. I always feel embarrassed. Anyway, celebrities are interested in hanging out with other celebrities, not tour guides!

W: What have you learnt from being a tour guide?

M: Good question. Well, you have to remember a lot of information – and get it all right. You don't want to say the wrong name or date and have somebody correct you. I don't forget things as easily now as I used to. There are also some useful skills I learned as a musician – speaking to large groups of people, for example. I'm good at that.

W: What do you recommend doing at the museum?

M: The museum has collected lots of artefacts since 1995, when it opened: guitars, posters, song notebooks – even motorcycles. There's so much to see. And don't miss the The Garage, a section where you can try out a variety of instruments. Another must-see, in my opinion, is the fashion. We have clothes worn by everybody from David Bowie and Prince, to Lady Gaga and Taylor Swift.

W: So, what's next for you?

M: Actually, I have just started a new job and I'm feeling a bit stressed out. They've made me tour manager, meaning that I organise all the tours now. Among other duties, I've got to train guides and most have little or no experience. This first week, well, it's been a bit tough, but I think I can handle it.

W: Well, best of luck with that Danny! And thanks again for coming on the show.

4.2

decision, passion, exhibitions, information

4.3

1 organise, organisation
2 explain, explanation
3 express, expression
4 celebrate, celebration
5 define, definition
6 produce, production
7 connect, connection
8 discuss, discussion
9 operate, operation
10 decide, decision
11 react, reaction
12 describe, description

5.1

W = Woman M = Man

1

You will hear two people talking about ice skating.

M: How long have you been ice skating?

W: Since I was a kid – my dad taught me. It's a lot of fun. I'm glad you are finally going to try it. Are you nervous?

M: A bit, yes. I'm not looking forward to people looking at me and thinking, "How funny, look at this guy who can't skate."

W: Just ignore them and concentrate on keeping your balance. You don't want to fall over and hurt yourself. That would really spoil the fun!

M: Good advice.

W: Have you tried on the skates yet? It's important that they're not too big or too small.

M: Yes, I have. At the shop, I put them on and walked around a bit. They seemed fine.

2

You will hear a man and woman talking about a documentary they saw.

W: Have you watched that new wildlife documentary I told you about, the one about chimpanzees?

M: Yes, I did. I saw it at the weekend. I loved the soundtrack.

W: Me too. It was great. And the photography was also lovely. How do you think they got so close to the animals?

M: I have no idea!
W: I didn't know much about chimpanzees and learnt a lot – they're fascinating creatures.
M: I actually read a book about them not long ago, so I wouldn't say there was much that was new for me. But I still really enjoyed it. Thanks for the recommendation.

3
You will hear two people talking about gardening.
W: Look at your clothes – they're so dirty!
M: I've been working outside in the garden.
W: Yes, of course. You're really enjoying this new hobby, aren't you?
M: I am. It's been good for me, I think. At first, I was just looking for an excuse to be outdoors. I often used to come home after work and just turn on the TV. But the real benefit, I've discovered, is that it gets my mind off work. In the garden, I forget about all those rude customers at the shop.
W: Not a bad way to keep fit, either.
M: Yes, it *is* quite tiring, but I don't mind that part.

4
You will hear a woman telling her friend about plans for the guest bedroom in her house.
W: I'm going to start working from home on Thursdays and Fridays.
M: Nice!
W: I'm going to set up a home office in the guest bedroom. Now I just need to buy a desk.
M: Don't you already have one?
W: Yes, I do. It's not that it's in bad condition or anything. It's just that I've got used to working with two computer screens and there isn't enough space.
M: What about the antique table with the plants? It's pretty wide.
W: I hadn't thought about that. It would easily fit between the door and the window. I could put the plants on top of the bookcase and take the desk to a charity shop.

5
You will hear two friends talking about a rock-climbing lesson.
M: How was your rock-climbing lesson?
W: Great. I went right up to the top of the first wall we climbed. According to the instructor, it usually takes people a few classes to do that. But I'm in good shape, so I didn't expect it to be hard.
M: On the website, the climbing gym looks absolutely enormous.
W: Yes, they have a few different rooms. The walls aren't as tall as they seem online, though. I think they used a special camera.
M: So, are you going back?
W: I might do. The day pass was reasonable, not too expensive. If I continue, though, I'll probably buy the monthly membership. That's even cheaper.

6
You will hear two students talking about a German course.
M: Hey! How are you?
W: Fine.
M: You haven't been going to our German course recently.
W: Yeah, I got a bit tired of it, to be honest.
M: Because the teacher speaks so fast?
W: No, it's not that. I just got bored of listening to him talk and talk. We never get to actually chat to the other students in class. Plus, the exercises are too challenging.
M: I'm with you there. get loads of answers wrong. But, going back to what you said before, I'm not sure I'd prefer to sit around talking all class. We're here in Germany, surrounded by people to speak German with.
W: You've got a point there.

5.2

Thank you for choosing the Iceland Travel Company for your tour of the south coast. I'd like to explain the travel arrangements for our day trip.
To begin with, I need to inform you of a change of plan: your group arrives in the capital city of Reykjavík on the 16th of September, and we were planning to go on our tour on the 17th. But we have to postpone it until the 19th of September because of bad weather. I hope that's not too inconvenient.
We're meeting at quarter past seven in the morning. Once everyone is on the bus, we'll need to get on the road at exactly half past seven. This is because we have to pick up a second group of tourists at quarter to eight.
Our first stop will be the amazing Skógafoss waterfall, one of the most beautiful in Iceland. We'll climb the stairs to the top of the hill, where the best views are.
After a short drive, we'll stop and have lunch beside a valley. We'll then take a short hike to see a cave made of ice. Unfortunately, the glacier in this area is quickly disappearing as a result of climate change, but it's still a very impressive place to visit. For this hike, we provide helmets and walking sticks, but please don't forget hiking boots. It's unsafe to walk in this area with regular shoes or trainers.
Our last stop is the Black Sand beach. It's amazing how many birds live here, including thousands of puffins. Maybe they should call it 'wild bird beach'! Together, we'll take a walk to Gardar cliff, which is made of strange rock columns. It looks a bit like a pyramid. On our way back to the bus, you'll also get a chance to see ...

5.3

1 Do you agree?
2 Do you like camping?
3 What is the best time of year to go camping?
4 Why do people enjoy spending time in nature?

6.1

W = Woman M = Man
M: Today I'm talking to Zoe, who is going to tell us about working on a cruise ship.
W: Hi, everyone.
M: So, Zoe, how did you get interested in working on cruise ships?
W: I studied marketing at university, but my first job was really dull. I started dreaming of a different life. One day a friend of mine from school was telling me about working on cruise ships, and I thought, "I think I'll apply. Why not?" To learn more, I watched loads of videos by cruise ship employees on social media.
M: Your first job on a cruise ship was in housekeeping, cleaning bedrooms. How was that?
W: I worked 10 to 12 hours a day, seven days a week. You see, weekends don't exist here on cruise ships. I knew that coming in, but it was difficult to get used to. It was also challenging for me emotionally, because I knew that I had gone to university and studied hard. But I survived thanks to the support I got from the other cleaners. They're incredible people.
M: You have a different position now, don't you?

W: Yes, now I'm a manager. I still work long hours, but my job has many benefits. You might think travelling the world would be the biggest one, but for me it's not having rent or bills to pay. Plus, I work with people from many different countries. The bad thing is that I'm constantly saying goodbye. Workmates come and go a lot.

M: Is it hard to be away from home for so long?

W: It can be, yes. But it helps to have a routine. I work out daily and also make some quiet time to read. I do miss my family, of course, but we have regular video calls. And I keep up with friends on social media. Unfortunately, those two things aren't always possible at sea, where internet access is limited.

M: Do you have a favourite place that you've visited?

W: It's easy of course to fall in love with the Bahamas. And I've seen famous monuments like Petra in Jordan, one of the Seven Wonders of the World. If I had to choose one place to go back to, though, it would be a wonderful place called Tauranga in the north of New Zealand.

M: What are your plans for the future?

W: Well, one day it would be nice to work in the tourism industry but on land. For now, though, I'm going to focus on my career here at sea. In fact, I'm meeting my boss tomorrow morning to talk about a new job. It's similar to the one I have but on a bigger ship, where I can earn a higher salary.

M: Best of luck with that, Zoe! Thanks for coming on the show.

6.2

W = Woman M = Man N = Narrator

1

What did the man do this morning?

W: How was your trip to the town centre?

M: A bit frustrating! I was planning to get a new passport photo taken at the photography studio, but there were so many people waiting that I decided to go back later. I went to the post office to pick up a package, but it was closed when I got there. I'd forgotten that they close early on Tuesdays. I stopped at a barber's to get my hair cut and then went back to the photography studio. Amazingly, the queue was even longer, so I just gave up and came back home.

2

What is the weather forecast for this afternoon?

W: Hi everyone and thanks for listening to *The Weather Today*. Well, it's going to be an interesting weather day here in River Falls. We'll start the day with a thunderstorm, so if you're walking to work or school, don't forget your rubber boots. Expect lightning and heavy rain. This should pass quickly, though. Around lunchtime the sun will come out. This nice weather won't last long, though, I'm afraid. This evening, you'll see the sky filling up with dark clouds again.

3

Where does the woman think she left her purse?

M: I thought you were going to buy a coffee.

W: I was, but in the queue at the café I realised that I didn't have my purse. I can't find it anywhere.

M: Oh no. Where do you remember seeing it?

W: Well, I had it at the train station for sure.

M: True. You paid for your ticket. What about the clothing shop?

W: I don't think so.

M: Maybe it fell on the floor while you were trying on that pair of jeans.

W: Yes, I think you're right. Do we have enough time to go back there before our train leaves?

M: Yes, I think so.

4

Which plate do the man and woman decide to buy?

M: Look at all these wonderful plates! Let's buy one to take back as a souvenir.

W: Great idea. I like this one with the lemons.

M: Yes, it's nice. It reminds me of the lemon trees we saw from the train. This one with flowers is nice, too.

W: It has such a beautiful design. Do you think they make all these by hand?

M: Yes, I think so. What about this one with the grapes? I love the colour of the leaves.

W: It's really nice, but I still like the first one the best.

M: Me too. Let's go for that one.

5

What time is the train expected to leave?

M: Attention all passengers of the 11 o'clock train to Stockholm. This train will experience an hour delay because of bad weather. There is currently a big storm near the city, and at the moment, there is too much snow for trains to pass safely. For this reason, the train is unlikely to depart until midnight. We also wanted to remind passengers that the restaurants, along with the other shops in the station, close at 11:30. We apologise for any trouble this delay causes and we will let you know if there are any further changes.

6

What book does the man recommend to the woman?

W: Have you read anything good lately? I'm looking for a new book to read.

M: Well, you know me, I love books about music. I've just finished one about a celebrity DJ that I bet you would like. I also read a biography of Miles Davis, a jazz musician who played the trumpet. It was excellent. You're not really into that kind of music, though.

W: I saw you reading a book about that rock star from the 80s. What's his name?

M: David Bowie. Yes, it was very popular, that book – a bestseller – so I expected it to be good. I found it a bit dull, actually.

7

Who was the woman's French teacher?

M: Look at this old photo!

W: It's from when I was in high school. These were my teachers. My favourite was Mr. Richard, my French teacher.

M: Is this him?

W: The man with the beard? That's Mr Gary. He taught us History. Mr. Richard is this one, the guy with the moustache.

M: He looks friendly.

W: He was. nother favourite of mine was Mr. Adams. I learnt so much from him about music. He taught me to play the piano and got me interested in classical music. The kids used to make fun of him for wearing these red glasses, but he never seemed to mind.

6.3

1 airline
2 hand luggage
3 car park
4 motorway
5 speed limit
6 window seat

7.1

Last year, I went to Antarctica for the first time. I was there because I'm a scientist. I worked with a team of people. When I got the job, I was quite nervous. The South Pole is quite a difficult place to live in, and I spent five months there. For the first two weeks, it was so exciting, but after two months, I was ready to go home.

My job was great though! I counted the penguins. It wasn't easy to count them, because they move a lot, and there are thousands of them! I had to get up really early every day because it's best to count them in the morning. They go looking for food in the afternoon. They are very busy animals!

I also had a special camera and took photographs of the area. This helped me to check my information.

The information can tell us a lot about how penguins live, and if they are doing well in the environment. It's normally a very cold place with a lot of snow, but when I went there was rain! Not much, but this is very unusual for the area. It's normally too cold for this weather. This shows how the temperature is changing there.

I loved the penguins! But life is hard in the Antarctic. I didn't miss things like restaurants, but there isn't any internet connection – and I couldn't talk to my friends or family. I missed them a lot.

The team is going back next year in March, and I will join them in May. It's only for two months, so I think it will be easier. There is a lot of work to do. And, of course, I can also see the penguins again.

7.2

W = Woman M = Man

1

What is the woman going to do after work?

W: Work is so busy at the moment. It's been such a long day; I'm so tired! I've got an exercise class tonight after work, but I think I'm going to cancel it. I am just too tired. I think I'll go and visit my mum instead. She hasn't been very well, so it will be nice to see her. I'd love to just relax on the sofa with a good film and a takeaway, but I'll save that for another day. Maybe I can do that at the weekend!

2

What job does the man's son do?

M: I thought my son would become a chef. He was always interested in cooking and, well, I'm a chef, so I thought he'd just do the same. But actually, he's really talented at something else. He's trying to become a successful musician! He performs in the restaurant I work at and he's really incredible ... the waiters think the music makes them feel more relaxed and the customers love it too! I'm sure he'll be a great success, and I think cooking will remain a hobby for him.

3

What has the woman lost?

M: Excuse me ... are you okay?
W: Oh, sorry ... I think I dropped my keys in here. They might be on the floor.
M: Hmm ... What table were you sitting at?
W: That one over there in the corner ... I was having a meeting on my mobile phone ... I think my keys fell when I was putting my phone away.
M: Hmm... someone handed in a lost notebook, but no keys I'm afraid. Let me have a look around the café for you.
W: Thank you. Normally, I'm so careful. I'll look in my bag again.
M: Don't worry. They will be somewhere!

4

Why did the man miss his flight?

M: I can't believe I missed my flight last week. I had a meeting in Hamburg on the Tuesday afternoon and my flight was leaving Tuesday morning. I got up very early because there are roadworks on the motorway at the moment. I took a taxi to the airport, but in the taxi, I started feeling very strange. I thought I might be sick! In the end, the taxi driver took me back home. We've rearranged the meeting for this week. I hope my next journey to the airport is more successful!

5

Where will the people have the meeting?

M: It was so good to see you today and I think we've had some good ideas. Shall we meet again to work on it some more?
W: Yes, I think that's a good idea ... How about the same time next week?
M: Good idea, but we won't be able to use the meeting room that day. We could do it online.
W: Well, I prefer meeting in person. We could go to a coffee shop or something. I find it much easier to concentrate outside of the house.
M: Yes, that sounds fine. Well, I'll email you later in the week and we can arrange a time.

6

What did the man forget to order?

W: We've got the Thompson meeting tomorrow, is everything ready?
M: I think so. I've booked the meeting room and ordered lunch – the sandwiches will arrive at midday.
W: That's great. But it starts quite early. Will there be tea and coffee for them when they arrive? I think we will need something like that before we start.
M: Erm ... No, I didn't think about that. I'll arrange it now.
W: And make sure there are some biscuits and sweet things for them when they come in too, please.
M: Okay.

7

How does the woman travel to work?

W: I work in the city centre, and there is nowhere to park, so I take public transport. The quickest way is to take the train but it's always so busy and unpleasant. I tried the bus for a while, but it was so slow, and quite busy too, so I went back to my usual route by train. I think next year I might start driving to work. It probably won't be any quicker, but the journey will be more comfortable!

7.3

W = Woman M = Man

1

M: Excuse me ... are you okay?
W: Oh, sorry ... I think I dropped my keys in here. They might be on the floor.

2

W: It probably won't be any quicker, but the journey will be more comfortable!

7.4

1 these
2 police
3 build
4 cheek
5 live
6 believe
7 system
8 evening
9 people
10 biscuit
11 key
12 village

7.5

1 Leave these biscuits in the tin.
2 Many people built this bridge.
3 This evening we'll leave the village.
4 She keeps fit in the gym every evening.

8.1

W = Woman M = Man

M: Today I'm talking to Hannah Chapman who is an assistant coach for a football team for girls under 15.

How did you get involved in this Hannah?

W: Um, I used to be on the football team when I was at university. And I've always enjoyed helping the local community. But I got involved with this team five years ago. It was when my daughter and some of her friends joined the team. At that time, the head coach was looking for more parents to help with training. I offered to help on Saturday mornings.

M: Did you know how to train teenagers when you started?

W: Not really, no! Although I taught my children how to ride their bikes, that was different. Teaching the rules of football to a large group of teenagers is hard. The good thing was that there were two other parents who joined at the same time as me. We decided to go on a short course. It really helped us understand what we had to focus on with a group of girls at that age. I think all the assistant coaches should do it.

M: How much time does your role take up?

W: Quite a lot, actually. I do two training sessions a week. On Wednesday evening and on Saturday morning. I know the girls would love to have more sessions, but we wouldn't be able to do that unless more parents offered to help. I understand parents don't have much free time these days. Recently we've been asking parents who live close to where the team trains.

M: Where does the financial support come from?

W: The team shirts have the logo of a restaurant in the town. It doesn't cost much to pay for the shirts and it's an easy way to advertise to families. But most of our money comes from some shops in the area who want to support us.

M: What would you do if you had more money?

W: I think the first thing would be to buy a new minibus to take the team to matches. There isn't much public transport in this part of the country. At the moment, parents have to drive their daughters. This isn't always convenient for everyone because sometimes the journey is over an hour.

M: And how is the team doing?

W: Oh, it's doing well. The girls lost a few matches at the beginning of the season, but they have won the last few games. I think it's because they're beginning to work as a team now. All the players felt awful when they were losing, so they made a big effort to change.

8.2

W = Woman M = Man

1

You will hear two friends talking about a sports event.

M: I can't believe that match. I've never seen anything so exciting. I'm so glad we decided to come to the stadium instead of watching it on TV.

W: Absolutely. I've never been to a sports event like this before.

M: Yeah. The tickets weren't as expensive as I thought, and they were definitely worth it.

W: You're right. I'd love to have the chance to go to something like this again!

M: That would be fantastic. We should try and book tickets for another match.

W: That would be great!

2

You will hear a man telling a friend about a shopping experience.

M: I went to the new sports shop last week to buy some new running clothes.

W: Oh really? What was it like?

M: Well to be honest it wasn't a great experience. I eventually found some good-quality running shoes, but I had to keep asking the assistants to help me find things.

W: What do you mean?

M: I thought all the running clothes would be in the same area, but the tracksuits were in a completely different section to the running T-shirts.

W: That sounds like a terrible idea.

M: I know. It was almost impossible to find anything.

3

You will hear a man telling a friend about a new exercise class.

M: I started a new gym class yesterday and when I entered the room, I was a little bit worried.

W: Oh really? Why?

M: The instructor looked very young, and I thought the class might be too easy. Sometimes that happens with less experienced instructors. Anyway, I was completely wrong. He's been an instructor for several years and was great. He was so good at giving instructions and he listened to everyone's questions carefully too. I think you should try the class.

W: Actually, that's a good idea. I'll check my schedule and see if I can join you next week.

4

You will hear two friends discussing a cycling trip.

W: Harry, can we talk about the cycling trip?

M: Of course.

W: I want to know what you think we should do for accommodation. I know some people go camping, but I don't want to carry a tent on my bike.

M: Okay. Why don't we stay in a hotel then? I'll have a look online and then we can choose together.

W: Okay. The trip is not going to be very long, so we don't have to take lots of things with us. Just a few tools to fix the bikes if something goes wrong.

M: Yes, you're right. I'll send you some links to hotels at the weekend.
W: Thanks!

5
You will hear a man telling a friend about a competition he is going to enter.

M: I'm really looking forward to the skateboarding competition next month.
W: Oh yes! It's not long now. I must get a ticket. You know I can get a discount because I'm a student.
M: That's great. I think it'll be fantastic to watch because a lot of people have entered. It's a shame that there isn't a big enough stadium for the competition to take place here though. It's quite a long way for everyone to travel.
W: But it's going to take place in the new stadium. What an amazing experience it'll be for you.
M: Yes, that's true.

6
You will hear two friends talking about a walking holiday.

W: I enjoyed most of the holiday, what about you?
M: Absolutely. I mean the weather was not as bad as I thought it would be. I didn't have to wear my rain jacket once during the whole trip.
W: But it was so difficult to know which path to choose without maps. I'm not surprised we got lost three times!
M: Yes, I didn't realise that the mobile phone reception would be so bad. I thought I could just use an online map.
W: Well, at least we know for the next holiday.
M: That's a good point.

8.3

1 column
2 comb
3 knee
4 wrote
5 scenery
6 doubt
7 muscle
8 climber
9 science
10 hour
11 where
12 autumn
13 sign
14 honour

8.4

1 Scientists don't always know all the answers.
2 The designer was honest about his mistake.
3 In the autumn, it's nice to walk for many hours.
4 I spent a whole hour listening to the audio guide.

9.1

W = Woman M = Man

M: I'm here with Nicola Martin, who's going to tell us about going back to education as an adult. Nicola, you decided to study car mechanics. Why did you choose that?
W: Well, I'd just bought a new car, and I always worried that it might go wrong ... and I wouldn't know what to do ... so I thought why not? I've always loved cars and wanted to know more about them. I didn't have a full-time job and the children were at school, so I decided to do a course!
M: And how did you study?
W: Well, I looked at some courses on the internet, but I didn't think it was a good subject for distance learning ... you need practical experience ... Then I heard about classes at the local college. They were from 9.30 to 11.30 am three days a week, so it was perfect, and my weekends were still free.
M: What was the course like?
W: It was brilliant. The students were so lovely, and I made some new friends. There were a lot of new words to learn ... some that I'd never heard of before, but it became easier when I started actually working on the cars. I loved that part.
M: How did you feel when the course ended?
W: I felt quite sad – I didn't want it to end! I wasn't the best student in the class, but I was very good, and I even did well in the exams! We had practical exams and a written test. I wasn't very confident about passing them, but I did well.
M: What do you do now the course has finished?
W: Well, I'm always busy, but I try to use my new skills as much as possible. I'm trying to repair some old cars at the moment, so I can sell them later. I also don't mind giving advice to people who want it, but I won't fix people's cars for free! It takes too long! Usually, I just tell them what the problem might be, so they can go to a garage.
M: Do you think you might make this a career?
W: I'm not sure ... I loved the course, but I don't think it will help me to study mechanics more. I think I know enough about it ... for what I need anyway. I'd quite like to find out how to run a business ... Perhaps I'll see if there are any good teachers who can help me with that next. I'm sure I could make a business out of what I'm doing now.

9.2

I didn't have a full-time job and the children were at school, so I decided to do a course!
I also don't mind giving advice to people who want it.

9.3

W = Woman M = Man

1
Where is the Newton building?

W: Excuse me, I'm new to the university and I'm looking for the Newton Building.
M: Oh, the Newton Building? That's a lovely place! It's not too far away. Just continue walking until you come to the lake ...
W: Oh yes, I think I saw the lake earlier!
M: You'll have to walk around the lake ... there's no bridge ... and then you'll see it. It's the building on the left. The other one is the chemistry block. I think it will take about 10 minutes to get there from here.

2
What subject did the woman do best in?

M: Did you get your exam results back today? How did you do?
W: Well, I did better than I thought in maths ... which I am quite happy about ... but I got top marks in science! I can't believe it ... I didn't think I was very good at maths or science!
M: That's great news! I was never good at science at school. I did well in my geography exams. I'm quite surprised really because I didn't study much.
W: I did! I was really worried that I might fail! I'm so pleased!

3
How will students receive a student card?

W: Before you start on your courses, you need to get a student card. You can use this to get into the buildings in the evenings and at weekends, and also to use the library. To get this card, please go to the library. You need to show your identification and complete a form. It normally takes three days to make the cards, so you will receive an email when they are ready. Then you should go back and collect them. If you want to book any rooms or reserve books, there is a mobile app you can use to do this.

4
What was the noise?

W: How was the exam?

M: A bit of a disaster to be honest! I arrived late because my 10-year-old was ill and I had to find someone to look after her. When I finally got to the exam I couldn't concentrate anyway ... It seems they were doing some work outside the building! They really should pick a better time!

W: Oh that's a shame. I'm sure you did well anyway! Give me a call when you know the result.

5
What does the woman plan to study?

W: Hello, is this Redburn College? I'm interested in taking an evening class with you. I wanted to do the dressmaking class, but I saw on your website that you're not doing that anymore. So, I think I'd be interested in the photography course. How many hours a week is it? I took the art class with you a while ago and I really enjoyed it .... Can you tell me ... are the prices for the evening courses still the same? Could you ring me back to confirm? Many thanks.

6
What does the man want?

M: Ermm ... Excuse me, are you using that?

W: No, not at the moment.

M: Do you mind if I borrow it? I need to plug my laptop in, but I've forgotten my charger! I only have about 10% battery left!

W: Of course. That's no problem, but I need it back in an hour. I've got to listen to a talk on my computer later and I will need it for that.

M: Yes, I'll give it back before then. Thanks!

7
How does the woman prefer to learn?

M: You always know the answers to these kinds of quiz shows. How do you know so much?

W: Well, it's not from school! Back then, I could never sit still for long enough to read all those text books we had. No ... I think actually I've got most of my knowledge from watching talks online ... I love them! My husband loves going to galleries and museums and learning about how the world works, but I'd rather be home with a cup of tea and a talk!

M: Well, it works for you!

9.4
hair here her

9.5
1 serve here term
2 work wear word
3 clear learn heard
4 nurse hurt wear
5 there bird shirt

9.6
/ɪə/ fear pier really steer we're
/eə/ fair pear rarely stare where

10.1
W = Woman M = Man

M: Today's programme is about holidays that went wrong. I'm talking to Marsha about her skiing holiday. So, tell us where you went and why.

W: Well, my sister and I decided to go on holiday to Austria. We usually spend the winter holiday with our families, but we wanted to do something with just the two of us. Although we like sightseeing, we both live in cities. So, we thought a sports holiday might be a bit different to what we normally do

M: And did you know how to ski before you went?

W: Yes, we went skiing a few times when we were younger. On the first day, we had a great time. We joined a class, and our instructor reviewed various things about the equipment and how to ski and stop without falling over. We practised on a few small slopes, and the instructor said we were ready for something a bit more advanced. However, the next day, it all went wrong!

M: Oh no, what happened?

W: We decided to challenge ourselves on a taller mountain, but as I was skiing, I hit a rock and fell over. I don't think we understood how hard it could be compared to the day before. We were too confident. I mean the last time we had been skiing was over ten years ago so one day was probably not enough practice. Anyway, I realised that my arm hurt a lot and I was a bit worried. Some other skiers carried me to the bottom of the mountain and called an ambulance to take me to the hospital.

M: What was it like at the hospital?

W: I thought that I'd had a serious accident, but the doctor told me that I hadn't broken any bones. I was really happy because I didn't need to have an operation. The doctor told me to take some pills for the pain and get some rest. But she also said that I couldn't go back to ski school!

M: So, what did you do instead?

W: I was going to read the books I'd brought with me, but I met two other people who had had accidents! We sat together in the sun and chatted and went on a couple of day trips to villages in the area. They were organised by the hotel.

M: So, it wasn't a total disaster?

W: Not at all. At the end of each day my sister told me all about the skiing. She said that she was learning so much in the class and she would teach me what she'd learned next year. It was a shame I missed it, but we're definitely coming back again. I can't wait to get back on the slopes – and I won't fall over next time!

10.2
Hi everyone! I'm David. Welcome to Talltrees! I'm the instructor on this yoga weekend. I'll show you to your rooms after this talk and you can get changed. Please put on some comfortable clothing. This is important as you need to stretch, and you don't need to wear shoes here – your feet can be free! We have mats here for you to use.

Most classes will be in this room, apart from the morning classes which are in the garden! We'll start at 7.30 am, and then at 8.15 we'll have breakfast. Breakfast is healthy – we have bread, yoghurt and fresh fruit. There's no tea or coffee, but there is lots of juice for you.

Now, Amira asked me if you had any free time in the morning. The answer is yes – until 11.30, when the second yoga class will start. This will be an hour, and then we're going to all cook lunch together. The chef here has offered to teach us some vegetarian dishes and I think it will be a great experience. She'll provide the ingredients and most of them are from the garden!

Some of you also asked what we were doing in the afternoons. We have two different activities planned. On Saturday, we'll go for a walk through the forest. It's a great opportunity to be close to nature, and you can often see wildlife there. Bring your cameras! And also wear some comfortable trainers. On Sunday, we're doing something different. Usually, we take our guests to the local market, but it's not open this Sunday, so we're going to have a painting class by the lake. We have all the materials for you. In the early evening there will be another yoga class to help us relax. This will be around 8 pm. Then, you can have a snack, and we'll go to bed at 10 pm. This might seem early, but I promise you will be tired! And relaxed too!

10.3

1 Amira asked me if you had any free time in the morning.
2 The chef here has offered to teach us some vegetarian dishes
3 Some of you also asked what we were doing in the afternoons.

10.4

1 pain / paint
2 neck / next
3 feel / field
4 lie / line
5 goal / gold
6 may / main
7 fine / find

10.5

1 paint
2 next
3 feel
4 lie
5 gold
6 main
7 fine

11.1

W = Woman M = Man

1

You will hear two flatmates talking about a washing machine.

W: Something is wrong with the washing machine. The light turns on, but nothing happens.

M: Yes, I noticed that. I looked for a new one online, but they are so expensive. The cheapest one I saw was about £300!

W: We can get one cheaper than that, surely! But anyway ... maybe we should try to have it repaired before we buy a new one. I don't want to spend so much money if we don't need to.

M: Yes, you're right. I know someone who might be able to help with it. I'll get in contact with him.

2

You will hear part of a town meeting.

W: ... So, that's the plan for the new office building.

M: Hmm ... I'm not too sure it will work. As the mayor of this town, I need to think about the people who live here.

W: But it will give people in the town lots more opportunities for jobs! We've already got three companies who want to move in when the offices are built.

M: I understand that, but I'm not sure we should be building on green spaces. I think we need to think of the children and families living in the area. It would be much better if it were outside the town.

W: But that will be far worse for traffic.

3

You will hear a man asking for directions.

W: Hello there. What can I get you?

M: Sorry, I've just come in to ask for directions. I'm trying to find this place ... it's a bakery ...

W: Oh yes ... I know the place, but it's on the other side of town. You shouldn't walk ... not in this weather.

M: It's just ... I've ordered my wife's birthday cake from there, and I've got to pick it up today.

W: Hmm ... it's probably best to take a taxi, I can call one. It's not a good day to be out walking!

M: That would be great! Thanks so much for your help.

4

You will hear two friends discussing their neighbours.

W: I am so sick of the people at number 43.

M: Oh, me too. We live right next door. We couldn't get to sleep until 4 am on Saturday.

W: I mean, I don't mind people having parties, but they should respect the neighbours.

M: I completely agree. In fact, my wife went around to speak to them about the noise on Sunday. They didn't think it was a problem.

W: Really? That's terrible. What do you think we should do about it?

M: I'm not sure. This isn't the first time, though. Perhaps we should try to speak to them again and go together.

5

You will hear a tour guide talking about a castle.

W: So, are there any questions about the castle?

M: Yes, I'd like to know why it was built here. It's very far away from any towns or villages.

W: Well, it is often believed that it was built here because it was a very safe place. It's on a rock in the sea, and it's hard to reach ... but actually this isn't true.

M: Really?

W: Yes. It was built here because this is where an old king died – so people thought it was a very important place. It was very difficult to get all the stone and other building materials to this location, but they did an incredible job!

M: Yes, and well ... here it is 800 years later!

6

You will hear two people talking about cleaning their houses.

W: I hate cleaning the house. It's a job that never ends. I'd like to get it cleaned by a professional, but my flatmates won't pay.

M: It's not a fun task, but it doesn't have to be that unpleasant, and you don't need a cleaner! Just make sure you and your flatmates clean different rooms. That's what my partner and I do. And we do it regularly.

W: Every day?

M: Twice a week is enough. but if you do little and often, that helps! And try putting on some music. That makes it more fun.

W: Well, I suppose we can try.

11.2

W = Woman   M = Man

1

Which hotel room does the woman choose?

W: I was trying to find us something for the weekend in La Rochelle. I wanted to get something with a nice balcony and sea view, but most of the accommodation was already booked. In the end, I got a room that also has a sofa bed for the twins. Unfortunately, we've got to share a bathroom, but that's not the end of the world. The hotel is in the centre of town and the price was excellent. Just 80 euros for the two nights!

2

What does the car need?

W: I'm really looking forward to getting away from the city this weekend. Did you get the car checked? It's going to take us at least three hours to get to the cottage.

M: Yes, I did. The mechanic looked at it last week, the engine is fine, but we've got to have two tyres changed. I've booked it in for later today.

W: Great! Should we clean it before we go too?

M: No, I don't think so. It will get dirty on the journey, so it's probably better to do it when we get back.

W: I suppose so.

3

Where is the saucepan?

W: Have you seen the big red saucepan?

M: No. Isn't it where it always is?

W: No. I've looked in all the cupboards and I can't see it at all.

M: Hmm ... Well I made that chicken dish in it yesterday; it's probably in the dishwasher.

W: Well, I put it on last night and it wasn't in there ... Have you left it in the oven?

M: I must have! Sorry.

W: Don't worry. Although it will be impossible to wash now. All the food will be stuck on it!

M: I'll clean it now so you can use it.

4

Where is the man's new flat located?

M: You must come and see my new flat! I need to do a lot of work on it, but it's in a pretty good location. I really wanted to buy a flat near the train station, so it would be easy to get to work, but the flats on that road were too expensive. In the end, I've got one just a five-minute walk from the station. But it's the same distance from the park and the shops too, so I think it's still a great location. I'm moving in next week!

5

How much does the company charge per hour?

M: Are you sick of all the chores you have to do in the house? Perfect House Services can help you! We offer house cleaning, clothes washing, ironing. We even prepare meals for you! And we can also fix anything that is broken around your house. If you have a garden, we can take care of that, too! We've lowered our hourly prices from twelve pounds fifty to ten pounds fifty per hour. And we have a fifteen percent discount for new customers! What are you waiting for? Give yourself more time to do what you really enjoy and leave the jobs to us!

6

Where do they decide to put the lamp?

M: So, where do you think we should put the lamp?

W: I think by the chair is a good place. What do you think?

M: Mmm ... I'm not so sure. I know you like to read there, but that table isn't very big, and you like to put your snacks and magazine on it ... I don't think that will work.

W: Okay, well why don't we move the plant from the bookshelf and put it next to the TV ... Then we can put the lamp there.

M: I think that's a good idea! It will look nice there.

7

Who does the building belong to?

M: Now, this building here is very special. It was home to the royal family around 300 years ago. It was bought by a group of local business people around 20 years ago. They wanted to attract visitors to the area, so it is open every day from nine till five. It's a beautiful place to look around, and there are even concerts in the garden in summer. In fact, it's a favourite venue of rock star Jordan Bright, who has played here at least five times.

11.3

tomorrow
remember
hospital
problem
survive
bigger

11.4

1 banana
2 comfortable
3 America
4 accurate
5 possible

11.5

Yesterday I went to London because I wanted to buy a present for my brother. I visited a lot of shops, but I couldn't find anything suitable. Finally, I saw an amazing pair of trainers, so I bought them.

12.1

Today on Tech Matters, I'd like to talk to you about the robot show that I went to last month in Japan. There were over 100 companies showing their robots, and almost all of these robots were designed to help people. One of these robots is the Robear. This is a robot that can lift elderly people from their beds to a chair. These are used in hospitals at the moment, but the company that made this robot has big plans. They want these robots to be in people's homes in a few years. This is great news for people who need help to move around.

Another robot, called Spot, can also help people. It's a robot in the shape of a dog, but it's not a pet! It's a robot that can be used in lots of different types of jobs. It's very useful for doing dangerous jobs that humans can't do, like going down a small tunnel. In fact, the number of these robots used in places like this is increasing!

Another invention in the show might not seem like a traditional robot. Café X is a totally automatic café, so it doesn't need any staff! These machines are available to buy now. It's a great idea, but I prefer speaking to someone when buying a coffee. Don't you?

Lastly, the most amazing robot I saw was Geminoid HI-1. It was made by Professor Hiroshi Ishiguro. The robot actually looks like him! It looks very realistic! He used artificial intelligence to make the robot, and Geminoid HI-1 even gives talks for the professor.

Robot development is changing year by year, and every year is more exciting. So, if you're interested in technology, I recommend you go to a robot show and see for yourself! The next one is going to be in London from the 29th of October to the 5th of November. Tickets are half the normal price if you book before the 19th of June.

12.2

W = Woman M = Man

1

You will hear two friends talking about buying a mobile phone.

W: Have you got a new mobile phone yet?

M: No, I haven't. I was looking on the website but there are too many to choose from. I don't know what the differences are between them all.

W: I know what you mean – it's all very confusing.

M: I'm going to go into one or two shops tomorrow. I think I should speak to someone before buying something. If I don't get some advice, I'll probably buy something that isn't right for me. I don't want to waste my money.

W: That sounds like a good idea. The shop assistants will be able to help you.

2

You will hear a man telling a friend about a technology problem.

M: Do you know much about computers?

W: Um, a little. I'm not an expert but tell me what's wrong and I'll see if I can help.

M: Okay. I need to print out this document later, but at the moment I can't even open it and I don't know what to do.

W: Hmm. Let me try ... Oh, yes ... I see what you mean. Is the printer working?

M: I haven't had any problems with it recently.

W: In that case, why don't you email it to me, and I can print it for you.

M: Oh, thank you, that would be great.

3

You will hear two friends discussing electric cars.

M: What do you think about electric cars?

W: I think they're great. You know if everyone had one, it would make a big difference to the environment. I'd like to see more of them on the roads in the future.

M: Me too. The government should definitely encourage everyone to get an electric car, but in my view, they still cost too much for a lot of people.

W: Well, they are very difficult to make – much more complicated than the old-style cars. The technology is amazing!

M: I don't know much about the technology, but I do think they're a great invention.

4

You will hear two friends talking about a robot cleaner.

M: I bought a robot cleaner for my house last week.

W: Oh really? What's it like? My friend told me that hers doesn't clean very well.

M: I'm really pleased with it. It wasn't very expensive, but I didn't just buy the first one I saw. I spent quite a lot of time reading about them online first.

W: Hmm. And did that help you?

M: Absolutely. I would have spent a lot more money if I hadn't read all those reviews. The one I bought works well for a small flat like mine.

W: Well, I'm glad you didn't spend a fortune!

M: Me too!

5

You will hear two colleagues talking about a conference.

W: I think the technology conference next week is going to be amazing. I can't wait to see all the new products and talk to some of the designers and engineers.

M: Unfortunately, I didn't know that it was happening. If I'd known about it, I would have bought a ticket, but I think it's sold out now.

W: Oh no, that's bad luck.

M: Well, it's okay. My manager is going, so she'll tell me about all the interesting things afterwards.

W: Oh, that's good.

M: And actually, I've got a lot of work at the moment, so I'd rather not take time off.

6

You will hear two friends talking about a mobile phone app.

M: Have you seen this hiking app?

W: No, I don't think so.

M: I think it's great. Look, all the walks in the region are listed and you can see them on an interactive map too.

W: Oh, yes. That looks amazing. Was it free?

M: No, but it only cost a few dollars. It would have been better if they'd used different colours, but it has all the walks in the region which is very good compared to other apps.

W: I agree.

M: I think I'll be using it a lot in future.

W: I'm going to download it too!

12.3

1 Have you switched‿off your computer?
2 I always‿send‿emails from‿my phone.
3 We do lots‿of‿experiments‿in science class.
4 Please print‿ten copies‿of your work.

12.4

Almost_everyone_owns_a mobile phone these days. These can be as cheap_as 40 pounds_or cost hundreds_of pounds, but_the most_expensive mobile phone_in the world is_an_enormous 40 million pounds. It_is made_of gold_and diamonds, and_it belongs to the wife_of the richest man_in_Asia.

Ready for Listening

0.1

W = Woman M = Man

What type of novel does the man most enjoy reading?W:
You've always got your nose in a book. Have you read anything good lately?

M: Yes, I have actually. This book's pretty interesting – it's about these young astronauts who go on a one-way trip to live on Mars. I can't put it down!

W: Cool. Is that the kind of novel you tend to read?

M: This novel is great, but I've always been really into detective stories – I mean, I'll read those before anything else.

W: I had no idea. Do you ever read horror stories? I absolutely love those!

M: They're all right, I suppose.

0.2

W = Woman M = Man N = Narrator P = Presenter
W1 = Woman 1 W2 = Woman 2

1

What's the woman's favourite souvenir from her last trip?

M: Did you buy any souvenirs from your trip to Canada?

W: Yeah, I got everyone in my family a keychain with a cute bear on it. I'm a bit sad I didn't keep one for myself, actually.

M: What else did you get?

W: A bracelet that I never want to take off. It reminds me of the incredible time I had over there. Oh, and I also got the T-shirt I'm wearing right now.

M: It's really cool!

W: Thanks!

2

What will the weather be like tomorrow?

P: Most regions have experienced light showers over the last few days, with temperatures gradually dropping. Despite this, roads will remain clear of ice and any sign of snowfall. However, expect heavy winds to pick up sometime shortly after midnight. This will continue throughout the day, so be aware that this may cause unexpected delays with the national rail service.

3

Where do the friends decide to go first?

W1: I still can't believe we're actually in São Paulo. I've got to put my backpack down soon, though!

W2: Yeah, my back's killing me, too. We should find a hostel right away, don't you think?

W1: Well, if we go to the tourist information centre – they'll tell us where there's one nearby.

W2: Good idea. Hey, did you know we're just around the corner from the Independence of Brazil monument? We could take a look at that on the way there.

W2: Okay!

4

What animal will the university student study for his research project?

W: What sea creature will you research for your ocean sciences course?

M: Well, Professor, my first choice was the great white shark, but someone else is doing that, and the same goes for the blue whale – another fascinating animal. I've been looking into the bottlenose dolphin, and I'm relieved I didn't go for anything else – particularly as it's a species that can recognise itself in mirrors, a sign of intelligence that few other sea animals have. I'm keen to explore this behaviour in more detail this semester.

5

What documentary series would the woman like to watch?

M: I'm thinking about watching *Blue Planet*. I've heard it's a brilliant documentary series about oceans.

W: It is – I saw it when it first came out, though. What about the one where two guys travel around the world on motorbikes? I've been dying to see that.

M: Possibly, or we could try that docuseries about the extreme rock climber.

W: If you're talking about *Free Solo*, I can't watch stuff like that.

M: How come?

W: It makes me anxious watching someone climb huge mountains without any ropes.

6

What did the man injure while on holiday?

W: Hi. I'm Dr Perez. What's the problem?

M: Well, I fell while on holiday, and walking on my left leg is still really painful.

W: Okay, let me see what's going on. Now, slowly bend your knee ... And move your toes around.

M: Okay.

W: So, it's not your leg giving you all this trouble. How does it feel when you move your ankle up and down?

M: Awful.

W: Right. You'll need to avoid putting any weight on it for two weeks, or you'll cause more damage. I'll also give you something for the pain.

7

What activity did the woman do last night?

W: Hey, Michael. We missed you last night! A bunch of us went to a club that was supposed to have this famous DJ playing house music all evening. But you'll never guess what? He didn't even show up, so there was just recorded music playing. That didn't stop us from going on the dance floor till it was time to go home, though. Call me when you get in, okay? I want to hear about the modern dance performance you went to. You seemed pretty excited about it. Okay, bye!

0.3

W = Woman M = Man

1

You will hear two friends talking about a music festival.

W: I had a great time at the music festival over the long weekend. Did you?

M: Of course! It was the best one I've been to in a long time, and the 3-day pass wasn't expensive, unlike other big festivals.

W: Really? I thought it was a bit too much – maybe that's why it didn't sell out. I didn't mind, though – I liked having room to dance, especially when my favourite bands were playing.

M: Me too. And they made sure everything ran on time.

W: I noticed that, too. That doesn't usually happen at big events like that.

2

You will hear a woman talking about visiting Machu Picchu in Peru.

M: Didn't you go to Machu Picchu while you were in Peru? I've always wanted to visit that historical site.

W: I did, and it was an unforgettable experience, You should go one day! I didn't mind climbing up the really steep path to get to it, but I was exhausted by the time I arrived there.

M: Was it worth all that effort?

W: I suppose so. You're only allowed to stay at the ruins for four hours – I was pretty irritated that I didn't manage to see everything even though I hurried as much as possible. It's a spectacular place to visit, though!

M: Sounds like it.

3

You will hear two colleagues talking about an invention.

M: Hi, Isabel. I'm working on an invention, and I'm pretty sure no one has done anything like it.

W: Sounds interesting. Am I the first person you've shared this with?

M: Yeah, I'm contacting you because you've invented things before.

W: Well, thanks for trusting me, but you need to protect your idea. Tell me, but don't tell anyone else about it until you've sent a patent application form to the Intellectual Property Office. Include a detailed explanation of how it works.

M: Right. How long will it be before I hear back from them?

W: You won't like this, but it usually takes over a year.

4

You will hear two friends talking about doing an escape-room experience.

M: That escape room was amazing! I can't believe we solved all those puzzles in just under an hour. I didn't think we'd get out in time, but we did!

W: It feels great winning these T-shirts by solving all those challenging puzzles together.

M: I know. Didn't you think the ones about numbers were quite hard?

W: Yeah, and the puzzles with text and letters were even more challenging. But the ones where you had to move objects seemed to take the longest to find a solution.

M: Absolutely. They were much more difficult than anything else we had to do.

5

You will hear two friends talking about a reality talent show.

M: Janine, you're an incredibly good singer. You should enter that reality talent show on TV.

W: You're talking about the one where the best performer wins a million dollars, right?

M: Yeah, and I've looked into it, and it doesn't cost a thing to enter. You just need to prepare a 90-second clip of you singing and send it to the judges.

W: That wouldn't be too hard to put together. But wait – I only sing other people's songs.

M: It doesn't matter – they just want to see if you can sing.

W: All right then. Maybe I'll be their next rising star!

6

You will hear two friends discussing a banking app.

W: What do you think about the banking app called Cash101? None of the other ones I've used have helped me to spend less money. Not like this one does!

M: Well, I can't compare it because I've only ever used this Cash101. And, like you, I found it helpful till it started crashing. They really ought to make sure that doesn't happen so it can work properly.

W: Maybe it's your phone rather than the app? I mean, I've never had that happen before.

M: I'm pretty sure that's not the problem. It's a shame because I liked how simple it was to use.

0.4

Hello. I'm Lars, your guide and here's what to expect on the half-day tour, where every attraction will be about the tulip, a popular flower in the Netherlands.

This morning, our first coach stop is a natural history museum where you'll learn more about the tulip. For example, this wild flower from Central Asia was brought to the Netherlands in 1593. By the mid-1600s, the Dutch considered it a luxury item and it was worth more than gold for a short period, causing the economy to rise and fall very quickly.

Next, we'll go to a region called Bollenstreek to visit a farm that grows over one million tulips. Nowadays, there are around 3000 types of tulip, and at this attraction, you'll see 700 of them, which always look fantastic in selfies!

We'll have lunch at noon at a 5-star restaurant, but don't expect a typical Dutch lunch of sandwiches and cheese. The chef is preparing a soup – the main ingredient is the tulip bulb, which is the bottom part of the flower. Don't worry, it's delicious!

Afterwards, the coach will take us to Keukenhof Gardens to see tulip gardens that are like art sculptures. I recommend going to the windmill for a view you'll never forget. There's a castle on the grounds with a pretty good view of the gardens, too.

Our last stop will be at Bloemenmarkt, which means *flower market* in Dutch, and it opened in Amsterdam in 1862. Most markets are in a public square, but this one's on houseboats and claims to be the only floating flower market in the world.

Finally, if you buy tulip bulbs to take abroad, you need a certificate. You can't take them out of the Netherlands if you don't show this at customs. When you buy tulip bulbs from official sellers, they should provide one with your receipt. I hope you enjoy the tour!

0.5

W = Woman M = Man

M: On today's podcast, I'm talking to Zara Cross, who went on a six-month working holiday in Ireland to run a bookstore called *Bookends*. Zara, what inspired you to do that?

W: Well, I'm a librarian at an American university, so I love being surrounded by books. I'd always wondered what running an independent bookstore was like, so I looked into working abroad to do something I'd always wanted to do ever since I could remember.

M: Were you surprised when you received the keys to the business?

W: I was thrilled! The whole point is to allow people like me to have this fantastic opportunity. One advantage I had was that I already knew a lot about the book industry. Even so, I had this romantic idea that I'd be sitting in a quiet bookstore reading for hours. Instead, I'd have the most amazing conversations with my customers – something I didn't expect.

M: Did you experience many challenges at Bookends?

W: Of course. I mean, no one likes rude customers, but anyone who deals with the public runs into people like that every now and again. Estimating which novels would be the most popular was probably the hardest job. To be honest, I was a bit nervous about doing the financial reports till I saw how well the bookstore was doing.

M: Did you hold special events there?

W: Yes, and some were more successful than others. For example, I gave a short-story course, but there was little interest. Then I tried live entertainment. I'm glad I did because local singers played almost every weekend in a store filled with happy customers. Occasionally, I'd invite authors to promote their work, too.

M: Most bookstores have interesting window displays. Did you do that?

W: Well, thinking of ideas for them wasn't my strength, and they took me far too long to arrange before they looked any good. To be honest, I'm not sure they made anyone want to come into the store because they lacked imagination. But I made sure everything was always tidy and well-organised.

M: I see. Can you give anyone who wants to go on this type of working holiday some advice?

W: Absolutely! It's essential you research how to run a business before you arrive. I'm glad I did, so I didn't do anything silly – like make the bookstore lose money. Some heavy lifting is involved when you work with books, so make sure you keep fit. And be realistic – sometimes you'll have good and bad days.

M: Thanks for sharing your experience with us, Zara.

Ready for Speaking

0.6

I = Interlocutor P = Pilar C = Carlos

I: Good afternoon. Can I have your mark sheets? I'm Helen Walker and this is Scott Harrison. What's your name?

P: My name is Pilar.

I: Where do you live?

P: In Cadiz, in the south of Spain.

I: Thank you, and what's your name?

C: I'm Carlos.

I: Where do you live?

C: In Valencia, in Spain.

I: Thank you. Do you work or are you a student?

C: I'm working.

I: What do you do?

C: I have got my own shoe shop.

I: Thank you, and Pilar, do you work or are you a student?

P: I'm a student, at university in my city, Cadiz. My career is medicine. But this summer, uh, this month, I'm studying English in London.

I: Thank you. Carlos, tell us about a good friend.

C: Sorry, I didn't understand. Can you say that again, please?

I: Tell us about a good friend.

C: Oh okay. Well, my friend Marco, he is a good friend. He has lived in the same city as me since we were children. I've known him for long time. But now he has got family and I ... I always work, I work a lot, so now we can't see each other like before, uh, every day like before.

I: Thank you. Pilar, what did you do last night?

P: I have gone to the cinema, to see a film.

I: Thank you, and what kind of websites do you like?

P: News websites. I like reading the news.

I: Why?

P: That's a good question. Well, I like know what happens in the world. You know, what happens in other countries, for example, um, information of the economy or new science discoveries.

I: Thank you.

0.7

I = Interlocutor P = Pilar C = Carlos

I: Now I'd like each of you to talk on your own about something. I'm going to give each of you a photograph and I'd like you to talk about it. Pilar, here is your photograph. It shows people in a supermarket. Carlos, you just listen. Pilar, please tell us what you can see in the photograph.

P: OK, so in this picture I can see two people, er, women, in a supermarket. I think they are friends because they are, um, they are smiling each other, laughing. Probably they are shopping for food ... to cook a meal together maybe. One woman, this one with curly long hair, she has a fruit. Probably it's a mango ... Yeah, um, that's it.

I: Talk about the people.

P: So, like I said already, there are two women, one is wearing a blue jacket ... a top, a red top, trousers and ... The other woman, she's wearing a blue skirt and, uh, I don't remember the name, er, a kind of top for women. In her hand she has...

I: Thank you. Carlos, here is your photograph. It shows people at the beach. Pilar, you just listen. Carlos, please tell us what you can see in the photograph.

C: It's a beach ... um a beach in summer, maybe ... There is sand on the beach. Um, at the top, I can see ... there are birds, uh, in the sky. The birds are flying in the sky. In the, uh ... here in the middle of the picture, there are two persons, one boy and one man ... I think, yes, a man. They are family, I think. They are not swimming, but, uh, talking maybe ... looking at the boats and birds. Relaxing. Um, there are many boats, uh, in the water ... six boats. Small boats, not big boats. The birds are ... in the sky, um, over the boats, flying in the ...

I: Thank you.

0.8

I = Interlocutor P = Pilar C = Carlos

I: Now in this part of the test you're going to talk about something together for about two minutes. I'm going to describe a situation to you. A young man wants to get fit and healthy. He is looking for a new way to exercise before or after he goes to work. Here are some activities he could try. Talk together about the ways to exercise and say which would be best. All right? Now talk together.

P: So I think, yeah, there are a lot of good options here, but maybe, uh, running is a good option.

C: Yeah, jogging ... jogging in the park.

P: It's good because it's not so expensive, you know, you ... you don't have to buy much, uh, much ...

C: Equipment?

P: Yes, equipment.

C: Yeah, only trainers, nothing more. Maybe shorts. And it's easy, if you, uh, have a park near to the house, but you also can ... it's also possible to run in the, uh, in the street before you work.

P: Everywhere, you can run everywhere you want.

C: But that is not true with, uh, swimming, you ... you need a pool.

P: But it's a good type of exercise, swimming, don't you think?

C: Yes, very good, if you want to be ... to get fit and healthy. But if you don't have a pool near the office or house, you don't swim. Maybe is also expensive?

P: Yes. Hmmm... What about dancing? I like that. It's a bit, um, different. You no ... you don't think about it, but it's .... it's a good way to exercise. And you can go with friends after work.

C: Yes, I agree. Um, hiking, it's a good idea too ... in the mountains, air fresh, trees.

P: But not with work. And it's, uh, you have got to go out the city ... far away.

C: But with a car ...

P: But going with a car is not exercise!

C: Yes, but when you arrive ... you walk much, you climb much. You're tired.

P: Okay, but it's not as good that running, I think. That's more convenient. You can run everywhere you want.

C: Hiking, yeah, it's less convenient ...

I: Thank you.

0.9

I = Interlocutor P = Pilar C = Carlos

I: Pilar, do you enjoy doing exercise?

P: Yes, uh, yes, I enjoying doing exercise. I go to the gym ... every week actually, now ... and I do Pilates. Exercise makes me to feel very well. I feel healthy after, uh, exercise.

I: And you, Carlos?

C: To be honest, no.

I: Why not?

C: Exercise is good. I know it's, ah, good, but I don't do exercise. I live in a city and I walk all the day. I am healthy ... I think I'm healthy, but I don't do Pilates or, ah ... the gym or jogging. I like swimming, but only in the sea, on holiday.

I: What ways of exercising are popular in your country? Talk together.

P: Shall I start?

C: Okay.

P: Well, in Spain, I think people, ah, people like to cycle. That is popular. I see many people cycling in the, um ... in the mountains ... in the countryside. It's not always nice to cycle in the city ... a bit dangerous.

C: Before, you said about practising Pilates. That is popular, definitely. In my city, they open many Pilates ... places, places to do Pilates. Recently. In the last 10 years. I have never tried. Why is it so famous?

P: I don't know! It's nice, yeah, easy to do. You feel ... good. Your body feels good – how do you say it? Um, flexible, you feel flexible when you do Pilates.

I: Is it better to exercise alone or with friends?

C: With friends.

I: Why?

C: I don't know. Exercise is boring, I think. I don't do it. With friends, probably is less boring.

I: Do you agree?

P: I disagree, I disagree completely. For me, exercise isn't boring, it's ... it's relaxing. I disconnect myself when I exercise. In my studies, I have a lot of stress, there are always many things to do ... reading, exams. When I exercise, I don't think about my studies! Instead, I think about me, where I am. Alone ... when you are alone, you can disconnect more, running, swimming ...

C: But with friends you can talk. That relaxes me, anyway. I relax that way.

P: Of course, that is true, it is nice and relaxing to stay with friends. I am agree. But I don't like talking while I'm doing exercise. Running and talking or doing Pilates and talking ...

I: Thank you. That's the end of the test.

ANSWER KEY

1 IN STYLE

Speaking Part 2 Extended turn

1

1 c **2** a **3** b **4** b
5 d **6** b **7** d **8** c

Vocabulary Clothing

1

a earrings **b** handbag
c belt **d** cap **e** ring
f tie **g** bracelet **h** necklace
i gloves **j** scarf
k watch **l** sunglasses

2

1 try on **2** fit **3** match
4 wear out **5** dress up ; wear
6 Take off; put on

3

1 fit **2** wear **3** try on
4 dress up **5** match
6 wear out **7** put on
8 take off

Reading Part 1 Multiple choice

1

b

2

2 to remind somebody about an art gallery tour

3 to advertise a used snowboard that somebody would like to sell

4 to give instructions on how to wash an item of clothing

5 to tell a friend that it's not a good day to play basketball

3

1 C **2** A **3** B **4** C **5** B

4

1 lift **2** fortnight
3 fine **4** Discounts
5 maximum **6** arrangements

Vocabulary Prepositions of time

1

1 on

2 at

3 in

3

1 in **2** at **3** in **4** on
5 in **6** in **7** on **8** at
9 in **10** in

4

months: in
dates: on
seasons: in
years: in
clock times: at;
days of the week: on

5

1 e **2** c **3** a
4 f **5** d **6** b

Language focus Present simple and present continuous

1

1 present simple
2 present continuous
3 present simple
4 present simple
5 present continuous

2

1 c **2** e **3** a **4** b **5** d

3 Ready for Grammar

1

1 they like **2** correct
3 correct **4** I'm cooking
5 It doesn't matter **6** correct
7 is escaping **8** seems

2

1 (well) is Molly playing?

2 bus does Megan take to work?

3 are Marek and Anna spending their summer holidays?

4 you like high heels?

5 's/is Robert working?

Language focus Present simple and present continuous

4

1 'm wearing **2** find
3 doesn't count **4** 'm not saying
5 looks **6** do you associate
7 are searching **8** Does anyone have

6

2 do you wear **3** do you prefer
4 Are you watching **5** are you learning **6** Do you know

Listening Part 1 Multiple choice

1

B

2

The correct answer is B. The line containing the answer is 'I think I'll have what I normally order,' which relates back to the line 'That's what you usually have.'
A is incorrect because the man suggests the risotto but the woman does not order it.
C is incorrect because the man decides to order the pasta, not the woman.

3

2 B **3** A **4** C **5** B
6 A **7** C

Language focus Adverbs of frequency

1

1 before **2** after **3** after
4 at the end

2

2 hardly ever **3** sometimes
4 often **5** usually **6** always

3 Ready for Grammar

1

1 every day **2** sometimes
3 always **4** often **5** once in a while **6** every week

2

1 We never wash

2 She always arrives

3 Sometimes he wears / He sometimes wears

4 your email every day

5 I am hardly ever

6 in trouble all the time

7 Usually the shop doesn't / The shop doesn't usually

8 work from home twice a week

Writing Part 1 Email

1

1 to your English-speaking friend Marc

2 to make plans with Marc for tomorrow.

3 You must: 1) agree to meet Marc; 2) say whether you prefer going to the shopping centre or the High Street in the city centre; 3) suggest which friends to invite; 4) thank Marc for inviting you to the cinema and explain why you can't go.

4 About 100 words

2

Yes

3

Responding to an email: *Thanks for writing.*
Making suggestions: *let's ..., Why don't we ...*
Ending an email: *Bye for now*

4

Responding to an email: *Nice/Good/ Great to hear from you.; Thanks for your email.*

Making suggestions: *Shall we ...?; You/We could ...*

Ending an email: *See/Talk to you soon.; Take care.*

5 Additional materials

Sample answer

Hi Clara,

Thank you for write. I believe a party is perfect manner to say goodbye to Laura.

Since we cannot eat food or playing music in the language school, I believe the park is a better option. There we don't worry about make noise and bother other classes.

Yes, let's all bring things to eat or drink. Shall I bring fizzy drinks?

As for the gift, what about football jersey from our city team? There are green ones and I believe Laura is big fan of team.

Write me soon.

Mila

92 words

Examiner's comments

Content: All the content is relevant and the writer addresses all four points.

Communicative achievement: The writer follows some of the conventions of an informal email, e.g. opening and closing salutations. She is able to communicate straightforward ideas and she provides reasons for her suggestions (e.g. *Laura is big fan of team* to justify buying a football shirt) and uses some functional language effectively, e.g. *let's all bring, shall I ...? what about ...?* However, the register is a bit too formal at times (*I believe, cannot*).

Organisation: In general, the different parts of the email are connected and there is a logical progression. She does a good job of using paragraphs and introducing each point by referring back to the input email, e.g. *Yes, let's ..., As for the gift*. Although she uses hardly any linking words, she is able to connect many of her sentence naturally using referencing, e.g. *there* = park, *ones* = football jerseys, *team* = local football team.

Language: Although she overuses some lexis (e.g. *I believe*), the writer uses a good range of everyday vocabulary, e.g. *play music, bother other classes, fizzy drinks, football shirt*. There are a number of errors (e.g. word choice, omitted articles and verb tenses) and some of these are with simple grammatical structures, such as the present simple. As a result, there is a lack of clarity at times.

Mark: Pass

1 REVIEW

Reading Part 5 Multiple-choice cloze

1

a cosmetics company

2

1 B **2** A **3** C **4** D
5 A **6** D

Vocabulary Prepositions of time

1

1 in **2** at **3** In **4** on
5 in **6** at **7** on **8** at

Language focus Present simple and present continuous

1 's staying **2** teach
3 is waiting **4** 'm wearing
5 play **6** 'm sitting
7 don't own **8** 'm leaving

Writing Part 2 Article

Sample answer

Clothes shopping? No, thanks.

I do not understand why people love shop for new clothes. Eating a cactus is more enjoyable. When you walk into the shop, the music is too loud and there is too much variety. Then you finally choose something and try on it, and the one that you like never fits, and the one that fits is very expensive. It is impossible to win. For some people, new clothes make them feel more interesting or successful. I only feel more uncomfortable. I think there is no thing worse that the feeling of a new clothing on my skin. Will you go clothes shopping soon? Do not invite me. I'm busy.

114 words

Examiner's comments

Content: All the content is relevant. The writer addresses both questions from the task instructions.

Communicative achievement: The writer successfully uses the conventions of an article, e.g. expressing opinion and describing personal experience. In particular, the writer is able to effectively engage the reader's attention through the use of humour. Straightforward ideas are expressed in a way that is clear and easy to understand. The writer gives reasons for their opinions, e.g. *the music is too loud and there is too much variety.*

Organisation: Despite only using one paragraph, the article is generally well organised. There is a clear overall structure. The article starts with an introduction to the topic and finishes with an appropriate ending. The writer contrasts their own point of view with those of others, e.g. *For some people ... I just feel ...* Some basic linking words (*than, and, when*) and referencing (pronouns: *one, it*) are used to connect the writer's ideas.

Language: The writer uses a range of everyday vocabulary, especially descriptive adjectives e.g. *enjoyable, loud, expensive, interesting, successful, uncomfortable.* They also use a range of simple and some more complex grammatical structures, such as relative clauses and comparatives. There are some errors with tenses, word order and word choice, but none of these impede communication.

Mark: Very good pass

Pronunciation /ʊ/, /uː/ and /ʌ/

1

1 good **2** put **3** food
4 move **5** true **6** come
7 sun **8** just

3

/ɪː/

4

/ʊ/: wool, look, pull, could, bull, bush

/uː/: juice, blue, soup, lose, suit, shoe

/ʌ/: country, colour, glove, cut, touch, nothing

2 TAKING IT EASY

Listening Part 2 Multiple choice

2

1 novel

2 Activities: storytelling for children and reading clubs for seniors. We know they are free because she says '... it doesn't cost a thing.'

3 She says, '... but not me. I prefer cafés.'

3

1 A **2** A **3** B **4** C
5 B **6** B

Language focus Past simple and *used to*

1

1 no longer; can also

2 only use the past simple

2

1 **Negative:** subject + *didn't use to* + infinitive without *to*

Questions: *did/didn't* + subject + *use to* + infinitive without *to*

2 chatted; went; stayed; studied

3 **Negative:** subject + *didn't* + infinitive without *to*

Questions: *did*/*didn't* + subject + infinitive without *to*

3 Ready for Grammar

1

1 did you do; got up; went

2 did you have; had

3 Did you enjoy; didn't like

4 did you grow up; lived

5 were you; got

6 did your parents teach; learnt/ learned

3

1 I used to work very long hours.

2 I didn't use to own a car.

3 I used to dream of becoming a rock star.

4 Did you use to do ballet?

5 Where did you use to live?

6 We didn't use to use this software.

4

Possible answers

1 At weekends, I didn't use to wake up until 9 or 10 am ... / I used to stay out past midnight and sleep late in the morning ...

2 I used to have a very low level of French ... / I didn't use to know any French ...

3 At my last job, I didn't use to wear smart clothes ... / When I was a student, I used to wear casual clothes every day ...

4 I didn't use to be interested in films ... / I used to prefer watching films at home ...

5 I used to drive to work ... / I didn't use to travel very often on public transport ...

Reading Part 2 Matching

2

1 E **2** C **3** H **4** B **5** F

Vocabulary *-ed* and *-ing* adjectives

1

1 *-ed* **2** -ing

2

1 surprised **2** embarrassing
3 relaxed **4** disappointed
5 satisfying **6** confused
7 frightening **8** frustrating

Language focus Past simple and past continuous

1

1 past simple
2 past continuous

2 Ready for Grammar

1

1 f **2** c **3** b **4** e
5 a **6** d

2

1 her finger while she was climbing.

2 video games when the internet stopped working.

3 coffee with Clara, my boss called to tell me the news.

4 her purse while she was sitting on the bench in the main square.

5 the package while I was making lunch.

3

1 was sitting **2** was registering
3 asked **4** didn't know
5 answered **6** was walking
7 started **8** saw **9** looked
10 grabbed **11** was putting
12 was doing

Writing Part 2 Story

1

1 Paula
2 at a party

2

Yes, the writer builds a story around the important elements from the first sentence: Paula (main character) and the party (setting).

3

1 When **2** soon **3** sudden
4 end

4

1 b **2** c **3** a

6

Sample answer

It was my first day on the course and I felt a bit nervous. I love art and I like to paint at my free time, but this is the first time to study with a teacher. Our first work is to paint a pile of books. While I am painting, my brush slips and one book appears more larger than the other books. I feel embarrassed, but I continue. Later, the teacher stops and looks at the picture. All of sudden she smiles. She says the other students that they come see my original idea. All the people are impressed!

101 words

Examiner's comments

Content: All the content of the story is relevant and there is a logical connection between the first sentence and the rest of the story. However, the first sentence is in the past and the rest of the story is told in the present.

Communicative achievement: The story has a clear beginning and ends with a clear resolution, and the events of the story are easy to follow. The writer successfully uses some conventions of storytelling, e.g. indirect speech (*she says the other students to ...),* description of how the characters feel and an unexpected event that creates a 'problem' to resolve.

Organisation: The text is generally well organised and coherent. The writer uses some basic linking words (*later*, *and*, *but*) and one more sophisticated discourse marker (*all of a sudden*) to connect the different parts of the story. At times, reference pronouns are used to create a connection within and across sentences (*she* = the teacher, *they* = the other students).

Language: The writer uses everyday vocabulary to describe the events of the story (*paint a pile of books*, *my brush slips*) and how the characters feel (*embarrassed*, *smiles*, *impressed*). Despite only using present tenses, the writer shows a good control of simple grammatical forms, e.g. *while I am painting, my brush slips ...* There are some errors with prepositions, word choice, and subject–verb agreement, but these do not impede communication.

Mark: Good pass

Vocabulary Leisure activities

2

1 eat out **2** go **3** take
4 see **5** do **6** spend
7 attend **8** go **9** use
10 play **11** read **12** go

3

1 doing exercise
2 playing video games
3 taking photographs
4 reading the news

4

Likes: I really enjoy ..., I'm a big fan of ..., I like ... a lot., I can't live without ...

Dislikes: I'm not really into ..., I can't stand ..., I don't like ... at all.

2 REVIEW

Reading Part 6 Open cloze

1 every/each 2 for 3 and
4 up 5 used 6 it

Language focus Past simple and past continuous

1

1 were waiting
2 didn't / did not meet
3 were; doing
4 didn't / did not hear
5 was rising
6 wasn't / was not wearing

Vocabulary Leisure *-ed* and *-ing* adjectives

1 saw; frightening 2 do; frustrated
3 relaxing; go 4 taking; satisfying
5 attend; disappointed

Writing Part 1 Email

Sample answer

Hi Kim,

Good to hear from you. I like the idea of fancy dress party. This is going to be fun!

It is okay to have the party on Saturday? On Fridays, I get up early for work, so I'm usually tired in the evening.

Takeaway food is good option. Why don't we order pizza?

I have a favour to ask: could you give me a ride? It takes a really long time to get to your house by bus. If you pick me up early, I can help you get ready for the party.

Talk to you soon.

Beth

101 wOrds

Examiner's comments

Content: The writer has addressed all four points from the input email. All the content is relevant.

Communicative achievement: The writer uses the conventions of an informal email, such as a friendly, informal tone and a consistent register. The opening and closing salutations are particularly appropriate to the context. While giving reasons for suggestions, the writer adds personal information, which makes the email sound very natural.

Organisation: The text is generally well organised. Although there are few linking words and phrases, the writer is able to connect her ideas both within and between sentences using referencing and some basic linking words. All punctuation is accurate and there is one very effective use of a colon to set up a question. Each paragraph has a clear focus, allowing the writer to clearly address each point one at a time.

Language: There is a good range of everyday vocabulary, including phrasal verbs and collocations (*get up early, order pizza, give me a ride, pick me up, get ready*). The writer displays very good control of simple and some more complex grammatical structures. Although there are a few errors with word choice and prepositions, none of these impede communication.

Mark: Very good pass

Pronunciation *-ed* endings

1

1 performed
2 searched
3 divided

2

/t/: searched, checked, fixed, walked

/d/: performed, answered, received, ordered

/ɪd/: divided, started, decided, repeated

3

/ɪd/

4

/d/: handled, informed, encouraged
/t/: knocked, stopped, announced
/ɪd/: tested, ended, interrupted

5

/d/: followed, answered, argued
/t/: knocked, pushed, introduced
/ɪd/: regretted, waited, skated

3 YOU ARE WHAT YOU EAT

Speaking Part 3 Discussion

2

Cooking videos on social media

3

1 which; about 2 agree; right
3 opinion; ask 4 shall; sure
5 option; go

Reading Part 5 Multiple-choice cloze

3

1 D 2 A 3 B 4 D
5 C 6 A

4

1 different 2 reply
3 interested 4 believe 5 asking
6 provide

Language focus Countable and uncountable nouns

1

1 Countable
2 Uncountable

2

Countable: problem, snacks, biscuits, recipe, dishes, people, shelves;
Uncountable: help, advice, seafood, pasta, rice, money, furniture

3

1 many, a few
2 a little, much
3 any, a lot of, some

4 Ready for Grammar

1

1 weather 2 luggage 3 rubbish
4 spaghetti 5 popcorn
6 research 7 toast 8 advice

2

1 I have (some) exciting news
2 correct
3 office furniture has arrived
4 correct
5 (some) toast
6 a lot of sugar
7 graffiti
8 correct

3

1 many 2 any 3 much 4 a little
5 any 6 a few 7 many 8 a little
9 some 10 much

Vocabulary Containers and amounts

1

Suggested answers

biscuits, chewing gum, crisps, nuts, sweets, sugar

2

1 b olive oil 2 e jam 3 a beans 4 c (frozen) peas
5 f cereal 6 d juice

3

Suggested answers

a bottle of ketchup / milk / water
a jar of honey / olives / mayonnaise
a tin of soup / tuna / peas / tomatoes
a bag of popcorn / rice / flour / ice
pasta / sweets / a box of chocolates
crackers / a carton of milk / soup

5

1 b 2 f 3 c 4 e
5 a 6 d

Listening Part 3 Gap fill

1

(Northern) Spain

2

1 (Northern) Spain
2 Marketing/marketing
3 eight/8 (o'clock)/8.00

4 patient
5 basket
6 rovellon

Language focus Articles

1

1 e   2 c   3 a   4 f
5 d   6 b

2 Ready for Grammar

1

1a the   1b –
2a –   2b the
3a –   3b the
4a The   4b –
5a –   5b the
6a the   6b –

2

1 a pilot; a week
2 sushi; Next Saturday
3 work; the last time
4 the future; the new retirement account
5 English; a cinema
6 talent; life

3

Because of social media, because it's healthy and because it's easy to prepare.

4

1 the   2 –   3 the   4 the
5 a   6 an   7 –   8 –   9 –
10 –   11 a   12 the

Vocabulary Food

2

1 boil   2 fry   3 barbecue
4 bake   5 roast

4

1 sweet   2 bitter
3 sour   4 juicy
5 salty   6 spicy

Writing Part 2 Article

2

Yes

3

Second paragraph: I like this dish because it's made with only a few basic ingredients.

Third paragraph: My advice is: if you love eating something, learn to cook it.

6

Sample answer

"Rin ran"

"Rin ran" it is a simple salad that consists of tomato, green pepper, onion, paprika, oil of olive, vinegar and salt. I love the dish because it remembers me of summer in my village in the north of Extremadura, Spain.

The food has a connection with memory very strong. When I prepare "rin ran," it brings me memories of the kitchen of my grandmother. I can see her kind face and hear the gentle sound of her voice. Almost I can taste the delicious tomatoes of her garden.

It's important that we learn to cook the food of our grandparents.

102 words

Examiner's comments

Content: All content is relevant. The writer addresses the first two questions, describing a traditional dish and explaining why they like it. However, they do not clearly state or explain whether it is important to learn to cook the food we like.

Communicative achievement: The writer effectively uses some of the conventions of an article, such as an engaging tone, expressing opinions and describing personal experience. The article has a clear beginning. The ending, however, is less appropriate and the article does not feel finished. The writer is able to hold the reader's attention by using specific and memorable details, e.g. the ingredients for the dish and the description of their grandmother's face.

Organisation: The article is generally well organised and coherent. Pronouns (*it* = dish), synonyms (*the dish* = rin ran) and basic linking words (*because*, *when*, *and*) are used to connect the writer's ideas. In the second paragraph, a topic sentence is used effectively to establish the focus of the paragraph.

Language: The writer uses a range of everyday vocabulary to describe the dish and explain why they like it, e.g. *consist of*, *kind face*, *gentle voice*, *delicious tomatoes*. Although the text is written entirely in the present simple, the writer shows a good degree of control of basic grammatical structures. Few complex structures are attempted. There are a few errors with word order, prepositions and articles, but these do not impede communication.

Mark: Pass

Useful language

1 satisfied   2 relaxed
3 confused   4 proud
5 keen   6 grateful

3 REVIEW

Vocabulary Containers and amounts

Across

2 bags   4 bottle   6 bar
7 slice   8 head

Down

1 jar   3 spoonful   4 bunches
5 loaf

Language focus Countable and uncountable nouns

1 cheeses   2 much
3 chewing gum   4 any
5 cakes   6 knowledge
7 a few   8 equipment

Language focus Articles

1 –   2 a   3 –   4 a   5 a
6 the   7 a   8 the

Writing Part 2 Story

Sample answer

Ali walked out of the restaurant into the cold rain. She opened her umbrella and waited. Suddenly, an enormous blue monster come from the dark. It had huge eyes and long, sharp teeth.

"Good morning, Ali," said the monster.

"Hi," Ali answered. She shaked the monster's hand.

"Where's the criminal?" it asked.

"He's inside. The one with the grey jacket."

The monster nodded. Then it kicked down the door and ran in. The criminal tried to escape, but he was too slow. The monster grabbed him with his huge hand and carried him out.

"You're under arrest," said Ali.

99 words

Examiner comments

Content: All the content is relevant to the story. There is a logical connection between the first sentence and rest of the story.

Communicative achievement: The writer successfully uses the conventions of storytelling, e.g. elements of mystery and surprise, narrative tenses and descriptive language. In particular, the writer uses direct speech to effectively engage the reader's interest. The story has a clear beginning, middle and end.

Organisation: There is a clear sequence of events and the story is easy to follow. The writer uses paragraphs to make it clear who is speaking. The writer uses some basic linking words (*then*, *but*, *and*) and one more sophisticated discourse marker (*suddenly*). They also use reference pronouns to create connections within and across sentences (*it* = the monster, *he* = the criminal).

Language: The writer uses a variety of everyday vocabulary (*umbrella*, *enormous*, *huge*, *shake hands*, *nodded*, *kicked*, *grabbed*) to describe the events of the story. Despite only relying on the past simple, the writer shows a good control of simple grammatical forms. There are a couple of errors with word choice and irregular past tense verbs, but these do not impede communication.

Mark: Very good pass

4 WHAT'S ON

Vocabulary Live entertainment

2

1 f 2 c 3 e 4 a 5 g 6 d 7 b

3

1 opportunity 2 costume 3 audience 4 show 5 review 6 admission 7 success

4

1 gave 2 attend 3 pay 4 surprise 5 wore / were wearing 6 posted 7 celebrate

Speaking Part 2 Extended turn

1

1 top 2 top right corner 3 left 4 middle 5 right 6 bottom left corner 7 bottom

Listening Part 4 Multiple choice

2

1 A 2 C 3 A 4 B 5 C 6 B

Language focus Present perfect simple

1

to have; past participle

2

1 c 2 a 3 b

3

1 c 2 a 3 c 4 b 5 a 6 b

4

1 Since
2 For

5 Ready for Grammar

1

1 I have just read your message.
2 How long have you been in Ireland?
3 Have you made a decision yet?
4 Have you ever won a prize?
5 I have already read this book.
6 We have just begun our journey.
7 She has not received an answer yet.
8 We have never had an accident.

2

1 We've been married <u>for</u> 20 happy years.

2 <u>How long</u> have you been involved in the theatre programme?

3 <u>I've/have known</u> my best friend since primary school.

4 He has been a cameraman <u>for five years</u>.

5 How long <u>has she worked</u> here?

6 I don't know – I've <u>never</u> thought about it.

7 <u>I've/have</u> just done the washing up.

8 We haven't spoken to him about it <u>yet</u>.

6

1 played the piano since she was a child.
2 studied Italian for 10 years.
3 bought a new phone charger yet.
4 you ever made/prepared this dish
5 heard from him since (last) Wednesday.
6 the children woken/got up yet?

Reading Part 4 Gapped text

3

1 E 2 H 3 C 4 F 5 A

4

1 Despite 2 why 3 fact 4 way 5 course 6 spite

Language focus Present perfect simple and past simple

1

a past simple
b present perfect

2

1 lived 2 has worked 3 Did Simon visit 4 have suggested 5 haven't eaten

3

Finished time expressions: *at the weekend, in September, last night/ week, two days ago, when I was a child*

Unfinished time expressions: *all my life, for the last 24 hours, these last few weeks, until now / so far*

4

Finished time expressions: *from 2010 to 2015, yesterday afternoon*

Unfinished time expressions: *in the last month, in recent months, these last few weeks*

5

1 Joe
2 Lucy is speaking in the morning. Eva might be speaking in the afternoon or evening.

6 Ready for Grammar

1

1 've lived 2 have been 3 arrived 4 climbed 5 felt 6 fell 7 hasn't happened 8 've travelled

2

1 gave; 've/have read
2 finished; got
3 tried; haven't / have not played
4 've/have never said; 've/have always thought
5 Have you found; seemed
6 bought; haven't / have not had

Vocabulary Social media

2

1 open 2 flat 3 proud 4 steep 5 quick

3

1 join 2 posting 3 update 4 tag 5 record 6 commenting 7 influence 8 share 9 notice; follow

Writing Part 1 Email

1

1 Say that you are also looking forward to the visit.
2 Choose and explain why you prefer the hip hop concert or the musical show.
3 Tell Stella if you think it would be nice to invite other friends.
4 Suggest one or two other activities you could do together.

4

1 too 2 but 3 and 4 because

5

Sample answer

Hi Guy,

Thanks for your email. The film night will be funny way for improve our English. Fantastic idea! For practising our speaking, we could discuss the film after watch it.

For me, Wednesday night is better than Thursday night. Because we have class on Wednesday afternoon, it will be easy stay and watch the film after.

You mention snacks. I can bring a big bag of crisps if you want. Are you sure we can eat food in the school?

Talk to you soon,

Lola

86 words

Examiner's comments

Content: All content is relevant to the task, but the writer does not recommend a film to watch, so she hasn't addressed the final point.

Communicative achievement: The writer follows the conventions of an informal email, including a friendly tone, a consistently informal register, and an opening and closing salutation. The writer also gives reasons to explain their decisions/ suggestions, e.g. *because we have class on Wednesday afternoon, it's easy [to] stay.*

Organisation: The text is generally coherent and well organised. The writer uses paragraphs effectively, each of which has a clear focus. The writer refers back to the input email to introduce points, e.g. *You mention snacks*. She uses some referencing (*it* = film), but very few linking words. Some of the sentences are quite short, limiting the number of linking words used.

Language: A good range of vocabulary is used appropriately, e.g. *improve*, *fantastic*, *stay and watch*, *big bag of crisps*. The writer shows a good degree of control of simple and some more complex structures, e.g. *is better than*, *I can ... if you want*. There are some errors (word choice, control of tenses, infinitives of purpose, etc.), but these do not impede understanding.

Mark: Pass

4 REVIEW

Language focus Present perfect simple

2 She hasn't / has not ordered a new microphone yet.

3 She has already downloaded video editing software.

4 She has already bought special lights.

5 She hasn't / has not created a timetable for posting videos yet.

Language focus Present perfect simple and past simple

1 At **2** In **3** So **4** When
5 Eight **6** These

Vocabulary Social media

1 photo **2** profile **3** video
4 trend **5** community

Reading Part 6 Open cloze

1

The Beatles

2

1 to **2** has **3** or **4** it
5 of/on **6** why

Writing Part 2 Article

Sample answer

Live music concert

My favourite artist of hip-hop is Octagon 3D. I love his music since I was a teenager. I went to see him in live music concert, but it wasn't a good experience. My friends don't like Octagon 3D, then I went alone. When I arrive, the queue is very long and I am very boring. Finally we enter, but we also wait for a long time inside, too. It's crowded. After Octagon 3D went out on stage and at first it's exciting, but soon it's disappointing. There is no DJ, only Octagon 3D that looks boring and tired, like he doesn't sleep. I think this is the last live concert that I assist.

117 words

Examiner's comments

Content: The writer only partly answers the questions in the task instructions. They talk about a number of bad things about one particular live concert (waiting in a long queue and it being crowded) but no advantages are mentioned. We can assume that hip-hop is their favourite type of music, but this is not clearly stated.

Communicative achievement: The writer successfully uses some of the conventions of an article, e.g. describing personal experience and expressing opinions. They hold the reader's attention by taking them step by step through the experience of attending the concert. However, the writer moves back and forth between present and past tenses, creating some confusion about whether the events are happening in the present or in the past.

Organisation: Despite only using one paragraph, the text is generally well organised. The writer effectively uses first-person narration to create a clear progression. There is a clear beginning and ending. Reference pronouns are used effectively to avoid repetition, e.g. *he* = Octagon 3D, *this* = concert. The writer also uses a number of basic linking words (*then*, *when*, *finally*, *after*), but not all of these are used correctly.

Language: Some everyday vocabulary is used appropriately, e.g. *experience*, *queue*, *crowded*, *stage*, *exciting*, *disappointing*. At times, the writer uses simple grammatical forms (present simple and past simple) with a good degree of control, but there are examples of limited control of basic structures. There are a number of errors with word choice, subject–verb agreement, relative clauses. There is at least one error that impedes communication, e.g. *... that I assist.*

Mark: Pass

Pronunciation Suffixes *-sion* and *-tion*

1

1 the second-to-last syllable

2 the /ʃ/ sound in 'show'

3 the /ə/ sound (op<u>e</u>n)

2

1 organisation **2** explanation
3 expression **4** celebration
5 definition **6** production
7 connection **8** discussion
9 operation **10** decision
11 reaction **12** description

4

1 station **2** competition
3 translation **4** conversation
5 fiction **6** question
7 population **8** conclusion
9 permission **10** solution

Ready for Reading

Introduction

1 F You should use a *pencil* to complete the answer sheet.

2 F You have 45 minutes to complete the exam, *including* writing your answers on the answer sheet.

3 T
4 T
5 T

1

1 d **2** f **3** e **4** b
5 c **6** a

2

B

3

B *the best time* and *from October to early November* is referring to *when I should go*, which is before the gap; *these magnificent creatures* is referring to *polar bears* in the first line of the text; after the gap *a few weeks off last autumn* is referring to *October to early November.*

A This sentence doesn't fit the gap because it doesn't link the sequence of events before and after the gap even though a *guide* leads a *tour*.

C This sentence doesn't fit the sequence of events after the gap because if the writer *permanently left [their] full-time job*, they would not have *managed to get a few weeks off work.*

Reading Part 1 Multiple choice

1

1 a text message **2** Mateo
3 Jemma **4** to give Mateo a concert ticket

2

B Jemma says *let me know what you think* about having the *ticket* because she knows Mateo is interested in going (*I know how much you want to go*).

C Jemma's cousin has *just given her his ticket*, so Mateo doesn't need to arrange to collect it from Jemma's cousin.

3

1 c **2** e **3** a **4** b **5** d

4

1 A **2** C **3** B **4** C **5** B

5 Additional materials

1 e **2** d **3** f **4** b
5 c **6** a

Reading Part 2 Matching

2

2 Elena is keen to meet someone who owns a cake business. She would like to learn more about creating cake recipes and stay in contact with other extreme cake makers after the course.

3 Christos would like some advice about his cake designs from someone who creates realistic-looking cake designs. He would prefer to make an extreme cake with other people.

4 Aiko wants to meet someone who writes cookbooks. She would like tips for taking photos of her cakes and how to advertise them.

5 Chima would like to receive advice about entering baking competitions. He hopes to exchange cake ideas with other extreme cake makers and receive information about the science of baking cakes.

3

A If you've heard of Christy Moore, it's probably from the extreme cake-making programme, *Over-the-top Cakes*. Her course teaches you how to make an incredible-looking cake that tastes delicious. With a background in photography, she offers tips and advice so your extreme cake-making skills get noticed on social media platforms.

B Parker Jones has a shop that only sells extreme cakes, and it's just as successful as his latest cookbook. His course teaches you that making your own cooking instructions for the perfect cake is possible. Once the course is finished, you join a private social media group to stay in touch with other talented bakers whose cakes look like pieces of art.

C Nila Michelsen is well-known for her simple recipes for creating the most amazing extreme cakes. In the course, students experiment with some of her recipes before they try to make their own. Nila will judge teams of students to see who can create a realistic-looking cake design that tastes great.

D After creating life-sized cake designs on the reality series *Extraordinary Cakes*, Bella Douglas became a celebrity almost overnight. She'll give you step-by-step instructions so the cake of your dreams becomes a reality! And you won't be following traditional recipes either. You'll experiment with a variety of ingredients no one expects in a cake, like wildflower honey and gold.

E Lilli Becker is well-known for making cakes that look so true to life that you wouldn't know they're actually cakes! If you want to improve the way your cakes look, then sign up for Lilli's extreme cake-making course. You'll also have the challenge of working in a team to make a huge dragon cake.

F Winning first place in an extreme cake-making contest isn't easy, and Chizoba Olutola will tell you why and how to do well in them. She also goes through the chemistry and laws of physics involved with baking cakes. During Chizoba's course, she encourages her students to share their recipes and extreme cake designs so they get inspired by one another.

G Dawid Adamski is a talented artist and baker whose extreme cakes have won international awards. All he asks his students to do is show up with some ideas for a cake design. Then, he gives you the skills to make it into a reality. Dawid also explains the scientific process of making a cake in his course.

H Jordi García is a bestselling author who has a new cookbook out. On his course, you'll do more than improve your baking skills. He'll show you tricks for making extreme cakes look incredible on social media posts – all you need is a phone. Not only that, he'll explain ways to promote your work so people will rush to buy your cakes!

6

1 D **2** B **3** E **4** H **5** F

Reading Part 3 Multiple Choice

2

1 D **2** D **3** C **4** A **5** B

Reading Part 4 Gapped text

2

1 F **2** H **3** D **4** E **5** B

Reading Part 5 Multiple-choice cloze

2

1 C **2** A **3** D **4** B **5** A **6** D

Reading Part 6 Open cloze

2

1 like **2** by **3** Because
4 to **5** One **6** whole

3

1 phrasal verb: *look like*
2 preposition: *by*
3 preposition: *Because of*
4 infinitive: *to show*
5 determiner: *One of*
6 idiom: *On the whole*

5 THE GREAT OUTDOORS

Vocabulary Nature

1

1 i **2** d **3** j **4** f **5** b
6 l **7** g **8** a **9** h **10** e
11 k **12** c

3

A hill is an area of land higher than the land around it, but not as steep or high as a mountain.

A stream is a moving flow of water that is usually shorter, narrower and contains less water than a river.

Speaking Part 4 General conversation

1

Useful Language
Possible answers

1 swimming / cooking / relaxing / stargazing / storytelling / playing cards / taking photos/ kayaking

2 food / water / map / insect repellent / clothing / hiking boots / backpack or rucksack /first aid kit / camping stove / blanket / pillow

Reading Part 6 Open cloze

2

1 be **2** care **3** a **4** There
5 of **6** was

Listening Part 2 Multiple choice

1

1 C **2** B **3** B **4** C
5 A **6** C

Language Focus Present perfect continuous

1

A Negative sentences: *has/have not* + *been* + *-ing* form; Questions: *has/have* + subject + *been* + *-ing* form

B Examples 1 and 3.

C Example 2

2

1 've/have been waiting

2 hasn't / has not been working

3 has been running

4 has; been studying

5 've/have been cycling

6 Have; been getting

7 've/have been eating

8 haven't / have not been doing

3 Ready for Grammar

1

1 has been spending
2 's/has been using
3 has been receiving
4 've/have been talking
5 's/has been trying
6 have been going

2

1 we've come **2** both
3 has belonged **4** Has he ever stopped **5** we've been watching **6** she's cancelled
7 both **8** I've been trying

Reading Part 3 Multiple choice

1

Number 3 is false. Giraffes are very quiet animals and for a long time people thought they didn't use any noises to communicate. However, it has been discovered that they do 'talk' to each other a bit using hums and hisses.

2

hunting, diseases, trees being cut down, heavy rain due to climate change

3

1 C **2** D **3** A **4** B **5** B

Language focus Relative clauses

Defining relative clauses

2

1 People <u>who know more than one language</u> make better researchers.

2 It's an organisation <u>whose members are dedicated to saving the environment</u>.

3 The café <u>where I met my wife</u> is just around the corner.

4

We can leave out *that, who or which* when they are the object of the verb in the relative clause – that is, when the person or thing they refer to is NOT doing the action.

When they are subject of the relative clause, we cannot leave out *that*, *who* or *which*, etc.

5 Ready for Grammar

1

1 who/that **2** whose
3 which/that **4** where
5 who/that **6** who/that
7 whose **8** where

2

Sentences 3 and 6

Non-defining relative clauses

2

a cannot

b cannot

c have to

3 Ready for Grammar

1

Suggested answers

1 This national park, which covers an area of 418 square kilometres, is located near the capital of Mongolia.

2 The Bogd Khan Uul mountain, which is 2261 metres high and takes 3–4 hours to hike to the top of, is a popular tourist destination.

3 On our walk, we got the chance to see a Siberian musk deer, which is a very rare, endangered animal.

4 Later, we also visited the Winter Palace of Bogd Khan, who was a rich and powerful Mongolian leader in the early 20th century.

2

1 who/that **2** whose **3** where
4 which **5** that/which
6 which **7** which **8** where

4

Possible answers

1 The flat, which looks over Central Park, is worth a lot of money.

2 Roberto, who lives in Munich, was home for the holidays.

3 Lisa and Tom are in Scotland, where they plan to go on a seven-day walking tour.

4 We all ate ice cream except for Julio, who was on a strict diet.

Listening Part 3 Gap fill

2

1 (the) 19/19th/nineteenth (of) September

2 7.30

3 waterfall

4 valley

5 (hiking) boots

6 Black/black Sand/sand

Vocabulary Environmental issues

2

1 Recycling **2** food waste
3 public transport **4** saving energy
5 Climate change **6** noise pollution
7 fast fashion **8** litter

3

1 pick up **2** keep on **3** rely on
4 switch off **5** go up

Writing Part 2 Story

3

1 were admiring **2** grabbed
3 replied **4** handed

4

1 Yes, the writer talks about seeing fish and feeling surprised. But they don't mention the characters hearing, touching or smelling anything.

2 Yes, there are four lines of dialogue.

3 Yes, this is particularly true in the third paragraph.

4 Yes, the title makes the reader wonder what the 'close call' will be.

5

Sample answer

A good view

When the two friends arrived, the field was full of people. The sky was full of hot air balloons. They waited an hour, the two friends, named Rose and Gabriela. They feel very exciting. And very nervous.

Finally, it is their turn. Soon they are many metres in sky, the view is incredible. In the sky, is peaceful and silent.

'Look, my house!' Rose said.

They watched Rose's mother, who is like a tiny ant, she open the door and walk to the car. Rose and Gabriela shout her name, but she can't hear them.

95 words

Examiner's comments

Content: All the content is relevant to the task. The story follows on logically from the prompt. However, it is clear from the first sentence that the story takes place in the past, but the writer moves between the present and past as they narrate the story.

Communicative achievement: The writer successfully uses some of the conventions of storytelling, e.g. direct speech, description of the setting and the characters' feelings. The events of the story are clear and easy to follow, and the story has a clear beginning, which introduces the characters and the setting. The ending, however, is less successful. It would be better if the narrative ended with a clearer resolution to a problem or conflict.

Organisation: In general, the text is well organised. It is easy to follow the characters as they move from one place to another. To this end, paragraphs are used effectively. The writer uses some basic linking words (*soon*, *and*, *but*) and referencing (*they* = the friends, *she* = Rose's mother). However, some sentences are punctuated with commas instead of full stops.

Language: The writer uses a range of everyday vocabulary, e.g. *hot air balloons*, *incredible*, *peaceful*, *tiny ant*, *shout*. They also use simple grammatical structures with limited control. More complex grammatical structures (relative clauses) are attempted, but not always successfully. There are errors with word choice, tenses, modal verbs, etc. but these do not generally impede communication.

Mark: Pass

5 REVIEW

Vocabulary Nature

1 islands 2 jungle 3 forest
4 waterfall 5 cave 6 lake

Vocabulary Environmental issues

1 d 2 e 3 f 4 b
5 a 6 c

Language focus Present perfect continuous

1 No, they've been eating snacks.

2 Yes, she's been studying it for years.

3 No, I haven't been paying attention.

4 How long has it been raining?

5 Yes, they've been talking about it all week.

6 How long have you been living in Copenhagen?

Writing Part 1 Email

Sample answer

Hi Bruna,

Good to hear from you. Yes, mountain biking this weekend seem fun! Can we go on Saturday? I have plans on Sunday.

As for the route, I'd prefer the one around the lake. This way we can go in a big circle and finish in same place we start. We can go also to a swim!

After do a lot of exercise, I've heard it's good to eat pasta. Shall we go to Italian restaurant?

Thanks for offer to drive us. Is 11 o'clock okay with you? At the weekend, I don't like getting up early!

Talk to you soon.

Krystyna

95 words

Examiner's comments

Content: All the content of the email is relevant to the task. The writer addresses all four points from the input email.

Communicative achievement: The writer has successfully used many of the conventions of an informal email, including opening and closing salutations and an appropriately friendly/informal tone. All the information is easy to understand. She has also given reasons to justify her choices, e.g. *At the weekend, I don't like getting up early!*

Organisation: The text is generally well organised. The writer uses paragraphs to address each point from the input task one by one. She references the input email while introducing some of her points, e.g. *As for the route ...* A variety of linking words and phrases (*because*, *that way*, *also*, *after*) are used effectively to link ideas together. There are also some examples of pronoun referencing (*one* = route) and ellipsis (*go* = go mountain biking).

Language: The writer uses a range of everyday vocabulary to express straightforward ideas, e.g. *prefer*, *big circle*, *same place*, *do exercise*, *get up early*. She also uses basic grammatical structures with relatively good control. There are some errors with word choice, word patterns, prepositions and missing articles, but none of these impede communication.

Mark: Pass

Pronunciation Intonation in questions

1

1 ↗ 2 ↗ 3 ↘ 4 ↘

2

1 rising
2 falling

6 AWAY WE GO

Reading Part 2 Matching

2

1 G 2 C 3 E 4 B 5 H

Vocabulary Adjectives

1

1 fascinating 2 ancient
3 peaceful 4 hilarious
5 magnificent 6 well-known

2

1 glad / pleased 2 typical / usual 3 essential / necessary
4 challenging / hard
5 incredible / wonderful 6 dull / uninteresting 7 odd / unusual

Language focus Comparatives and superlatives

1

1 T

2 F (India became the most populated country in 2023)

3 T

4 T

5 F (New York is a more popular tourist destination than London)

6 T

7 F (Greenland is the least densely populated country, but the country with the smallest population is Vatican City.)

2

1 wider, further, more popular

2 the largest, the most expensive, the busiest, the least populated

3 We use *-er/-est* with all one-syllable adjectives and some two-syllable adjectives ending in *-y*

4 We use *more/most* with all adjectives with three or more syllables.

5 further (from adjective 'far')

3

1a *as... as...*

1b *not as... as*

2 No

4 Ready for Grammar

1

1 calmer, the calmest; fresh, the freshest; greater, the greatest

2 more surprising, the most surprising; more powerful, the most powerful; more convenient, the most convenient

3 earlier, the earliest; heavier, the heaviest; sillier, the silliest

4 bigger, the biggest; hotter, the hottest; thinner, the thinnest

5 further, the furthest; worse, the worst; better, the best

3

1 more talented than me
2 better than the last one
3 older than Dina
4 as long as I expected
5 tallest student in our school
6 interested in studying abroad than Khaled

Vocabulary Travel compound nouns

2

Chat A: good experience (very friendly staff)

Chat B: bad experience (damaged hire car, traffic jam, stopped by police, invalid driving licence, couldn't drive anymore)

3

1 airlines 2 window seat
3 hand luggage 4 return ticket
5 check-in desk 6 car park
7 motorway 8 traffic jam
9 speed limit 10 driving licence

4

1 backpack; suitcase
2 tour guide
3 seaside; countryside
4 sun hat; sunglasses
5 guidebook
6 credit card

Listening Part 4 Multiple choice

2

1 C 2 A 3 B 4 B
5 A 6 C

Language focus Future forms

1

1 present continuous
2 going to
3 will

2

1 B 2 A 3 B 4 B 5 A

3 Ready for Grammar

1

1 I'll turn 2 He's going to visit
3 Are you doing 4 I'll donate
5 I'm picking 6 she's going to do

2

1 ✓
2 I'll stay here and tidy up.
3 I'm going to Leeds
4 ✓
5 ✓
6 When are you meeting / going to meet Samuel for coffee?
7 I'll pay for you.
8 ✓

Writing Part 1 Email

3

1 rock climbing
2 exploring a cave
3 in May
4 to the mountains

4

Sample answer

Hi Boris

Yes, let's go to trip together the next weekend! I think is a great idea. In my opinion, the small village is better that the city. Because we both live in big cities, where there is lots of contamination and noise, I think is nice to spend time in a more quiet place. Do you are agree? Did you ever look at www.bestcheaphotels.com? You always can have a good price there. I used it last time I go to holiday and I pay only the half of normal room price. Anyway, write to me back soon.

Miguel

99 words

Examiner's comments

Content: All the content is relevant to the task. However, the writer only addresses the first three points in the input email. He doesn't say whether it's possible to take his car.

Communicative achievement: The email is written in an appropriately informal and friendly tone. The writer adds some personal information (we both live in big cities), which helps make the email sound more natural. He also gives reasons for his suggestions, e.g. his prior experience with the website. Asking a question engages the reader's attention e.g. *Do you are agree?* However, the number of errors creates some difficulty for the reader, making the message less clear at times.

Organisation: In general, the text is well organised. There is a clear progression from the beginning to the end. The writer uses some basic linking words (*because*, *and*, *anyway*) and referencing (*it/there* = website) to connect their ideas within and between sentences. However, clear paragraphing would help the reader better see where the writer moves from one point to another.

Language: The writer uses some everyday vocabulary, e.g. *noise*, *spend time*, *quiet*, *good price*, *room*. He can also use some simple grammatical structures with some degree of control. However, there are a number of errors (word choice, tenses, articles, etc), and some of these are related to quite basic structures, e.g. using present simple to refer to the past. More complex structures like relative clauses and comparatives are attempted, but with only limited success. The number of errors is distracting at times, but none impede communication.

Mark: Pass

Listening Part 1 Multiple choice

1 C 2 C 3 A 4 B 5 C
6 A 7 B

Language focus *So, such, too* and *enough*

1

1 enough 2 such 3 too
4 so

2 Ready for Grammar

1

1a ii 1b i
2a i 2b ii
3a i 3b ii
4a ii 4b i
5a ii 5b i

2

1 too 2 so 3 enough
4 so 5 such 6 too
7 such 8 so

6 REVIEW

Reading Part 5 Multiple-choice cloze

1 C 2 B 3 C 4 D
5 A 6 D

Language focus Comparatives and superlatives

1 the 2 not 3 than
4 than 5 most 6 as
7 The

Vocabulary Adjectives

1 wonderful 2 odd
3 challenging 4 usual
5 pleased 6 essential 7 dull

Language focus *So, such, too, enough*

1 such; so much 2 too many; too
3 too little; such 4 so; fast enough

Writing Part 2 Article

Sample answer

When you are a tourist, it's easy to visit a city and to learn nothing of it. It's easy to only going shopping and drinking coffee at trendy cafés. For me, this is a pity because every city has a story to tell, for example, when you go for a walk through the old parts of European cities, you can admire the old beautiful buildings. In the narrow streets, I imagine life in past, many hundreds of years ago. This experience it is more better with a tour guide, they know all of the city and can tell you many interesting stories of the people who has lived there.

109 words

Examiner's comments

Content: All the content is relevant. The writer has answered both questions from the task instructions.

Communicative achievement: The writer uses the conventions of an article (e.g. expressing opinions, describing personal experience) to engage the reader's attention. The writer communicates straightforward ideas and provides reasons and examples for these ideas. The tone is consistently neutral.

Organisation: Despite only using one paragraph, the article is connected and coherent. The writer uses basic linking words (*when*, *and*, *because*) and some more sophisticated discourse markers (*for me*, *for example*) to connect their ideas. Reference words such as *this* are used to make connections both within and between sentences (*this = only going shopping and drinking coffee, this experience = when you go for a walk through the old parts*). The article starts appropriately, with a sentence to catch the reader's attention. However, the ending is less successful, as it does not bring the article to a satisfying end.

Language: The writer uses everyday vocabulary (e.g. *tourist*, *trendy*, *admire*, *imagine*, *tour guide*). They also use simple grammatical forms and attempt more complex ones (e.g. relative clauses, comparatives). There are a number of errors with prepositions, word choice, word order and subject–verb agreement, but these do not impede communication.

Mark: Good pass

Pronunciation Word stress

2

first

3

sunglasses, swimsuit, guidebook, sun cream, raincoat, earphones, passport, credit card, notebook, toothbrush, sun hat, newspaper

7 WORK LIFE

Listening Part 3 Gap fill

2

Time = 1, 2 and 6.
Nouns = 3, 4 and 5.

3

1 5/five months
2 morning / Antarctica
3 photographs
4 rain
5 internet (connection)
6 May

Vocabulary Jobs

1

a chef **b** receptionist **c** nurse
d businessperson **e** cleaner
f dentist **g** engineer

2

1 An actor **2** A reporter
3 An architect **4** A police officer
5 A lawyer

3

Sample answers

A chef cooks/prepares food/dishes/ meals for customers/diners.

A receptionist answers the phone / welcomes people.

A nurse helps/cares for people / gives people medicine.

A businessperson manages people / makes decisions/deals / organises projects.

A cleaner washes floors/windows / tidies rooms.

A dentist checks/fixes/cleans teeth.

An engineer designs things / solves problems.

4

-ER: *reporter, builder, cleaner, engineer, farmer, lawyer, photographer, police officer*

-IST: *receptionist, dentist*

-OR: *actor, director*

Listening Part 1 Multiple choice

2

1 B **2** C **3** C **4** C **5** A
6 B **7** A

Language focus *Will, may* and *might*

1

1 might **2** won't; will

3

1 may/might (not) **2** will (not)

4

1 may **2** won't **3** will
4 might not **5** might **6** won't

5 Ready for Grammar

1

1 b **2** c **3** e **4** d
5 a

2

1 won't **2** might **3** may
4 won't **5** will

Writing Part 2 Story

3

1 adjectives **2** the weather
3 gorgeous **4** simple
5 anxious, polite, relaxed, calm, shocked

Useful language

job: *enjoyable, professional, stressful*

people: *clever, confident, friendly, helpful, honest, professional, strict*

place: *bright, modern, professional, spectacular*

4

Sample answer

It was only a summer job, but I will never forget my first day. I got a job in a company of travel. The building was the most tallest in the city and the views from the top floor are fantastic.

After arrived, the sales manager gave me a tour and said me about my tasks. I was nervous, but she help that I relax. Just then the mobile phone rang. After, she looked to me and said, "My assistant is sick today, so you are my assistant." I was shocked, but there was no time to worry me. That day it was too exciting, and I knowed that work in the office was exciting.

115 words

Examiner's comments

Content: The story follows on logically from the first sentence and all the content in the story is relevant.

Communicative achievement: The writer uses elements of storytelling to communicate straightforward ideas and hold the reader's attention. The story has a clear beginning, middle and end. The writer also introduces a problem to resolve, uses direct and reported speech, and provides descriptions of both the setting and the character's feelings.

Organisation: The story is connected and coherent. Paragraphs help to give the story a clear structure, with the setting introduced first, followed by the characters and problem/conflict. The writer uses some linkers (*but*, *after*, *just then*) to help the reader follow the sequence of events.

Language: There is a variety of everyday vocabulary (*top floor*, *mobile phone*, *shocked*, *exciting*) that is appropriate to the task. The writer uses simple grammatical forms and attempts some more complex ones, but there are a number of errors with simple forms, e.g. past irregular forms (*I knowed*) which can impede communication. The writer also moves between the present and past tenses.

Mark: Pass

Vocabulary Work life

1

Suggested answers

read newspapers, look online, ask other people, go to an agency

2

1 earn 2 apply 3 quit
4 send 5 found 6 fill in
7 retired 8 look for / find

3

1 manager 2 department
3 staff 4 temporary
5 employees

4

1 An employer gives people jobs. An employee is a person who works for a company.

2 *To retire* is to stop working, usually when you're 65 or 70 years old. *To quit* means to leave a job or stop doing something.

3 *To earn* is to get money from a job and *to win* is to get money by chance or in a competition.

4 *To apply* is when you ask for a job or place at university in a formal way, (usually in writing). *To ask* is informal (usually in speech).

5 A temporary employee usually works for a short time. A permanent employee has a job for a long time.

5

1 career 2 temporary
3 manager 4 employee

Reading Part 3 Multiple choice

2

1 C 2 A 3 D 4 B 5 C

Language focus Zero and first conditional

1

A present simple + present simple
B present simple + future simple

2

1 sentence B 2 sentence A

3 Ready for Grammar

1

1 I won't get hungry if I eat something now.

2 If you don't practise, you won't improve your tennis skills. / If you practise, you will improve your tennis skills.

3 I go to bed when I am tired. / I'll go to bed when I'm tired.

4 She'll be late if she misses her train.

5 If the weather is nice, I'll go to the beach later.

6 Will I get the job if I apply for it?

2

1 she takes 2 I'll meet
3 I'll buy 4 won't succeed
5 go 6 it is

3

1 d 2 f 3 e 4 a
5 c 6 b

4

1 try 2 won't get 3 are
4 will/ 'll feel 5 dress

4

1 finish; will go 2 visit; have
3 won't have; don't start
4 doesn't arrive; will miss
5 want; ask

Speaking Part 4 Discussion

Useful language

1 Working with old people is good because ~~of~~ it's important.

2 Working with animals is fun. ~~Too~~ The animals are very sweet, too.

3 Helping people get fit is most enjoyable. The reason why is (that) you can change their lives.

4 Being a police officer is fun because ~~why~~ you can meet lots of people.

7 REVIEW

Vocabulary Work life

1 d 2 f 3 b 4 a 5 c
6 e 7 h 8 g

Reading Part 6 Open cloze

1 been 2 one 3 their
4 than 5 be 6 If

Language focus Conditionals

1 do 2 go 3 want
4 email 5 have 6 will
7 don't 8 will 9 gets
10 won't 11 look 12 send

Writing Part 1 Email

Sample answer

Hi Paula,

Thank you for the email. I am really very happy also that you come to work here on my company. It is great! I tell you about the company: first, is really big. There are 400 employees at office, and there 4 offices more in different cities. It's much more bigger that the company where we used to work together before. People is nice. To work, it is best to go to work in train or bus. Do not go in car! The office does not have the car parking.

I looking forward to see you the first day!

See you soon,

Li

105 words

Examiner's comments

Content: In this email, all the content is relevant and the reader is generally well-informed. However, the writer only addresses three of the four points. Although they mention seeing Paula on the first day, they do not suggest a place where they can eat.

Communicative achievement: In their email, the writer uses a friendly, positive tone, which would be appropriate in an email to a former workmate. The email begins and ends with appropriate salutations. Throughout the email, the writer communicates straightforward ideas, at times providing explanations for their suggestions, e.g. not driving because the company does not have a car park.

Organisation: The text is connected and coherent. The writer uses reference pronouns (*it = my company*) to create a link across sentences. The writer makes good use of punctuation, in particular the colon. However, many of the sentences are quite short and the writer uses few linking words and phrases. As a result, the writer at times jumps from one idea to the next without providing a link between these ideas.

Language: The writer uses everyday vocabulary related to the task (*happy*, *employees*, *offices*), but at times displays a lack of range, e.g. referring to a *car park* as *car parking*. The email is mostly written using simple grammatical forms, and these sometimes contain errors, but the writer does use *used to* successfully to refer to past situation. There are some noticeable errors with prepositions, word order, missing subject pronouns, etc. but in general the meaning is clear.

Mark: Pass

Pronunciation

1

1 these 2 police 3 build
4 cheek 5 live 6 believe
7 system 8 evening 9 people
10 biscuit 11 key 12 village

2

/ɪ/ like *chip* = build, live, system, biscuit, village

/iː/ like *cheap* = these, police, cheek, believe, evening, people, key

5

1 L**ea**ve th**e**se biscuits in the tin.

2 Many p**eo**ple built this bridge.

3 This **e**v**e**ning we'll l**ea**ve the village.

4 She k**ee**ps fit in the gym **e**v**e**ning.

6

(underlined letters: /ɪ/ bold letters: /iː/)

prett**y**, recover, activit**y**, minute, betw**ee**n, lettuce, imagine, myster**y**, rec**ei**pt, give, insect, fix, d**ee**p, cit**y**, manage, beaut**y**, cr**ea**m, depart, thick, women, b**ea**ch, disagr**ee**, thi**e**f, maybe, bus**y**, n**ei**ther, symbol, rec**ei**ve, **e**ven, quickl**y**, c**ei**ling, m**ee**t, million, recip**e**, quit, luggage

Ready for Listening

Introduction

1

1 4 2 25 3 30 4 1
5 20 6 45 7 6

2

1 c 2 b 3 a 4 e 5 d

3

1

dialogue or monologue

Listen for *specific information*

multiple choice

2

dialogue

Listen for *gist*

multiple choice

3

monologue

Listen for *specific information*

gap fill

4

dialogue

Listen for *detailed understanding of attitudes or opinions*

multiple choice

Listening Part 1 Multiple choice

1

1 A crime fiction; B science fiction/ sci-fi; C horror

2 Suggested answers

crime fiction – detective, investigation, criminal

science fiction – space, planets, spaceship

horror – frightening, scary, monster

2–3

Option A ✓ M: I've always been really into detective stories – I mean, I'll read those before anything else.

Option B × M: This book's pretty interesting – it's about these young astronauts that go on a one-way trip to live on Mars. I can't put it down!

Option C × W: Do you ever read horror stories? I absolutely love those! M: They're all right, I guess.

4

1 What's the woman's favourite souvenir from her last trip?

2 What will the weather be like tomorrow?

3 Where do the friends decide to go first?

4 What animal will the college student study for his research project?

5 What documentary series would the woman like to watch?

6 What did the man injure while on holiday?

7 What activity did the woman do last night?

5 Additional materials

trousers = pants
lift = elevator
football = soccer
crisps = potato chips
film = movie
pavement = sidewalk
university = college
chips = French fries

6

1 C 2 B 3 B 4 A 5 B
6 C 7 A

Listening Part 2 Multiple choice

1

1 both speakers 2 the woman
3 the woman 4 both speakers
5 the man 6 both speakers

2

1 B 2 C 3 A 4 B
5 B 6 A

Listening Part 3 Gap fill

2

1 economy 2 700 / seven hundred 3 soup 4 windmill
5 houseboats 6 certificate

Listening Part 4 Multiple Choice

2

a 5 b 4 c 3 d 6
e 2 f 1

3

1 B 2 A 3 C 4 B
5 A 6 B

8 GET SET, GO!

Vocabulary Types of sports

1

a skiing b handball
c rock climbing d basketball
e skateboarding f athletics
g karate h mountain biking
i windsurfing j table tennis
k rugby l ice hockey

3

Track: athletics; Pitch: rugby; Court: basketball, handball; Ice rink: ice hockey

4

Possible answers

a basketball, handball, table tennis, rugby, ice hockey

b mountain biking, rock climbing, skateboarding, skiing, windsurfing

c athletics, karate

Vocabulary Sports collocations

1

1 scores 2 bring
3 take part; achieve
4 enter; accept 5 deal; treat

Reading Part 4 Gapped text

2

1 D 2 E 3 A 4 G 5 C

Language focus Second conditional

1

1 lived; would go

2

1 imaginary 2 past

3

1 went; would need
2 didn't work; would have
3 wouldn't be; woke up
4 would be; invited
5 had; would buy
6 would go; wasn't
7 lived; would be
8 did; would feel

4 Ready for Grammar

1

1 If I had the time, I'd go to the gym more often.

2 If you could swim, you wouldn't worry about travelling by boat.

3 We 'd/would go and see more matches if we lived nearer the stadium.

4 If Paulo had the money, he'd buy a new car.

5 What would you do if you were a superhero?

6 I wouldn't speak to him again unless you paid me!

2

1 wouldn't speak 2 were 3 'd/would love 4 would; do 5 'd/would travel 6 wouldn't go

3

1 would; choose
2 would play
3 were
4 became
5 would be
6 joined

5

1 If you moved to another country, where would you go?

2 If you found (some) money in/on the street, what would you do?

3 Who would you ask if you needed (some) help?

4 What would you buy if you had more money?

5 Who would you meet if you could / were able to meet anyone from history?

Listening Part 4 Multiple choice

2

1 B 2 A 3 A 4 B
5 C 6 C

Language focus – Modals of permission, advice, obligation and prohibition

1

1 should 2 have to

2

1 advice
2 obligation
3 without 'to'

3

1 c 2 d 3 a 4 e 5 b

4 Ready for Grammar

1

1 must take
2 mustn't / must not leave
3 do not / don't have to pay
4 can play
5 shouldn't feed
6 can't / cannot have

2

1 don't have to 2 can
3 shouldn't 4 can't 5 mustn't
6 must

3

1 can't 2 don't have to
3 both 4 should
5 wasn't allowed to 6 both
7 ought to 8 can't

Speaking Part 2 Extended turn

1 Useful language

1 can't 2 might 3 must

2

Picture 1:

1 This is true. We do not know if he is lost or not.

2 This is false. He is pushing a bike up a hill. He is probably tired.

3 This is true. He is high up, so he might feel a little scared.

4 This is false. We cannot see any other people. It is possible he is in a race, but he is going slowly and there are no clues from the picture.

5 This is false. The weather is sunny and he is exercising and wearing a T-shirt. He is probably not cold.

Picture 2:

1 This is false. They haven't started the race yet, so it is unlikely that they are tired.

2 This is true. They are in a field, they are not in a stadium. And there are no other people around.

3 This is true. They look similar. It is possible they are brother and sister.

4 This is true. They are doing the activity so it is probable they like it.

5 This is false. She is the only one running, the man is timing her.

Reading Part 1 Multiple choice

1

1 Chad 2 No
3 Chad can swim, his sister can't swim

2

C

3

2 C 3 B 4 A 5 B

Writing Part 2 Article

2

1 Swimming

2 It's nice to be outside in the sun and it's fantastic exercise.

3

Places: *pools, lakes, rivers, sea, outside*

Equipment: *swimsuit, trunks, goggles*

People: *swimmers, professionals*

Other nouns: *sunshine, competitions, benefits*

Verbs: *protect, exercise, watch, play*

Adjectives: *amazing, fantastic*

Useful language

1

1 stick 2 gloves 3 match
4 boots 5 pitch

2

1 helmet 2 hoop 3 goggles
4 racket 5 knee pads 6 net

5

Sample answer

"Sport in the winter sun!"

My favourite sport is the skiing. I live near the mountains, so it's a very popular sport in winter. I started skiing when I was six, so I'm a good skier. In my opinion, skiing is great because you can pass time in the mountains which everything look beautiful. I love the white snow, the blue sky and the sun. Remember that you should wear warm clothes and goggles to protect yourself! For me, it's better going skiing than to watch other people. Ski fast down a mountain gives an amazing feeling. If I could go somewhere skiing, I would go to Canada.

108 words

Examiner's comments

Content: The article answers all three questions from the task instructions, so the reader is fully informed. All the content is relevant.

Communicative achievement: The text is written in a way that is generally appropriate for an article. The writer uses some conventions of an article to hold the reader's attention, e.g. including a catchy title, addressing the reader directly and mixing general description with personal opinion. They express straightforward ideas in a way that is easy to understand.

Organisation: Despite using only one paragraph, the text is generally connected and coherent. There are some basic linking words and phrases (*so*, *because*, *and*) and some more sophisticated discourse markers (*in my opinion*, *for me*). Punctuation is used accurately. However, in certain places, some of the ideas could be better connected, in particular the ones in the last three sentences.

Language: The writer uses a range of everyday vocabulary that is appropriate to the task, e.g. *skier, beautiful, warm clothes, goggles, amazing feeling*. The writer demonstrates the ability to use both simple and some more complex grammatical structures (second conditional) with a good degree of control. There are a few errors with articles, word choice, word formation and relative clauses but none of these cause difficulty for the reader and the meaning is clear.

Mark: Very good pass

Listening Part 2 Multiple choice

1

1 B 2 C 3 A 4 B
5 A 6 C

8 REVIEW

Language focus Modals

1 shouldn't 2 have to 3 can't
4 must 5 can 6 don't have to

Vocabulary Sports

1 played 2 handball 3 play
4 ice rink 5 going
6 does 7 competition 8 deal
9 pitch 10 scored

Reading Part 5 Multiple-choice cloze

1 C 2 A 3 B 4 D
5 B 6 D

Writing Part 2 Story

Sample answer

It was a great day for mountain biking, but as we set off, we had no idea what was going to happen. The sun was shining, and I was excited about the race. I had been practising, and I had been hoping that I do good.

Some of the riders started quickly and soon they were riding fast, I decided go slowly at the beginning. After about half an hour, I looked and saw a strange thing. A lot of riders were looking to the side of mountain.

I didn't know what was happening, so I stopped too. Then I looked them – a large group of monkeys swinging by the trees. Suddenly, no one cared for the race, they only wanted to watching the very amazing animals.

127 words

Examiner's comments

Content: The opening sentence clearly connects to the rest of the story and all the content is relevant. The reader is fully informed about what happens in the story.

Communicative achievement: The writer tells the story in a clear straightforward way, using some of the conventions of storytelling, such as narrative tenses and description of the setting and the characters' emotions. The writer successfully creates an element of mystery and suspense by making the reader wait to find out what the cyclists are fascinated by.

Organisation: In general, the story is well organised. The sequence of events is clear and the writer connects ideas within and across sentences using reference pronouns and linkers (*after*, *then*, *suddenly*, *so*). Paragraphs are also used effectively to break up the events of the story.

Language: The writer uses a suitable range of everyday vocabulary, e.g. *set off*, *shining*, *strange*, *swinging*, *amazing*. The writer uses a good range of simple grammatical tenses and attempts some more complex ones (past perfect continuous). There are a few mistakes with word choice and verb patterns, but these do not impede communication.

Mark: Good pass

Pronunciation Silent letters

1

column, comb, knee, wrote, scenery, doubt, muscle, climber, science, hour, where, autumn, sign, honour

4

Silent b: comb, climber, doubt
Silent c: scenery, muscle, science
Silent g: sign
Silent h: hour, honour, where
Silent k: knee
Silent n: column, autumn
Silent w: wrote

5

1 Scientists; know; answers
2 designer; honest
3 autumn; walk; hours
4 whole; hour; listening; guide

6

1 lamb 2 knife 3 ghost
4 scissors 5 knee 6 whale
7 thumb 9 comb 10 sign

9 LIFELONG LEARNING

Vocabulary Student life

1

1 homework 2 marks
3 essays 4 exam
5 instructions 6 projects

3

1 took 2 failed 3 get
4 borrow 5 have

Reading Part 1 Multiple choice

2

Suggested answers

price, location, what the item is like, condition, how to get/collect it, etc

3

1 B 2 C 3 B 4 A 5 C

Language focus Past perfect simple and continuous

1

1 he had already prepared the dinner
2 We hadn't studied all of the topics
3 it had changed a lot
4 Had you studied any English
5 I'd ever attended

2

before

3 Ready for Grammar

1

Amira had never danced before she joined the Salsa Academy. She'd always wanted to try it, but she wasn't brave enough. She thought she'd be terrible at it – but actually, she was great! In just a few months, she could dance salsa like a professional! She'd been dancing at the Academy for a year when she decided to enter a competition. She had the chance to win €1000 and to dance on TV! When she was at the competition, she felt nervous – she thought she hadn't practised enough. In the end, she came second. She didn't win the prize, but she had a wonderful day, and she still dances salsa now.

2

1 had ~~been~~ met
2 the plane had left
3 had been ~~rained~~ raining
4 I'd ever done
5 The film had just started
6 I'd been shopping

3

1 hadn't studied
2 had been learning
3 had been running
4 had already started
5 hadn't finished
6 'd/had ever had
7 Had; left
8 had been talking

4

1 already 2 ever 3 until
4 by the time 5 just 6 before

4

1 'd / had been thinking
2 decided 3 arrived 4 had already set up 5 hadn't / had not managed 6 got

5

1 'd/had bought a car; she passed her driving test

2 'd/had been practising the piano; he decided to take a break

3 hadn't / had not arrived at the bus stop; the bus came

4 'd/had been trying to fix his PC; started working

Writing Part 2 Story

2

2 Yes, the story is good. It has a context, a middle and an end, and the grammar and vocabulary are appropriate.

4

1 very = really

2 almost = nearly

3 how something happened = slowly, suddenly, quickly

5

Sample answer

I'll never forget how embarrassed I felt on my first day of the course. I was excited and I was nervous also. Many new things and the college, it was huge, a lot more biger than the school. All morning I go to classes and meeting my teachers and other students, after I go to the café for the lunch. This is when a disaster happened, I let fall my food tray, and everything bang fall on the floor. It made a super loud bang nose, and all the people didn't talk and only looked at me. However, the worst thing about it was another, the food and drink was on my clothes, I didn't know to decide to go home or pass the afternoon in coffee and spaghetti sauce.

130 words

Examiner's comments

Content: The opening sentence mentions the first day of course, but the story instead focuses on the first day at a new college. Despite this slight misinterpretation of the task, the content of the story is relevant and the target reader is still informed about the events of the story.

Communicative achievement: The story has a clear beginning, middle and end. The writer appropriately describes the school and the embarrassing incident. At the end, the reader is able to imagine what the character looked like with their clothes covered in food. However, the number of errors and the fact that the writer moves between the present and past tenses leads to an occasional lack of clarity.

Organisation: Despite using a single paragraph, the story is connected and the series of events is clear. The writer is able to move the reader through the story using referencing and some basic linking words and phrases, but these are not always used accurately. At times, the writer connects sentences with commas where full stops would be more appropriate.

Language: The writer uses a range of everyday vocabulary to describe the events of the story, e.g. *huge*, *disaster*, *tray*, *bang*, *spaghetti sauce*. To narrate the story, the writer mainly uses the present simple and past simple, and these structures are not always used accurately. They attempt some more complex structures (comparative forms). There are a variety of errors with spelling, word choice and tense control. One of these slightly impedes communication (*nose* instead of *noise*).

Mark: Pass

Listening Part 4 Multiple choice

2

1 C **2** B **3** A **4** A
5 B **6** A

Vocabulary – Different types of study

1

1 distance learning
2 full-time; part-time
3 evening classes
4 professor; degree
5 trainer; instructor

Language focus Gerunds and infinitives

2

1 to do **2** giving

3 Ready for Grammar

1

1 f **2** c **3** e **4** b **5** a
6 d

2

1 Learning **2** to pass
3 to talk **4** keeping **5** to build
6 starting

3

1 to have **2** Teaching
3 to get **4** to help
5 learning **6** studying

4

1 studying **2** to do **3** to learn
4 to study **5** developing

Listening Part 1 Multiple choice

2

1 B **2** C **3** B **4** A **5** C
6 A **7** B

9 REVIEW

Language Focus Gerunds and infinitives

1 to find **2** to help **3** playing
4 to fix **5** Studying **6** to be
7 applying

Vocabulary Student life

1 d **2** f **3** c **4** a **5** h
6 e **7** g **8** b

Reading Part 6 Open cloze

1 her **2** as **3** had **4** to
5 the **6** how

Writing Part 1 Email

Sample answer

Hi Jake,

Thanks for your email, I am exciting too! Do not worry for your first day.

The college is small, and everyone is very friendly. The first day, you bring pens and paper and go to secretary. They will to help you! Don't arrive late to your classes, it is very important.

My first day at the college was great, the classes were really great and I knew some other old students. They were working and studying, like me, we had in common many things. Additionally, the teachers were very great and helpful. I did not feel nervous on the first day, because I knew so many great people!

Kisses,

Anna

112 words

Examiner's comments

Content: The writer responds to each of the four notes in the input email, as well as including extra information where relevant. The reader is fully informed.

Communicative achievement: The writer uses a polite, friendly tone that would be typical of an email to a friend. They are able to communicate straightforward ideas and hold the reader's attention. In general, the style is appropriately informal, although *additionally* sounds too formal for this context. The email starts appropriately, but *kisses* would be an uncommon way of ending an email in English.

Organisation: In general, the email is well organised and it has a clear, logical structure. The writer uses paragraphs to arrange their ideas, although the second paragraph lacks a clear focus. The writer uses some linking words (*because*, *and*, *additionally*), but most of the sentences are quite short, limiting the possibility of using a wider range of linkers and cohesive devices.

Language: The writer uses appropriate vocabulary, including *excited*, *friendly*, *reception*, *arrive late*, *had in common*, *nervous*. However, the word *great* is overused, indicating a lack of range. The writer relies mainly on simple grammatical structures, but these are used accurately. There are some minor errors with articles, prepositions, and there is at least one error that creates a bit of confusion for the reader (*know* instead of *meet*).

Mark: Pass

Pronunciation /ɜː/ /eə/ and /ɪə/

1

1 hair 2 here 3 her

3

1 here 2 wear 3 clear
4 wear 5 there

4

/ɪə/ fear, pier, really, steer, we're

/eə/ fair, pear, rarely, stare, where

6

/ɜː/: herb, search, girl, worse, turn, earn
/ɪə/: beard, hear, cheer
/eə/: stair, bear, their, pair, care

10 GETTING BETTER

Reading Part 3 Multiple choice

2

Yes, she did

3

1 A 2 C 3 C 4 B 5 D

Vocabulary Health

1

1 take some time off

2 get a prescription

2

1 d 2 a 3 f 4 c 5 e
6 g 7 h 8 b

3

1 a fever 2 sick 3 medicine

4

1 call; ambulance
2 make; appointment
3 take; temperature
4 get; rest
5 go; diet
6 broken
7 take; pill

Language focus Reported speech: statements

1

Another student told me that he had worked for Doctors without Borders.

When I told my parents what I wanted to do, they said that I was crazy!

The sentences in the text are in a different tense and use different pronouns:

I've worked = he had worked

What I wanted to do = I want to work

I was crazy = You're crazy

2

1 said 2 told 3 that

3

1 say 2 tell 3 that

4 Ready for Grammar

1

1 said 2 wanted 3 me
4 that 5 her 6 would
7 didn't

2

1 A 2 C 3 B 4 C 5 A

5

1 said 2 said 3 were
4 us 5 wanted 6 'd/had had

6

1 Ivan said (that) he needed to buy a new jacket for winter.

2 Amir said (that) he was going to the doctor the next / following day.

3 The children told their mother (that) they hadn't cleaned the kitchen yet.

4 Ella and Harry told us that they hadn't gone to the concert the week before / previous week.

5 Oliver said that his friend Jana played tennis really well.

Listening Part 4 Multiple choice

2

1 B 2 A 3 C 4 A
5 C 6 B

Vocabulary – Strong and weak adjectives

1

extremely good: brilliant, fantastic

extremely bad: awful, terrible

2

1 very 2 absolutely 3 really
4 quite 5 really

3

1 delighted 2 shocked
3 freezing 4 miserable 5 tiny
6 enormous, huge 7 exhausted
8 beautiful

4

1 freezing 2 exhausted
3 shocked 4 beautiful
5 delighted 6 enormous/huge

5 Additional materials

Suggested answers

1 shocked 2 beautiful
3 freezing 4 miserable
5 delighted 6 exhausted

Speaking Part 2 Extended turn

1

Photograph 1: cold, off work, sneeze, tissues

Photograph 2: appointment, toothache, dentist, pain

Listening Part 3 Gap fill

2

1 comfortable clothing
2 7.30
3 juice
4 cook (lunch)
5 lake
6 snack

Language focus Reported speech: questions

1–2

1 b 2 a 3 b

3

1 b 2 c 3 a

4

1 c 2 a 3 b

5 Ready for Grammar

1 offered to help me cut the grass in my garden.

2 asked me if I had finished painting my house yet.

3 asked us if we had seen the accident the day before / the previous day.

4 asked if I could call the restaurant and book a table.

5 offered to make the children some lunch.

6 asked to borrow / asked if he/she could borrow my car.

6

1 offered to drive
2 asked her if she had read
3 asked us what we had learnt
4 asked if we needed
5 asked the tourists where they were

7

1 My doctor asked me if I ate healthy food.

2 I asked (my flatmate) Lina to buy some more coffee.

3 (My friend) Amanda asked me where I went running.

4 Daniel asked us what we were listening to.

5 Our English teacher offered to help us.

Writing – Part 2 Article

2

The plan answers all the questions. There is one piece of information which shouldn't be there 'follow advice to exercise every day' – the student hasn't said who gave that advice before.

3

Yes, it does follow the plan mostly.

4

1 Healthy habits, healthy life!

2 Have you ever watched TV and eaten pizza all day?

3 It's very important to move around and eat healthy food.

4 My doctor told me to eat vegetables with every meal and not to drink too much coffee.

6

Sample answer

A happy life is a healthy life!

Do you think eating salad is bored or going to the gym is too hard? Don't worry. I am healthy, but I don't try too much. It's possible!

I don't go to the gym, but I like to play sports. I eat the vegetables, but I eat the pizza too! My doctor told me that it's better the things that are easy but good. I agree, because if you try too hard, it is difficult to do all the days.

For be healthy, you must be happy! Then, find the vegetables you like and eat those sometimes, and find the sports you like and do those some times!

115 words

Examiner's comments

Content: The writer answers the three questions from the task instructions, so the reader is fully informed. All the content is relevant.

Communicative achievement: The writer uses some of the conventions of an article to hold the reader's attention, such as including a catchy title, addressing the reader directly, and using a friendly informal tone. There is also a good mix of general views and personal opinion. The writer expresses straightforward ideas in a way that is easy to understand.

Organisation: The writer uses a logical structure, answering each question from the task instructions in a separate paragraph. There is a clear beginning and ending. The writer uses some basic linking words (*or*, *but*, *because*), but one (*then*) is used incorrectly. They also use reference pronouns (*it* = *being healthy*, *those* = *vegetables*) to make connections within and across sentences.

Language: There is a variety of everyday vocabulary that is appropriate to the task, e.g. *going to the gym*, *possible*, *play sports*, *vegetables*, *hard/difficult*, *healthy*. The writer also shows a good control of simple grammatical forms and some more complex ones (conditional sentences). There are a few errors with word choice, spelling and articles, but these do not create difficulty for the reader and the meaning is clear.

Mark: Good pass

10 REVIEW

Language focus Reported speech

1 Jona told me that he had seen Pavel and his family at the cinema the ~~day~~ previous day.

2 She asked if ~~that~~ I wanted tea or coffee for breakfast.

3 I called Richard and he said ~~me~~ that he ~~is~~ was walking home from work. / I called Richard and he ~~said~~ told me that he ~~is~~ was walking home from work.

4 My teacher offered to give me some extra worksheets to prepare for the exam.

5 My friend told ~~we~~ us that she ~~will~~ would come to visit next summer.

6 My parents told ~~to~~ me ~~no~~ not to open the presents before my birthday.

7 She told me that she didn't want to come to my party.

8 My brother asked me to go to the chemist's to buy him some pills.

Vocabulary Health

1 have **2** make **3** take
4 get **5** take **6** go

Reading Part 6 Open cloze

1 most **2** to **3** been
4 than **5** of **6** If

Writing Part 1 email

Sample answer

Hi Emily,

I'm looking forward to seeing you too. It's a pity that you've broken the arm! How has it happened?

When you come, we don't need to go to the beach. There are many other things we can do. For example, we can go to the cinema. There's lots of good films there, or if you don't like, we can only stay at my house and play computer games!

You asked about what to bring. You don't need to bring anything for me, only bring some clothes for you and anything else you need.

See you on Saturday!

Inés

100 words

Examiner's comments

Content: The writer addresses the first, second and fourth points, but they do not tell their friend whether it's possible to meet at the train station. Given the context, this note is perhaps the most important one to address, which means the reader is not fully informed.

Communicative achievement: The email begins and ends in an appropriate way. The overall tone of the email is friendly and polite, and the writer uses a suitably informal style. In general, the email is clearly written and it is easy to follow. At one point, the writer refers back to the input email, which would be a natural thing to do in this context.

Organisation: The email has a logical structure and the writer effectively organises their ideas into paragraphs. The ideas in the text are well connected, and there are examples of reference pronouns, basic linking words (*and*, *when*, *or*) and a discourse marker (*for example*).

Language: The writer uses a good range of everyday vocabulary, e.g. *it's a pity*, *computer games*, *anything else*. They demonstrate the ability to use both simple and more complex grammatical structures, including conditional sentences, with a good degree of control. There are a few minor errors with prepositions, word choice and tense control, but these do not impede communication.

Mark: Good pass

Pronunciation Word endings

1

1 paint **2** next **3** field
4 line **5** gold
6 main **7** find

3

1 paint **2** next **3** feel **4** lie
5 gold **6** main **7** fine

Ready for Speaking

Speaking Part 1 Interview

1

1 c 2 a 3 e 4 b 5 d

2

Possible answers

Which do you prefer, watching films at home or going to the cinema?

What's your favourite type of food?

What did you do last summer?

How often do you do exercise?

Tell us about your family.

4

2 He asks the examiner to repeat the question. This is not a problem on the exam and you will not lose points.

3 At times, she could expand her answers more. Toward the end, the examiner asks her two questions in a row to get her to speak a bit more, even using the back-up prompt 'why?' to encourage her to give a supporting example or reason.

Speaking Part 2 Extended turn

3

2 The examiner uses a prompt, "Talk about the people" to encourage her to keep talking.

3 Pilar describes the pictures in a coherent way, starting with a summary and then going into more detail about the people and place. She uses a good range of vocabulary, e.g. *smiling*, *laughing*, *skirt*, *cook a meal*, etc. In addition, she is able to use paraphrase successfully when she can't remember the word *blouse* ("a kind of top for women"). Carlos is able to keep talking for a full minute. He correctly uses phrases with prepositions of place (*at the top*, *in the middle*, *in the sky*, *on the beach*) to say where things are.

4 Pilar does not speak for a full minute and needs help from the examiner to continue. Carlos' extended turn is not very well organised, which results in repetition, e.g. boats and birds. In general, he could use a wider range of vocabulary.

4

1 **seasons:** *autumn, spring, summer*

2 **weather:** *cloudy, stormy, sunny*

3 **furniture:** *bookshelf, sofa, table*

4 **types of room:** *dining room, kitchen, living room*

5 **age:** *adult, child, teenager*

6 **clothing:** *skirt, T-shirt, trousers*

5

Possible answers

1 winter

2 snowy, hot, cold

3 bed, bedside table, wardrobe

4 bedroom, bathroom, home office / study

5 baby, in his/her 40s/50s/60s, etc., middle-aged / elderly man/woman

6 boots, trainers, jeans

Speaking Part 3 Discussion

3

1 c 2 a 3 b

6

1 He provides the word *equipment* when she can't remember it.

2 They discuss four of the options: running / jogging, swimming, dancing, hiking.

3 No, but this isn't a problem. It is clear they're on their way to reaching an agreement.

Speaking Part 4 General conversation

2

1 To get Carlos to extend his answers, the interlocutor uses the prompts "Why?" or "Why not?"

2 Pilar and Carlos interact very well, listening and responding to what the other person says. For example, Carlos refers back to Pilates, which Pilar mentioned earlier. They have different points of view about exercise, but each of them shows they have understood the points made by the other person.

11 HOUSE AND HOME

Vocabulary Buildings

1

1 skyscraper 2 monument
3 tower 4 block of flats
5 palace 6 office block
7 apartment 8 cottage

2

1 People live in apartments, blocks of flats, skyscrapers, cottages. People work in office blocks, skyscrapers (and sometimes from their apartments). People visit towers, monuments and palaces.

2 Kings, queens and royal families often live in palaces.

3 Cottages are usually in the countryside.

Writing Part 1 Email

3

1 , 2 ! 3 . 4 ?

4

Do you like your new home?
I really love my new flat and the neighbourhood where I live.

What is the area like? And what is your new flat like? There are lots of skyscrapers and so many cars, people and shops. My flat has two bedrooms and it is on the 20th floor of a building in the city centre.

Do you prefer it? I prefer it here to my village in France. It was a bit quiet there and I enjoy having lots of things to do. New York is perfect for that.

I'd love to come and visit you. You can visit me soon. Can you come next month?

5

Sample answer

Hi Arnie,

Thanks for your email. How are you?

I love my new home. The area is very relaxing. It's on a small town with lot of country nearby. Also, my flat is really nice. It has three bedrooms and it has big terace on the roof. I can see horses and river from terace!

I definitely prefer it to my flat in the city. It was so small, and the area it was too busy for me.

You can visit me any time you like. There is a bedroom in which you can stay here. You let me know when you will like to come!

See you soon,

Maria

110 words

Examiner's comments

Content: All the content is relevant and the writer addresses the four points from the input email. The target reader would be fully informed by the information provided.

Communicative achievement: The writer uses an appropriately friendly tone for an email to a friend. The email is written in a suitable format. The writer makes effective use of opening and closing salutations, and they finish the email with an invitation that would require a response from Arnie. Throughout the email, the writer provides explanations to support more general statements, e.g. saying exactly why she prefers her present flat to her former one in the city.

Organisation: The email is generally well organised and coherent. The writer addresses each note from the input email and they break the texts effectively into different paragraphs. However, the writer only uses a few high frequency linking words (*and*, *also*), relying mainly on reference pronouns to connect ideas within sentences and paragraphs.

Language: The writer uses a good range of everyday vocabulary to describe the place where they live, e.g. *relaxing*, *big terrace*, *roof*, *busy*. Apart from one attempt at a conditional sentence, the email is written mainly using simple grammatical forms, but these are used with a good degree of accuracy. There are a few mistakes with articles, prepositions and spelling, but these create no difficulty for the reader and the meaning is clear.

Mark: Good pass

Reading Part 2 Matching

2

1 F **2** G **3** B **4** D **5** C

Language focus Passive

1

1 will be opened
2 is cleaned
3 was built

3

1 was **2** will

4

1 No
2 No

5 Ready for Grammar

1

1 speak **2** designed
3 was **4** is being watched
6 will ever be caught

2

1 started
2 is/was named
3 became
4 needed
5 was found
6 are made
7 aren't sold / are not sold
8 includes

3

1 A local artist is invited to the studio once a month.

2 Will this report be finished by Friday?

3 This jacket was given to me (by Lucas). / I was given this jacket (by Lucas).

4 Tickets to the concert are being sold online.

5 Has the cat been fed today?

6

1 is known **2** was built
3 is used **4** is visited
5 are talked **6** was given
7 is; surrounded

7

1 built **2** filmed **3** watched
4 born **5** used

8

Possible answers

1 The Colosseum, The Tower of London, The Royal Alcázar of Seville

2 Students' own answers

3 football, basketball, cricket, tennis

4 Students' own answers

5 smartphone, smartwatch, tablet, 3D printer, AI / artificial intelligence

Vocabulary Household objects

1

1 i **2** e **3** k **4** d **5** l **6** g
7 b **8** n **9** a **10** q **11** h **12** f
13 p **14** j **15** o **16** c **17** m

Vocabulary Chores

1

1 make **2** put **3** makes
4 makes **5** tidy **6** do
7 throw **8** do **9** switch
10 doing

2

1 tidies **2** makes **3** does
4 does **5** puts

Listening Part 2 Multiple choice

1

1 A **2** C **3** C **4** B
5 C **6** A

Language focus – Get/Have something done

1

1 The speaker wants to ask someone else to repair it.

2 The speaker wants to repair it themselves.

2

1 b **2** a **3** a **4** b

3

1 *have* **2** past participle

4

1 We didn't get pizza delivered last night.

2 Has Amanda had her kitchen decorated?

3 They had their photo taken by a professional.

4 Where did you get your jacket cleaned?

5 Our neighbours are having an alarm installed in their house.

6 David is going to get his eyes tested tomorrow.

5 Ready for Grammar

1

1 have/get; delivered
2 had/got; fixed
3 have/get; tested
4 have/get; painted

2

1 Gina had her necklace repaired ~~her necklace~~ at a jewellery shop.

2 You can't visit this month because we ~~have~~ are having the kitchen redecorated.

3 We're going to ~~make the table~~ have the table made by a carpenter.

4 The museum will have the objects ~~check~~ checked by history experts.

6

Possible answers

1 I had my hair cut last week.

2 My sister has had her mobile phone stolen twice.

3 I get my car fixed by a mechanic.

4 We usually get food delivered to our house at the weekend.

5 My friend Ana has her nails painted once a month.

Listening Part 1 Multiple choice

1

1 C **2** B **3** A **4** B **5** A
6 B **7** C

11 REVIEW

Language Focus Passive

1 is collected **2** was taken
3 wasn't cleaned **4** were sent
5 is being built **6** will be signed

Vocabulary Chores

1 makes **2** tidies **3** makes
4 makes **5** do **6** does
7 throw **8** switch **9** does

Reading Part 5 Multiple-choice cloze

1 C **2** B **3** D **4** C
5 B **6** A

Writing Part 2 Article

Sample answer

My dream house is an old cottage because I prefer houses that made from stone in the traditional style. In my opinion, old houses have personality, but all of the modern houses, they built in the same boring manner.

I enjoy living in the countryside more than in the city, there houses are larger that apartments in the city. My dream house would have a large garden with much flowers.

For me, I like to paint my house bright colours. I put always lots of photo in the walls and I've much plants in the kitchen and salon.

98 words

Examiner's comments

Content: All the content is relevant. The writer answers all the questions in detail and there is some development of the topic.

Communicative achievement: The writer successfully communicates straightforward ideas in an appropriately neutral style. The article includes a mix of personal opinion and general views, which is characteristic of articles. There is also some good description, e.g. paint colours, photos on walls and plants in the kitchen. These details help the reader imagine the house being described and therefore engages their attention.

Organisation: In general, the writer explains straightforward ideas in a way that is easy to follow and understand. There are three paragraphs, each with a different focus. There is a clear introduction to the topic, but there is no clear ending. Some basic linking words (*because*, *but*, *and*) are used to link ideas and there is some use of reference words (*there* = *in the countryside*) to connect ideas within sentences.

Language: In this article, there is a good range of everyday vocabulary, e.g. *stone*, *traditional style*, *personality*, *large garden*. The writer displays a fairly good control of simple grammatical forms (present tenses) and attempts some more complex structures (passives and comparative structures). There are some noticeable errors, but these do not create difficulty for the reader, with the exception of one impeding error: the use of the word *salon* for *living room*.

Mark: Pass

Pronunciation The schwa /ə/

1

1 They all contain the same sound – the schwa /ə/

2

tomorrow remember hospital
problem survive bigger

3

1 unstressed

4

1 banana 2 comfortable
3 America 4 accurate
5 possible

6

Yesterday I went to London because I wanted to buy a present for my brother. I visited a lot of shops, but I couldn't find anything suitable. Finally, I saw an amazing pair of trainers, so I bought them.

8

extra magazine
banana computer cousin
leisure tonight correct survive
disagree stadium happen
together stomach alone
remember enormous
communicate exercise given
again machine arrive condition
hospital

12 TECHNOLOGY TODAY

Reading Part 4 Gapped text

2

a

3

1 D 2 H 3 B 4 E 5 A

Vocabulary Computers and devices

1

1 switch on 2 collect 3 print
4 connect 5 begin

2

1 deleted 2 shut down
3 remember 4 send
5 installed

Language focus Third conditional

1

1 *did*
2 the past
3 past perfect
4 *would* + *have* + past participle

2

1 c 2 b 3 d 4 a

3

1 zero 2 second 3 third

4 Ready for Grammar

1

1 wouldn't have won; had given up
2 had been; would have gone
3 would have made; had had
4 had known; wouldn't have

2

1 c 2 b 3 g 4 e 5 d
6 h 7 f 8 a

3

Zero conditional: 2, 8

First conditional: 3, 6

Second conditional: 4, 7

Third conditional: 1, 5

5

1 have 2 hadn't
3 wouldn't 4 had

6

1 want 2 order
3 would our lives be
4 didn't have 5 hadn't done
6 wouldn't have grown 7 use
8 will continue

Vocabulary Changes and amounts

1

1 improve 2 decline
3 grow; increase
4 decrease; drop

2

a 2 b 1 c 4 d 3

Listening Part 3 Gap fill

1

1 adjective (to describe people)
2 noun (probably a place)
3 adjective (to describe activities)
4 noun
5 verb
6 date or day

2

1 elderly
2 (people's) homes
3 dangerous
4 (any) staff
5 looks like
6 29/29th (of) October / October 29th

Vocabulary Knowledge and invention

1

1 e 2 a 3 f 4 b 5 g
6 h 7 d 8 c

3

1 discoveries 2 machines
3 solution(s) 4 diagrams
5 research 6 experiments
7 data 8 ideas

Listening Part 2 Multiple choice

1

A 2; 3

B 1; 5

C 4; 6

2

1 A **2** B **3** A **4** C
5 B **6** C

Language focus Future Continuous

2

be + -ing

3 Ready for Grammar

1

1 She will/'ll be cycling in the mountains.

2 She will/'ll be doing homework.

3 She will/'ll be walking around the city.

2

1 No, she won't. She will/'ll be taking the train.

2 No, she won't. She will/'ll be visiting a museum.

3 No, she won't. She will/'ll be going on a boat tour.

4

1 will be living
2 will be learning
3 will be running
4 won't be driving; will be flying

Writing Part 2 Article

3

what technology you prefer; how technology improves your daily life; reasons why you like using some technologies

5

Yes, the writer answers all the questions.

6

1 b **2** c **3** a **4** d **5** d
6 d **7** e

Useful language

1 exciting **2** quickly
3 like **4** What

7

Sample answer

Great Inventions

Everybody uses technology a lot. The internet is the most important invention of the last 100 years, surely. Some people love their phones, but I love my e-book reader. In my opinion, it's more useful than books because it's small and I can download hundreds of books. Think of how many of the trees we cut to make paper! E-reader is better for environment, and it doesn't take space in your bag. Also, it's quick to buy books with e-reader, so I shop from everywhere no problem.

For me, the invention of e-readers and other modern technology give me many choices and improve my daily life too much. I can't imagine the life without them!

117 words

Examiner's comments

Content: All the content is relevant, however the writer says what they think is the most important invention but doesn't expand on this point or explain why.

Communicative achievement: In this article, the writer is able to communicate a number of straightforward ideas about e-readers. They use some common features of articles to effectively hold the reader's attention, e.g. addressing the reader directly (*take space in your bag*) and including a mix of personal opinion and general ideas. They also include an appropriate title, which sparks the reader's interest.

Organisation: The text is generally well organised, with a clear beginning and end. The writer separates their discussion of the topic into paragraphs. The second one, however, feels like a collection of different ideas and lacks a clear focus. The writer uses basic linking words and some cohesive devices to connect ideas across the text (*also*, *or*, *and*, *in my opinion*).

Language: The writer uses a good range of everyday vocabulary that is suitable to the topic, e.g. *useful*, *download*, *environment*, *modern technology*. Although most of the text is written in the present simple, there are examples of both simple and some more complex grammatical structures and these are used with a fairly good degree of control. There are some mistakes with word choice, but none of these impede communication.

Mark: Good pass

12 REVIEW

Language focus Third Conditional

1 had left
2 would have caught
3 would have remembered
4 hadn't been
5 had seen
6 would have said

Vocabulary Computers and devices

1 d **2** a **3** f **4** b
5 e **6** c

Reading Part 5 Multiple-choice cloze

1 B **2** C **3** D **4** B
5 D **6** A

Writing Part 2 Story

Sample answer

As I entered the laboratory, I knew my life would never be the same. It was my last day of training to be astronaut. The doctors checked my health. Finally, they said I was ready for my travel to the moon.

After, I went to home and spent the evening in family, relaxing. We sat and looked up at space and the millions of stars, I was feeling very scared but very excited also!

The next day, I sat with other astronauts and we heard the numbers 10 ... 9 ... 8 ... 7. Then suddenly, up to the sky we went. We stayed 3 days there in space, we made experiments and bring rocks home. It was the most amazing experience in my life!

119 words

Examiner's comments

Content: The target reader is well informed about the events of the story, which follow on logically from the first sentence. All the content is relevant.

Communicative achievement: The story communicates straightforward ideas and holds the reader's attention throughout. There is a clear sequence of events. Given the short word count, the writer is able to move the main character very economically through the events of the story. There is also some description of the character's feelings. An element of suspense is used effectively in the first paragraph, where the trip to the moon is mentioned at the very end of the paragraph, which engages the reader's attention and makes them want to keep reading.

Organisation: The text is well organised and the narrative is quite well controlled. Paragraphs are used effectively to move the main character from one event to the next. There is some use of narrative tenses, as well as linking words and phrases, to connect the sequence of events. Referencing is used effectively (*we* = main character + family) to create connections between sentences.

Language: A range of everyday vocabulary is used to describe the events of the story and the feelings of the main character, e.g. *last day of training, checked my health, excited, bring rocks home, amazing experience*. The writer uses a range of grammatical forms with a good degree of control. There are some errors, but the meaning is clear and they create little or no difficulty for the reader.

Mark: Very good pass

Pronunciation Connected speech

1

1 switched off 2 send emails
3 of experiments 4 print ten

2

a and d are true

4

Almos**t-e**veryo**ne-ow**n**s-a** mobile phone these days. These can be as chea**p-as** 40 pound**s-or** cost hundred**s-of** pounds, bu**t-th**e mos**t-ex**pensive mobile pho**ne-in** the world cost**s an en**ormous 40 million pounds. I**t-is** ma**de-of** gol**d-an**d diamonds, an**d-it** belongs to the wi**fe-o**f the richest ma**n-in-A**sia.

5

Connected words: switch on, catch up, lost email, almost all, share ideas, web browser

Not connected words: video game, tv screen

Collocation revision Units 1–12

Adjective + noun

1 clothes 2 course 3 food
4 musician 5 trip 6 area 7 job
8 degree 9 class 10 building

Verb + noun

1 win 2 play 3 do 4 enjoy
5 attend 6 spend 7 get
8 take 9 have 10 make

Ready for Writing

Introduction

Marking

1 c 2 d 3 b 4 a

Writing Part 2 Article

Useful language

Giving examples

For example
For instance
Such as
Including
Like

Contrasting ideas

However
Yet
Despite
Still
While

Showing cause and effect

Because
Due to
Therefore
For this reason
As a result of

Expressing time

During
Finally
Next
Meanwhile
Previously

Adding information

Also
In addition
As well as
Besides
Not only that

Macmillan Education Limited
4 Crinan Street
London N1 9XW

Companies and representatives throughout the world

Ready for B1 Preliminary Student's Book with Key ISBN 978-1-035-12142-7
Ready for B1 Preliminary Student's Book with Key with App & Digital Student's Book ISBN 978-1-035-12155-7

Written by Fiona Aish, Ethan Mansur, Jo Tomlinson with contributions by Roy Norris

The authors have asserted their right to be identified as the authors of this work in accordance with the Copyright, Designs and Patents Act 1988.

First published 2025

Designed by EMC Design Ltd.
Illustrated by Keri Green (Beehive Illustration) pp90, 91, 98, 99, 110, 111, 138, 139; Irina Golina-Sagatelian (Beehive Illustration) pp110, 111, 169, 172, 173; Szilvia Szakall (Beehive Illustration) pp111, 131, 138, 139, 161, 172
Cover design by The Restless
Cover photograph by Getty Images/AsiaVision.
Picture research by Emily Taylor

Authors' acknowledgements
Fiona Aish would like to thank the team at Macmillan and Roy Norris for their constant and valuable support throughout this project.
Ethan Mansur would like to thank Roy Norris for his invaluable help and encouragement, as well as everyone at Macmillan Education who worked on the course. Thanks also to Christina Anastasiadis, Ian Sowers, Alex Makenzie, Michael Agganis, Natalia Piekarowicz, Heidi Russell and Sam Draffin at International House Madrid for their help piloting materials, and to Javier Fruns at the Instituto Cervantes for his always insightful feedback. Finally, he would like to express his deep gratitude to his wife, Antonia, and his two children, Lola and Dylan, for their continued support and inspiration.
Jo Tomlinson would like to thank everyone who worked tirelessly on the project, including Roy and the team at Macmillan.

The publishers would like to thank: Andrea Littlewood, International House Madrid (Madrid), Frank Carrizo Zirit (Madrid), Ian Sowers, International House

The authors and publishers would like to thank the following for permission to reproduce their photographs:
Alamy Stock Photo/Al Kancello p38, Alamy Stock Photo/Ingo Arndt p64(inset), Alamy Stock Photo/Art Directors & TRIP p34(tr), Alamy Stock Photo/Clarence Holmes Photography p46, Alamy Stock Photo/Ian Dagnall Commercial Collection p132, Alamy Stock Photo/Julian Elliott News Photography p115, Alamy Stock Photo/Fredrick Kippe p127, Alamy Stock Photo/kwcg p121(3), Alamy Stock Photo/Chris McLennan p68(l), Alamy Stock Photo/PhotoEdit p34(a), Alamy Stock Photo/photonic 20 p94(notebook), Alamy Stock Photo/Jozef Polc p125, Alamy Stock Photo/Pumkinpie p34(d), Alamy Stock Photo/theatrepix pp44(tr), 45(1), Alamy Stock Photo/Varbes p116(a), Alamy Sock Photo/Wavebreakmedia p147(br), Alamy Stock Photo/Olga Yastremska p116(j);
Corbis p116(f);
Getty Images p121(2), Getty Images/4FR p70, Getty Images/10'000 Hours p97(b), Getty Images/Fuad Afandi p180, Getty Images/AGuyWhoClicks p164(5), Getty Images/Aletheia97 p122, Getty Images/Alter_photo p34(e), Getty Images/Andresr p137, Getty Images/Artpartner-images p128(3), Getty Images/Asia-Pacific Images Studio p186(tl), Getty Images/Gonzalo Azumendi p78(tl), Getty Images/William Barton p88, Getty Images/Carlos Barquero p51(bl), Getty Images/Jeff Bergen p154, Getty Images/Bet_Noire p94(guide books), Getty Images/Anastasia Bid p148(tr), Getty Images/Blend Images p68(k), Getty Images/Matjaz Boncina p63, Getty Images/Borut Trdina p68(b), Getty Images/Oleg Breslavtsev p235, Getty Images/Brothers91 p182(3), Getty Images/Brusinski p130(bm), Getty Images/Peter Cade p97(g), Getty Images/Caia Image pp158(1), 163, Getty Images/Carbonero Stock p130(t), Getty Images/Cavan Images pp97(e),134, Getty Images/CBS Photo Archive p215, Getty Images/Yuichiro Chino p183, Getty Images/Choness p94(passport), Getty Images/Chuvipro p175, Getty Images/Matteo Colombo p65, Getty Images/Compassionate Eye Foundation/David Oxberry p51(br), Getty Images/David Merron Photography p96(b), Getty Images/Gregory_DUBUS p167, Getty Images/DGLimages p174, Getty Images/Dima_sidelnikov p150(1), Getty Images/dlerick p94(hat), Getty Images/Digital Vision pp60(4), 76(5), Getty Images/E+ p76(t), Getty Images/Fcafotodigital p37, Getty Images/FG Trade pp30(tr), Getty Images/Filrom p48(inset), 44(tl), Getty Images/Finn Bjurvoll Hansen p206(br), Getty Images/Flashpop p60(5), Getty Images/Franckreporter p213, Getty Images/David Freund p76(7), Getty Images/Jamie Garbutt p60(1), Getty Images/Georgeclerk p114, Getty Images/Geraint Rowland Photography p211, Getty Images/Gilaxia p171(tl), Getty Images/GlobalP p128(1), Getty Images/The Good Brigade p97(c), Getty Images/Gorodenkoff p34(bl), Getty Images/Jonas Gratzer p229, Getty Images/Nicolas Hansen p82(3), Getty Images/Hemera Technologies p34(c), Getty Images/Hero Images pp76(1), 119, Getty Images/Marie Hickman p96(t), Getty Images/Hispanolistic pp171(tr), 182(1), Getty Images/Bjorn Holland p94(credit card), Getty Images/ImageSource pp82(2), 170, Getty Images/Interim Archives p141, Getty Images/istockphoto pp60(3), 61, 68(c), 83, 94(toothbrush), 116(d), 128(8), 155, 207, Getty Images/ivotheeditors p78(tr), Getty Images/JackF p116(g), Getty Images/Jacky Parker Photography p65(inset), Getty Images/Javier Zayas Photography p233, Getty Images/kickstand p94(toothpaste), Getty Images/Vlad Kochelaevskiy p181, Getty Images/Joff Lee p33, Getty Images/Johner RF p124, Getty Images/Justin Lewis p116(c), Getty Images/LightFieldStudios p97(d), Getty Images/David Madison p95, Getty Images/Matthias Makarinus p121(4), Getty Images/Emilija Manevska p135, Getty Images/Antonio Masiello p93, Getty Images/Maskot p189, Getty Images/Mbbirdy p148(tl), Getty Images/Ryan McVay p223, Getty Images/Mendowong Photography p56, Getty Images/Metal Hammer Magazine p45(2), Getty Images/Metamorworks p182(2), Getty Images/MoMo Productions p82(4), Getty Images/Monkeybusinessimages p106, Getty Images/muminінan p34(b), Getty Images/Michael Ochs Archives p55, Getty Images/Mixetto p153, Getty Images/Daniel Milchev p116(e), Getty Images/Dean Mitchell pp97(f), 107, Getty Images/Karen Moskowitz p129, Getty Images/Camilo Morales p166(t), Getty Images/Morsa Images pp82(1), 130(bl, br), p146, 166(1, 2, 4), Getty Images/Aleksandar Nakic p81, Getty Images/Nadezhda Nazarova p94(suncream), Getty Images/Mark Newman p194, Getty Images/Nico_blue p169, Getty Images/Nicolesy p100, Getty Images/Nico De Pasquale Photography p68(a), Getty Images/Mikel Oibar/Nervio Foto p112, Getty Images/Martin Novak p225, Getty Images/Ondacaracola photography p69, Getty Images/Dimitri Otis p166(3), Getty Images/Ozgurcankaya p150(2), Getty Images/Andre Panneton p82(5), Getty Images/P_A_S_M Photography p32, Getty Images/Isabel Pavia p191, Getty Images/PEDRE p75, Getty Images/Peopleimages.com p116(k), Getty Images/Charday Penn p178, Getty Images/Phynart Studio p126(tr), Getty Images/The Picture Pantry p41(bl), Getty Images/PNCp68(g), Getty Images/Popovaphoto p94(coat), Getty Images/Prostock-Studio p140, Getty Images/Puneet Vikram Singh p89, Getty Images/RealPeopleGroup p136, Getty Images/Recep-bg p150(b), Getty Images/RelaxFoto.de p43, Getty Images/RichLegg p201(1), Getty Images/Riou p128(9), Getty Images/Richard Rodriguez p66, Getty Images/RossHelen p187, Getty Images/Aleksander Rubtsov p35, Getty Images/Andy Sacks p68(f), Getty Images/Santiaga P118, Getty Images/Joaquin Sarmiento p182(4), Getty Images/Science Photo Library RF p128(6), Getty Images/SaskiaAcht p68(i), Getty Images/SDI Productions pp53, 147(tl), Getty Images/Davide G. Seddio p68(e), Getty Images/Seremin p94(headphones), Getty Images/SerrNovik p72, Getty Images/Ilan Shacham p116(h), Getty Images/Simonkr p116(l), Getty Images/SimonSkafar p145, Getty Images/Hugh Sitton pp144, 147(bl), Getty Images/SKashkin p66, Getty Images/Robin Skjoldborg p76(6), Getty Images/SolStock pp130(cl), 201(2), Getty Images/Paul Souders p77, Getty Images/Alexander Spatari pp164(1), 185, Getty Images/SrdjanPav pp34(br), 103, Getty Images/Armin Staudt p128(4), Getty Images/Sturti p221, Getty Images/Surangaw p168, Getty Images/Issarawat Tattong p128(5), Getty Images/Tbralnina pp36, 164(3), Getty Images/Tetra Images pp126(bl), 130(cr), 162, Getty Images/The_burtons p113, Getty Images/David C Tomlinson p87, Getty Images/TravelCouples p206(br), Getty Images/Trexdigital p94(sunglasses), Getty Images/Triloks p166(5), Getty Images/Kentaroo Tryman p117, Getty Images/george tsartsianidis p34(f), Getty Images/Universal Images Group p68(h), Getty Images/Urbazon pp143, 209, Getty Images/Dedé Vargas p49, Getty Images/Vkyryl p164(4), Getty Images/VorDa p186(tr), Getty Images/Vostok p164(7), Getty Images/James Warwick p68(d), Getty Images/AJ Wattamaniuk p60(2), Getty Images/We Are p76(3), Getty Images/Roberto Westbrook p71, Getty Images/Tom Werner p116(b), Getty Images/Westend61 pp41(br), 76(2, 4, 8), 152, 158(2), 177, 188, Getty Images/Stuart Westmorland p195(cm), Getty Images/Wilpunt p67, Getty Images/Art Wolfe p92, Getty Images/Worakit p149, Getty Images/Gary Yeowell p164(2);
IMAGE SOURCE p97(a);
Courtesy of Klahoose Resort p64;
Macmillan Publishers/Paul Bricknell p94(swimsuit);
PHOTOALTO p68(j);
PIXTAL p128(7);
PureStock p116(i);
Shutterstock/Dean Drobot p101, Shutterstock/Kuznetcov_Konstantin p121(1), Shutterstock/Pcruciatti p164(6);
Stockbyte pp128(2), 164(8).

Printed and bound in Spain

2029 2028 2027 2026 2025

14 13 12 11 10 9 8 7